ARETHA FRANKLIN:
THE QUEEN OF SOUL

ARETHA FRANKLIN:
THE QUEEN OF SOUL

MARK BEGO

Tribute Edition

Skyhorse Publishing

Skyhorse Publishing books may be purchased in bulk at special discounts for
sales promotion, corporate gifts, fundraising, or educational purposes. Special
editions can also be created to specifications. For details, contact the Special Sales
Department, Skyhorse Publishing, 307 West 36th Street, 11th Floor, New York,
NY 10018 or info@skyhorsepublishing.com.

Skyhorse® and Skyhorse Publishing® are registered trademarks of Skyhorse
Publishing, Inc.®, a Delaware corporation.

www.skyhorsepublishing.com

10 9 8 7 6 5 4 3 2 1

Library of Congress Cataloging-in-Publication Data is available on file

ISBN: 978-1-5107-4507-0
eISBN: 978-1-5107-4508-7

Printed in the United States of America

TO DON KEVERN:

My junior high school English teacher who taught me
to appreciate the written word.

CONTENTS

ACKNOWLEDGMENTS

From the 1989 edition of this book:

The author would like to thank the following people for their help, assistance, and encouragement: Vince Aletti, Bob Altshuler, Bob and Mary Bego, Fran Boyar, Nathaniel Brewster, Ray Bryant, Joe Canale, Andy Carpenter, Mark Chase, John Christe, Rita Coolidge, Paul Cooper, Jack Cunningham, Billy Davis, Clive Davis, Sandra DeCosta, Brad DeMeulenaere, Simo Doe, Jack Donaghy, Shellie Ellis / *Oklahoma Daily*, Tisha Fein, Dennis Fine, Joann Forsyth, Neil S. Friedman, Stacia Friedman, Gary Graff / *Detroit Free Press*, Rita Griffin / *Michigan Chronicle*, Dan Hartman, Isiah James, Randy Jones, Marilyn and John Kelly / WXYZ-TV Detroit, Barb Knudson, Virginia Lohle, Toni Lopopolo, Diane Mancher, Bob Margouleff, Sindi Markoff, Peter Max, Walter McBride, Sue "Muffy" McDonald, Joe McEwen, Charles Moniz, Terry Morgan, Ernie Needham, Carolyn O'Connell, Clyde Otis, Greg Porto, Stephen Pullan, Kenneth Reynolds, Sherry Robb, Melani Rogers, David Salidor, Barbara Shelley, Brendan Thompson, Ted White, Mary Wilson, and special thanks to Glenn Hughes . . . AND all of my "confidential" sources.

For the 2011 / 2012 edition of this book:

Cindy Adams, Sam Alexander, John Botticella, Marten Brandt, Mary Anne Cassata, Jay Cassell, Tom Cuddy, Sarah Dash, Dan DeFilippo, James Edstrom, Sasha Goodman, Yvette Grant, Giovanni Jackson, Ronit Jariv, Dave Marken, Scott Mendel, Kevin Milburn, David Nathan (Thank you for quoting this book in the liner notes of all of Aretha's great Atlantic repackages!), Luke Nicola, Mark and Bonnie Olson, Christopher Pavlick,

Freda Payne, Anne Raso, Marsha Stern, Derek Storm, Ann Treistman, George Vissichelli, Beth Wernick, Patrick Wood, and to Aretha Franklin herself—thank you for the in-person interview that started me on the path to writing this book.

I would like to dedicate this new edition of this book to the memory of my dear friend John Klinger (1962–2011): "Dude, the coffee will always be on here for you, and I will always love you and never forget you!"

For the 2018 edition of this book:

Cindy Adams, Jay Cassell, Tom Cuddy, Dave Marken, Scott Mendel, David Salidor, Mary Wilson. Skyhorse Publishing, you have been great to me!

I would like to dedicate this special "tribute edition" of this book to the memory of Kenneth Reynolds and to Barbara Shelley. You both worked closely with the late Aretha Franklin at Arista Records and beyond, and you were very dear supportive friends to me throughout my career and in my life. Didn't the three of us have fun at Studio 54 and all the NYC hot spots? We sure did! The two of you are sincerely missed.

INTRODUCTION TO THE
TRIBUTE EDITION

On August 16, 2018, the world was stunned by the sad news that Aretha Franklin had passed away at the age of seventy-six, following a long illness. With her roller coaster-like weight gains and losses in the past six years, the public was well aware that she was suffering from some sort of undisclosed ailment. Although her millions of international fans had long suspected that something was not right with her health, when the final news came, it was like the universe had suddenly lost something of great value.

The beginning of the swirling dark clouds of doom had started in February of 2017 when Aretha made a public announcement that she was set to retire by the end of the year, and that she was planning on recording one last album. According to her, "I will be recording, but this will be my last year in concert. This is it." The album she had hoped to record was to be one with several guest producers at the helm, including her longtime friend Stevie Wonder.

At the time of her death, her final solo studio album was *Aretha Franklin Sings the Great Diva Classics*, and it was released in 2014. It was her reunion with longtime friend Clive Davis as the project's co-producer, and it was a concept album with Franklin delivering her rendition of hits by The Supremes, Barbra Streisand, Gloria Gaynor, Gladys Knight & The Pips, Adele, and several other divas.

Although it was met with mixed reviews, it indeed proved a final high point to one of the most legendary and enduring careers in the music business. The album's lone single was billed as "Rolling in the Deep (The Aretha Version)," and was Franklin's soulful interpretation of Adele's composition and worldwide Number One hit. Aretha showed that she was still musically agile enough to keep up with the new talent in the music world.

Franklin's version of "Rolling in the Deep" hit Number One on *Billboard*'s Dance Music Chart, and the album hit Number 13, Number Three R&B. It was her first album to chart that high since her "Who's Zoomin' Who" had also hit Number 13, and Number Three R&B in 1985. It was an affirmation that her talent and unflagging stature as a hit-maker had endured and continued after nearly sixty years as a recording artist.

Aretha's final public concert was on August 26, 2017, at The Mann Center in Philadelphia, Pennsylvania. She then performed at an event held for Elton John's AIDS Foundation on November 7, 2017, at The Cathedral of St. John the Divine in New York City. She appeared to be frighteningly thin, setting off further alarms that something was gravely wrong. Franklin appeared gaunt and frail on stage. Considering her trademark hearty weight and unwavering energy, the way she looked and moved was alarming at best.

During the ensuing months Aretha remained relatively quiet. She had three concerts booked for the spring of 2018, including a performance at

The New Orleans Jazz Fest. Ultimately, all of them were canceled. Then suddenly, on Sunday, August 12, 2018, the news hit the internet, and instantly circulated that Aretha Franklin was in "ill health," and most likely would not recover. It was Franklin's longtime press friend Roger Friedman who first broke the news on his web-based news site *Show Business 411*. When Friedman noted that her family "is asking for prayers and privacy," it confirmed to the world that this would likely be her final battle.

People magazine on August 13 disclosed, "Aretha Franklin's death reportedly 'imminent': She's been ill for a long time." When *TMZ* also reported that day Aretha was "down to 85 pounds," it was further confirmation that the end was near. The public could see the handwriting on the wall.

Aretha was all over the television with CNN, Fox News, and *The Today Show* following updates on the beloved soul diva's condition. On August 14, *Us* magazine reported, "Stevie Wonder says goodbye to Aretha Franklin as she receives hospice care." Other guests who came to Aretha's house to wish her well were her long-time friend Jesse Jackson and ex-husband Glynn Turman.

That same day came the announcement that there was already a big gala tribute concert planned in memory of Aretha set for November 14, 2018. There was no information at that time who would be performing, but it was already being billed as "Clive Davis Presents: A Tribute to Aretha Franklin." It must have buoyed Aretha's spirits in her last days to know such an honor was going to be bestowed upon her.

Then, on August 16, the saddest news of all hit the media: "Aretha Franklin Dead." The tributes began pouring in from her countless celebrity friends and devoted fans.

What an amazing legacy Aretha Franklin leaves behind her. She will always be remembered as a true original. Her voice was so strong and pure, it was like a force of nature, and it brilliantly redefined the word "soul." Franklin's famed producer Jerry Wexler once told me that when he sat Aretha down at the piano and let her be herself, her true brilliance came pouring out. How true that was. The music world would never be the same.

Aretha's songs like "Respect," "Think," "Rock Steady," and "Freeway of Love" will forever represent an era of sheer musical brilliance. She also had the unique ability to take the hits of others—like "Bridge Over Troubled Water" and "I Say a Little Prayer"—to breathe new life into them, and to make them all her own. I will always recall my one-on-one interview with Aretha in 1985 at her Detroit area home as one of the most unique afternoons of my entire writing career. It wasn't so much an interview as it was a visitation with royalty. Aretha Franklin's legend and her amazing body of recorded music will live on as proof of her unflagging reign as "The Queen of Soul."

INTRODUCTION
ALL HAIL THE QUEEN!

The book you are reading is one I have been writing—in one form or another—for forty years. The first time I wrote about Aretha Franklin was when I was a journalism student at Central Michigan University. I wrote a record review column for my college newspaper, and that very first year of its existence, I declared Aretha's *Young, Gifted and Black* to be one of my "Ten Best Recordings of 1972." At the time, I had no idea I would be consistently writing about her life and her music for the following four decades!

In 1985 I interviewed Aretha Franklin in person in her Detroit area home, and this book was conceived that very day. The first edition of *Aretha Franklin: The Queen of Soul* was published by St. Martin's Press in 1989. It was not only the first full biography ever published about Aretha Franklin, it was also critically acclaimed. The original book comprised nine chapters and a conclusion, labeled *"Dénouement"*—which is the French term for the final outcome or "resolution" to a story.

Da Capo Press published the second version of this book in 2001. It comprised the original 1989 edition, plus an additional chapter, entitled "A Rose is Still a Rose," and an updated Discography section in the back of the book to take the book from 1990 to 2001.

By the end of 2010, Aretha Franklin was back in the headlines again. She had been continuing to record and to perform across America, when she was hospitalized, battling a mysterious and life-threatening illness. The world drew a collective gasp, worried for her health. At the same time, the rights to this book again reverted back to me, and suddenly it was time to update this book again.

This time around I had to do more than just add a new chapter and update the growing list of Aretha's recordings presented in the Discography. Since the original book written in 1989 was such a favorite of Aretha's fans, I have chosen to leave it more or less intact and to build some new pieces around it.

While everything in the 1989 and 2001 editions of this book is included, this new version has been completely updated. In addition, I have added over one dozen Aretha Franklin stories and two new chapters in order to bring the story all the way up to 2012 and to make this edition of the book completely unique.

The new chapters, entitled "So Damned Happy" and "How Does Aretha Keep the Music Playing" discuss Aretha's final recordings with Arista Records, her alarming weight gain, the highly-publicized feud she started with Tina Turner, her 2010–2011 health issues, her sudden weight loss, an all-star salute to Aretha on the 2011 *Grammy Awards* telecast, rumors of a film about her remarkable life, her first Number One pop album appearance, and an overview of her amazing career.

As concerns about Aretha's health grew in 2010 and 2011, record labels scrambled to issue new compilations of her iconic music. So, in an effort to make certain that this book remains the "definitive" book on Aretha, it needed a new up-to-the-minute list of all of her recordings. I decided that, rather than adding a separate updating section to the segmented Discography that appeared in the 2001 version of this book, I needed to reconstruct the whole thing so Aretha's devoted fans will now have a new "ultimate" list of her recorded music at hand. Since it was Aretha's music that first made us all fall in love with her, I am able to present a "new and improved" Discography that is truly fit for rock and roll royalty.

Since this soul-singing Detroit diva is such a unique performer, this new version of *Aretha Franklin: The Queen of Soul* had to be unique, exciting, up-to-date, and filled with information that is unobtainable anywhere else. This has offered me the opportunity to revisit one of my all-time favorite books and to give it a new lease on life. In addition, for the first time, this book will not only be available in America, it will also be published in several different languages in several countries, around the world.

The great soul man James Brown once claimed in song that "It's a Man's World." That's not Aretha's side of the story. After you have read this book, I am confident you will come to the conclusion that it is Aretha Franklin's world and clearly she is and always will be the "Queen of Soul."

—Mark Bego
2012

PROLOGUE
DETROIT 1989

Aretha Franklin rarely grants interviews, and when she does, she never discusses the details of her personal life. In the summer of 1985 I had the unique opportunity of spending several hours at her home in the Detroit suburb of Bloomfield Hills, interviewing her for a national radio broadcast. Although Aretha was a bit shy at first, as the interview progressed, she relaxed and became quite warm and talkative.

Since the interview was for radio broadcast, we stopped the tape recorder a couple of times so that she could light up a cigarette and just chat off the record. I found her to be charming, and very down-to-earth. Having grown up in Detroit myself, I had known of Aretha as a local legend for three decades. As our interview progressed, I was pleased to find that she was not a prima donna. She opened up when she discovered that my interviewing technique was more like having a friendly conversation.

During one of our breaks in taping for the radio broadcast, I told her I was the author of several biographies of celebrities. I confessed that it was a dream of mine to collaborate with her someday on her autobiography. "I'm not interested in doing that," she said, "I don't want to write a book." I was disappointed, but at least I had gone on record as having asked.

We completed the interview, and it went quite smoothly. As she had requested, I stayed away from several topics of her personal life—especially the recent death of her father. But she was comfortable enough with me to poke fun at herself, to discuss her very real fear of flying, and to talk about her French lessons. "*Moi?*" she said, laughingly referring to herself in French. When our interview was over, Aretha took me on a tour of her backyard to see the swimming pool and her vegetable garden.

Although I had met her before, backstage at Radio City Music Hall in New York City, that afternoon in the Detroit suburbs I felt that I had met a charming, witty, suburban "lady next door" who was proud of her home and her garden. The fact that she was an international superstar was almost incidental.

I have been asked several times during my career, "What is the one book you would most like to write?" That afternoon at Aretha's house, I had my answer. With that interview, I officially began work on this—the most challenging and rewarding book I've ever written. There had never been a book published about Aretha Franklin. I have endeavored to write the most in-depth biography possible without her complete cooperation. Some of the information I have uncovered is shocking.

During the course of my research, I was fortunate enough to be able to interview not only Aretha Franklin, but several key people in her life as well. Three of the most important people I spoke to were record producers Clyde Otis and Jerry Wexler, and Arista Records president, Clive Davis. I cannot thank these talented gentlemen enough. Clyde Otis is responsible for writing and producing several of Aretha's most memorable songs from her years at Columbia Records in the 1960s. At Atlantic Records in the late sixties and early seventies, Jerry Wexler crafted the most famous string of hit recordings in her career. And Clive Davis is the mastermind behind Aretha's incredible Gold-and-Platinum resurgence in the 1980s.

Unfortunately, during the writing of the original edition of this book, two important figures in Aretha's life died. Record producer John Hammond passed on in July of 1987, and her sister, Carolyn, succumbed to cancer in April of 1988. Their memory is preserved on these pages.

Jerry Wexler has stated that an underlying sadness surrounds Aretha's personal life. When I asked him to clarify his comment, he replied, "Well, it wasn't caprice or temperament, it was just sadness." I set out to discover the cause of Aretha's sadness.

Just when I thought I had reached a dead end on several issues of Aretha's personal life, suddenly new doors opened to me, and several people from her past decided to speak. After twenty years of silence,

Aretha's first husband, Ted White, talked to me. Although he answered questions in a guarded fashion at first, we ultimately began a dialogue that shed much light on his life with Aretha—as both her husband and her manager. I cannot thank him enough for his insights.

There are at least two sides to every story. The stories in this book are no exception. In several instances I was told conflicting information. In an effort to tell the story of Aretha's life objectively, in many cases I have presented both views. Since controversy and rumors often hold truth, I have investigated her life from several different angles in an effort to present, for the first time, the real Aretha Franklin.

Before Aretha was a pop legend and a rock & roll star, she was a gospel and blues singer. Like Bessie Smith, Billie Holiday, and Dinah Washington before her, she has had several disappointing events in her life that have caused her to become introverted and sad. Fortunately for the rest of the world, Aretha has been able to channel her feelings into some of the most memorable and soulful music of the Twentieth Century. On the other side of the coin, Aretha has had much in her life to rejoice about, and often she has sung of optimism and happiness too.

At what point does Aretha—the taken-advantage-of blues singer—end, and Lady Soul—the steadfast woman who commands "R-E-S-P-E-C-T"—begin? In writing this book, it has been my goal to provide the answers to these questions.

ARETHA FRANKLIN:
THE QUEEN OF SOUL

CHAPTER ONE

THE QUEEN OF SOUL

It is a hot July afternoon in suburban Detroit, in 1985. Aretha Franklin is comfortably seated next to me on one part of the dark brown ultrasuede sectional sofa that winds its way across her spacious and modern living room. Through the sliding glass doors I can see the tree-lined backyard. Outside, a warm summer breeze sends a ripple across the surface of the huge swimming pool.

Aretha is smoking a Kool cigarette, and she takes an occasional sip from her glass of ginger ale. It strikes me as odd to be sitting next to a woman whose voice I have spent years admiring, and to watch her chain-smoke. After years of going through two packs of cigarettes a day, for Aretha it is still a habit that she can't seem to break.

The room is painted a creamy shade of off-white, and several walls are hung with framed Gold records and laudatory citations. Behind us is a black grand piano, and on top of it sit several gold statuettes and an impressive bust of a woman. The short gold statuettes are just a few of her many Grammy Awards, and the bust is of Egyptian Queen Nefertiti, who is Aretha's favorite historical figure. On the shelf by the fireplace, there are two clear Lucite obelisks, which are better known as American Music Awards. Across the cream-colored wall-to-wall carpeting and against another wall, is a modern-looking entertainment center complete with a stereo and a wide-screen television set on which Aretha watches her favorite soap operas. Fresh-cut flowers are arranged in vases, and a recent portrait of Aretha is framed and hung on one of the walls.

With her well-manicured fingernails she plays with her gold necklace as she prepares to reflect on her long and eventful career in show business. She is dressed in a casual but smart blue pantsuit, and on one of her fingers she wears a large rectangular art deco ring, sparkling with dozens of diamonds.

Aretha takes one last drag from her cigarette, and stamps it out in a large ashtray on the coffee table before her. It is the signal that she is now ready to begin a rare press interview.

After over thirty years as a singing star, she's known around the world. In Italy she is called *"La Regina del Soul."* In France she is referred to as "Aretha Franklin *La Magnifique*." She is also known as "Sister Ree," "Lady Soul," *"La Diva* Franklin," and "The Queen of Soul." But to her millions of followers, the one word "Aretha" says it all. She is the most celebrated female artist in the history of recorded music. With more Grammy Awards and Top Ten chart hits than any other woman in the realms of rock & roll, pop, jazz, soul, or gospel music, her career is definitely one of legendary proportions.

She began singing in the choir at her father's church at an early age. "I love gospel music!" Aretha proclaimed in our interview. "Gospel music means everything to me. It certainly was part of my beginnings, the church being my background." When she found stardom in the late 1960s, she embodied the heart and the sound of "soul" music. She became a symbol of black pride, and her songs spoke of unbridled passion and heartbreak.

I found that Aretha especially glowed when she talked about her glory days at Atlantic Records in the 1960s and 1970s. "Jerry Wexler signed me to the Atlantic label," she recounted proudly that afternoon, "and of course I had many, many great days in the studio with him. 'Respect' was produced by Jerry Wexler, who produced so many hits for me. And there was [co-producer] Arif Mardin, whom I love and love to work with. Magic things happen when Arif and I work together. And let's see: [recording engineer] Tommy Dowd, who I think is just one of the best in the business. That man can do things—editing with tape—that I have never seen before."

Her image has been largely shaped by the songs that have made her famous. She is the uncompromising "earth mother" who is steadfast and strong. Her singing is blisteringly honest and charged with emotion. Her voice is unmistakably pure, unrestrained, and soul-stirring. The mention of her name cultivates a vivid mental picture of Aretha—the Survivor. It is easy to envision her as the no-nonsense woman, musically commanding "Respect," threatening her man that he'd better "Think" before he looks at another woman, announcing that she has discovered "The Spirit in the Dark," or enticing someone to take a ride on "The Freeway of Love." However, Aretha's shattering encounters with personal tragedy and pain have earned her the right to sing the blues as well.

Aretha has so much for which to be thankful. She possesses one of the most emotionally expressive five-octave voices of the rock era. She has been able to span three decades with Number One hit records, from 1967's "Respect" to 1987's "I Knew You Were Waiting (For Me)." The royal command performance, the unsurpassed total of twenty Grammy Awards, the movie and video performances, the sold-out concerts, the white Rolls-Royces and pink Cadillacs, and the highly publicized romances that stardom has brought her, are all part of the glamorous life she has led.

Yet, on the other side of the coin, Aretha's life hasn't been one long joy ride down "The Freeway of Love." Fate has thrown several obstacles into her path that have caused her anguish. Desperation, domination, disappointment, prejudice, frustration, teenage pregnancy, weight problems, and devastating emotional trauma are all part of her closely guarded private life.

In Jerry Wexler's eyes, Aretha's personal life is so sad that he refers to her as "the mysterious lady of sorrow." Clyde Otis claims that he was amazed she could sing at all in the sixties because she was so depressed that she appeared to be carrying the weight of the whole world on her shoulders. John Hammond once said that Aretha had "terrible luck" with the men in her life, and that they all made her suffer.

Although she bears several emotional scars, Aretha Franklin is clearly a survivor—not only in her career, but in her personal life as well. Although she has experienced a lifelong series of personal tragedies and disappointments, for each of her emotional low points, she has overcome her pain by channeling her frustration into creative energy. In turn, her determination has made her into an enduring star. The erratic highs and lows of her life—public and private—have obviously given her an inner strength that is both powerful and inspiring. Her inner faith has seen her through the worst of times.

A list of "forbidden" topics relating to her personal life is given before an interview is granted, and she would much rather talk about her music than her life. That afternoon at Aretha's home, I learned several things I did not know about her. But I was left wanting to know more:

- What it was like to grow up in a big inner-city house, raised by housekeepers and family friends?
- What was it like to grow up as the daughter of a local celebrity of the black community?
- What are the details of her relationship with her father, and what kind of power did he have over her?
- What was it like to become a soloist in the church choir at the age of twelve?
- Is gospel music really her first love, or is it merely a creative outlet into which she escapes?
- What kind of things was young Aretha exposed to while traveling on a bus from city-to-city with a gospel roadshow?
- How old was Aretha when she had her first child, and who was the father?
- Who was the black male pop star with whom she fell in love, and how did he inspire her?
- In what way did Aretha become a symbol of black pride in the 1960s?
- How much of her music was drawn from her own tragic personal life?
- Did she sing the blues because she was living them?
- When her first marriage broke up, into whose arms did she run?
- What kind of emotional toll did her father's five-year coma and eventual death have on her?

◆ Why does Aretha almost never leave Detroit? Like Scarlet O'Hara drawing her strength from the red earth of Tara, does Aretha derive her confidence from Detroit—or is she simply hiding there like a frightened child?

I felt as if I had just encountered one of the great unsolved mysteries of the show business world. The answers to these questions are all pieces of the puzzle that is the mesmerizing story of Aretha Franklin.

CHAPTER TWO

THE GOSPEL YEARS

Aretha Louise Franklin was born on March 25, 1942, the fourth child in a family of five children. "There's Vaughn, the oldest, who was a career man in the Air Force," she says of her siblings. "Then Erma, then Cecil—who's my manager—then myself, then Carolyn."

Their household was infused with religion. Their father was a Baptist minister who was known for his emotional deliveries from the pulpit, and their mother was a renowned gospel singer. Aretha inherited her father's sense of drama and her mother's vocal talents. These talents helped to create a show business legend.

Much is known about Reverend Clarence LaVaughn Franklin and his vivid flair for life. Born on January 22, 1915, he rose from modest beginnings amid the cotton fields of rural Mississippi, to be heralded as "The Man with the Million-Dollar Voice." In the 1950s he reputedly commanded up to four thousand dollars per sermon. In the 1960s *Time* magazine claimed that his obvious success could be measured by his attraction to glitzy Cadillacs, diamond stickpins and expensive alligator shoes. He became known as a flashy *bon vivant* in the middle of the Detroit ghetto. With an inner-city congregation all his own, he delivered impassioned invocations with fervent charisma, and when he passed around the collection plate it always came back filled.

Time wasn't the only observer of Reverend Franklin's financial prosperity. The Internal Revenue Service also took note of the fact that passing the collection plate was an unaccountable "cash" business and in the late sixties he was audited and fined for tax evasion.

Throughout her life, Aretha's father remained a key figure in her personal life *and* in her career. Regardless of who she married or where she was living, Reverend Franklin's thoughts and opinions were often to guide her. "He had a tremendous influence over her," recalls one family friend. "I don't know if it was just as a father figure or what."

Far less is known about her mother. Her maiden name was Barbara Siggers, and those who knew her often recalled her glorious singing voice. It is said that as a gospel singer, Barbara Siggers was in the same league with Mahalia Jackson and Clara Ward. According to John Hammond, "Mahalia always told me that Aretha's mother was one of the really great gospel singers. She said she had more talent than Reverend C. L. Franklin."

Aretha explains of this period of her life, that from Memphis "we moved to Buffalo, then to Detroit. I was raised in Detroit, the north end. Then we moved to the west side, then further out."

In spite of his marriage to Barbara Siggers in 1936, Reverend C. L. Franklin had quite a reputation with the women and girls in his church. In 1940 Reverend Franklin caused a scandal when he had an affair with Mildred Jennings, a thirteen-year-old member of his congregation at New Salem Baptist Church in Memphis. She became pregnant by him, and gave birth to a daughter, Carl Ellan Jennings.

In 1948 Barbara suddenly packed her bags and left Detroit, Reverend C. L. Franklin, and the four children they had together: Aretha, Erma, Carolyn, and Cecil. She moved to Buffalo, New York with her oldest son, Vaughn, to whom she had given birth prior to her marriage to C. L. Franklin.

Whatever caused Barbara Franklin to leave her husband and her four youngest children appears to have been too traumatic for anyone to discuss. One is left to guess what might have caused her sudden flight. Was it marital strife? Another man? Another woman? A liquor problem? Was she finally done with his infidelities? The matter remains a tightly-kept family secret to this day.

There are two ways to look at this story. Many sources view what happened as Barbara having "deserted" Aretha and her siblings. However, Aretha later recalled that this was not the case since she, Erma, Carolyn and Cecil would go to Buffalo to see their mother during their summer vacations.

Barbara and Vaughn had moved into Barbara's parents' home in Buffalo and Aretha remembers her summer visits there fondly. Her mother had taken a job as a nurse's aide at Buffalo General Hospital, and Aretha and her siblings recalled riding their bicycles through the streets of Buffalo in the warm summer sun. Aretha was so impressed with her mother's job at the hospital that as a child she contemplated making nursing her life's work. One Christmas Aretha and Carolyn were given little toy nurses kits, and they would prescribe little candy pills to each other as make-believe medicine.

However, the carefree memories of her childhood were soon clouded by tragedy. When Aretha was just ten years old, her mother suffered a massive heart attack and died. Reverend C. L. Franklin called Aretha, Carolyn, Erma and Cecil into the kitchen of their Detroit house one day, and plainly but solemnly delivered the sad news. It was a devastating blow to them. The children all went to their mother's funeral, but Reverend Franklin reportedly did not attend.

What is most recalled about Barbara Siggers Franklin are the widely-spread statements about her *alleged* "desertion" of the family and her sudden death. In Aretha's eyes, her mother never deserted her children, it was her marriage to C. L. Franklin she deserted. Family friends recall that her mother's untimely disappearance from Aretha's life caused the young girl to change from an outgoing, happy youngster to a shy and insecure child. Mahalia Jackson once commented, "After her mama died, the whole family wanted for love."

Detroit in the years immediately following World War II was the scene of economic expansion and growth. Although racial prejudice existed, compared to Memphis, the Motor City was a liberal land of opportunity. There were jazz clubs, dance halls, theaters, burlesque houses, bars, and a booming nightlife scene. In other words, come the Sabbath, there were plenty of souls in need of Sunday-morning redemption. That's where Reverend C. L. Franklin's oratorical powers came into play.

In Memphis, Reverend Franklin was the pastor of the New Salem Baptist Church. Upon moving to Buffalo, he was called to Friendship Baptist Church. When he took over the New Bethel Baptist Church, at the corner of Linwood and West Pennsylvania in Detroit, he made it clear that his Sundays spent before the congregations in Memphis and Buffalo were just "dress rehearsals" for his true calling.

When Reverend Franklin began preaching and the choir started rejoicing, enraptured parishioners would stand up and shout a heartfelt "Praise the Lord!" Often, members of the crowd gathered in the 4,500-seat church would become so frantic with their "testifying" that nurses in starched white uniforms had to revive them. On hot summer Sundays, the air would be stirred with complimentary cardboard fans. Mounted on wooden sticks, the handheld cardboard fans were printed with advertisements for local funeral homes. Clearly there were only two realities in Reverend Franklin's church—life and death.

Word spread fast and people traveled from great distances to hear the gospel according to Reverend C. L. Franklin. Eventually a glowing blue neon crucifix was installed over the altar to match the electricity of his oratory delivery.

Reverend Franklin became so famous for his sermons at the New Bethel Baptist Church that he was often asked to make guest appearances across the country. When he was called away from Detroit on business, his four children were left in the care of a series of housekeepers and family friends. For a while, Aretha's grandmother, Rachel, moved in and took care of her and her siblings. The children called her "Big Mama," and she was their father's mother. She had a reputation for being a strong disciplinarian if any of the children did anything wrong. Big Mama was one of the women who taught Aretha how to cook, along with the Franklin family's regular housekeeper, Katherine. Another household guest was Lola Moore, whom Aretha referred to as "Daddy's special friend." Three of the most frequent visitors who took care of the Franklin children were Frances Steadman and Marion Williams, who were both gospel vocalists with the Clara Ward Singers, and Mahalia Jackson.

Mahalia Jackson was already a singing legend when she came to visit the Franklin home. She was to become a lifelong inspiration for Aretha. In her own opinion, Mahalia felt that she was "ordained to sing the gospel."

Mahalia Jackson was born in New Orleans in 1911, the daughter of a stevedore / barber / preacher and his wife. Her mother died when she was four years old, and she was raised by her aunts. By the time she was twelve, Mahalia had vowed to spread the gospel. According to her, "Ever since that day, I promised the Lord that I'd dedicate my life to song."

When Mahalia was sixteen, she went to Chicago to live with another aunt. It was there that her professional singing career took off. For seven years she was a member of the gospel quintet, The Johnson Singers, and in 1941 she became a soloist. Four years later, she recorded "Move On Up a Little Higher." The inspirational record sold eight million copies and made her a star. She continued to record hit after hit with "Upper Room," "Even Me," and "Silent Night."

In 1954, Mahalia debuted her nationally broadcast CBS radio show, becoming the first gospel performer to have a regular network program. While her recording career flourished, she also appeared in several movies, including *Imitation of Life* with Lana Turner (1959) and *The Best Man* with Henry Fonda (1964).

It was Mahalia's clear and strong contralto voice that made her such a huge success. Her singing was emotion-charged, and everyone who heard her was genuinely touched by her inspiring strength and spiritual fire. Her faith in God was unwavering, and everything she sang was deeply felt. This was a trait that young Aretha gleaned from Mahalia and applied to her own music.

Although she had become the most famous singer in gospel music, Mahalia never lost her down-home sincerity. She once described herself as "just a strong Louisiana woman who can cook rice so every grain stands by itself." Aretha has fond memories of Mahalia—in church and in the kitchen.

There were times when the Franklin house buzzed with music and excitement. "There was always music in our house," Aretha recalls. "The radio was going in one room, the record player in another, the piano banging away in the living room. During my upbringing, people like Art Tatum, Arthur Prysock, Dinah Washington, Lionel Hampton, Sam Cooke, James Cleveland, and Clara Ward used to come to our house. So I was accustomed to being around famous people. Mahalia would come in, put a pot of greens on the stove, sit around and talk and eat, and maybe somebody would start toying with the piano and something would start up."

It is easy to see how young Aretha and her sisters, growing up in a household that played host to a virtual *Who's Who* of popular black music, all gravitated toward singing and playing the piano. When she was "about eight or nine," Aretha began playing around with the piano while listening to Eddie Heywood on the record player. She recalls that she was "just banging, not playing, but finding a little something here and there." Her father encouraged her daughter's interest in the piano and hired a teacher to give her lessons. However, playing the piano became too much like school, and Aretha rebelled. "I used to run and hide when she came," she recalls of her teacher. "She was going along too slowly for me. Too much 'Chopsticks.' She stopped coming because every time she did, I wasn't there."

Eventually, without the help of formal instruction, Aretha taught herself how to play the piano and also discovered that she could sing.

Instead of being influenced by the many negative aspects of inner-city life, the Franklin children seemed to stay away from trouble, and they learned to channel themselves in positive directions. Their house was shaded by trees and there was a grassy lawn. In spite of cockroaches in the kitchen and an occasional rat in the basement, they had it better than several of the children with whom they played and attended school.

According to Aretha's brother Cecil Franklin, "The people that you saw who had any measure of success were the pimp and the hustler, the numbers man, and the dope man. Aretha knew what they were all about without having to meet them personally."

"We were very good kids," Aretha recalls. "We roller-skated, sat on the back porch—some people would call it a stoop—and told a lot of jokes late into the midnight hours. I had a piano right off the back porch, and sometimes I'd sing . . . all day, every day, with my sisters and my friends. Mostly what we heard on the radio—the Drifters, LaVern Baker, Ruth Brown. Oh, it was real nice. Of course in the end we'd argue, because they were tired. And I wanted to sing all through the night."

She was especially encouraged by the household of visiting celebrities. One of her first mentors was James Cleveland, who taught her how to reach notes she didn't realize were in her range. "He showed me some real nice chords," she remembers, "and I liked his deep, deep sound. There's a whole lot of earthiness in the way he sings and what he was feeling. I was feeling but I just didn't know how to put it across. The more I watched him, the more I got out of it."

Another one of Aretha's prime influences was Clara Ward. When one of Aretha's aunts died, Ward sang at the funeral. Caught up in the fervor of the song "Peace in the Valley," Ward grabbed the hat off her head and hurled it to the ground. "Clara knocked me out!" Aretha recalls of the emotional gesture. "From then on I knew what I wanted to do—sing!" The spirit and the stirring emotion of that afternoon stayed with her for a long time.

At the age of twelve, Aretha sang her first solo in church. "I stood up on a little chair and sang," she recalls. She and her sister, Erma, also joined a gospel quartet directed by Reverend James Cleveland. At times Aretha played piano for the choir, and she eventually became one of the church's three featured soloists. After her first solo performance, several parishioners flocked around Reverend Franklin and exclaimed, "Oh, that child sure can sing!"

She was regularly highlighted in the choir after that, and was quite taken by the attention that she received. Since her role model was Clara Ward, who also played the piano, Aretha decided she wanted to play just like Ward did. "I liked all of Miss Ward's records," Franklin remembers, "and I learned how to play them because I thought one day she might decide she didn't want to play [in church] and I'd be ready."

Aretha has several fond memories of her school days. According to her, she enjoyed most of her courses. "My favorite classes were health, science, art, and lunch!" she recalls with a laugh. "I was a good student. A's, B's, some C's. Maybe one D here and there. I used to get called from my classes a lot because the auditorium teacher would need me to entertain the kids. They'd be throwing spitballs or fighting and I'd have to play the piano to entertain. She'd always call me when I was in Phys. Ed. and I'd have to walk in wearing my gym suit, with the shorts and the blouse that you had to sew your name on. I hated that. I really wanted to get down with the kids and do a little screaming myself, but I had to sing. That was my first experience with a tough audience."

Two of Aretha's favorite pastimes, in addition to singing, were roller-skating and watching boxing matches on television. When she was singing with her choir as a soloist, she was paid fifteen dollars a week for her services. Little by little, she saved her earnings to purchase one of her most prized possessions: her own pair of roller skates. "I bought my first pair of roller skates with Raybestos wheels. They were about thirty dollars a wheel, so I had to really save for those skates," she recalls.

As amazing as it seems, Raybestos skate wheels were that expensive, and were only manufactured for a short period of time. The Raybestos Company was famous at the time for making superior auto brake linings for Cadillacs and other high-profile cars. If Aretha was going to have skates that would make her the envy of the entire neighborhood, then she had to have top-of-the-line Raybestos wheels!

The hot spot for roller skating was the nearby Arcadia Roller Rink on Woodward Avenue. All of the area kids would hang out there, skating for hours to the latest hit records. "I lived in the roller rink!" Aretha exclaims.

Her lifelong interest in boxing began when she was a kid. She used to sit for hours with her father in front of the television, eating ice cream and watching the fights. She explains, "I've loved boxers since I was a little girl. I kept up with Joe Louis, Rocky Marciano, Johnny Bratton, Kid Gavilan, Muhammad Ali, Joe Frazier. I met Ray Robinson at the Hollywood Bowl once. That was a real treat. When I was a child I used to think he was so handsome."

Combining her love of singing and her passion for watching boxing matches, Aretha developed her own formula for a vocal TKO. By the time she was fourteen years old she was stunning people every Sunday at the New Bethel Baptist Church with her expressive gospel singing.

Just as Mozart had entertained the crowned heads of Europe with his piano playing as a child prodigy in the Eighteenth Century, young Aretha Franklin sang her heart out with the voice of a world-weary woman four times her age. Before long, New Bethel Baptist Church wasn't enough to contain her vocal gifts alone; it was time for the rest of the world to marvel at the wonder of her voice.

In the late 1940s, Reverend Franklin had begun to expand his realm beyond the boundaries of Detroit through personal appearances and recordings. It all started on the radio. A local Detroit radio station persuaded him to allow his sermons to be broadcast to a listening audience unable to attend church. A record producer in town, Joe Von Battles, heard Reverend Franklin on the radio one Sunday and began recording his sermons on LPs to spread the gospel. After Revered Franklin recorded several sermons on Battles' own label, JVB Records, Battles licensed them to Chess Records for national distribution. According to Aretha, her father left quite a legacy of preaching on record. "He has about fifty volumes on Chess Records, meaning fifty sermons. He usually prefaced his sermons with a hymn," she explains.

Since the records were distributed nationally, it wasn't long before religious radio stations across America began broadcasting Reverend Franklin's sermons. This made it possible for him to organize a traveling revival show, complete with a choir, gospel singing stars, and, of course, Reverend Franklin and his oratory as the centerpiece of the show.

With the encouragement of Clara Ward, James Cleveland, and her father, the teenage Aretha would spend her summer vacations away from Detroit's Northern High School touring the country with the revival show. For a young girl, life on the road was quite an education. It wasn't long before she was exposed to several aspects of life that none of the long talks with Mahalia Jackson around a simmering pot of greens in the kitchen of her house ever covered. She witnessed drinking, carousing, all-night partying, and heavy doses of Southern prejudice on these out-of-town jaunts. While her father traveled from city-to-city by plane for his appearances, young Aretha and her siblings stayed with the rest of the troupe on cross-country buses.

Of the racial prejudice she encountered, Aretha reveals, "When my father and I traveled in the South, we ran into it from time to time, usually in restaurants with [separate] black and white sections. Racism is more sophisticated and subtle today [in the 1980s], but still prevalent."

Her brother Cecil adds that "driving eight or ten hours trying to make a gig, and being hungry and passing restaurants all along the road, and having to go off the highway into some little city to find a place to eat because you're black—that had its effect."

"When you were singing gospel," says Erma Franklin, "it was very hard to get your money after the program was over. The promoter would run off with all the money, so it was almost a knock-down-drag-out fight to get on the show with Revered Franklin because then you wouldn't have to worry about your money."

Erma also remembers that "blacks had to stay with blacks in the South. You had to stay at black motels, so you had your gospel groups and your rhythm & blues stars would come up to my father and they would say, 'We heard your album and we think it's great.' They'd introduce themselves and they'd become fast friends with everyone else who were stars on the road. So when they would come to Detroit they would call my dad and come over to the house. He'd have dinner fixed for them and they'd stay. Invariably, they'd start singing then there would be one big party! Anything that you had heard them sing, you would just holler it out and they'd do it! You didn't have to beg 'em. We were hams, we all were."

Aretha especially remembers those long hours spent on the road. "We'd drive thousands and thousands of miles," she recalls. "I've been to California from Detroit about four times through the desert. Never again! Never again! That's the way people traveled back then. Baby, those steep mountains with no railing! That was worse than coming across in a horse and buggy, I'm sure."

Traveling on those gospel caravan extravaganzas prepared Aretha for the concert tours she would embark on in the 1960s and 1970s. "I traveled from about the age of thirteen to sixteen with my dad, singing with the Roberta Martin Singers, the Clara Ward Singers Caravan—real gospel giants. It was great training." She also made several lifelong friends along the way such as Mavis Staples, who sang along with her father, "Pop" Staples, and with her sisters, Yvonne and Cleo, performing gospel as the Staples Singers.

During this time, Reverend Franklin gave his daughter constant guidance. "He encouraged me to sing," says Aretha. "He taught me to conduct myself as a lady." When she would rush through a song out of nervousness, he would say to her, "Take your time; say what you want to say." She took his advice and her reward came during one of the cross-country gospel caravans—a chance to record her singing at Oakland Arena.

"We weren't in the studio," Aretha explains. "It was a church service in Oakland, California. My dad appeared in many of the major auditoriums throughout the country and I appeared with him on weekends as a featured vocalist. So Chess Records, after having recorded many of his sermons, came out to California and recorded that service." That same year, a compilation of several of her gospel performance from New Bethel Baptist Church was assembled on one album and Chess released it under the title *Songs of Faith*. (In 1964, it was re-released as *The Gospel Sound of Aretha Franklin* and in 1982 it was reissued again, as *Aretha Gospel* on Checker Records.)

The album itself is a true piece of recorded history. With only a piano backing her, and the voices of the church choir on one of the tunes, the pure and untrained sound of fourteen-year-old Aretha singing hymns and spiritual songs is an amazing preview of the greatness to come. Her performances on this album are underscored by the excited shouts of "Amen!" and "Oh Lord!" On "There Is a Fountain Filled with Blood," young Aretha's singing is clear and strong. When she wails in the middle of "Precious Lord (Part Two)," she demonstrates the passion she later unleashed on her Atlantic recordings. Like the formula she would use throughout her career, she took several songs from someone she admired, reinterpreted them, and made them all her own. In this case it was Clara Ward's "Never Grow Old" (as well as the two previously mentioned songs) she took hold of and improved upon.

On "He Will Wash You Whiter Than Snow" Aretha is heard singing the lead with the church choir answering her vocal pleas. This album previews several of her late-sixties hits, on which the Sweet Inspirations sang the choral accompaniment. On this particular song, the recording quality echoes the sound of the great blues singer Bessie Smith. In fact, Aretha's vocal on "He Will Wash You Whiter Than Snow" is reminiscent of Bessie's blues delivery.

While Aretha was discovering her vocal capacities on the altar of the New Bethel Baptist Church, the surrounding Detroit neighborhood was humming with music of all sorts. Otis Williams recalls hearing wonderful things about that little Franklin girl who had people in awe of her voice when she sang on Sundays. In 1964, Williams became world-famous as one of the Temptations. A skinny little neighborhood girl named Diane Ross joined two school friends, Mary Wilson and Florence Ballard, and together they became the Supremes. (When she became famous, Ross changed her name from Diane to Diana.) Friends of the Franklins, the Robinsons, had a little boy named William, and he was interested in becoming a pop singer. Everyone called William by his nickname, "Smokey." It is amazing to think that such a concentration of musical talent was centered in that one area of Detroit.

According to Smokey Robinson, "When Aretha was a child she could go to the piano and play—nearly like she plays now! None of the rest of us could just go sit down and play the piano and sing like that!"

Aretha remembers all of these singing stars as kids in the neighborhood with little more than their dreams and their vocal talent. "I didn't really know Diana," she reminisces. "On my way home, I would see her from time to time. She was screaming off the back porch one night at somebody, and I said, 'Oh, that's that Diane Ross girl.' Smokey and I—our families had been friends going back till I was nine, ten years old. Smokey would come over with his group [The Miracles] to rehearse. Erma and I used to love the Flamingos. We did 'I Only Have Eyes for You.' We knew all the Flamingos' dance routines, so when Smokey was trying to put something together for the Miracles, we showed him what we knew. That was probably one of their first bits of choreography. And we did it gratis!"

Music industry executive Billy Davis distinctly remembers that era in Detroit. "In hindsight, there certainly was a lot of young talent who was inspired by each other," he recalls, "and inspired by groups like the Dominoes, the Four Buddies, Ruth Brown, the Ravens, and groups who gained their popularity in the mid-fifties. Independent record labels began to spring up because all this talent was there. It was easy to put out a record in those days, and very cheap. In 1956, with five hundred dollars you could record it, press it, and take it around to your local stations and get it played. Within two or three weeks, you might have yourself a hit. It was very active and alive and inspiring. You could discover a talent one day, have them in the studio within a week and have a record out and on the air within two weeks. It was an exciting time in Detroit. A lot of kids who would probably have ended up in all types of trouble were singing on street corners instead of doing things that they might have been getting into. I was one of them, so I'm talking to you from experience."

Before Motown Records was founded and made million-selling stars out of the Miracles, the Supremes, Martha & the Vandellas, and the Temptations, the local musical marvel was clearly Aretha Franklin. Don David, who grew up to own a recording studio in Detroit called United Sound (where Aretha now records), remembers those days when all eyes were on teenage Aretha. "We spent an awful lot of time as kids in Reverend Franklin's church," says Don. "Those Sunday nights when he would finish preaching, we would listen to little Aretha up on-stage, and she'd turn the whole church on its cheek. Man, we'd look forward to that!"

"We belonged to her father's church," Mary Wilson recalls of Aretha and her sisters. "We went there every Sunday from 1956 up until 1963. That's when I first heard her. In fact, it was Aretha and Erma who were singing all the time, and they were fantastic! When I first heard Aretha, I adored her style. I adored everything she was doing, because she had a way of singing gospel that transcended all musical boundaries. Sometimes in gospel music you can only enjoy it in the framework of religion. Gospel was part of my religion, but I was into pop and R&B music. Aretha had a way of making me enjoy my gospel roots in a pop context. In church she would make you feel that you were listening to good music and not being preached to from the Bible. That was the beauty of her style."

Mary vividly remembers Aretha's younger sister, Carolyn, from Algers School which they attended together. "Carolyn Franklin was very tough," says Wilson. "She was the baby in the family, but she always had street gangs, and she was the gang leader. She was a little bully. With everyone in the family being such great singers, they were all local celebrities, and she usually used her family position to get her own way."

Especially impressive in young Mary's eyes was C. L. himself. "Reverend Franklin was the kind of man who had so much charisma that everyone was fascinated by him. Women absolutely loved him. He was a ladies' man! My mother adored him. That charisma he had. He was so charming that people were drawn to him. He was also a very eloquent man and very popular. I can see why his children would be as enamored of him as everybody else. It's as if none of the men in Aretha's life could ever match her father because he was so dynamic."

While Aretha was becoming locally famous as a gospel-singing child star, the music industry was changing and growing around her. Although she still loved gospel music, she was becoming fascinated by the hot new music she was hearing on the radio. One of the first R&B singers to grab Aretha's attention was the girl they called "Miss Rhythm"—Ruth Brown. Like Aretha, Ruth had begun singing spiritual songs in her father's church. She became an R&B singing sensation and later a pop star. Brown was known for her hits "5-10-15 Hours" (1952) and "Mama He Treats Your Daughter Mean" (1953) on the R&B charts, but in 1957 she crossed over to pop fame with her huge hit "Lucky Lips." "She was the singer when I was a girl," Aretha exclaims. "It was her records I liked, along with the Clovers ['Love Potion No. 9'], Clyde McPhatter ['A Lover's Question']— and these were all Atlantic [Records] artists, too. But Ruth Brown was my favorite."

Soon afterward, Aretha began toying with the idea of becoming an R&B singer as well. Her fascination was fueled by a close friend of hers who went from gospel fame to mainstream pop success. Aretha had followed his transition from singing at New Bethel Baptist Church to making gospel records, to becoming an R&B star, to his transformation into a hit-making pop star. Her friend's success opened her eyes to what was possible for her own singing career. His name was Sam Cooke.

Like so many of the gospel singing stars—including Mahalia Jackson—Sam Cooke came from Chicago. It wasn't uncommon for many Chicago stars to drive over to Detroit to appear at Reverend C. L. Franklin's church. When he was still in high school, Sam began singing gospel songs with his brother in a group called the Highway Q.C.'s, and in the 1950s he was the lead singer of the religious group called the Soul Stirrers. Sam made several recordings including "Touch the Hem of His Garment" and "Pilgrim of Sorrow."

After appearing at Reverend Franklin's church, Sam would come over to the Franklin house and socialize with Aretha and her sisters. He was very handsome and charming and Aretha developed a huge crush on him. She loved hearing him sing, and she even kept a Sam Cooke scrapbook.

"Oh, I loved that man," Aretha sighs at the mention of his name. "I was a great Sam Cooke fan. I had a little book of everything on him, down to his Kent cigarettes. I had a pack of those. He was young, handsome, and quite dashing. He was a very down-to-earth and beautiful person." Aretha was so in love with Sam that for years to come she saved that crumpled cigarette package he had left behind. She cherished it because it was his.

When Sam made the move from gospel singing to pop, he recorded two singles for the Soul Stirrers' gospel label, Specialty Records. When the staff at Specialty Records couldn't seem to market the two songs "I'll Come Running Back to You" and "Forever," in 1957 he switched to Keen Records.

As Sam's career grew, instead of coming to Detroit to perform at New Bethel Baptist Church, he would instead headline at the hottest club in town, The Flame Show Bar. Unhappily, Aretha was too young to be admitted when Sam played there, and she longed desperately to see his new act. "The Flame!" Aretha exclaims. "Oh, how I died to get into The Flame. Everybody who was anybody in soul played there, and for a couple years I was just underage. When I finally got in, I played with Smokey Robinson, the Temptations, Ben E. King—everybody. Yeah, those were wild times!"

Right before his debut single on Keen Records was released, Sam came over to the Franklin home and gave Aretha a special preview. "I learned a lot from Sam Cooke," she recalls. "He did so many things with his voice—so gentle one minute, so swinging the next, then electrifying, always doing something else. Sam brought his dub recording of 'You Send Me' to our house for us to hear when he was still singing with the Soul Stirrers. The song became a hit and Sam went pop."

When Sam's song, "You Send Me," became a huge Number One pop and R&B smash, it left a lasting impression on Aretha. According to her, "When he made the change [from gospel to soul], I said, 'I'd sure like to sing that too.'"

With this new goal in mind, Aretha decided she wanted to branch out with her vocalizing. Now all she needed was the right opportunity and she would try her hand at singing contemporary songs. She wasn't the only one who saw potential in her singing. Through her performances in her father's church on Sundays, she had already gained a reputation around Detroit as a legend in the making. Two of the people who regularly came to New Bethel Baptist Church to hear Aretha sing were a pair of young songwriters from the area. The duo longed to get involved in record producing. Their names were Berry Gordy, Jr. and his partner Billy Davis.

Eventually, Gordy went on to establish the company that put Detroit on the musical map—Motown Records. But in 1956 and 1957 he was just beginning his career in the recording business, and he had his first streak of luck as a songwriter. At the time, Billy Davis had assumed the pen name of Tyran Carlo. As the writing team of Gordy and Carlo, the pair helped to launch the solo career of a local Detroit singer named Jackie Wilson.

Wilson had been singing with the Dominos since 1953, when he replaced Clyde McPhatter as the lead singer of the group. McPhatter went on to form another group which brought him international fame: the Drifters. Jackie Wilson stayed with the Dominos for four years. Although the original group had scored a number of hits with McPhatter singing lead, Jackie at the helm of the quintet found itself mainly coasting on the fame of their former hits "Do Something for Me" (1951), "Sixty Minute Man" (1951), and "Have Mercy Baby" (1952). Although they performed in Las Vegas and at New York City's famed Copacabana, their songs were not making the charts. When their 1956 single "St. Therese of the Roses" hit the charts, Wilson took that as his signal to spring off onto a solo recording contract.

A solo engagement at Detroit's premier club, The Flame Show Bar, brought Jackie Wilson the career package that he needed: a recording contract and a hot songwriting team. Signed to Brunswick Records, Jackie Wilson began carving out his own unique place in music history by recording seven consecutive songs penned by the writing team of Gordy and Carlo. Those hits included "Reet Petite (the Finest Girl You Ever Want to Meet)" (1957), "To Be Loved" (1958), "Lonely Teardrops" (1958), "That's Why (I Love You So)" (1959), and "I'll Be Satisfied" (1959). [Note: Berry's sister Gwen is credited as co-writer on all of the above Jackie Wilson hits except for "Reet Petite."]

Berry Gordy and Billy "Tyran Carlo" Davis were having such luck with Jackie Wilson's career, they decided that what they needed next was a female R&B singer to perform their songs. Billy Davis had several contacts at Chess Records, the same company that released Reverend Franklin's sermons and Aretha's gospel album. Gordy and Davis came up with a plan: they would sign Aretha Franklin to a production deal, and she would record their songs for Chess.

To this day, Davis still remembers the first time he heard teenage Aretha singing in her father's church. "The impression that I had," he recalls, "was that she was a child genius. Everything that she sang was with such emotion that you felt every word. She had just terrific control over her expressions. So, as far as I was concerned, she *was* a young genius."

"This was actually about 1958," Davis explains. "This was prior to Motown, when Berry and I were first starting—just recording and signing acts. The Motown concept came out of our frustration in dealing with the late Nat Tarnopol who was Jackie Wilson's manager. I was working with Chess Records independently. I had an association with Chess because I had a couple of hits on other artists of theirs—the Moonglows and the Flamingos. And I was working with Chuck Berry and Bo Diddley."

Impressed by Aretha Franklin's voice, Davis and Gordy decided to sign her to an immediate recording deal. According to their plan, Aretha would become a teenage R&B star, singing Gordy and Carlo compositions. However, Aretha's father was opposed to the idea of his young daughter entering the music business at such an early age. "That's why he wouldn't let her record," says Davis. "He was opposed to it initially—because he felt she was too young, as opposed to not liking that style of music. He just didn't want her getting into the music business at that age."

"But," Davis explains, "he had consented to our recording Erma Franklin, her older sister. Erma is a terrific singer as well. We rehearsed her and wrote songs for her, two of which later became hits. Aretha played the piano when we were rehearsing Erma, preparing her to record. Her father wasn't going to let her sing, but she was a hell of a player as well, so she actually played the piano. Of course, we had to pay her. I forgot what it was—probably something equivalent to movie money or something like that—a couple of bucks. But she was phenomenal even then. But how it turned out is that Erma turned to jazz. Erma preferred to sing jazz over R&B and rock music, so we never recorded either one of them."

Had the timing been just a little different, Aretha and Erma might have both gone on to become Motown Records' first two female stars. But that was not to be. Ultimately, the two songs Billy Davis and Berry Gordy wrote with Erma Franklin in mind went on to become hits for other people. "You've Got What It Takes" became a Top Ten pop smash for Marv Johnson in 1959, and Etta James scored her first Top Forty hit with "All I Could Do Was Cry."

Billy Davis still remembers those rehearsal sessions with teenage Aretha Franklin playing piano for her older sister. According to him, she was very strong-willed and not the sad, insecure, and withdrawn adult that so many people claim she later became. "I don't think she was shy," says Davis. "She was a little introverted. I would never describe her as shy. She was a strong individual and had a mind of her own, there's no doubt about it. Aretha wasn't anyone that you walked over or pushed around or manipulated too easily, even at that age."

That particular character sketch makes what happened to Aretha later that year even more devastating. At the age of fourteen she was a talented piano player and a teenage gospel singing sensation, and she was just beginning to get over her childhood disappointments and the loss of her mother. She became pregnant. Suddenly she was forced to face a highly emotional adult problem. She dropped out of high school to await the birth of her first child. Although she was technically just a child herself, this marked the sudden end of her carefree adolescence and the beginning of her troubled adulthood.

Unfortunately for so many young girls growing up in inner-city Detroit in the 1950s, being unmarried and pregnant was nothing unusual. "That was not uncommon in our environment," Mary Wilson recalls. "Many of the neighborhood girls had babies when they were thirteen, fourteen, and fifteen years old. That was the bad part about being in the projects, because that kind of thing was happening all around us. So many people living in such close proximity has a lot to do with it. I grew up in a strong family environment and my parents would have killed me! The Franklin children were there without a mother and in the care of housekeepers, so it was not a normal household."

Over fifty years after the birth of her first son, Aretha still refuses to explain the circumstances surrounding her teenage pregnancy. When questioned about the subject, she answers firmly, "Well, that's very, very personal, and nothing I care to discuss."

The unanswered question of who is the father of her first child, has left the door wide open to rumors and conjecture. Under what circumstances could the daughter of such a prominent and highly visible minister have gotten herself into such a situation? Was the pregnancy the result of an affair with someone on one of the chaperoned gospel tours? Or was it a rape or a teenage romance? Was it a stranger, a relative, or did someone she knew and trusted take advantage of her? All that is known for certain is that Aretha gave birth to a son that year, and that she named him Clarence Franklin—after her father.

What exact information is known about the first child born to Aretha in the mid-1950s? The documented birth records for that time remain confidentially filed in Michigan. Although birth certificates from 1893 to the present are stored in the City County Building in Detroit, the certificates for all illegitimate births are stored in the state capital, Lansing. The only people who are legally allowed to request copies of them are the subjects and the subjects' mothers. So, to this day, the father's identity remains a secret. Only Aretha knows the facts.

Additionally, Aretha became pregnant again not long afterward, and gave birth to her second son when she was just sixteen years old. She named him Edward Franklin. She has never revealed the name of Edward's father either.

What happened to Aretha as a teenager, set a pattern of victimization by the men in her life. If it is true that an adult is the product of his or her experiences as a child, then this traumatic situation must have affected the emotional makeup of her later life. With such a promising career already in the making and her whole life ahead of her, she somehow endured this trauma. Having given birth to two children by the age of sixteen, Aretha Franklin had already earned her right to sing to the blues.

CHAPTER THREE

ARETHA SINGS THE BLUES

Having dropped out of high school to have her first baby, Aretha spent a lot of her time at home listening to music and playing the piano. Although she had grown up immersed in the world of gospel music, in the mid-fifties she began expanding her musical horizons. Not only was she interested in the popular R&B music she heard on the radio, but she was also introduced to the melancholy and heartfelt sound of the blues. Mahalia Jackson once said, "Anybody that sings the blues is in a deep pit, yelling for help." In Aretha's case, this certainly applied.

It wasn't just the blues in general that fascinated Aretha; it was the music of one particular blues singer: Dinah Washington. There were a lot of similarities between Aretha and the famous blues singer. At her birth, in Tuscaloosa, Alabama, Dinah Washington's name was Ruth Jones. Her family moved north to Chicago in the mid-1930s, and as a teenager she played piano in a Baptist church. Like Aretha, she had begun to establish a name for herself locally by the age of fifteen. This came about for Dinah by winning several Chicago-area talent contests. When she was eighteen she changed her name to Dinah Washington and embarked on a career of awe-inspiring proportions.

From 1943 to 1945 she was the featured vocalist with the Lionel Hampton band, where she received her first taste of national fame. After leaving the Hampton band, she embarked on her career as a solo jazz singer.

In 1949 she signed a contract with Mercury Records, where she was destined to find her greatest success. Her first single release that year, "Baby Get Lost," marked the beginning of a long and harmonious relationship with Mercury. From 1949 to 1958 Dinah joined the ranks of Bessie Smith, Billie Holiday, Sarah Vaughan, and Ella Fitzgerald as one of the most popular blues and jazz singers of all time. Her string of jazz hits from this era included "Long John Blues" (1949), "I Wanna Be Loved" (1950), "Cold, Cold Heart" (1951), "Wheel of Fortune" (1952), "Trouble in Mind" (1952), and "Make Me a Present of You" (1958).

In July of 1958, along with Benny Goodman, Joe Turner, Mahalia Jackson, Thelonius Monk, and George Shearing, Dinah was one of the headliners at the prestigious Newport Jazz Festival, held annually in Newport, Rhode Island. Although she had a strong jazz following, Mercury Records wanted to market her in a way that would appeal to a more mainstream audience. To accomplish this, they teamed her with their new A&R director, Clyde Otis, who became her producer.

Dinah was reluctant at first to sing the songs Clyde had chosen for her, in the style he wanted her to sing them. She eventually complied, and with their first recording sessions together, she created the greatest solo commercial smashes of her illustrious career.

"Well, how that came about is, in early '59 Mercury asked me to add Dinah to my roster," Otis remembers. "Up until then, Dinah had recorded either straight blues songs or big-band numbers. In our first session together, we made 'What a Diff'rence a Day Makes.' That was the first time she ever sang to strings in that manner. But the point was, I said, 'Honey, put your heart in the song.' Once she realized that I wasn't trying to prostitute her talent, she just went ahead from that point on."

"What a Diff'rence a Day Makes" became Dinah's first solo Top Ten pop hit. From there she went on to score a string of Top Forty smashes, including "Unforgettable" (1959) and the poignant Clyde Otis composition "This Bitter Earth" (1960). Not only did Aretha fall in love with these songs, but she was later to record all three of them. Ultimately, she would record with Clyde Otis as well. Clyde was also responsible for pairing Dinah Washington with Brook Benton, and he produced their two Top Ten pop duets of 1960: "Baby (You've Got What It Takes)" and "A Rockin' Good Way (to Mess Around and Fall in Love)."

In 1958, 1959, and 1960, while the teenaged Aretha was sitting at home tending to her babies, she decided that the person after whom she most wanted to fashion her life was Dinah Washington. When Dinah came to Detroit, she would perform at either the Flame Show Bar, or the Frolic Show Bar; the latter was located at the intersection of John R. and Garfield Streets. Whenever she rolled into town, Dinah was treated like visiting royalty.

Dinah Washington became a very important catalyst in Aretha's life. Not only was Dinah her idol, but it was through her that Aretha met several of the people who would become important figures in her adult life.

Ted White, Aretha's first husband, says his earliest memory involving Aretha was of a visit he made to the Franklin home with Dinah. According to him, "I first saw Aretha when Dinah and I were guests in her father's home. She was a teenager then. I didn't meet her, we just saw her, she was standing on the steps—she wanted to meet Dinah."

"I knew Dinah through friends back in the fifties, and she worked Detroit continuously," says White. "At the time, I owned some music boxes—we were in the jukebox business—and some mutual associates kind of flung us together. We used to hang out quite a bit. She was a character, a loveable person, a very strong personality, and a great performer. And she's the only individual I ever knew who *loved* to sing—I mean, just *loved* to sing! She wouldn't care if it was just two guys standing on the corner at a bus stop, she'd stop and sing. She didn't care—she just loved to sing. It was always fun to go into a club with her. You know—some third-rate act is on-stage, and all of a sudden Dinah walks up the aisle and quietly lifts the mike out of their hand and just tears the house up. She was super!"

According to Aretha, "My dad loved giving parties. The great jazz, soul and gospel artists of the day performed in our living room. On this occasion Dinah was there. I was too young to go downstairs, so I'd sit at the top of the staircase and sneak a peek. That's when I first spotted Dinah. She had one too many [drinks] that night and the man who carried her out was Ted White, who I wound up marrying."

Billy Davis remembers meeting Dinah around the same time he got to know Aretha. "Aretha worshipped Dinah Washington," he recalls. "Her father used to know Dinah, and Dinah used to come in and stay at their home. As a result, she became very good friends with Dinah Washington. As I listened to Dinah Washington [records], I think Aretha was largely inspired by Dinah."

"Dinah was a character," Davis continues. "She was another one that didn't take anything from anybody, and was definitely totally independent and flamboyant. She was pretty difficult at times to get along with. But she was a star and she knew it. She acted the part in every sense. But beneath all of that, and behind all of that, she was a decent human being."

According to Davis, "Dinah respected Aretha's talent, and she met her through Reverend Franklin, who was a friend of hers. She took a liking to Aretha, and Aretha liked and respected her as a vocalist as well."

It was after one of Dinah's performances during this same era that Clyde Otis first met Aretha. He had never heard of the young singer. In fact, he recalls that when he first met her, Aretha was an awestruck teenager gushing with adoration for Dinah.

"During that time, when I was working with Dinah, we did on occasion run into Aretha. Dinah was one of Aretha's idols," Otis explains. Of his initial introduction to her, he claims, "I didn't have an impression, because she was just like a groupie. Aretha came on like a groupie! I didn't even know who she was, frankly. And I didn't hear her sing, it was just that she introduced, because she was there to see Dinah and to pay homage."

On the one hand, it is amazing to think of Aretha Franklin as an enraptured teen, waiting backstage in a grimy hallway for the chance to say "hello" to her favorite singing star. On the other hand, it is quite easy to envision young Aretha being mesmerized by the self-confident and flamboyant Dinah Washington. Dinah was exactly what Aretha longed to become—a magical songstress who could mesmerize audiences with her emotional blues singing, and who seemed to be in total control of her personal life.

In those final two years of the 1950s, Aretha defined what she wanted to do with her life, and she found someone to model herself after. She began to plan how she was going to leave her family, and to try to succeed on her own. She decided to leave Detroit, to head for New York City, and to become a successful blues singer like Dinah Washington.

"The transition from gospel to blues was very nice," Aretha remembers. "I was encouraged by my father to do what I would like to do, and I began choreography classes with Cholly Atkins. It was very exciting, new, and nice." Although her father encouraged her to branch out into other forms of music, several sources claim he was not too keen on the idea of her leaving Detroit to seek her fortune in New York City.

Eventually, Aretha convinced her father she should shift from gospel music to secular singing. According to Aretha, "I gained a lot of experience on the road with him, and then I decided I wanted to change fields, so I let him know, and he felt that if this was what I wanted to do, this was what I should do." Another problem arose when several of her father's parishioners complained that Aretha's pop-and-jazz aspirations were nothing short of blasphemy. Reverend Franklin believed that Aretha should share her singing with the world. He would explain things to his congregation.

Sensing that she was despondent about her personal life and her unexpected role as a teenage mother, several family friends encouraged her to immerse herself in her music and to turn her natural talent into a successful career. One person who was most supportive in her progression to the next step was musician Major "Mule" Holly, who was the bass player for jazz pianist Teddy Wilson.

With Holly's help, in early 1960, at the age of eighteen, Aretha packed her suitcases. Leaving her young boys, Clarence and Edward, in the care of family and friends, Aretha left Detroit and headed for New York City. Mule Holly took Aretha into a recording studio and produced a demo of her singing a blues song. Aretha's first residence in Manhattan was the YWCA on East 38th Street, and when she arrived in town, one of the first people she met was a woman named Jo King, for whom Aretha auditioned. King was later to recall of that initial audition: "Aretha did everything wrong, but it came out right. She had something—a concept of her own about music that needed no gimmickry. She was a completely honest musician."

As Aretha recalls, "Mule Holly is the person responsible for my getting to Columbia [Records]. He used to be a friend of my dad's, and he kind of set me up for that. I did stay at the Y for a couple of days, and then I moved in with my manager. Her name was Jo King, and she was working for Broadway Recordings then. She lived in the East Seventies."

According to John Hammond, who, at the time, was working for Columbia Records, his first introduction to Aretha Franklin's singing was through the demo she recorded, which Mule Holly produced for her. As Hammond later wrote in his memoirs, *Hammond on Record*, published in 1977, a black composer named Curtis Lewis came to his office one day with four demos of songs he had written. He played the first three and Hammond wasn't very impressed. However, the fourth one really caught his attention. It wasn't the song, but the singer. The song was called "Today I Sing the Blues," and it was performed by a woman playing the piano and singing. Upon hearing the rudimentary demo, Hammond exclaimed, "This is the best voice I've heard in twenty years!"

Not long afterward, Jo King telephoned Hammond and said, "I know you're interested in Aretha Franklin. If want you want to meet her, she'll be in my studio today."

John Hammond went over to 1697 Broadway, to the small recording studio Jo owned, and he met the eighteen-year-old singer who, he was convinced, was the future of the blues. If anyone should have been qualified to make that judgment, it was John Hammond, who had discovered Billie Holiday when she was just seventeen years old, in the 1930s. There was no question—Hammond wanted to sign Aretha Franklin to an immediate recording contract at Columbia Records.

To fully appreciate the historic significance of Aretha's being "discovered," signed, and produced by John Hammond, one first has to have a knowledge of Hammond's relationship with Billie Holiday, Bessie Smith, Teddy Harris, and Columbia Records. A relative of the affluent Vanderbilts, John Hammond was born into a wealthy Manhattan family in 1910. He was in an ideal position to choose his life's work because of his love for it and not out of financial necessity. His passion was music—particularly jazz. Having dropped out of Yale in 1931, he chose his combined interest in jazz and journalism over his college degree. His first writing assignments were as a jazz critic for the British publications *Melody Maker* and *Gramophone*.

His first record production came in September 1931, when he financed the recording of a pianist named Garland Wilson. The session produced two songs that were never released, but it brought him the experience he needed, and provided him with a production demo that he used to get himself a job with a record company. In 1933 he received his big break, producing American jazz records for the European market, to be released by Columbia, Parlophone, Decca, and Okeh.

In the autumn of that year he recorded two historic sessions by the two most phenomenal female blues singers of the Twentieth Century: Bessie Smith and Billie Holiday. On November 24 he produced Bessie Smith's last four recordings: "Do Your Duty," "Gimme a Pigfoot," "I'm Down in the Dumps," and "Take Me for a Buggy Ride." Only three days later, Hammond was back in the studio, producing Billie Holiday's very first recording: "Your Mother's Son-in-Law" which she sang with Benny Goodman's orchestra. Bessie's career was just ending, as Billie's was just beginning, and it was John Hammond who captured both historic events on 78 rpm discs the very same week.

Hammond discovered Billie Holiday in a dingy little jazz spot on 133rd Street in Harlem: Monette Moore's Club. Generally, Monette was the headliner, but since she had landed a role in a Broadway play, she had Holiday fill in at the club for her. According to John, "She was seventeen, and she'd been scarred by life already. But she was the first girl singer I'd come across who sang like an improvising jazz genius." The first song he heard her sing was a Johnny Mercer tune called "Woudja for a Big Red Apple?"

In 1935, Hammond teamed Holiday with Teddy Wilson and they recorded the classic "I Wished on the Moon." It was a fascinating twist of fate that twenty-five years later Aretha Franklin would make her first blues recording with Teddy Wilson's bass player, and that the recording would bring her to Hammond's attention.

Over the years, Hammond made dozens of jazz recordings for several different record labels. Another one of his monumental signings was big band leader Count Basie, whom Hammond had heard on a late-night radio station in Kansas City. Trumpet player Harry James, and vocalists Helen Hurnes, Alberta Hunter, Paul Robeson, and Joe Williams were all among the recording stars he produced in his long career, for several labels including Vanguard, Mercury, Okeh, Vocalion, and Victor.

In 1959 Hammond returned to Columbia Records, where he was to remain on staff until his death came in 1987. His last major discovery for

Columbia was in 1972 when he supervised the signing of an unproven guitarist / songwriter who he believed had potential. The artist's name was Bruce Springsteen. At the time of his death, Hammond was supervising the release of several compact discs comprising material from Columbia's vaults, including Billie Holliday's classic *Lady in Satin*.

When he had rejoined Columbia in 1959, his responsibilities included choosing which 78s from Columbia's vaults should be re-released as LPs. His other task was signing new talent to the label. His first five signings were jazz pianist Ray Bryant, the legendary folk balladeer Pete Seeger, a folk singer from Texas named Carolyn Hester, a young social-commentary folksinger / songwriter named Bob Dylan, and his jazz / blues discovery— Aretha Franklin.

Hearing Aretha sing "Today I Sing the Blues" on the rough demo tape had struck the same chord with him that Billie Holiday did twenty-seven years before—singing "Wouldja for a Big Red Apple?" Like Holiday at seventeen, Aretha at eighteen had also "been scarred by life already." Hammond called Aretha "an untutored genius—the best voice I've heard since Billie Holiday."

Signed to a six-year contract at Columbia, Aretha recorded ten different albums and released two "greatest hits" packages. The material from the original ten albums was subsequently repackaged onto over twenty other albums, which shuffled the same series of songs by category—often including "alternate takes" and "previously unreleased" songs from the Columbia vaults. Aretha's recordings from the Columbia years encompassed several different styles: blues, jazz, pop, standards, show tunes, ballads, and R&B. By far the finest testament of Aretha's years at Columbia is the exceedingly impressive compilation album *Aretha Sings the Blues*, released in 1985.

During her years at Columbia, Aretha worked with producers Bob Mersey, Clyde Otis, Billy Jackson, Bob Johnston, Bobby Scott, Al Kasha, and John Hammond. Although each of them produced some brilliant sessions, the bulk of the material failed to find an audience. There were many factors that prevented Aretha from achieving the recognition, fame, and commercial glory she sought. Much of this was the result of Columbia's indecisiveness as to how to market her, the lack of definition of a target audience for her, and her traumatic personal problems during this era.

John Hammond was the first producer to take Aretha into the studios at Columbia. She was his discovery, and he was going to have the first shot at recording her vocal talents. For her debut album on the label, Hammond decided that he would combine two of his new protégés by having Aretha sing with Ray Bryant's jazz combo. The resulting album was originally entitled *Aretha*, and it was released in 1961 (later released as *The Great Aretha Franklin—The First 12 Sides*). Although it is stylistically inconsistent, the album provided Aretha with an effective showcase of jazz, pop standards, blues, and show tunes.

John had first introduced Aretha to Ray Bryant to make sure that they were musically compatible. In the summer of 1960, Hammond threw a party for Aretha at the Village Vanguard in Greenwich Village. Reportedly, Aretha and John made the evening an all-night fête, and from 3:30 to 4:00 a.m., Aretha sang on-stage with Bryant, to the delight of the night-owl guests of the famed jazz club on Seventh Avenue South.

Nearly thirty years later, Ray Bryant distinctly remembered that evening. "One night John called me," he recalls. "It was pretty late at night, maybe nine or ten o'clock, and he said, 'Could you please come down to the Vanguard?' I said, 'Why?' and he said, 'Well, I signed this young girl singer from Detroit; she's coming in tonight, and we're having a little get-together for her. We'd like for you to come down and meet her.' I guess he had the idea for us to make a recording together even then. So, that's when I first met Aretha, at the Village Vanguard. She had come into town with her father, and that's how I met her and her father. There were lots of people there, like a big party. Everybody just got up and did something. I played a little bit, she sang, and it was just sort of a welcome-to-New-York party for Aretha. She was a very nice young lady—sort of shy. But when I heard her sing, I said, 'This girl can *sing!* She loved to sing—that was *it!*"

Ray was very impressed with Aretha and her father that evening. "He had come to New York with her," he explains. "She was only eighteen years old at the time. He seemed to be a very nice guy. Of course I was impressed, because he was a minister, [and] my mother is a minister—a Pentecostal minister. So, Aretha and I really had something in common right there. We had similar musical backgrounds. I guess that this is one of the reasons that convinced John that he should try to get us together."

John Hammond's intuition proved correct, and Ray Bryant and Aretha hit it off almost immediately. Soon afterward, Aretha's first Columbia recording sessions were set with the Ray Bryant Combo. "Some people know me as the guy who made Aretha's first record with her," according to Ray in 1989. "That's always a pleasant distinction. In the beginning, I'd see her quite often, because we used to meet for rehearsals and things like that. And, I'll never forget, I had a record that was going pretty good on CBS that was a hit, 'The Madison Time,' and 'Little Susie,' so I had a big Cadillac car—a 1960 Cadillac. I was driving her—we were going someplace one day, and she was in the car with some people, and she said, 'This is such a nice car, maybe someday I'll be able to have a car like this.' And I said, 'I think you will!'" He laughs. (Who could have suspected that big Cadillacs with tail fins would become an Aretha trademark twenty-five years later, when she recorded "The Freeway of Love?")

On August 1, 1960, John Hammond, Ray Bryant, and Aretha Franklin went into the CBS 30th Street recording studio and began working on the album. Aretha recalls, "Some of the best musicians in the business were on my very first sessions. Mr. Hammond surrounded me with the very best."

That first recording date was an evening session, which, John Hammond was later to claim, ranked among the three or four most exciting sessions of his entire career in the music business. He felt that of all of Aretha's material on Columbia, this first album was the one that most strongly carried the feeling of improvisational jazz that so intensely appealed to him.

The musicians on the initial session included Ray Bryant on the piano, Lord Westbrook playing guitar, Bill Lee on the bass, Osie Johnson on drums, and Tyree Glenn on the trombone. On one of the songs ("Right Now,") Skeeter Best was heard on guitar.

As with his historic Bessie Smith session in 1933, Hammond decided that they would cut four songs that first evening. He knew precisely how he wanted to record Aretha's first album. Although Aretha wanted to follow Sam Cooke's footsteps and go directly after an R&B audience, neither Hammond nor Columbia was interested in pursuing that segment of the market. What Hammond wanted to do was select material that would catch the attention of jazz devotees, while retaining as much of the natural gospel delivery in Aretha's voice as possible. At Aretha's insistence, one of the songs she recorded in that first session was the Judy Garland signature song, "Over the Rainbow." The other three songs were John Hammond's selections: "Today I Sing the Blues," "Right Now," and "Love Is the Only Thing."

The first song they tackled that evening was the tune that was responsible for bringing Aretha to Columbia: "Today I Sing the Blues." Every one of the cuts on the album were recorded live in the studio to maintain that intimate improvisational feeling. There was no overdubbing, no stereo rechanneling, and no additional tinkering with the sound.

The rest of the album was recorded in four additional sessions, with minor changes in the lineup of the musicians. In fact, Aretha herself played the piano on several of the cuts, in place of Ray Bryant. As a matter of historic interest, the additional sessions, which took place from November 1960 to January 1961, unfolded as follows:

November 17, 1960: "By Myself" and "All Night Long" (Ray Bryant, piano; Bill Lee, bass; Lord Westbrook, guitar; Sticks Evans, drums; Al Sears, tenor sax; Quentin Jackson, trombone).

November 29, 1960: "Sweet Lover" and "Won't Be Long" (Ray Bryant, piano; Bill Lee, bass; Belton Evans, drums; Aretha Franklin, piano [on "Won't Be Long" only]).

December 19, 1960: "Ain't Necessarily So" (Ray Bryant, piano; Warren Luckey, tenor sax; Lord Westbrook, guitar; Bill Lee, bass; Belton Evans, drums).

January 10, 1961: "Are You Sure," "Maybe I'm a Fool," and "Who Needs You?" (Aretha Franklin, piano; Al Sears, tenor sax; Lord Westbrook, guitar; Milt Hinton, bass; Sticks Evans, drums).

True to Hammond's established forté, the slow-paced, lamenting blues numbers on the album were the most successful cuts. "(Blue) By Myself," "Maybe I'm a Fool," "All Night Long," and "Today I Sing the Blues" are all four-star classics of that genre. On those cuts, the clarity and purity of Aretha's voice is remarkable to hear, especially in contrast to her later "soulful" work at Atlantic Records. On this particular album, the blues songs were all excellently executed. While Aretha immediately found an audience in the R&B market, it was not necessarily the type of music that was selling in a big way to the mainstream pop market at the time. In the record business, the bottom line is always the chart position, *and* the sales figures.

"Today I Sing the Blues" was the natural choice as Aretha's debut single on Columbia Records. Based on record sales and radio airplay, it shot up the R&B charts and became her first Top Ten recording. Although "Today I Sing the Blues," released in October 1960, did not cross over to the pop chart, her strong support from the black radio stations was an encouraging sign to the record company that they were on the right track. "Won't Be Long," the upbeat Johnny McFarland tune, was released in February 1961 as the second single from her debut Columbia album. It became her second Top Ten R&B hit, peaking at Number Seven on that chart and it crossed over to the pop chart for three weeks, peaking at Number Seventy-six. The *Aretha* album was released on February 27, 1961, and it immediately drew strong reviews in the music trade papers. *Billboard* Magazine was especially impressed by Aretha's performance on the LP, noting at the time that "she brings a true and strong gospel accent into a fine full-blown blues." While the album never made the pop LP charts, Aretha became an instant hit with the jazz audience.

During the months between Aretha's signing of her Columbia recording contract and the release of her first non-gospel album, she had begun to take piano lessons. According to the press biography that Columbia sent out to newspapers in early 1961, "An expert pianist, Aretha accompanies herself on records and in nightclubs. She was self-taught musically until the summer of 1960, when she began studying with Leora Carter, a coach she considers without peer. Aretha is an expert swimmer, likes skating and horseback riding, Miami, her puppy, French couture, Chopin, Duke Ellington and 'making people happy.' 'If I have any advice to give,' Aretha says, 'it's to work hard and have faith in the guidance of God.'"

There was conspicuously no mention of the fact that teenage Aretha had two small children living in Detroit at the time. Her personal life as a single mother was completely glossed over and would not be revealed to the public for several years to come. At that time, the focus was on the fact that she was a normal, talented eighteen-year-old, with a budding musical career, and an incredible voice.

Under the tutelage of Jo King, Aretha also took several courses to round out her education. "I took lots of classes," she recalls. "This was all in the CBS building on 54th and Broadway, where the Ed Sullivan Theater is. That building had all kinds of classes going on in it—dancing, ballet, you name it. I'd spend a couple of hours with my vocal coach Lenora Carter, and then if there was somebody hot at the Apollo, I'd go there. I saw the Supremes when they were still singing in little black skirts and white blouses. They weren't starring yet, but they were on the show. And I saw a lot of gospel artists there too."

Although the *Aretha* album didn't exactly set fire to the record charts, it gave the talented eighteen-year-old a solid foundation in the recording business. On the album, Hammond had obviously chosen songs like George and Ira Gershwin's "It Ain't Necessarily So" for its references to Bible characters like David and Goliath, Jonah, and Methuselah to highlight her roots in gospel. The inclusion of Billie Holiday's "Who Needs You?" presented her in a blues context and was a nod to Hammond's own association with "Lady Day." The album worked as a cohesive package because of the crisp sound of the recording and the emotion that Aretha brought to it.

According to Ray Bryant, "I always figured that Aretha just sang 'Aretha,' not pop or jazz. She had her own sound and her own feeling, which she would carry to whatever they decided to call the finished product. Of course the album that she did with me was sort of jazz oriented. I recall that as more of a pure jazz album than some of the ones she did afterwards, possibly because John made sure that it had all of the pure jazz guys on it with her. Even though, some of the things she was singing were more or less pop, like 'Over the Rainbow.' 'Won't Be Long' sounds like more of a pure gospel. It was more or less just Aretha's sound, and it was just a matter of putting a different sort of background to it. In our case, we leaned more towards a jazz background, because we were jazzmen."

After the album was completed, on a couple of occasions Aretha performed with the Ray Bryant Combo. "We shared the bill once in New

York in a club," says Ray. "I had my group, and she was playing opposite me, on the other part of the bill, at a place called the Jazz Gallery." Not long afterward, Ray and Aretha went off in separate directions. "I'm sorry that we sort of lost contact as the years went by," he recalls, "but she got married, and shortly after I just stopped seeing her at all."

Following the release of her debut Columbia album, Aretha spent a large portion of 1961 touring the country, playing a series of small, smoke-filled jazz clubs. With her sincerely sung blues songs, her expressive voice, and her expertly interpretive piano-playing, she became a big hit with the small and selective segment of the record-buying audience who followed jazz singers.

Aretha had just turned nineteen when she went out on the road, making the rounds of the jazz circuit. Unlike the Sunday performances at her father's church, singing in small jazz clubs where people were drinking and smoking and talking, was a new experience for her. Instead of being up before an altar with dozens of choir members behind her for support, she found herself seated at a piano with a spotlight on her, in a small, dimly lit room. Instead of the camaraderie of having a huge assembly of choir members behind her for support, she suddenly felt alone on-stage with just a handful of musicians accompanying her. Occasionally she would experience stage fright. She remembers how she felt at first: "I was afraid. I sang to the floor a lot."

Columbia Records, and John Hammond in particular, have unnecessarily taken a lot of heat for getting Aretha's career off to a false start. If one only looks at the overwhelming success she had at Atlantic Records in the late sixties and early seventies as the "Queen of Soul," it can be viewed that way. But in reality, Aretha's recording career has been longer and much more involved than that.

When John Hammond visited Jo King's recording studio that fateful day in 1960 to meet Aretha Franklin for the first time, he was very up-front with his vision of her career and Columbia's intentions. Jo King told him that day that Sam Cooke was trying to lure Aretha over to his label, RCA Records, as an R&B singer. Hammond explained to Aretha that he saw her as a gospel-edged jazz singer. When he offered her a recording deal on the spot, Franklin and King accepted the deal with their eyes wide open. Yet Aretha was later to complain that she was uncomfortable with being marketed as a jazz star.

Was John Hammond successful with the direction that he chose for Aretha with her first Columbia album? His track record with jazz performers, and the way in which the jazz audience accepted Aretha, makes the answer a conclusive "yes." She was so successful on that level, in fact, that the prestigious jazz magazine *Down Beat* named her as its "New Female Vocal Star of the Year" when it tallied their International Jazz Critics Poll in 1961. Hammond did not turn Aretha into an instant pop star, because that was never his intention. What he did accomplish was to make her an overnight jazz-singing sensation with two Top Ten R&B hits to her credit.

In his mind, he had the new Billie Holiday on his hands. When Billie died in 1959, she was a drug-plagued disaster. Her once-beautiful voice had been ravaged by years of abuse. With Aretha, Hammond knew that he had on his hands a young woman who possessed more expressive vocal power than he had heard since Holiday in the 1930s. Aretha's voice was still fresh, pure, and unravaged by years of abuse.

When Aretha embarked on her debut jazz tour in 1961, she was billed in clubs as "The *New* Queen of the Blues." So, when it came time to return to the recording studio with Franklin, Hammond chose songs that would befit the successor to Billie Holiday's crown. Hammond wasn't aiming this album at the youth market at all, it was directed straight at hard-core jazz fans.

When Aretha and John commenced work on her second Columbia album, *The Electrifying Aretha Franklin*, instead of showing off her voice in another simple jazz setting, this time Hammond would give her the full treatment. For many of the songs, he chose to set her in the middle of a 1940s-style big band, complete with horns and strings. Oddly enough, this was the album that provided Aretha with the only Top Forty pop single of her entire Columbia career: "Rock-A-Bye Your Baby with a Dixie Melody."

The Electrifying Aretha Franklin was a continuation of the jazz exploration from the *Aretha* album. Not only is the instrumental accompaniment a bit different, but her vocals ring with a new sense of confidence. Aretha's singing on the standard "You Made Me Love You" is a mesmerizing example of the emotional vocal control she possessed in the early 1960s. Singing to a horn section worthy of the Glenn Miller Orchestra on "I Told You So," one can imagine Aretha as a big-band songstress of another era. This was obviously the vision that struck John Hammond.

Other standards on this album included "Exactly Like You," "Ac-cent-tchu-ate the Positive," and "That Lucky Old Sun." Like her debut album on the label, there were also several straightforward blues numbers out of the jazz mold: "Blue Holiday," "Nobody Like You," and "Just For You."

There were two musical arrangers who worked on *The Electrifying Aretha Franklin*. The majority of the songs were arranged by Richard Wess, but on two of the cuts ("Rock-A-Bye Your Baby with a Dixie Melody" and "I Surrender, Dear,") Robert Mersey was the arranger. Mersey was fascinated by Aretha's voice, and he was later to play an important role in her recording career.

Again, on this album there were subtle references to Bible characters—just to include a touch of church on the LP to remind people of Aretha's gospel roots. In the lyrics of Johnny Mercer and Harold Arlen's "Ac-cent-tchu-ate the Positive," she sang about Noah's Ark and Jonah inside the whale.

The album, which was released in early 1962, actually contained three hit singles. Not only did "Rock-A-Bye Your Baby" become a Top Forty pop hit, but a subsequent single containing "I Surrender, Dear" on one side and "Rough Lover" on the other became a two-sided hit, with both cuts charting: at Number Eighty-seven and Number Ninety-four respectively.

After she recorded *The Electrifying Aretha Franklin*, her business relationship with John Hammond ended. As Hammond was later to explain, when the album was completed in late 1961, he and his wife Esmé left for a European vacation. When they returned to the States, he was informed that the company had decided to turn Aretha over to other staff producers. They told him he couldn't produce hits.

The executives at Columbia explained to Hammond that while he was more than qualified as a jazz album producer, he had no concept of how to deliver a hit single. In his absence, Aretha went into the recording studio with a staff producer named Al Kasha, and recorded a single called "Operation Heartbreak." Released in September 1961, the song became Aretha's third consecutive Top Ten R&B single. However, it did not cross over to the pop charts.

John Hammond had gotten along well with Aretha on their two albums together, and he was surprised he wouldn't be working with her any longer. Reflecting about this in his autobiography, Hammond claimed that he suspected the reason for his being removed from the Aretha Franklin project was related to factors other than just his abilities as a producer. According to him, Columbia's sales and promotion staff were so impressed with Aretha's singing that they encouraged Columbia's subsidiary label, Epic Records, to do something that inadvertently incensed Aretha. Dave Kapralik, of Epic's A&R (Artists & Repertoire) department, signed Erma Franklin to a recording deal, which meant that Aretha's own sister had become in-house competition for her. Although Hammond denied having anything to do with Erma's signing, he suspected that Aretha somehow blamed him and had requested another producer.

"I think I made some very good records with Aretha at Columbia," Hammond argued. "I wanted to keep her to a degree as a jazz singer, but Columbia wanted to make a big pop star out of her, which I thought would ruin her integrity."

Bob Altshuler was the director of press and public affairs at CBS Records in the 1960s, and he was a friend of John Hammond's. According to Altshuler, "I don't know what caused the separation. Whether it was Aretha who said, 'Let's try something else,' or the company who said, 'Let's try something else.' John Hammond's great strength has always been his ability to recognize a great talent at a very early stage—long before most other people could even recognize that this artist had such enormous potential, in terms of audience support. That was true of Dylan, it was true of Springsteen, it certainly was true of Aretha. It was true of all of the jazz discoveries, whether it was Billie Holiday, or the Count Basie Orchestra, or the work that he did in establishing the sound of the Benny Goodman Orchestra. He always had that ability to recognize what could be the future of such a talent, very early on, during an embryonic stage in its career. And he certainly recognized that in Aretha."

"However," Altshuler concludes, "that was his great strength. If he possessed the same astuteness as a record producer that he had in recognizing talent at a very early stage, I think the Aretha Franklin story would have been an all-Columbia story rather than an Atlantic story."

In 1961, Aretha Franklin made two more changes in her life. Not only did she end her relationship with John Hammond, but also her relationship with her manager, Jo King. Aretha had met a man in Detroit with whom she had fallen in love and ultimately married. His name was Ted White, and she not only made him her husband, but her manager as well. According to people who worked with Aretha during this period, Ted White had no prior management experience before becoming her manager. She was to spend most of the decade in the middle of a tug-of-war between Columbia Records and her husband.

To this day, Aretha refuses to discuss any aspect of her relationship with Ted White. She also refuses to speak to him. They have had only two conversations since their divorce in 1969.

In 1961, Aretha traveled back and forth between New York City and her father's home in Detroit. It was during one of her trips to Detroit that she was introduced to Ted White, and she immediately became infatuated with him. "I was introduced to her by Della Reese," White recalls, "at a club in Detroit—The 20 Grand." Six months later they were married. White had remembered seeing Aretha on the steps at her father's home, when he visited in 1959 with Dinah Washington. This time it was more than a casual meeting—it was love.

Reportedly, Reverend Franklin was not at all happy about Aretha's sudden marriage. He and Ted were to become bitter enemies, and Aretha was torn between her relationship with her father and her love for Ted. As soon as they took their vows, Ted took over the reins of Aretha's career.

Ted White readily takes credit for getting John Hammond out of the picture. "I came in and kind of upset the apple cart by not wanting John Hammond to produce another one of those Al Jolson-type albums, so he didn't carry a lot of good blessings [towards me]," he claims.

There was no question that during this period in her career, Aretha Franklin was the new darling of the jazz set. To make this point even clearer, in July 1962 she was one of the headliners of the Newport Jazz Festival, like Billie Holiday and Dinah Washington before her. The other jazz stars at the festival that summer included Carmen McRae, Duke Ellington, the Charles Mingus Sextet, the Max Roach Quartet, the Clara Ward Gospel Singers, the Oscar Peterson Trio, the Thelonius Monk Quartet, and the trio of Lambert, Hendricks and Bavan. It was a three-day festival held July 6, 7, and 8, 1962, and Aretha performed on the evening of the third day, accompanied by her rhythm section. To illustrate her stature in the jazz community at that time, Aretha and her jazz combo followed Duke Ellington and his orchestra, and preceded the Thelonius Monk Quartet.

There were two "panel discussions" at the festival, on the subject of jazz. On the afternoon of July 7, the discussion topic dealt with "The Economics of the Jazz Community." Charles Mingus, Joe Williams, and John Hammond were on the panel.

Ted White distinctly remembers Aretha playing at the Newport Jazz Festival that year. "That was when we had just started putting her career into some shape," he recalls. "We had some arrangements that were written by some arrangers that she liked, and it was just starting to happen. It was enjoyable to have the security of knowing, 'Hey, I don't have to go up there and hope these guys can read my music.' You know, they've got a trombone part to this one, and a piano part to that one. It just started falling into place. It was like a heavyweight situation, 'cause it was like Duke Ellington, Thelonius Monk, and all the heavyweights of the day were there. So it was great to compete in that atmosphere."

According to him, Aretha was so hot on-stage during this era, that as the opening act she would often intimidate the headliner. Often, the star of the show would think of some excuse to cancel his or her set, afraid that they couldn't match the intensity of Aretha's singing as the opening act. As Ted explains, "The strangest thing about those years—every time we had the opportunity to work with the 'biggies,' there was always a lull afterwards. Somebody got sick, or the amps went out, and nobody wanted to go on the stage [after] her. I mean—seriously! We were working in Chicago with Otis Redding the first time, and always," he laughs, "every time she would finish—and this was early on, when she was not the 'closer'—something always happened when she went on-stage. Nobody would dare get up there after she sang. That audience would be on fire."

Ted was busy booking Aretha in small jazz lounges across the country. Among those dates she played was the famous Flame Show Bar in Detroit, the Thunderbird Lounge in Las Vegas, and several clubs in the Caribbean.

White was not popular with the brass at Columbia Records, but he was headstrong and determined to prove himself as a manager. "Columbia had not been dictated to before," he explains, "and they didn't have a great relationship with Aretha, because she had missed a few scheduled recording sessions. There wasn't a lot of good blood between them, but we came in and healed that. We did some very good work and we got some good product out there."

In mid-1962, Aretha Franklin began working with her new record producer, Robert Mersey. He had been the musical arranger on the *Electrifying* album, and now he was given complete control of her next release. Together, Aretha and Robert would record three albums, including the brilliant *Unforgettable*.

Since Ted White claims that he was responsible for getting John Hammond out of the picture, was Mersey his personal choice as her next producer? "Not particularly," says White, "but he was the one that was available at the time. He did some great things with [Barbra] Streisand [after his association with Aretha], and he was producing for Andy Williams, and we wanted to try her in a different area. So we tried him."

Aretha's first album with Mersey at the helm was *The Tender, the Moving, the Swinging Aretha Franklin*, which was released in August 1962. Although there were plenty of strings used on this particular album, Mersey moved away from the horn-laden big-band sound of Aretha's second Hammond-produced album. With the exception of a couple of up-tempo tunes, the majority of the songs were on the "tender" and "moving" side of things. The "swinging" element was represented by the snappy "I'm Sitting on Top of the World," the bluesy "Don't Cry Baby," and a jumping "Lover Come Back to Me."

Although this album had less of a central focus than her two subsequent albums with Mersey, this was her most successful Columbia LP from a sales standpoint. Her touching version of "Try a Little Tenderness" and her songwriting debut on "Without the One You Love" are amongst the album's high points. Aretha also tackled Billie Holiday's trademark composition "God Bless the Child," delivering a knockout version of the classic song that is both sensitive and soulful.

"Don't Cry Baby" was released as a single in July 1962, and spent one week on the pop chart at Number Ninety-two. In September, "Try a Little Tenderness" hit Number 100 for one week. A Mersey-produced version of Aretha singing the Dinah Washington hit "Trouble in Mind" was released as a single in December of that year, spent five weeks on the charts and made it to Number Eighty-six. This studio version of the song wasn't included on any of her subsequent albums. *The Tender, the Moving, the Swinging Aretha Franklin* proved quite popular, and peaked at Number Sixty-nine on the LP chart.

In an attempt to introduce Aretha to the teenage record-buying public, on August 2, 1962, she made her debut appearance on the TV show *American Bandstand*. This was years before she was dubbed the "Queen of Soul" by the American youth market. On the show that afternoon she sang both "Try a Little Tenderness" and "Don't Cry Baby." Unfortunately, those songs were completely out of place with the sounds that were hitting the top of record charts in the United States. The three songs that hit Number One in *Billboard* magazine that month were "Roses are Red" by Bobby Vinton, "Breaking Up is Hard to Do" by Neil Sedaka, and "The Loco-motion" by Little Eva. (Years later, the composers of "The Loco-motion," Carole King and Gerry Goffin, were to write one of Aretha's biggest hits, "[You Make Me Feel Like] A Natural Woman," with Jerry Wexler.)

Aretha's second album with Robert Mersey, *Laughing on the Outside*, was an all-ballad masterpiece. Her version of Johnny Mercer and Hoagy Carmichael's "Skylark" was one of her best performances of the entire decade, and Aretha's reading of the song is one of the vocal high points of her career. Although a brilliant performance, the song "Skylark" was never released as a single, and the album never even made the pop LP chart.

The material Aretha tackled on *Laughing on the Outside* was more in the "adult contemporary" mode than in a purely jazz framework. Among the songs that she sang on her fourth Columbia album were Lerner and Loewe's "If Ever I Would Leave You" from the Broadway show *Camelot*, Duke Ellington's "Solitude," and Irving Berlin's "Say It Isn't So." One of the songs included on this album was an expressive composition written by Aretha and Ted White, entitled "I Wonder (Where You Are Tonight)." Although a technically beautiful album, *Laughing on the Outside* wasn't one of her biggest sellers when it was released, but it is now looked upon as one of the most underrated classics of her Columbia years.

Although Columbia executives were beginning to become perplexed with what direction to take Aretha—as far as material, market, and promotional outlets—other people in the music business were looking on with wonder. One person who was fascinated with Aretha at this point in her career was Jerry Wexler at Atlantic Records. "A lot of people missed the great licks* she did on Columbia," he recalls. "It's become traditional to say, 'Well, Atlantic is where she really broke out.' But people are negating some of the beautiful things she did on Columbia—some of the ballads, some of the show tunes. They tried everything with her. They tried Broadway show tunes, they tried jazz, everything from Nina Simone to Dinah Washington. They did make a couple of R&B records with her. They did other wonderful things, like the ballad from *Camelot*, 'If Ever I Should Leave You.' Her rendition of that is just superb, like the way Ella Fitzgerald would do Gershwin. Her articulation and her lyric intelligence are other things that people don't realize . . . they just see her as a belter, a soul screamer."

[*In musical terms, a "lick" is a trademark sound, note, expression, or vocal pattern that a singer or musician uses time and again to uniquely personalize his or her performance.]

Columbia Records knew they had a masterpiece with *Laughing on the Outside*, and they tried to introduce it to a wider audience than that which had bought Aretha's previous blues and jazz albums. The way in which a hit record could be created was television exposure, and the one television show that was counted upon to reach the heartland of America was the Sunday-night institution, *The Ed Sullivan Show*. Aretha really knew her singing career was on the right track when she was booked to appear on the *Sullivan* show in 1963. She spent hours finding the right gown to wear, and working with choreographer Cholly Atkins, she came up with a complete routine to accompany the song. Unfortunately, that evening's show was running long: "I was booked once to go on *Ed Sullivan*, and I got bumped and ran out the back door crying," she recalls. "Of course, I had told everybody in the world, 'I'm going to be on *The Ed Sullivan Show*! I had the most beautiful gowns, I was going to sing 'Skylark.' I had worked with Cholly on that, and we had done the rehearsals [at the TV studio]. I remember one of my gowns was cut a little low, and a voice from up in the booth said, 'We don't like the cut of the gown—change it.' So we brought out two others that were higher-cut, and they seemed to be satisfied with those, but then at the last minute they said, the show was overbooked, and somebody had to be bumped—and that was me."

The third and last album Aretha recorded at Columbia with Robert Mersey is considered by many to be the greatest disc that she cut at that company. It was also the most inspired project, and her seriousness about the material shows brilliantly on every cut. The album is titled *Unforgettable*, and it was a complete tribute to Aretha's idol, Dinah Washington.

According to Clyde Otis, what Aretha and Dinah most closely shared was the pain in their lives. "Aretha ached in the same way that Dinah did," he claims.

On December 14, 1963, Dinah Washington met a needlessly tragic end. Following her string of hit records at Mercury Records, in 1962 she moved to Roulette Records and placed several songs on the charts, including "You're Nobody 'Til Somebody Loves You," "For All We Know," "You're a Sweetheart," and the rousing "Soulville." In July 1963 Dinah had gotten married for the seventh time. Husband number seven was Detroit Lions football pro Dick "Night Train" Lane, and they lived together in Detroit. Dinah's death resulted from a combination of sleeping pills and liquor, and was assumed to have been accidental and not an attempted suicide.

Aretha was crushed when she heard of the death of her idol. Even though Aretha was being sold as "The *New* Queen of the Blues," she stated to the press, "*The* Queen of the Blues was—and still is—Dinah Washington!" Recording an album of Dinah's hits was a natural choice for Aretha. She had already recorded "Trouble in Mind" and "For All We Know," and she loved evoking the moody expressiveness of her favorite star. Aretha's *Unforgettable* album is without a doubt her most artistically successful Columbia LP. Decades later, original vinyl copies of it are considered prized collector's items, as well as a creative milestone in Aretha's career.

Said Aretha at the time, "I first heard Dinah when I was a kid, back around the time she made 'Fat Daddy.' I never got to know her personally in those days, though she and my father were good friends. The idea of recording a tribute to her grew out of the way I've always felt about her. I didn't try to do the songs the same way she did them, necessarily—just the way I felt and will always feel about Dinah. I regretted not knowing her better; even just sitting around listening to people speaking about her makes me wish we had been close personal friends."

In October 1963, just two months before Dinah's death, Aretha was performing at a Detroit jazz club, and one night during the engagement, Dinah showed up to catch her act. After the performance, Dinah was quoted as saying, "That girl has got soul!"

Aretha recalls, "Last time I saw her was in Chicago. She was walking across a parking lot on her way to the Roberts Hotel. I admired her outfit—she had this hip short jacket—and [I] noticed how her stylish hat broke so beautifully. That's the image of Dinah I like to keep."

Stricken by the death of Dinah Washington, Aretha and Robert Mersey hurried into the recording studio to produce *Unforgettable* in a matter of weeks. The finished album was released in March 1964 to capitalize on the sudden public interest in Dinah's music. Aretha once stated that "all my songs are very personal to me. I always give everything I have to give to every song I sing. That's the only way I know how to sing." That was never more true than on *Unforgettable*.

The album starts out with a slow and dreamy version of "Unforgettable," and ends with a rousing version of the bawdy "Soulville." Every one of Aretha's performances on this album is searingly emotional—from the teasing "Evil Gal Blues" to the pleading "This Bitter Earth," to the poignant "If I Should Lose You." However, the most effective song on the album is the melancholy "Drinking Again." To get the mood just right, Robert Mersey dimmed the lights in the recording studio to give it an "after midnight" feeling. Listening to Aretha singing the song, it is easy to imagine her at a small table in a jazz club, smoking a cigarette, with a glass, and the bottle of Seagram's whiskey that she mentions at the end of the song.

Taking her time on her delivery of the first half of "What a Diff'rence a Day Makes," she shows off the different colorings of her versatile voice. The song then builds to a dramatic close that finds Aretha confidently in her element. This album is the height of her blues-and-jazz phase at Columbia. Received well by critics at the time, *Unforgettable* is still considered an outstanding album, even though it never appeared on the album charts, or contained a hit single. The songs on *Unforgettable* were originally Dinah's, but on this album Aretha redefines them and makes them all her own.

According to Bette Midler, Aretha's *Unforgettable* album was responsible for shaping her own singing style. Midler refers to the first time she played the album as "a real awakening. It was like I had no idea what music was all about until I heard her sing. It opened up the whole world."

Not only does Aretha sound great on the *Unforgettable* album, but the music and production are also exquisite. It is easy to see how Robert Mersey went from *Unforgettable* directly to the top of the charts on his next project. As he had defined, distilled, and directed Aretha to perfection on the Dinah Washington tribute, he did the same for his next subject— Barbra Streisand. The album that Streisand and Mersey came up with was *People*, Barbra's first Number One LP, and her fifth consecutive certified Gold album in a year-and-a-half.

In the spring of 1964, Aretha Franklin was a guest star on a couple of episodes of the late-night network TV program, *The Steve Allen Show*. She was seen on millions of television screens, singing and playing her own piano accompaniment on the popular variety program. Aretha's performances on the show included: "Lover Come Back to Me," "Rock-A-Bye Your Baby with a Dixie Melody," "Won't Be Long," and "Skylark." It was one of America's first chances to witness Franklin in the era in which she was a fresh-faced, pert, focused, and fashionably coiffed twenty-one-year-old. Playing her own piano accompaniment, Franklin was seen on the black & white TV screen dressed in a sequin spangled shoulder-strapped dress, singing her heart out on a track from her latest album: Dinah Washington's "Evil Gal Blues."

Meanwhile, time was marching on for Aretha, and some decisions had to be made about the direction that her career should take. There is a logical progression to the subsequent chain of events. Aretha had hit her creative peak on the Dinah Washington album. Dinah was a respected blues singer in the 1950s, but she had not been a big seller until she hooked up with Clyde Otis and he converted her into a hit-making star. Why not put Aretha in the studio with Clyde Otis, and let him turn her into a contemporary singing star? This idea occurred to Robert Mersey.

"It came about because of Bob Mersey, who was the head of A&R [artists & repertoire] at Columbia—reporting to Clive Davis—was my neighbor," Otis recalls. "We lived just a few doors from each other, here in Englewood, New Jersey. He kept stopping by and asking me if I wouldn't come over [to Columbia] and help him salvage a few situations—especially the Aretha Franklin one. Finally I consented. I went over there, I worked for less than a year, and I cut five albums with Aretha."

Her career wasn't the only thing on her mind at the time. Aretha had recorded her first five albums at Columbia before she was twenty-one years old. Since she had married Ted White, and handed him the reins of her career, she had also given birth to another son, Ted, Jr. In addition to her responsibilities as an entertainer, she also recalls the pressures of "getting up at four o'clock in the morning to change diapers." She felt overworked and unhappy.

At this point, Aretha and Ted moved to a quiet, middle-class neighborhood on the West Side of Detroit. The Colonial-style house they lived in was located on a street called Sorrento, and the neighbors still talk about the loud all-night parties that Aretha and her husband gave. Cathy Maloney married and moved out of her parents' house in 1960, but she remembers her parents complaining about the noise emanating from Ted and Aretha White's home next door.

"I'll be frank—my parents' memories of her are not very pleasant, for a variety of reasons," says Maloney, whose mother and father were especially aggravated by the noise that emanated from Aretha's home, the throng of cars parked out front, and the fact that people came and went at all hours of the night. "That was bothersome to them," she recalls. "My parents were very quiet people, and for entertainers and musicians, the middle of the night is just when they're getting groovin'. The houses were situated in such a way that Aretha's basement family room was underneath my parents' bedroom window. She would have friends over, and as I recall, there was a piano there. In the summertime, when the windows were open, it was a burst of aggravation to my parents that she would come home from a job, and at three o'clock in the morning they would entertain."

Describing the block that Aretha and Ted lived on, Maloney explains, "These were all nice brick Colonial-style homes: living room, dining room, and kitchen on the main floor, and the bedrooms upstairs. The particular house that she lived in was built some time after the majority of the houses on the block. I don't think that the house was built until after the war, because it was really like a house and a half. It was bigger than the rest of the houses on that street, and newer.

"Middle-class to upper-middle-class," is how Cathy recalls the neighborhood's makeup. "There were several doctors that lived—maybe not on our street, but in the surrounding blocks. By that time there were many black families in the Northwest section of Detroit."

Several people claim that Aretha and Ted's home life was less than perfect at the time. Aretha often found herself in the middle of conflicts, with her husband / manager on one side, and Columbia Records on the other. According to several accounts, Ted was less than pleasant to deal with, and consequently, Aretha usually lost her battles with him.

A stylistic conflict regarding her music also began to develop. Aretha longed to try other types of music, while Ted was in favor of keeping her rooted in the jazz mode. However, she was going to have to make a clean break away from jazz if she was ever going to reach the mainstream record-buying audience. Finally, everyone agreed with Bob Mersey's idea of having Clyde Otis move her into contemporary music.

After several requests from Mersey, Otis agreed to see what he could do to resolve Aretha's situation and help her find a wider audience with her next album. "He took Barbra," Otis recalls, "and gave me Aretha." In mid-1964, Aretha and Clyde—and Ted—went into the recording studio to produce the Columbia album that was designed to make her a pop and R&B singer: *Runnin' Out of Fools*.

The year 1964 was a milestone in the music business. There were exciting new sounds, and fresh new singing stars on the charts. The stiffness of the Connie Francis and Steve Lawrence era was ending, and a new wave of creativity had taken over. It was the year of the Beatles and the "British Invasion." Mary Wells hit Number One on the pop charts, and the whole Motown scene was exploding. The Supremes produced three consecutive Number One hits that year, and suddenly there was a hip, exciting, glamorous new standard for black female singers to emulate. Dionne Warwick produced her first two Top Ten hits that year, and the radio airwaves were filled with an assortment of dynamic new music.

The plan was obvious: Immerse Aretha in the compositions of the contemporary pop charts, get her into the mood by recording her own versions of the songs, and complete the album with a handful of originals cut from the same cloth. To introduce Aretha to the music that was selling at the time, Otis produced Franklin "covers" of no less than seven Top 20 smashes: Betty Everett's "The Shoop Shoop Song (It's in His Kiss)" (recorded in 1964 / peaked at Number Six), Mary Wells' "My Guy", Barbara Lynn's "You'll Lose a Good Thing" (1962 / Number Eight), Brenda Holloway's "Every Little Bit Hurts" (1964 / Number Thirteen), Dionne Warwick's "Walk on By" (1964 / Number Six), Inez & Charlie Foxx's "Mockingbird" (1963 / Number Seven), and the one "oldie" in the batch—Brook Benton's "It's Just a Matter of Time" (1959 / Number Three).

"I think that was a moment of truth in her career," Clyde Otis claims. "Knowing that she came from a gospel background, I knew that just doing the heavy soulful thing would not at all be appropriate. So she and I decided that these kinds of songs would be best suited for some degree of success. So it *was* planned to that degree."

The "moment of truth" that came during the recording of the *Runnin' Out of Fools* album, was when Aretha found she could handle rock, pop, and R&B material. Clyde Otis' plan succeeded artistically, and commercially. The album showed Aretha off to the record-buying public in a whole new light. Her first recording sessions with Otis yielded Aretha's second-highest-charting album (at Number Eighty-four), and the second-highest-charting pop single with the album's title song "Runnin' Out of Fools" (at Number Fifty-seven). It didn't exactly set the charts on fire, but she was finally seen as a contemporary performer. When *Runnin' Out of Fools* was released, Columbia hoped Aretha would finally break through to the same audience who purchased millions of Supremes and Dionne Warwick records. Unfortunately, that was not to be the case.

"It had nothing to do with the material," says Clyde Otis, explaining why *Runnin' Out of Fools* fizzled. "There were a couple of major problems. One was a lack of promotion and merchandising for Aretha—that was on the part of the company. And on the part of Aretha—she refused to really blast vocally. But then she had been there four years, and knew that singing a song like she sang '(You Make Me Feel Like) A Natural Woman' was not the way to go, to get the support from CBS [Columbia's parent company]. Because they just weren't into that kind of soulful record, so she toned her style down. Between her toning her style down and CBS not promoting what she did give them—well, it was just very frustrating. Even with them [CBS executives at the time], we almost had a couple of real big hits."

Ted White echoes Clyde Otis' frustration with Columbia's lack of promotion. "We went in and waged a campaign to let them know that we were there to really do some work, as opposed to the attitude that they had about Aretha at the time. And they kind of opened the door a bit for us. They were very cooperative from that time on, [but there was] very little money and very little outside support. In fact, I remember the first time we went to L.A. to work. I had to go down to Compton, in some very out-of-the-way record stores to buy old Aretha albums and singles, because I couldn't get product from the local Columbia PR person. I had to take a taxi down there and promote it myself. There just wasn't any product out there. They knew she was going out there. They weren't overly concerned. If you got a hit—great! If you didn't then, 'We'll see you later.'"

After years of being locked into an older-than-her-years jazz mode, while she was touring to publicize *Runnin' Out of Fools*, for a brief time she was treated like an emerging pop artist—for the first time in her career. She appeared on shows with people her own age, and had the opportunity to meet some of her singing contemporaries. Looking back on this era in her career, she remembers the first time she met Dionne Warwick. "Dionne and I began our careers around about the same time," says Aretha, "and we frequently were on the same shows together. I remember back in '64, we did one show where I was promoting *Runnin' Out of Fools*, and she was promoting 'Walk on By,' but we never really had a chance to talk with each other." (Two decades later, both stars would be label mates together at Arista Records, where each of them would experience a huge career resurgence.)

In addition to their dissatisfaction with Columbia, Clyde Otis and Ted White also agreed on their mutual dislike of each other. According to Clyde, in the recording studio he would try to get Aretha to loosen up and have a good time with the material she was singing. This would infuriate Ted. Clyde was appalled to find that if Aretha smiled at anything, Ted's temper would flare—regardless of how many people were present. Clyde recalls, "He'd come in, and if she wanted to have a little bit of fun by cutting loose, he'd either look at her or slap the shit out of her, and that was it."

According to Otis, Ted White was making a nice living, working with Aretha at the time. As her manager, he was paid for booking her in jazz clubs, and when she recorded his compositions on her albums, it provided him with music publishing money. Many people from this era of Aretha's life recall that whenever she opposed his authority, Ted would become abusive toward her.

Instead of continuing to build mainstream audience support by recording another R&B / pop album, at Ted White's insistence, Clyde Otis produced Aretha's next album as a live nightclub jazz LP, complete with an audience. The resulting album, *Yeah!!!*, was artistically successful, but the return to jazz killed all interest from contemporary record buyers. "The live album was something that she had discussed doing," says Clyde, "and something that Ted White wanted done, because he was working her in jazz-type situations, and that's why he didn't want her to be too soulful in her singing. On the *Runnin' Out of Fools* album, or the subsequent sides that I recorded, I kept hoping that she would let go. As you can see, the moment she went over to Atlantic, and they got rid of Ted White, it all came together. Boom! The rest is history."

According to White, the motivation was quite different. With regard to going pop with *Runnin' Out of Fools*, he says, "We all [Aretha, Clyde, Columbia, and Ted] agreed that we would try this direction and see what happened. So we called in some various arrangers and writers, and came up with some what-was-happening-then type product. We were pretty happy with it."

On the subject of shifting back to jazz on *Yeah!!!*, White explains that, "Aretha was so multitalented, we didn't want her to get bottlenecked into one particular idiom at that time. We thought she was broad enough to attract people from all audiences. So we felt that was the best way to present something that they would accept, and that's what we tried to do. We wanted a little of the jazz, a little of the pop, and a little of the so-called rock & roll. And we just touched on all bases. There are few artists that can do it, because most of them are limited."

Arguably, Aretha *is* talented enough to sing all sorts of music, but Ted's scattershot tactics confused record buyers, retailers, and disc jockeys alike. Instead of becoming a star in every musical market, she was missing the boat altogether. No one knew how to categorize her, so she ended up ignored.

"Clyde Otis was a 'star,'" Ted complains. "He wasn't a producer, he wasn't a support for Aretha, he wanted to overwhelm everything, he was rigid, and it just didn't work. There were a lot of things that could have been done a lot better had he had a little more flexibility, and he was kind of a dictator."

Ted found that Clyde was trying to force Aretha to go in musical directions that were more appropriate for Dinah Washington. "There was a whole difference there," says Ted. "Dinah was an old-line, hard-core singer and a twenty-year professional. And there is a difference in how you would handle people of that stature at that time, and he just wasn't geared for it at that particular time. He did a decent job, but I wasn't totally overwhelmed with his work. It really didn't come off 100-percent—it came off 80-percent, I'd say, or 70-percent."

In reality, Aretha was being pulled in several different directions when Ted was her manager / husband. On one hand, he wanted her to be revered as being a classy jazz singer like Dinah Washington, yet he wanted her to have huge pop and soul hits like Dionne Warwick and Mary Wells were producing at the time. While Ted wanted her to have jazz appeal so that he could book her in jazz clubs like The Flame Show Bar, he also wanted her to produce mainstream hits. It seemed that whatever Clyde Otis had her record, Ted was dissatisfied.

In the meantime, while everyone was arguing back and forth about what she should be singing, what was Aretha's opinion? What direction did she think she should be taken in? "I don't think she ever even thought about it," Ted White claims, "because she knew she had that gift. There was no question in her mind as to 'how high.' I guess it was just a matter of when. She had experienced it to from the age of twelve or thirteen—the raw power—and that's a great weapon to be equipped with at an early age. Things don't worry her. She'd never been hungry. She was born with a Cadillac in the driveway, you know, so it was just a matter of time. So she let other people worry about the semantics, and when it came her time, she did her job."

As mentioned earlier, in less than a year, Clyde Otis cut enough material for more than five albums. He recalls that his assignment was to record as many songs with Aretha as possible because her contract was going to lapse in 1966 and CBS knew that she was going to go elsewhere and ultimately become successful.

"It was a Catch-22 situation," he says of his position at the time. "CBS didn't want her to go, but they could not reverse themselves to help her become a star. So they said to me, 'Well, look—cut as much stuff on her as you can,' because they felt that they might lose her—and in fact they did lose her. The way they talked about it was, 'Look we've only got one more year left on her contract, and we'd like to have as much product on her in the can as possible.' So that's why I was given free reign to cut all that product. Normally you wouldn't cut that much product with anybody."

In December 1964, a month after the release of *Runnin' Out of Fools*, another one of Aretha's idols met with a tragic end. Under somewhat seamy circumstances, Sam Cooke was shot and killed at a Los Angeles motel after picking up a young girl at a party. In his hotel room, Cooke had taken off his clothes and gone to the bathroom. When he returned to the bedroom, he discovered that the girl had left—dressed in most of *his* clothes. Clad only in his sports jacket and shoes, Cooke began pounding on doors, looking for the girl. When he went to the door of the motel manager, ranting and half naked, the woman who managed the motel shot him three times and finished him off by beating him with a club. His death set off a wave of mass mourning among his fans in the black community, that was paralleled by the effect of the death of Elvis Presley on that star's mostly white fans.

Sam Cooke's passing was especially unfortunate in that he died at the peak of his creative popularity. During the years that Aretha had been singing the blues—literally and figuratively—Sam had been enjoying extreme pop and R&B success on the charts. Earlier that year he had a huge hit with his song "Good News," and his career in the early sixties was one smash after another. When she moved to Atlantic Records in the late sixties, Aretha cut several of Sam's songs in remembrance of their friendship.

Yeah!!! was released in May 1964. Although the finished product is a wonderfully produced jazz album, it found her back in the "standards" and "show tunes" mode. The cuts on the album included "If I Had a Hammer," "More," "Misty," and "Once in a Lifetime" (from *Stop the World—I Want to Get Off*). Her versions of the jazz classics "Muddy Water" and "Trouble in Mind" sound wonderful in the "live" nightclub atmosphere in which they were recorded. Along with the *Unforgettable* album, *Yeah!!!* is considered a real prize by album collectors. It is a great opportunity to hear Aretha sing jazz without the heavy string arrangements that were ever-present in her studio recordings at the time. Unfortunately, *Yeah!!!* peaked at Number 101 on the LP charts in 1965, when it was released. The disappointing sales figures at that time prove that her return to jazz eradicated the gains in popularity that she had made with *Runnin' Out of Fools*.

During the months that Clyde Otis worked for Columbia Records, he cut dozens of songs with Aretha, but he wasn't happy with the whole situation, nor did he care for Ted White. "The point was simply that I didn't enjoy it. Columbia at that time wasn't really into her kind of music, and they certainly were not into her. During that year, when I was at CBS and cutting those albums, they went through a lot of trauma, she and Ted, and I rescued her so many times—financially—and him even, financially. I was very accommodating on the part of the company, and very receptive to their problems, whatever their needs were. So it became very frustrating for me, and I just walked away from it," Clyde recalls of his fast exit from Columbia.

It was during this era that Bob Altshuler joined CBS Records as Director of Press and Public Relations. Previously he had worked at Atlantic Records, where Aretha would ultimately find her greatest success. Comparing the two companies at the time, Altshuler remembers the contrast: "At the end of the day, when people were listening to music at

Atlantic Records, they were listening to Otis Redding or Rufus Thomas or Ray Charles. At the end of the day, when people listened to music at Columbia, they would be listening to Doris Day and Ray Conniff and Percy Faith."

Before Aretha's contract with Columbia lapsed, the company released one more album of her music. After she signed with Atlantic, Columbia released five more Aretha albums (mainly comprised of Clyde Otis productions) *and* two "greatest hits" packages before the decade was over.

Aretha's *Soul Sister* album was released in May 1966, and although the title sounds as if this was to be Aretha's big breakthrough to the R&B market, it was misleading. *Interview* magazine has referred to this album as containing "hints of things to come." *Soul Sister* comprises what seems a schizophrenic variety of songs. Anyone who was hoping for a follow-up to her youthful *Runnin' Out of Fools* must have been disappointed. *Soul Sister* is a hodgepodge of soul, jazz, and schmaltzy standards. Whatever prompted her to re-record "You Made Me Love You"? Once was enough.

Comparing the version of "You Made Me Love You" that John Hammond recorded with Aretha in 1961 and the rendition Clyde Otis produced in 1965, it is clear that the more recent one takes a much more mature approach to the song. In playing these songs back to back, it is fascinating to see how Aretha's voice had deepened and gained expressive character in four years' time.

"Can't You Just See Me" is as close to a rock & roll beat as Aretha comes on this album; it is indeed a nice preview of coming attractions. And on Ashford & Simpson's "Cry Like a Baby," Aretha does show off the beginnings of the style of singing that would make her famous at Atlantic.

However, in spite of these fresh selections, *Soul Sister* also contains two show tunes from the heart of Dixie: swinging jazz versions of "Ol' Man River" and "Swanee." One of the high points on this disc is Aretha's first version of Van McCoy's touching "Sweet Bitter Love." She also sang McCoy's "Follow Your Heart" on this set, and she would continue to record his songs throughout her career.

Ted White agrees that "the Van McCoy things" were among his favorites of Aretha's recordings with Clyde Otis. "And," White continues,

"Clyde brought in the Warwick Singers, which Dee Dee was heading up [Dee Dee Warwick is Dionne's sister]. Cissy [Houston] was in the group also, and Myrna [Smith]. And there were a lot of good things that came out of that contract with Clyde," he admits in retrospect.

Cissy Houston and Myrna Smith later formed their own group, called the Sweet Inspirations. They ended up working with Aretha at Atlantic Records, and she became very close friends with Cissy.

The most touching song on *Soul Sister* was the Clyde Otis composition "Take a Look." The lyrics of the song are meant as a message aimed at fellow black Americans. "I felt that to a large degree, many blacks were not pushing themselves," Otis explains. "They were standing around, waiting for somebody to pay them a debt that could not be paid. That's how the whole concept of the song came about. I had established a foundation for the song. If you look at the first four lines, it tells you what the philosophy of this foundation was. Self-help, I think, is the key to success, and self-analyzation. I feel that America is the greatest melting pot for success of any place on the face of the Earth. You can accomplish it here, if you are willing to work."

The single of "Can't You Just See Me" was released in January 1966, and made it to Number Ninety-six on the pop charts. *Soul Sister* was released in August of that year, and its peak chart position was Number 132. There seemed to be total confusion as to what category to put Aretha Franklin in. Originally she had been marketed as a straight jazz singer, then she was shifted to pop tunes, and just when that started to happen, she went back to jazz. From that point forward, she was all over the board—soul, jazz, rock, standards, ragtime, blues, ballads, and everything in-between.

During this same period, Aretha scored two Top Forty hits on the R&B charts. In 1965 a song called "One Step Ahead" was released and made it to Number Eighteen; and in 1966 "Cry Like a Baby" peaked at Number Twenty-seven.

Aretha's contract with Columbia Records lapsed in the second half of 1966, and the company began recycling everything that was left "in the can." *Take It Like You Give It* (1967) was the last Columbia album of Aretha's that was made up in its entirety of previously unreleased material. Eight of the cuts on it were produced by Clyde Otis, two by Bob Johnson, one by Bobby Scott, and one song was left over from her sessions with

Robert Mersey. The Mersey cut was a Ted White composition called "Lee Cross," which was released as a single in 1967.

The strongest cuts on the album are the ballads: the lush "Her Little Heart Went to Loveland," and the sentimental and bluesy "Only the One You Love," and Aretha's own composition, the beautiful violin-laden "Land of My Dreams." Most of the up-tempo material is dreadful by comparison. "A Little Bit of Soul" is style without substance and "Tighten Up Your Tie, Button Up Your Jacket (Make It for the Door)" is just plain silly.

The *Take a Look* LP (1967) combined three previously unreleased album cuts ("Operation Heartbreak," "Bill Bailey, Won't You Please Come Home," and "I Won't Cry Anymore,") with six re-released numbers from every phase of her Columbia career. The recycled material included "Blue Holiday" (1962) through "Lee Cross" (1967). Aretha's success at Atlantic in 1967, 1968, and 1969 was the greatest thing that ever happened to the material she recorded at Columbia. "Take a Look" was released as a single by Columbia in August of 1967, while "Baby I Love You" (Atlantic) was still on the charts, and it made it to Number Fifty-six. It was, however, eclipsed by "(You Make Me Feel Like) A Natural Woman" (Atlantic), which was released only a few weeks later.

In 1969 Columbia released Aretha's *Soft and Beautiful* album, produced by Clyde Otis, which was comprised of 90-percent previously unreleased material. (The one exception was "A Mother's Love" from the *Soul Sister* LP.) These songs were recorded during the era in which Robert Mersey had gone on to produce three consecutive smash albums by Barbra Streisand. On this LP are two of Streisand's 1960s hits, as interpreted by Aretha Franklin: "My Coloring Book" and "People." The deep-down blues of "Only the Lonely," and the jazzy despondency of "(Ah, the Apple Trees) When the World Was Young," make this album well worth listening to. It is the most consistently-paced album of her later Columbia years, and her version of "My Coloring Book" is a little-known gem.

Years after her contract with Columbia lapsed, the company was still pumping out albums by Aretha. Over the years, the company has packaged and repackaged these songs over and over again (see the Discography section). In the 1980s, Columbia released three repackaged retrospectives of classics from this period of her career: *Sweet Bitter Love* (1982), *Aretha*

Sings the Blues (1985), and *After Hours* (1987). Joe McEwen coordinated the album packaging and personally chose the material for the most recent two.

According to McEwen, when he joined CBS Records, he was curious to see what kind of material was in the vaults from Aretha's Columbia years. He remembers being pleasantly surprised. "I felt that they really got a bad rap," he explains. "Her voice was amazing then, she was really young. And even though a lot of things didn't work then, surprisingly the material does hold up pretty well, especially her piano playing in the quartet stuff. Some of the violin arrangements aren't really as good as she is. There's some awkwardness in the arrangements and just the general approach. They tried a lot of different things, and those things just didn't really work. There were definitely a number of great records that she made here [CBS]. Even though she didn't approach the kind of intense style that really catapulted her at Atlantic, they were a lot better than I think generally they've been given credit for."

What was it that made Aretha Franklin unique during the early 1960s? In Joe McEwen's opinion, "Her passion, her voice, her vision of reading a song—that's a big thing. Just the way that she would accentuate lines in a song, or the songs that she would do. Often they would be songs that you'd think would be unlikely vehicles for her, yet they became completely convincing in every way. That's what makes anyone a great singer—like Frank Sinatra, or anybody who is convincing, is real, is warm, is tender. All of the elements that go into great styles—*and her voice!* No one has a voice like that!"

Looking back more than twenty years to her days at CBS, Aretha recalls, "On Columbia I cut a lot of good stuff, and I feel that I gained an audience there. But I was having what is commonly known in the business, at Columbia, as a lot of 'turntable hits.' I was getting a lot of play, but not a lot of sales, and I think that it was largely due to the kind of material that I was doing. I was being classified as a jazz singer, and I never, ever felt I was a jazz singer. I can sing jazz, but that was not my forté to begin with. I think the move from Columbia to Atlantic was about commercial success."

In 1966, Aretha's CBS contract expired. Just as in her version of "My Coloring Book," Columbia Records could simply take out their crayons and "color Aretha—gone!"

CHAPTER FOUR

ARETHA ARRIVES

By the fall of 1966, Aretha Franklin was ready to explode creatively. At the age of twenty-four, she had already spent ten years in the recording business, holding her own emotions inside while being forced to mimic the styles of others. On *Songs of Faith* she had done her best imitation of Clara Ward and Mahalia Jackson. When she recorded her pair of albums with John Hammond, he had directed her to emulate his vision of Billie Holiday. On *Unforgettable*, she had echoed the songs and singing style of Dinah Washington. With *Running Out of Fools*, she had delivered her version of Mary Wells and Dionne Warwick. Even on her final 1960s album for Columbia, *Soft and Beautiful*, she had tried to mold herself into a black Barbra Streisand with her interpretations of "People" and "My Coloring Book." Now it was time for her to show the world who she was. It was as if one of the identity-concealing charades on the television game show *To Tell the Truth* had just come to an end and the master of ceremonies had just said, "Will the real Aretha Franklin please stand up?"

When the "real" Aretha Franklin finally did stand up on her own, the whole world was to take notice. After a decade of trying to become everyone else's vision of who she was, the moment had finally come when she could unleash her singing with all of the unrestrained passion that had been welling up inside her for all that time.

Unfortunately, throughout her life, Aretha has leaned too heavily on the men who surrounded her. In the 1950s she was her daddy's little girl—the favorite daughter of a preacher man, a prodigal child of New

Bethel Baptist Church. When she left for New York City, John Hammond temporarily took her under his wing, and became her father figure in the recording studio. When that relationship came to a swift conclusion, she found a new man to become her paternal decision-maker: Ted White. According to her co-workers, the emotional toll taken of her by her marriage eroded her own personal confidence.

Clyde Otis recalls the emotional difficulties she underwent: "Ted beat her down so unmercifully. This is a woman who is so insecure. She knows that she can sing well, but she's been so stepped upon and put upon by people who were close to her. She's never been able to stand and say, 'This is what I will do, and this is why I want to do it.'"

Several people who worked with Aretha from 1966 to 1970 claim that the minute Ted was deposed as her central authority figure, she soared. Otis claims that, much to his disappointment, he never had the opportunity of working with Aretha without the oppressive Ted White to contend with. According to him, Aretha would defer to Ted for all of her decisions, and more often than not, his judgment would prove unwise.

Likewise, Billy Davis claims that Ted White was not pleasant to work with. In the mid-1960s, Davis had moved from Chess Records in Chicago, to a job in New York City, working for the advertising agency of McCann-Erickson. His most famous advertising campaign was as the producer of radio spots for Coca-Cola. In the late sixties, Aretha recorded a couple of Coke commercials for him. He too was shocked by the way Ted would treat Aretha in front of other people. "I recorded her several times," Davis recalls. "One of the times she was married to Ted White—unfortunately." On the subject of White's treatment of Aretha, Davis comments, "It was a shame, and it took its toll on her too. And fortunately, thanks to God, she recovered from it all, but it hindered her in her career for quite a few years."

Was Ted holding Aretha back at Columbia? "He was doing that," Davis admits. "He was her husband, her lover, her friend, her father, her manager, her agent, and anything else. But certainly, the demise of him certainly helped her in more ways than one."

In other words, Aretha's big burst to the top of the charts was more complicated than simply changing record labels. Did Ted White have to be grounded before Aretha could fly to new heights? Clyde Otis remembers when Aretha made her transition from Columbia to Atlantic. When asked about the breakup of Aretha and Ted, Clyde replied, "Look, I don't want to deal with that too much. All I can tell you is this: he [White] negotiated the deal [with Atlantic Records], and the moment the deal was signed—two days later he was on his way back to Detroit. Don't ask me what happened."

Ted White tells a different story. According to him, "During the Columbia years we knew we weren't going to stay there. We were waiting the contract out, so meanwhile, I started reaching out in my area to get writers and we started writing. We would lock ourselves in for three or four days at a time, where we'd just write, write, write. And we came up with a lot of great stuff—and a lot of garbage. But we had a portfolio [of songs] that was dynamite—and we knew it."

"We weren't just negotiating with Atlantic. In fact, Irv Steinberg from Mercury Records came over, and he brought me a couple of contracts and told me, 'Just keep them in your briefcase, and whenever your contract's over, just sign it and bring it on in. You've got money, you've got the world.' But we thought Atlantic could do the job. They offered the right kind of numbers and the right type of situation. After they heard what we had, the door just jumped off the hinges, because we were ready," Ted claims.

If the above statements from Ted White are to be taken literally, it would seem that Atlantic was more interested in his song compositions than in Aretha's singing talent. This is absurd. To his credit, Ted and Aretha did compose five songs together that were recorded at Atlantic—including "Think" and "Dr. Feelgood." But to say that these compositions closed the deal at Atlantic stretches the imagination.

"We initiated the contract with Atlantic," Ted White claims, "and we signed as the first black female million-dollar recording artist in the history of the world. So we feel that we've been praised enough in having done what we set out to do. We were paid well for what we did, and we're satisfied. You won't find any press on me [at that time]; you *will* find a chain of million-sellers during the time I was involved with Aretha's career." He further asserts that he chose all of the material contained on

Aretha's first four albums for Atlantic Records. This version of the story seems a bit at variance with everyone else's memory of this era.

According to everyone who dealt with Ted at Columbia Records, they considered him a huge thorn in their side. Yet, when Aretha shifted to Atlantic Records, Jerry Wexler claims that with the exception of Aretha's first recording date, Ted was either absent from the sessions or as docile as a kitten. "I never had any problems with Ted," he says, "in terms of interference or attempting to take control away or anything. He didn't always come to the studio, he would come sometimes. He didn't attempt to get involved in the production of the music. If she discussed material or ideas with him at home, I have no idea. If Ted White was interfering at CBS, maybe he saw that we had our hand on the tiller." Was it that Ted realized who controlled the tiller . . . or the till?

What actually did happen? Aretha became a major-league star, and as she did, Ted White was eased out of the picture. Since Aretha flatly refuses to talk about her relationship with Ted, the only other person who can objectively discuss the chain of events that began Aretha's rise is Jerry Wexler of Atlantic Records.

Wexler's interest in Aretha Franklin began in the 1950s, when she recorded her first gospel album at the age of fourteen. "I heard her before I signed her," Jerry explains. "I heard a record on the Chess label, called *Precious Lord*, that she made at her father's church. That was the record that made a big impact on me. Then, of course, all during her tenure at Columbia I tracked her. I had a tremendous sense that she was a superior singer.

"I heard her doing her various things on Columbia," he recalls, "everything ranging from 'Today I Sing the Blues,' which I thought was maybe one of her best records on Columbia, to the show tunes. The thing from *Camelot* ['If Ever I Would Leave You'] I thought was beautiful. I thought she made a lot of great records on Columbia, except there were a lot of scattershots. They didn't focus their direction. They didn't focus on an idea—a sound in the studio. They went all over the map. That was it—they made a lot of great records because it's hard to make bad records with her. But they were not focused.

"I was the 'body finder' for the label. I put my interest on the back burner, just waiting for her to be free." Wexler explains of his role at Atlantic

Records at the time of Aretha's signing, "At the time, Louise Bishop was working in Philadelphia under the name Louise Williams. Louise knew I was interested in Aretha. I was in Muscle Shoals cutting Wilson Pickett, and I got a call from Louise and she said, 'Call this number; it's Aretha and she's waiting for your call.' She had finished up at Columbia. I called her. She said, 'Sounds good. I want you to talk to my husband.' They came to New York and made the deal; it was as simple as that—no lawyers, no nothing. People ask, 'Did you know she was going to be that great?' Of course not, but I knew she was going to be good."

It was Wexler's idea to take Aretha to Rick Hall's Fame Studio in Muscle Shoals, Alabama. Jerry had gotten bored with the sounds being produced in New York City, and he found that the Southern flavor of the rural Alabama setting enhanced his hit-making formula. He had recently produced Wilson Pickett's "Land of 1,000 Dances" and "Mustang Sally" in the South, and he felt the change of pace would be perfect for Aretha.

Wexler recalls, "Bringing Wilson Pickett to the Stax Studios in Memphis changed my whole approach to music, to the Southern style of recording. Just sitting around with the chord changes and building tracks from there. I had gotten very stale and burned out in New York, and I didn't know what way to turn. I don't think Aretha was clued in on Stax in Memphis or Muscle Shoals. I had to do a little convincing. Maybe I played her some Wilson Pickett things. Aretha and her then husband, Ted White, were ready to take some cues from me. They had tried a variety of approaches at Columbia and were ready for something different."

"Jerry's one of the giants of R&B," Aretha proclaims. "When I was a teenager buying records, I listened to Atlantic artists like Ruth Brown and Ray Charles. I knew Jerry's product, but I didn't know his name until we met in 1966 at the Atlantic offices in New York. The meeting was very brief, just a get-acquainted thing. We talked about some of the things I had done at Columbia that he especially liked. Mostly I was struck by how enthusiastic he was with having me on the label. I always felt Jerry had my interests at heart and always tried to obtain the best for me."

"So," Wexler explains, "I took her to Muscle Shoals. I had planned to be there for a week, which would have been enough in those days.

We were supposed to do a whole album. We wound up with one night's recording."

What ended up happening that night was a drunken argument between Ted White and one of the white trumpet players at the studio. The date was January 27, 1967, and it was a night that Jerry Wexler will never forget. It was the recording session that yielded the single song that would make Aretha Franklin an international singing star. Ironically, the song was "I Never Loved a Man (The Way I Love You)." In the lyrics of the song, Aretha sings about being in love with a man who lies and hurts her emotionally. How odd that she was to record that particular song on the night of one of Ted White's most talked-about conflicts. Several people have theorized that the song could have been about her relationship with Ted.

"There was a big ruckus because a couple of guys in the band got drunk," Wexler recalls. "I had asked Rick Hall to hire a certain brass section, either Wayne Jackson and the Memphis Horns, or a horn section led by Bowlegs Miller. I wanted a black horn section because it was an all-white rhythm section. I didn't want to present Aretha and her husband, Ted White, with the spectacle of a wall-to-wall white band. And second, I wanted the sonority of a certain brass section. But Rick didn't bother to get 'em, so the whole thing was white, including Charlie Chalmers on saxophone, who was great."

At first, things went quite smoothly in the studio. Unfortunately, it wasn't long before a conflict arose between Ted and one of the white trumpet players—whom Jerry described as "real obnoxious trash." According to Wexler, Ted and the trumpet player were drinking, and getting drunk, out of the same bottle. However, as time passed their camaraderie turned ugly. As the trumpet player got more inebriated, he began using racist slang words, to which Ted took instant offense. It wasn't long before an irrational argument broke out between them which ended up ruining the recording session.

"That night, I got to sleep early," recalls Wexler, "but the guys were drinking and carrying on and I heard footsteps, doors slamming, I thought I heard shots going off; it was a nightmare. At six in the morning, Aretha called from a diner and told me that she and Ted had had a fight and she ran away. This big brouhaha had developed, and Ted got into [an argument] with Rick Hall. So I wound up in Ted and Aretha's room at seven in the morning. Ted laid me out,* said, 'Man, why did you bring her down here with these rednecks?!' It was pretty heavy. So they [Aretha and Ted] split, and I went back to New York."

[*Slang for "berated."]

Who started the fight—was it Ted or was it the musician? Whether Wexler actually heard guns going off, or merely the sounds of a drunken brawl, no one has ever explained. If there were shots fired, "who shot them?" and "at whom?" has never been revealed. "I have never attempted to assess the blame, because what good is it?" says Jerry Wexler. With regard to the fight that Aretha had with Ted—was that the reason for their suddenly fleeing Alabama? "This was not a Ted White-versus-Aretha situation, it was jus a general 'rat-fuck' going on," says Wexler. "There was some drinking, and there were some problems between the band and Ted White." When asked for more specific details about the night of fighting and racial bickering, Wexler declined to comment. According to him, when the morning came, "they were back on the plane for Detroit."

When the incident is brought up in conversation, Ted White explains, "Well, it was some racial overtones, so we decided that it would be better to just not do the sessions [there], and they [Atlantic] didn't like that too well. So I told Jerry we would pay for their air transportation to New York to continue the sessions—or we couldn't do it. At that time, if you will recall, that was during the Freedom Riders [the civil rights movement of the 1960s], and there was a lot of racial tension in the country. So we just left. We brought the key musicians into New York. We finished the album—no problem."

Although Wexler remembers the completion of the album a little differently, the one thing everybody agreed on was the success of the song from that Muscle Shoals session. The resulting recording was well worth all the trouble. According to Wexler, "The very first record, 'I Never Loved a Man (The Way I Love You),' I couldn't believe it was that good. I said, 'That's my first record with her, and it can't be *this* good. I'll cool out in the morning. It will sound different in daylight.' I had to get used to that kind of greatness!"

"Now we had only one side completed, 'I Never Loved a Man,' with the horns and everything. And also we had a three-piece track on another song that turned out to be 'Do Right Woman—Do Right Man,' we had drums, bass, and rhythm guitar. That was all. I ran off some master tapes and sent them to the R&B deejays and I got this incredible reaction. They started playing it, but I couldn't put the record out, because I didn't have a 'B' side! And I couldn't find Aretha! She'd split up with Ted—it was temporary, as it turned out—and nobody knew where she was.

"I couldn't locate Aretha, because she had been traumatized by this incident, and she was hiding someplace," he remembers. "I finally caught up with her a couple of weeks later. I brought her to New York with her two sisters and finished 'Do Right Woman.' We finished the record with just the three of them. She put piano and an organ on [it] herself, sang the lead, and then went and did the backups with her sisters, and then we had a record. Aretha came out to my house in Great Neck [Long Island, New York], and we prepared the first session there. She played me a lot of things and I played her some things. She had songs ready to go that she had written on the piano." Some of the compositions she had written, which appeared on her debut Atlantic album, were "Don't Let Me Lose This Dream," "Baby, Baby, Baby," "Dr. Feelgood (Love Is a Serious Business)," and "Save Me."

"We didn't go back to Muscle Shoals to finish the album," Wexler continues. "Instead, I brought the band up—that same band. I took a big chance. I also used Wayne Jackson and the Memphis Horns, plus King Curtis. I used to work very closely with Curtis on all my sessions. He had a great nose for musicians. He always found fantastic people, including Jimi Hendrix. We kept recording singles, then put them together as the album. 'Respect' was the next really important record after 'I Never Loved a Man.' If you listen to the original Otis Redding version of 'Respect,' there's no bridge in it. It's just straight ahead chorus, chorus, chorus."

"Respect" was a song that Aretha had a real passion for. She had taken an apartment in New York City, and one night while there she and her sister Carolyn began playing around with the song, and together they came up with the idea of spelling out the word "R-E-S-P-E-C-T" in the song, and repeating the impromptu line "sock it to me." According to

Aretha, "Otis Redding, as you know, cut that [originally]. And my sister Carolyn and I collaborated on that one evening, and came up with the 'sock it to me' line, which became quite popular worldwide. We coined a phrase there."

"Respect" was recorded on Valentine's Day, 1967, at the Atlantic Recording Studios in New York City. Aretha and her sisters amazed everyone present when they began singing the song in the studio, complete with the "sock it to me's" and the spelled out the title in the middle of the song. "When she started singing, all the parts became obvious—and it was just: 'Boom! Here it is!'" recalls recording engineer Tom Dowd. "Her sister Carolyn was instrumental in the tempo aspect of it, the way they did the 'R-E-S-P-E-C-T' lines and so forth. I fell off my chair when I heard that!"

"When we got serious about recording the song," Wexler elaborates, "we took a look at it and realized there was no bridge. It's something you'd never notice with Otis because of his incredible projection and magnitude. We came up with using the chord changes of Sam & Dave's 'When Something Is Wrong with My Baby.' They're very jazzy, a very advanced chord progression."

When I asked Jerry Wexler if Ted White started any trouble during the recording session for "Respect," Wexler stated quite clearly, "He was not with her." With Ted White absent from the recording session, Aretha was able to blast the song out with newly unleashed passion and fire. The lyrics of the song, combined with Aretha's incredible delivery, spoke a universal language. "It could be a racial situation, it could be a political situation, it could be just a man-woman situation," says Tom Dowd. "Anybody could identify with it. It cut a lot of ground."

"Aretha added another dimension to the song," Jerry Wexler claims. "This is almost a feminist clarion. Whenever women heard the record, it was like a tidal wave of sororal [sorority-like] unity. 'A little respect when you come home' doesn't only connote respect in the sense of having concern for another's position; there's also a little lubricity in there—respect acquires the notion of being able to perform conjugally in optimum fashion. It was just a very interesting mix: an intuitive feminist outcry, a sexual statement, and an announcement of dignity. And a minority person making a statement of pride without sloganeering."

The song went on to become Aretha's lifelong trademark. Decades later, it still holds up with all of the sizzle and excitement that it had when it was released in 1967. When *Rolling Stone* magazine tallied its choices of "The 100 Best Singles of the Last 25 Years" in 1988, "Respect" ranked in the publication's all-time Top Ten.

When Aretha teamed up with Jerry Wexler, they created a magical chemistry. Between her raw emotions and his proven taste in popular music, they proceeded to write several pages of musical history. Once she saw what Wexler had planned for her career, she had implicit trust in his taste. When she began following his creative intuition, instead of Ted's shortsighted judgments, she saw immediate results. In a business sense, Aretha's trust in Ted was being dismantled piece by piece.

Aretha's association with Jerry Wexler spanned nine years and eighteen albums. From a musical standpoint, Wexler became the most important person in her career from 1966 to 1975. Like John Hammond in the black jazz scene, Jerry Wexler has always been a champion in the arena of rhythm & blues. Both white businessmen, Hammond and Wexler dedicated their time and their know-how to promoting black music and to developing black recording artists. Hammond had been born into a wealthy Manhattan family, but Wexler was the offspring of working-class immigrant parents. During the Depression he worked with his father as a window washer, delivered liquor, and hung out at a local pool hall in New York City.

After graduating from high school in 1932, Jerry studied journalism at the City College of New York, at New York University, and at Kansas State. He became fascinated with jazz and blues in Kansas City when he visited the bars and nightclubs on Twelfth Street. When he returned to Manhattan, his new haunts became the jazz clubs on West 52nd Street and the famed nightspots in Harlem. He wrote for a publication called *Story Magazine*, and was eventually hired as a copywriter for Broadcast Music Incorporated (BMI). Later he accepted a job at *Billboard*. When he joined the staff of that magazine, the "Soul" music charts were labeled "Race Music." Wexler is credited with being instrumental in changing that designation to "Rhythm & Blues."

In 1953, Jerry Wexler began his music-making career with Atlantic Records. Not only was he a record producer, A&R director, and a member of the promotion department, but he was also a senior partner in the whole operation. At the time he joined Atlantic, the company was so small that during the day Wexler shared an office with company founder Ahmet Ertegun, and after five o'clock they would stack the desks on top of each other, haul out the microphones, and that was the recording studio. If they needed an echo effect, they would simply take a microphone onto the fire stairs and let the sound reverberate off the brick walls surrounding the staircase.

Throughout the 1950s and 1960s, Jerry Wexler worked with several of the most influential R&B singers ever to hit the charts: Wilson Pickett, Otis Redding, Clyde McPhatter, the Drifters, Joe Tex, Ray Charles, Ruth Brown, The Clovers, Joe Turner, and LaVern Baker, to name a few. *Rolling Stone* has gone so far as to christen him "The Godfather of Rhythm & Blues." In view of his musical accomplishments, the honor seems quite apt.

When Jerry Wexler and Aretha Franklin connected in the recording studio, something very special happened. Together they were to create the most enduring music of both of their careers.

Of her recordings with Wexler, Aretha recalls, "In the studio he was very relaxed, which I liked a lot. I guess you could describe him as a creative perfectionist. He always tried for really tight, clean tracks, and his input was especially good. My sessions with Jerry Wexler are among my favorite sessions. I feel the things we did together were dynamite, and I would also say that they were some of the finest records of the sixties, and early seventies. I enjoyed everything I did with him."

Wexler also remembers those sessions with special fondness. "With Aretha it always went like cream," he claims. "If I had something to say that she didn't agree with, we worked it out. There was never an impasse or any ridicule or abrasiveness. She had superb musicality, this gift—so unsophisticated, like a natural child, a natural woman. There was no gloss, there was no attempt at gloss."

Nineteen-sixty-seven was another landmark year in the music business. Just as 1964 had witnessed a complete change in the music that was played on the radio and had ushered in a new roster of stars, 1967 also represented a whole new scene. It was the year that the Beatles released *Sgt.*

Pepper's Lonely Hearts Club Band, and in San Francisco it was the "Summer of Love." By contrast, in Detroit and Newark it was the summer of race riots and vast social change. At the top of the pop charts in America, the year began with the Monkees' "I'm a Believer," and ended with the Beatles' "Hello Goodbye." The biggest hit-makers of the year were the Supremes, the Beatles, and the Monkees. However, in the first week of June, dead-center in the middle of the year, Aretha Franklin's "Respect" topped the charts. Somewhere amid the bubble-gum sound of Lulu's "To Sir with Love," the effervescent pop stylings of the Seekers' "Georgy Girl," and the psychedelia of the Strawberry Alarm Clock's "Incense and Peppermints" there came another sound wafting its way through the airwaves. Like the sassy fragrance of a side of barbecued spareribs amid the sweetness of the bubble gum, Aretha Franklin arrived on the scene—and redefined the sound of R&B music.

While the Supremes were celebrating "The Happening," Martha Reeves & the Vandellas were singing the praises of "Jimmy Mack," and Gladys Knight & the Pips were announcing "I Heard It Through the Grapevine," another Motor City girl had a different story to tell. While Dionne Warwick was trying to find what it was all about with "Alfie," and white country singer Bobbie Gentry was telling her "Ode to Billy Joe," Aretha released five consecutive Top Ten singles that really laid it on the line. With her unique singing style she announced that she was "A Natural Woman" who demanded "Respect" in spite of the "Chain of Fools" she had been hanging around with. Although her man had done her wrong, she wailed shamelessly that "I Never Loved a Man (The Way I Love You)," in a way that everyone—black or white—could understand.

During her years at Columbia Records, Aretha's clothes and makeup were decidedly conservative. However, in 1967 she began to radically change her image, and to show off a flashier side of herself. She began wearing high-teased Dynel wigs, and developed a Supremes-like penchant for sequin-spangled gowns. She had missed so much of the decade by trying to become the new-age Dinah Washington that she had some catching up to do. While the cover photos on her first couple of Atlantic albums found her made up à la Diana Ross, the way she sang was a decidedly different story. Her music was raw, forceful, and earthy in a way that no one who came before her had ever expressed. Lady Soul had hit the airwaves, and all of a sudden everyone knew who Aretha Franklin was.

Between the gutsy and emotional confidence of her singing and the sharp freshness of her music, she turned heads. When she sang "Do Right Woman—Do Right Man," you knew that this woman was speaking from experience. When she proclaimed that she wanted some "Respect," you immediately recognized that her life up until then had clearly lacked just that.

Comparing her recordings at Atlantic with those from her previous incarnation at Columbia, Aretha concluded, "It wasn't selling, but I liked very much what I did at Columbia. When I went to Atlantic, they just sat me down at the piano and let me do my thing. The hits started coming."

She refers, of course, to Wexler's famous line, "I took her to church, sat her down, and let her be herself." He was later to elaborate, "To say we took her back to church, that merely means we were trying the same recording context as we already were recording with Ruth Brown and LaVern Baker, and of course I also realized the value of her piano playing. Atlantic Records was like the West Point for rhythm & blues. It was our main focus. We just applied what we knew about rhythm & blues to a rhythm & blues artist, instead of trying to make her a pop artist like Judy Garland or Peggy Lee.

"Atlantic Records had already earned its spurs as a temple of rhythm & blues, so she came to the right place. And we put her in church. We used what we knew how to do. CBS was a pop record company with an R&B department—it's a different story. Also, there's a lot of luck. We lucked up on the right thing. We lucked up on the right approach and with the very first record and we had our direction focused. I didn't go in there saying, 'There's no way we can miss'—I've never gone into a session like that—or that we were in on the beginning of a fabulous roll and in on the genesis of a great star. I didn't know any of that. All I knew was that I had a great, great artist who thrilled me to death. And if I could help to provide the right context for her, we could make some good music."

When her first hit single on Atlantic Records leaped onto the charts, there was no question that Aretha Franklin was in a totally different category from Judy Garland or Peggy Lee. In her first year at Atlantic, she broke as many records as she recorded. Wherever that emotional sound came from, it cut through every musical barrier.

Roger Hawkins, who played drums on several of Aretha's first hit recordings at Atlantic, had never met a singer quite like her. "Aretha's emotion made everything work," he recalled. "I played to her voice."

In various combinations, Tom Dowd and Arif Mardin assisted Jerry Wexler on all of the recordings of this era. At times they would serve as co-producers, on other recordings they were the recording engineers and they would also handle the musical arrangements, often alongside Wexler.

"One of the world's greatest singers," is how Mardin describes Aretha. "The excitement she generates in the studio is unmatched. I've seen musicians stop playing to listen to her sing. She backs up that God-given voice with her genius—her choice of phrases, notes. She did three-part backup harmony on one cut and remembered every intricacy. She can do those things. She can go anywhere. All the possibilities are there. With a person like that, there's no stopping."

"Most singers will have a bad night or make a bad record," Dowd explains. "She couldn't. But she could make better ones. If you gave her enough input, she could get close enough to grasp it and come up with something that was one step beyond what you'd given her."

According to Wexler, he was amazed by her musical intuition and her knowledge of that glorious instrument that is her voice. "When she overdubbed her vocals, she would do these incredible inversions and licks, and I would think, 'That's it!' 'No,' she'd say, 'wait a minute there,' and she'd do one better. You never knew what visions she has about another lick, another inversion, another variation that would top the last one. She might even sing eight bars to get one note in. All singers have that to a degree, but not the way she did. She had a perfect fix on what she was doing and whether it came off or not, and how it could be improved."

Describing her own approach to recording during this period, Aretha explained, "If a song's about something I've experienced or that could've happened to me, it's good. But if it's alien to me, I couldn't lend anything to it. I look for a good lyric, a good melody, the changes. I look for something meaningful. When I go into the studio I put everything into it. Even the kitchen sink! I *love* to record. I love music. I do background vocals because I like the sound I get when I harmonize with myself."

From February 1967 to February 1968, Aretha released an unprecedented six Top Ten pop singles and three Top Ten albums. Five of the singles were certified Gold (sales in excess of one million copies), and two of the albums were certified Gold (sales of 500,000 copies). Only one other solo performer in history of recorded music had accomplished that feat in a single year: Elvis Presley. The record-buying public had crowned Elvis "The King of Rock & Roll," and it wasn't long before they began to refer to Aretha as "The Queen of Soul."

Aretha's soulful conquest of the record charts began with the single "I Never Loved a Man (The Way I Love You)." It was released on February 10, 1967, hitting Number Nine on the pop charts, Number One on the R&B charts, and it became her first million-seller.

At the time, Bob Rolentz was the head of Atlantic Records' promotion department. "She started from zero, from zip, no hits, no one knew who she was," he recalls. "It was that voice. It just grabbed people by the collar. That first record, 'I Never Loved a Man,' in three months was a national treasure. She just exploded. Now this was a black woman, a hefty black woman, certainly handsome and charismatic, but so damned unlucky [in her personal life]."

The record was such a smash that the "B" side of the single, "Do Right Woman—Do Right Man," charted on the R&B charts. It peaked at Number Thirty-seven.

The single "Respect" was released on April 10, 1967, and by the week of June 3, when it was the Number One record in America, it also made it into the British Top Ten. Not only was the song "Respect" a Number One pop hit, but it topped the R&B chart as well.

Otis Redding first recorded the song "Respect," which was his own composition. His version peaked at Number Thirty-five on the pop charts in 1965. When he heard Aretha's blistering cover version of his song, he is quoted as having exclaimed, "I just lost my song. That girl took it away from me!"

"Respect" has an interesting history all its own. In 1965, Redding was recording his album *Otis Blue*, with the group Booker T. & the MGs. The drummer of the group was a man name Al Jackson. During a break in the recording session, Otis sat down with Jackson and began to complain about the ups and downs of his career, and how difficult touring was. According to Jackson, "I said, 'What are you griping about, you're on the road all the time? All you can look for is a little respect when you come home.' He wrote the tune from our conversation." Coincidentally, Tom Dowd was the engineer on Otis' recording of the song, and he was also the engineer on Aretha's Number One version of the same song.

Meanwhile, Aretha's debut Atlantic album, *I Never Loved a Man the Way I Love You*, was released in March of 1967. It peaked on the LP charts at Number Two, was certified Gold, and eventually sold 800,000 copies. In 1987, *Rolling Stone* proclaimed it one of the "100 Best Albums of the Last 20 Years," in a special issue of the publication. According to the magazine, "With her first album for Atlantic, Aretha Franklin unleashed the gospel-bred vitality that had been bubbling under her tepid Columbia pop and jazz sides. It remains the best of her highly successful Atlantic efforts."

Aretha's second Atlantic album, *Aretha Arrives*, was released in August 1967, and hit Number Five on the LP charts. One single was pulled from the album, the hit "Baby, I Love You," which made it to Number Four on the pop charts and Number One on the R&B charts.

Before she was due in the recording studio to begin work on *Aretha Arrives*, Aretha was hurt while she was giving a concert performance in Georgia. She fell off the stage when she moved too close to the edge of it, and the accident left her with a shattered right elbow. Although her elbow was in a cast, and in spite of her doctor's opposition, she was determined to play the piano on her second Atlantic LP. On the album's faster paced songs, she was unable to play with her right hand, so on songs like the cooking cut "You Are My Sunshine," she was forced to pound out her part on the keyboard using only her left hand.

"When it came about that she couldn't play," recalls Jerry Wexler, "we really had to work hard to generate a good personal sound, to make sure that her essence came across on record."

According to him, Aretha's piano playing was an essential ingredient in his formula for musical success. "In my opinion, one of the reasons that we clicked right away," he explains, "was because I put Aretha at the piano. When a musician who writes songs can play anything, I like to have them play on that record—whether he can play or not. It happens that Aretha is a magnificent player. At CBS, they didn't avail themselves—or only occasionally—of having her be part of the rhythm section. But by having the soloist, or the featured artist who's going to be singing on the record, by having him put his input into the track, it puts you in a whole different level of the game."

Aretha Arrives features one of the most diverse song lineups of any of her LPs. Only Aretha could sing the Rolling Stones' "Satisfaction," and Frank Sinatra's "That's Life" on the same album, and pull it off. She also tackled Willie Nelson's "Night Life," and ? & the Mysterians' "96 Tears." These songs represented what Aretha had in mind for herself to record, and Jerry Wexler claims he would never have chosen some of the material for Aretha that she inevitably picked for her albums. "I don't really like 'That's Life' myself," he says; however, he admits that she somehow made it work. "It's because of her magic, man. She put the magic to it. You see, part of Aretha's genius is the unspoiled naiveté that she brings to songs like 'That's Life.' There's a side of Aretha that respects—and almost adulates—that big Las Vegas aspect. There's some bad parts, but there's some good parts to it too. It's the same innocence that the Supremes brought to their early songs. It's believing in those little soap operas, and those little dramas."

The song "Baby, I Love You" was written by Ronnie Shannon, who had written "I Never Loved a Man." Aretha distinctly remembers the recording session: "It was done at Atlantic's studios in New York, in that one big room. It was big enough for the rhythm section, but intimate enough for the vocals. Those sessions were a lot of fun, and there was a lot of good food coming in and out of the studio. Lots of burgers, cheeseburgers, fries, milkshakes. In between takes we would sit and chat with whoever was producing, Jerry or Arif. They'd be enjoying those burgers so much I couldn't wait until mine came!"

"Baby, I Love You" was certified Gold, but the album was not. Probably, if another hit single was released off of the album, it too would have gone Gold, but there was such a demand for Aretha by the end of the summer of 1967 that the next three singles all came off her third Atlantic album, the triumphant *Lady Soul.*

Her next smash was a song written by the hit-making team of Carole King and husband Gerry Goffin, with Jerry Wexler. The song is considered by many to be the finest performance of her career: "(You Make Me Feel Like) A Natural Woman." Released September 7, 1967, the single peaked at Number Nine on the pop chart, and it became a Number Two R&B hit.

The title of the song was a concept Jerry Wexler envisioned. He, in turn, suggested to Carole King and Gerry Goffin that it would be a great idea for a song for Aretha Franklin. "The expression 'he's a natural man' is one of the rubrics of the blues. So I came up with the idea: 'You make me feel like a natural woman,' that line. And they were kind enough to give me a [writer's credit on] the song."

Its follow-up was the Gold single "Chain of Fools," which was written by Don Covay. At first the song was about field hands at work down South, but Aretha's version was slanted to become about a chain of unworthy lovers. Covay rewrote some of the lyrics of the song, which had been composed with Otis Redding in mind. "I did some minor surgery to the song to adapt it to Aretha," Covay says. "Originally it was far more of a blues thing." According to Jerry Wexler, "When we finished recording, [songwriter] Ellie Greenwich ['Da Doo Run Run'] came by the office and I played it for her. She heard another [possible vocal] part there in the background. She sang it for me and I pulled her into the studio with her girls for another vocal background that filled out the record."

Aretha's sixth single released in her first year at Atlantic was "(Sweet Sweet Baby) Since You've Been Gone." It was released on February 9, 1968 (her first was released on February 10 of the previous year), and it became a Number Five pop hit, and her fifth Number One smash on the R&B chart. In January of 1968, her third Atlantic album *Lady Soul* was released, and it became a Number Two LP on the album charts, and was certified Gold. Like her debut Atlantic album, the *Lady Soul* LP was also rated by *Rolling Stone* magazine as one of "The 100 Best Albums of the Last 20 Years." That particular issue of the magazine (August 27, 1987) proclaimed that "on *Lady Soul*, Aretha Franklin sat down at that piano and earned her title, playing and singing her heart out in a way truly fit for a queen . . . packing whole lifetimes of emotional trauma, romantic yearning and physical release into *Lady Soul*'s three-minute blasts of soul dynamite."

Since shifting record labels from Columbia to Atlantic, Aretha had logged a year in the music business that was phenomenally triumphant. No one was more surprised or overwhelmed than Aretha herself. In the summer of 1967, as the song "Respect" made Franklin the hottest new voice on the airwaves, she suddenly found herself very much in demand. She was almost instantly swept up into playing in the major leagues of what she referred to as "the game of show business." After lingering on the fringes of stardom, she was beginning to reap the rewards. In the second week of August, 1967, she made a splash on late-night TV's *The Tonight Show*, flew to Atlanta to entertain a convention of black radio deejays, and then zipped back to Manhattan to headline the New York Jazz Festival on Randall's Island.

After seven years on Columbia Records in virtual obscurity, her popularity skyrocketed, and the world couldn't get enough of Aretha. From February to August of 1967, she sold over 3.5 million copies of her albums and singles. She confessed to *Newsweek* magazine, "I'm very surprised about the whole thing. I thought that we'd have another five years on the edge of success before we went over."

For Aretha, one of the most exciting events of the year was having her first Atlantic release, the single "I Never Loved a Man (The Way I Love You)" certified Gold. "It had looked for the longest time like I would never have a Gold record," she confessed at the time. "I wanted one so bad!"

When the year ended, all three of the major music industry trade magazines—*Billboard*, *Cash Box*, and *Record World*—each proclaimed her the top female vocalist of 1967. From that point on, the accolades just kept coming.

Aretha became the embodiment of a new meaning for the word *soul*. Ray Charles tried to explain what soul was by saying, "It's like electricity—we don't really know what it is." Mahalia Jackson claimed that blues and soul began with "the groans and moans of the people in the cotton fields . . . before it got the name 'soul,' this musical thing has been here since America's been here. This is a trial-and-tribulation music."

But is soul something that only black people can emulate or feel? Aretha didn't think so. "It's not cool to be Negro or Jewish or Italian or anything else," she explained. "It's just cool to be alive, to be around. You don't have to be Negro to have soul. I can think of lots of white people who have soul: Eileen Farrell [the opera singer], Charles Aznavour [the French singer / songwriter] are two. It's something creative, something alive. It's honesty."

Although her fans still had to compare her raw, emotional singing with that of the great ladies of the past, it was clear that Aretha was someone unique and special. The British press proclaimed that she was "the new Bessie Smith," and a soulful white girl named Janis Joplin exclaimed that Aretha was "the best chick singer since Billie Holiday." Ray Charles ranked Aretha as "one of the greatest I've heard anytime."

The arrival and acceptance of Aretha Franklin's music signaled that the times were definitely changing. When the Grammy Awards were created in 1958, there was only one category for R&B music: "Best Rhythm & Blues Recording." When Aretha Franklin began to dominate the record charts in 1967, a new category had to be created: "Best Rhythm & Blues Recording, Female." In early 1968, Aretha's "Respect" took two trophies, and began her reign as the most-awarded female singer in Grammy history.

The one concept that seemed to run through everyone's definition of the word soul seemed to be pain. Whether it was physical or emotional, everyone seemed to agree that suffering went with the territory. Although the stance of "Respect" suggested strength and confidence, it was strength gained at a high emotional price. On the record charts, Aretha was everyone's shining new musical savior, but when she was at home, was she the victim of a painful marriage? Although she never spoke of the emotional abuse she endured, there are several reports that claim she was confused and unhappy.

A cover story in *Time* magazine (June 28, 1968) zeroed in on this aspect of her life, and caused Aretha to stop giving press interviews for several years. In fact, the article proved so embarrassing to her that it made her leery of all journalists. The article spoke of pain in Aretha's life, and explained that "what one of these burdens might be, came out last year where Aretha's husband, Ted White, roughed her up in public at Atlanta's Regency Hyatt House Hotel. It was not the first such incident." Ted was later to sue *Time* magazine over this statement.

Her friends and family were very concerned for her at the time. Her brother Cecil commented, "For the last few years, Aretha is simply not Aretha. You see flashes of her and then she's back in her shell."

During her initial burst of international fame, several articles pointed out her gospel background. At the time, Aretha confessed, "My heart is still there in gospel music. It never left." She even went so far as to tell Mahalia Jackson that "I'm gonna make a gospel record, and tell Jesus I cannot bare these burdens alone." Does this sound like the kind of statement that a twenty-six-year-old woman would make right after she had become an international singing star? There was obviously something very wrong.

At the time, Mahalia Jackson said with concern, "I don't think she's happy. Somebody else is making her sing the blues."

The *Time* cover story depicted Aretha as a sad woman who stayed at home and "wrestle[d] with her private demons. She sleeps till afternoon, then mopes in front of the television set, chain-smoking Kools and snacking compulsively."

Letting down her guard at the time, Aretha explained, "Trying to grow up is hurting, you know. You make mistakes. You try to learn from them, and when you don't it hurts even more. And I've been hurt—hurt bad. I might be just twenty-six, but I'm an old woman in disguise—twenty-six goin' on sixty-five."

The article painted a rather unflattering picture of Ted White, describing him as a "streetcorner wheeler dealer." "They really did a hatchet job on us," he proclaims twenty years later. With regard to the subject of striking Aretha, he says, "It's libelous, because it's untrue. We sued *Time* magazine, and we did win the case. Andy Fine [Andrew J. Feinman] handled that case."

When asked how *Time* could have reached such conclusions, White says, "Well I'll tell you what it was, they talked to a lot of those little yes-men, that were hang-arounders, and I was a straightforward guy. I didn't have a lot of BS around me. It was all business with me, and lot of those people didn't care for me very much, but they all got paid, you see, so a lot of stories developed that weren't true."

The case of *Theodore R. White v. Time, Inc*, was filed in the United States District Court for the Southern District of New York, on July 10,

1968. The "complaint" claimed that *Time* magazine's statements were "false and defamatory." White sued for $10 million in damages.

According to the "answer" from *Time*, filed in the same district court on September 12, 1968, the story in question was "true" and "was published in good faith, in reliance on reliable sources and reports, and the defendant had no reason to doubt the truth or accuracy of those sources and reports."

The official court records show that the case was dismissed without prejudice and without cost," by a stipulation dated November 3, 1971. Those records do not indicate whether any payment was made in settlement. According to *Time* magazine, the case was simply "dropped."

In spite of her emotional problems, Aretha maintained an optimistic front. "Things can never be that bad," she says with a shrug. "For the blind man, there is always the fellow with no feet. I've been hurt. You can't get over it all, but you can go on living and keeping on looking. You know, I like people today more than I ever did. Sometimes it takes something bad to bring you out of yourself. Maybe it's not as bad as it seems. It's nice to socialize, meet lots of people, but it's nice to stay at home with your own. There is strength in that. I'm not free yet, but I will be. I will be! It takes time, exposure, and a lot of going out to the woodshed."

In 1968, Aretha was a vastly successful singing star with million-selling albums and sold-out concerts. After years of hard work, she had established herself as an innovative force in the music business. What was it that she wanted or needed to become "free" of? Was it Ted White?

Meanwhile, Aretha's father, Reverend C. L. Franklin, was having some problems of his own. Because he had failed to disclose his income and failed to file income tax returns, the government slapped a $25,000 fine on him. The government estimated that Reverend Franklin's annual income from 1959 to 1962 had been in excess of $76,000—which, in those days went a long way, especially when one didn't pay the taxes on the income. As reported in *Rolling Stone*, Reverend Franklin was also charged with marijuana possession during this era.

Through all of her highly publicized personal problems, one thing was never compromised in Aretha's life: her music. Owing to the overwhelming success of her records, the hottest concert ticket in 1967 and 1968 was

Aretha on-stage. In October 1967, when she appeared at New York City's Philharmonic Hall in Lincoln Center, *Look* magazine said that "she oiled the good grained walls of New York's Philharmonic Hall with the bleating beat of gospel rock."

Aretha hadn't always been as confident and comfortable on-stage as she became during this era. She confessed that in the beginning of her career she wasn't certain about her material or her approach to her singing, and her uncertainty led to bouts with stage fright. "Like 'Over the Rainbow,'" she explained, "I started out with it more like a quiet ballad. But I didn't seem to be going over, so I went back and tried *to go over* the rainbow! It's taken me a long time to get over that rainbow—a long time to get to the other side." Ever since "Respect" had hit the top of the charts, Aretha had learned to leave her troubles behind her when she was on-stage. She was finally getting to the pot of gold that was waiting for her on the other side of the rainbow. Regarding the stage fright she felt during her jazz-club era, she claimed, "I once had this problem about actually walking out on-stage. Sometimes I still have that problem . . . you know? It's a thing about whether everything is hanging right, whether my hair looks okay . . . all those people sitting out there looking at me, checking me out from head to toe. Wow! That really used to get to me, but I've overcome it by just walking out on-stage night after night, year after year."

She not only successfully recovered from her stage fright, but there were times when she wanted to come too close to her audiences. That was how she fell off the stage in Georgia in 1967, right before the recording sessions for *Aretha Arrives*. "I always move toward the edge of the stage to get to the audience," she explained. "If they don't happen, I don't happen. I sing to people about what matters. I sing to the realists, people who accept it like it is. I express problems. There are tears when it's sad, and smiles when it's happy. It seems simple to me, but for some people, I guess feelin' takes courage. When I sing, I'm saying, 'Dig it, go on and try. Ain't nobody goin' make ya. Yeah, baby, dig me—dig me if you dare." Well the whole world was starting to "dig" Aretha, and for her hour on the stage she learned to leave her own troubles—and thoughts about Ted White—behind her.

It was as if the audience who was clamoring for her every move became a sea of personal friends who were missing from her day-to-day life. It got to the point where she would talk to them like intimates. According to *Look* magazine, at Philharmonic Hall she caught the heel of her shoe in the hem of her gown, and sang mid-verse, "I'd feel better if I got this here heel out of my dress." On another song she asked, "Mind if I sit down? My feet sure hurt."

In December of 1967, Aretha made her prime-time network television debut, singing on *The Kraft Music Hall*. The following month she was a guest star on *The Jonathan Winters Show*. Aretha's big production number on the Winters show was her performance of "Chain of Fools." She stood center-stage on a circular platform, while the Sweet Inspirations danced in circles around her. Aretha wore a silver-spangled minidress that had a high neck and half sleeves. The Sweet Inspirations wore low-cut pink minidresses, white stockings, and white shoes. They looked like flamingos dancing around Aretha in this classic piece of sixties video.

On February 16, 1968, Aretha was back in Detroit to headline a concert at Cobo Hall in front of 12,000 cheering fans and to receive several of her greatest honors. First of all, Detroit's Major Cavanaugh declared the date "Aretha Franklin Day." In addition to delivering a 90 minute musical performance with the Sweet Inspirations backing her up, Aretha was given a series of plaques and certificates from all three of the music-trade publications for her clean sweep of the previous year's music charts. Bernie Blake of *Cash Box*, Ted Williams of *Record World*, and Rodger Bass of *Billboard* each presented her with "Female Vocalist of the Year" awards.

That night, Aretha was dressed in a very sophisticated-looking dress that was a bright lime green. It was trimmed with boa-like lines of flowing, lime-green ostrich feathers at the neckline and encircling her hips. Her makeup was done in the height of 1968 fashion, with blue eye shadow and Cleopatra-style eyebrows. Her hair was coiffed in a soft-looking but high-stacked dome, and white spherical earrings danged from her earlobes. That night she was every inch the conquering heroine, triumphantly returning to her hometown.

The greatest honor of all came from Reverend Martin Luther King, Jr. He had flown to Detroit on that day to attend Aretha's concert, and to bestow her with a special award from the Southern Christian Leadership Council. When Dr. King took the stage to present Aretha with her award, the crowd burst into a wild round of applause, and a complete standing ovation.

While Dr. King was the leader of the civil rights movement in America, in Aretha's first year of international fame she had become an inspiring symbol of black equality. With her own sense of pride and her dignified stance, she represented the new black woman of the late 1960s. In her own way she embodied the social and cultural change that was taking place in the country, merely by being herself without pretense. Respected by black *and* white America, she was the "natural woman" that she sang about. That evening in Detroit when King and Franklin were together on the same stage was a moment of inspiring history.

"That evening stands out in my mind," says Rita Griffin, the managing editor of a Detroit newspaper, *The Michigan Chronicle*. "The thing that I remember most is just the feeling of the crowd. King had laryngitis that night and couldn't say a word. That was the 'love swell' that I recall. You know, they talk about waves of emotion, well this was a 'love wave.' Everybody just stood on their feet. He never said a word, because he couldn't. But you could just feel the impact his presence had—just him being there. It really made for a great historic evening. That's what I remember most about it—the feeling, the love that people had for him. At the time, people were said to be wishy-washy about King, that he wasn't militant enough. Well, all 12,000 people in that room cared for him—you could feel it."

According to Jerry Wexler, Aretha was very friendly with Dr. King and supportive of the civil rights movement. She was greatly honored by King's presentation that evening. "She was very much involved with Dr. Martin Luther King, Jr. in the early days," Wexler recalls. "She wouldn't talk about it—this was private. And yet I never heard the slightest expression of animosity or anti-white anything. And God knows she would have had a reason, because of some of the experiences she went through in her early days."

"Dr. King was a wonderful, wonderful, fine man as well as a civil rights leader," Aretha said fondly, years later. "He and my dad were great friends. My dad brought him to Detroit, and introduced him to the city of Detroit through the New Bethel Baptist Church. He very definitely had an appreciation for gospel music. One of his favorite songs was 'Precious Lord,' and he would always ask me to sing that for him." In April 1968, Aretha sang "Precious Lord" one last time for Dr. King, at his funeral in Atlanta.

A few days after the Cobo Hall concert, Rita Griffin recalls going over to Aretha and Ted's house. "*Billboard* was coming up to take some photos and do a little piece, because it had been her first sold-out concert in her hometown. We had posters that had 'Sold Out!' printed across them. I can remember going up to her home that day, and the reporter from *Billboard* and I sort of sitting around till she finished cooking dinner. Then she freshened up and posed for the photos. That was the homey side of Aretha that I saw that day," she remembers warmly.

In the spring of 1968 came Aretha's first triumphant concert tour of Europe. During her two-week series of engagements, she visited seven major cities, in England, France, Germany, the Netherlands, and Sweden. She drew rave reviews wherever she appeared. On Monday, May 7, 1968, Aretha performed at the famed Olympia Theater in Paris, and she had the City of Light singing to a new tune. That evening's performance was recorded in its entirety and yielded the "live" album *Aretha in Paris*. Instead of the Sweet Inspirations, her background singers on this tour were her sister Carolyn, along with Wyline Ivey and Charnessa Jones.

To look fashionably like the global star she had become, when Aretha appeared on-stage at the Olympia, she dressed in an outfit befitting the capital of fashion. She wore an empire-waisted light blue chiffon dress, and a wig shaped like a huge bubble, with a single pageboy flip on one side. She was taking the role of "Lady Soul" quite seriously.

In August 1968, Aretha was in Chicago to open the National Democratic Conventions with her unique version of "The Star-Spangled Banner." That same month she was booked to perform in Denver, Colorado, for the fee of $20,000. A riot nearly occurred when the concert promoter came up with only half of the fee and Aretha refused to perform. Her television appearances during this era included guest spots on *The Merv Griffin Show*, *The Mike Douglas Show*, *The Les Crane Show*, *The Joey Bishop Show*, and *The Steve Allen Show*.

While she was in Chicago that August, Aretha demonstrated her generosity when a fourteen-year-old girl came running up to her, claiming to have been abandoned by her family. Actually, the young girl was a runaway from Milwaukee, living by her wits on the street. Her name was Oprah Winfrey.

According to Oprah, she was expecting to stay with a girlfriend of hers in Chicago, but when she arrived, she found no one home. When she spotted Aretha's limousine, Oprah was struck with a scheme to get out of her moneyless fix. "She was getting out of her limo in front of the Sheraton," Winfrey recalls, "and I ran up to her crying my eyes out. I told her I had been abandoned, though actually I'd run away from home and was just walking the streets. By the time we reached the front door of the hotel, she pulled a hundred dollars out of her purse and gave it to me. It was a great acting job. Ever since that time, I bought every Aretha Franklin album ever."

In 1985, when Oprah was the hostess of a morning television show called *A.M Chicago*, she made an offer to Aretha. If she would appear as a guest on Winfrey's show, Oprah would return the money she had "borrowed" seventeen years before. Aretha was appearing at Park West in Chicago in April of 1985, and laughingly commented about Winfrey's offer. "I really don't recall the incident. Tell her to come see my show and pay me back!"

Another incident that took place in Chicago in 1968 was the "official crowning" of Aretha as the "Queen of Soul." She recalls, "I was crowned in Chicago. It was a deejay named Purvis Spann. One night after the show he brought the crown out and crowned me [on-stage]. I was delighted and thrilled. Thereafter the journalists and people started using the term."

In 1968, Aretha scored another triumphant year on the record charts. The song "Ain't No Way," which was the "B" side of "Since You've Been Gone (Sweet Sweet Baby)" hit the charts, peaking at Number Sixteen on the pop charts and Number Nine on the R&B charts. "Ain't No Way," like several of Aretha's most popular songs, was written by her sister Carolyn. "Carolyn was a terrific songwriter," Jerry Wexler recalls. "I gave her the title of 'Ain't No Way.' I said, 'Carolyn, I've just got a feeling "Ain't No

Way" is a good phrase for a song.' She said, 'Sounds good!' I said, 'You've got it for nothing.'" The song went on to become one of Aretha's most popular songs from this era of her career.

It is especially interesting to note that Aretha's success from 1967 to 1969 was so solid that it also catapulted her sisters into their own recording careers. Since Atlantic Records had Aretha, RCA Records quickly signed Carolyn to her own record deal, and Erma released several songs for Shout Records and for Brunswick Records.

In 1967, Erma scored a Top Ten R&B hit with "Piece of My Heart," a year before Janis Joplin made the song one of her trademark tunes. In fact, Erma's version of "Piece of My Heart" was so popular it was nominated for a Grammy Award under the category "Best R&B Vocal Performance, Female." She was competing against Aretha, whose song "Chain of Fools" ended up with the trophy.

Carolyn's biggest hits were "It's True I'm Gonna Miss You" in 1969, and "All I Want to Be Is Your Woman" in 1970. She continued to record for RCA Records into the 1970s, releasing the album *I'd Rather Be Lonely* in 1973 and *If You Want Me* in 1976.

Jerry Wexler worked with all three of the Franklin sisters on sessions for Aretha's albums. He especially liked the way their voices sounded together. "It's because of the blend," says Wexler. "Sisters are naturally harmonic—if they have any music in them, they are gonna be a bet to have a smooth blend, because they match vibratos as well as timbres. The three had three entirely different sounds, but they blended well. Erma's voice was a little grittier, and Carolyn's was a little thinner and prettier. Being the youngest sister, Carolyn was plugged in a little more to the pop / contemporary scene. Erma as more gritty—like her records of 'Piece of My Heart' and 'Big Boss Man.' They were dynamite recordings."

Meanwhile, Aretha continued to produce hit after hit. On May 2, the single "Think" was released, and became her sixth Number One R&B hit, her sixth Gold single, and her sixth Top Ten pop hit. In July, her fourth album for Atlantic, *Aretha Now*, was released and immediately climbed into the Top Ten on the LP Charts and was certified Gold. She continued to score R&B and pop Top Tens that year with "I Say a Little Prayer for You" (Gold) and "The House that Jack Built" (Gold).

In November of 1968 the album *Aretha in Paris* was released, peaking at Number Thirteen on the LP charts. It contained live versions of thirteen of her songs from her first four Atlantic albums. It was produced by Jerry Wexler, with recording engineer Jean-Michael Poudubois, and the orchestra was conducted by Donald Townes. Aretha was captured in strong voice at the peak of her first plateau of international fame. This was one of the most enjoyable "live" albums released in the 1960s, and her performance—as captured here—reaffirms her title of Lady Soul.

While her singing on *Aretha in Paris* is crisp and exciting, her accompaniment is a bit bland and the arrangements a little Las Vegas-like. "That album embarrassed me!" Jerry Wexler exclaims. "Ted White's only interference at this time, came not in the studio, but in the fact that he selected the band that accompanied her on live appearances, which was a *horrible* band."

According to Wexler, the Donald Townes band was even disliked by club owners. "I went to Las Vegas with [Aretha and] that Donald Townes band. And the manager or the entertainment director of—I forget which of the casinos it was—came up to me and started vilifying me for this band. I said, 'Hey, man—it's not my band. Give me a break!'"

Wexler hated the band so much that on the back of the original *Aretha in Paris* album, he is listed—at his request—as "Supervisor," not "Producer." [The 1994 CD version of *Aretha in Paris* carries the credit: "Original Recordings Produced by Jerry Wexler"]. According to him, "I was the one who finally brought about . . . how should I say . . . I don't want to say 'the demise of Donald Townes' . . . but I brought about the institution of King Curtis & the Kingpins—who by that time were working with her in the studio—to be her regular band out on appearances."

The single "See Saw" was released on November 1, 1968. It peaked at Number Fourteen pop, Number Nine R&B, and was certified Gold. On February 4, 1969, the single "The Weight" was released, reaching Number Three R&B and Number Nineteen pop. Aretha took her third Grammy Award in early 1969 for her hit single "Chain of Fools," which seized the "Best R&B Performance, Female" prize.

Although Aretha was gathering a nice little collection of Grammy Awards in the late sixties, the awards ceremonies weren't anything like the glitter spectacles they are nowadays. These were not evenings when Aretha put on one of her outrageous beehive-like wigs and a beaded gown and accepted her statuette. The Grammys were not even televised until 1971, which was actually the first year that Aretha picked up her trophy herself. She was later to explain, "When I started getting Gold records and Grammys, I said, 'Wow! This is really something!' I mean, I never even knew the Grammys were that important. Jerry Wexler used to pick up the awards for me."

Although her career was soaring, her home life was making her miserable. Her marriage to Ted had turned into a nightmare and it took its toll on her. She was depressed, and to distract herself from her problems, she chain-smoked and over-ate. Photos from the later part of the year show her as round-faced and overweight. To mask her added weight, she started wearing chiffon dresses with huge, wing-like sleeves.

Now that Aretha Franklin had been crowned the "Queen of Soul," she started taking her role very seriously. And, she wasn't above fighting for her crown. She has had a career-long history for starting feuds with other female singers. Detroit's own Martha Reeves was one of the first to find out just how territorial Aretha could be. She had a run-in with Franklin during this era following a performance in New York City. Martha & the Vandellas were riding high on their own latest hits "Jimmy Mack" and "Honey Chile," when Aretha paid them a surprise backstage visit, and Franklin wasn't at all happy.

Martha explains, "At The Apollo, we were proudly doing a tribute to our own Aretha Franklin, Detroit's 'Queen of Soul.' It was an arrangement of Maurice King's featured on our *Live* album. 'Respect' and "Do Right Woman' were combined in a way where we did bits and pieces of each song, then on with our hits. Suddenly a parade proceeded up the aisle and backstage during our song, and it was perfectly timed. We finished our show and returned to our second-floor dressing room. Shortly afterward, 'the Queen' was let into our room. I saw her backup singers Margaret Branch, Carolyn Franklin, Brenda Franklin, and about seven or eight more members of her entourage gathered like a gang, ready for violence."

According to Reeves, she had no idea what to expect. "Aretha finally spoke, saying curtly: 'I heard you have been singing my songs,

Miss Martha.' I was waiting to hear her say more, maybe, 'Thanks for the tribute,' or 'Nice arrangement,' but she was finished and remained solemn." Clearly, Aretha was unamused at the thought of another Detroit diva singing her hits.

After a moment of dead silence, Martha continued, "'Well, you won't hear that anymore,' I replied. She appeared satisfied with this decision. I guess it bothered her to hear another singer doing her hits. I know the feeling. She turned and walked out, with everyone following her except Carolyn, whom I was always in constant contact with and always greeted with open arms. She nervously tried to explain that her sister was truly upset that we were singing her songs. I had only been following directions, doing material prepared for us at Motown's artist development department. Although the brilliantly designed arrangement was a definite showstopper and a fine work of art, we dropped it from our show and it wasn't missed. Besides, I still had several of my own new songs to sing!"

In January 1969, Aretha released her sixth Atlantic album, *Soul '69*, which represented a whole new approach to her music. Her first four studio albums had created a strong basis for her career and for her musical identity. From this point on, she was free to experiment musically. If she wanted to go off into a whole jazz phase, as she did with *Soul '69*, she had such a strong and devoted audience that she could experiment, and her fans would go along with her. She later did that with her gospel albums as well.

Aretha's first four Atlantic albums set the tone for a solid seven years of Number One million-sellers. Recording them solidified several lifelong friendships. In addition to her working relationship with Jerry Wexler, Arif Mardin, and Tom Dowd, Aretha also cemented her friendship with Cissy Houston and The Sweet Inspirations, who sang background vocals for several of Aretha's most memorable hits, right up through the 1980s. She also established a strong rapport with several musicians who gave those first four Top Ten albums their distinctive sound. Aretha especially became very close with drummer Roger Hawkins and sax player King Curtis.

During this, Aretha's first golden era, she wasn't afraid to attack any type of material. One of the reasons for her across-the-board appeal, and her instant popularity with the rock & roll record buyers, was the fact that she recorded her own exciting versions of several of the hottest rock hits of the 1960s. In her first two years at Atlantic, Aretha rocked with her own distinctive versions of the Rolling Stones' "Satisfaction," the Rascals' "Groovin'," and ? & the Mysterians' "96 Tears." In addition, she also recorded three Sam Cooke compositions: "You Send Me," "A Change Is Gonna Come," and "Good Times."

Jerry Wexler distinctly remembers the several Cooke songs that appeared on Aretha's early Atlantic albums. "She loved Sam, and usually if you saw a Sam Cooke song, it was her idea. Like 'A Change Is Gonna Come,' on which, incidentally, James Booker played organ."

On the R&B side, she recorded James Brown's "Money Won't Change You," Ray Charles' "Come Back Baby," and Curtis Mayfield's "People Get Ready," which was a big hit for Mayfield's group, the Impressions. She also recorded seven of her own compositions (five of which were written with Ted White, one with Carolyn Franklin) including "Don't Let Me Lose This Dream," "Think," and the lowdown blues classic "Dr. Feelgood (Love Is a Serious Business)."

Jerry Wexler recalls that Aretha's scope for musical appreciation was virtually boundless. "It was amazing how much rock & roll she liked, and there was absolutely nothing racist about her attitudes. She was totally open to anything from any quarter if it was good," he claims. "Only once did we have to stop the session because we weren't going anywhere. I even remember the song, it was The Box Tops' 'The Letter.' She always wanted to do that song; we tried it a couple of times and never could get a handle on it."

One of the cuts on *Aretha Now* was a Clyde Otis song called "A Change." Aretha had stayed in touch with Clyde since they had both left Columbia Records. To capitalize on her success with Atlantic Records, Columbia had released Aretha's single of Clyde's composition "Take a Look" in the fall of 1967. The song "A Change" was a hot song out of the same snappy mold as "See Saw" and "Think." In fact, it was such a hot record that Atlantic wanted to release it as a single. However, Clyde Otis and Jerry Wexler got into an argument over the royalties on the music publishing rights, and this caused a rift in Clyde and Aretha's friendship that hasn't been resolved in the ensuing twenty years.

"We fell out on 'A Change,'" Clyde Otis recalls, "because with that one, they wanted to use it for a single, and it probably would have been a great single, but I felt that they wanted to rip me off regarding the ownership of the publishing. I wouldn't go along with their terms, and that was really the beginning of when we didn't really talk, or communicate any further."

According to Otis, he was angry Aretha didn't step in and resolve his reported stalemate with Wexler. "She was hiding behind Wexler's coat, and he was saying, 'Clyde, my God, you ought to give up the publishing [rights].' And I was thinking to myself, 'Jesus Christ!' I just got real pissed, and she didn't intercede. She didn't say anything. I offered them a deal which I felt was fair, and that was to give them half, but they wanted more than half. The wanted at least a two-thirds share in the publishing, and I said, 'No way! I'm not going to do that.' We got real pissed at each other, and that was really when I stopped seeing her. She would have recorded more of my songs, but we just sort of hit a stone wall with that particular song." Since that time, he claims, "I've stopped in to see her when she's appearing someplace, and it's been cordial, but it was never as warm again."

Naturally, there are two sides to this story. Appraised of Otis' comments, Wexler laughingly exclaimed, "Oh, balls! All that I have to say about that is 'balls'!"

Of all of the lasting relationships that Aretha cemented during this period, the most enduring is her friendship with Cissy Houston. Cissy has recorded with Aretha throughout three decades. Cissy and the Sweet Inspirations have appeared on Aretha's albums starting with the Clyde Otis sessions at Columbia in 1965, to her Atlantic albums beginning with *Aretha Arrives* (1967), through her Arista era with Luther Vandross on *Jump to It* (1982) and *Get It Right* (1983). Originally, Cissy was the choir director of a gospel group in Newark, New Jersey. One of the members of her choir was her niece, Dionne Warwick. In the early sixties, Dionne started making demo recordings with a newly formed songwriting team, Burt Bacharach and Hal David. Beginning with "Don't Make Me Over" in 1962 and proceeding through "I'll Never Fall in Love Again" in 1969, the triumvirate of Warwick, Bacharach and David had one of the biggest strings of Top Forty hits of the decade.

Meanwhile, Cissy and the Sweet Inspirations began doing background vocals for everyone in the music business from Wilson Pickett to Elvis Presley, from Connie Francis to Bette Midler. In 1968 they even had their own Top Twenty pop hit, "Sweet Inspiration."

According to Arif Mardin, "The soul sound of Atlantic in the sixties depended on some tightly played horns and a great rhythm section, playing danceable and hard rhythmic patterns. And then the Sweet Inspirations would be called in, and Cissy would come up with a background vocal arrangement. You had the singer, the star—it could be Aretha Franklin, it could be Solomon Burke, it could be Wilson Pickett, or—you name it—all the greatest singers. You could call it an artistic assembly line, in a way, and Cissy Houston actually was part of this mechanism."

The first song Aretha worked on with the Sweet Inspirations at Atlantic was a cut from *Aretha Arrives* called "Ain't Nobody (Gonna Turn Me Around)." Until that point at Atlantic, Aretha had done the background vocals along with her sisters Carolyn and Erma. For this particular session, however, her sisters weren't available.

Tom Dowd recalls, "When it came to getting someone to sing with Aretha, we had the ideal solution. Because we had these girls that had the same basic musical root as Aretha, which was a church root, or a gospel root, and that chemistry just worked beautifully."

Aretha immediately formed a rapport with Cissy and the Sweet Inspirations, because they had both come from strong gospel backgrounds. "That's one of the reasons that we grooved together so good, because we do come from the same place," Aretha said. "Different churches, but the same place. Whenever we got together, we knew that we were going to sing, that we were going to do some good singing, wherever 'here' was. It's always going to be like that."

Aretha and The Sweet Inspirations really started cooking in the studio on *Lady Soul*. The unmistakable sound of Cissy Houston and her group can especially be heard on "Chain of Fools," "Groovin'," and "Ain't No Way." In fact, on "Groovin'" and "Ain't No Way" Cissy can be heard singing solo background vocals mid-song.

Jerry Wexler credits Cissy Houston with coming up with some of the most memorable background vocals on Aretha's albums in the late

1960s. "They'd come into the studio," Wexler recalls. "She'd listen to the tape, and they'd gather around the microphone and start working out. It was a collaboration, it was a communal thing. Most of it came from Cissy Houston and the girls. Most of the ideas, most of the lines, and most of the parts."

Whenever possible, Aretha also took the Sweet Inspirations on the road. According to her, "They have worked together for so long, if you spring something on them, they can go with it. Because they know you, and they know you so well, it doesn't have to be rehearsed. They can ad-lib and stay right with you."

Cissy and her group weren't with Aretha in 1968, when she did *Aretha in Paris*, because Cissy had a family to raise and she didn't travel overseas often. In fact, during several of her recording dates with Aretha, Cissy would bring her daughter Whitney to the studio, and the little girl would peer through the glass from the control room and watch her mother and Aretha sing.

"I remember when I was six or seven, crawling up to the window to watch my mother sing," Whitney Houston says. "And I'd be talking to Aunt Ree. I had no idea then that Aretha Franklin was famous—just that I liked to hear her sing, too! I just remember being in an atmosphere of total creativity. When I heard Aretha, I could feel her emotional delivery so clearly. It came from deep down within. 'That's what I want to do,'" she recalls.

Whitney has stated many times that one of her greatest musical inspirations was and continues to be, Aretha Franklin. It all began in those recording sessions at Atlantic Studios in New York City, when Whitney used to watch "Aunt Ree" sing with her mother. According to Aretha, "Cissy toured with me on a number of dates, and we're old and very good friends, and she used to bring Whitney to some of my recording sessions. I read some of her [interviews] and I think that it's fabulous she's been influenced by me. I had no idea that Whitney felt as close to me as she does—but it's lovely."

There were also several star musicians on Aretha's first four Atlantic albums. Eric Clapton, who at the time was a member of the rock group Cream, played the guitar obbligato on the song "Good to Me as I Am to You" on the *Lady Soul* album. Bobby Womack, Joe South, and King Curtis were all heard on these classic Aretha albums, and guitar player Duane Allman played on several of her sessions. Duane later united with his brother Gregg Allman to form the Allman Brothers Band. One of the concert dates that included Cissy Houston and the Sweet Inspirations was Aretha's triumphant return to New York City's Philharmonic Hall on October 13, 1968. *Variety* raved, "More than 4,500 fans turned out for two shows Sunday, ready to clap, stomp and holler in celebration of this soulful superstar, and they got even more than they had bargained for in the superb performance of Cissy Houston and the Sweet Inspirations . . . The audience's appreciation of the Inspirations was most strikingly expressed in the second show, during 'Ain't No Way.' Four times the house exploded with applause for Miss Houston's high soprano counter-singing to Miss Franklin's lead."

That night, in the middle of the show, Aretha's father bounded onto the stage to present his daughter with Gold record certifications for her single "I Say a Little Prayer" and for her album *Lady Soul*. Aretha's first two years and her first four albums on Atlantic Records had established her as *the* solo female singing star of the decade. Throughout 1967 and 1968, she had certainly made up for lost time. She now had a career basis from which she could grow, stretch, and experiment—which is exactly what she did on her next album.

Soul '69 represented a departure from her debut quartet of albums on Atlantic. Her singing on this record shows off the soulful delivery she had perfected on her previous albums for the label, but the material was mainly jazz. However, the music on this album was not the type of smoky, nightclub-style jazz she had recorded on her *Unforgettable* album; this was swinging, funky, fully orchestrated jazz. In a very real sense, *Soul '69* combined the best aspects of her jazz recording on Columbia with the confidence and vocal power she had gained by singing songs like "Respect" and "Think."

Although it was titled *Soul '69*, Jerry Wexler believes that "the title is a misnomer. That should have been called *Aretha's Jazz Album.*" This album is actually a patchwork quilt of different sessions, stitched together into one album. There is some straightforward jazz—including

"Ramblin'" and "I'll Never Be Free." There are some jazzy treatments of country & western tunes—on Rudy Clarke's "If You Gotta Make a Fool of Somebody" and John Hartford's "Gentle on My Mind" (which was a hit for Glen Campbell). And she even chose a couple of recent pop hits to reinterpret: Smokey Robinson & the Miracles' "Tracks of My Tears" and Bob Lind's "Elusive Butterfly." In addition, she also re-recorded her first Columbia song, "Today I Sing the Blues."

"I love that album. People don't know that Aretha made a jazz album, because of this unfortunate title," Wexler still laments. "It's a jazz album, and it is terribly misnamed, and I'm ashamed of myself. And the reason I permitted to happen is because my then-partner Nesuhi Ertegun had some kind of promotion going on at that time, which he thought would be beneficial if we called it *Soul '69*, rather than *Aretha's Jazz*, which it should have been called. And I permitted him to euchre [trick] me into this."

Although *Soul '69* was not a huge pop or R&B smash—commercially it is an absolutely brilliant testament to the genius and scope of Aretha's singing. Although Latin bongos and jazz saxophones on "Elusive Butterfly" were not what her new allegiance of R&B fans wanted to hear at the time, this was music that was meaningful to Aretha at the time, and she gave it all of the emotion and feeling that she gave any music she sang.

Jerry Wexler remembers being a bit taken aback by Aretha's insistence on recording "Gentle on My Mind" and "Elusive Butterfly." However, Aretha was the songstress of the day and if she had wanted to record her version of the Manhattan Yellow Pages, he wasn't about to stop her. According to Wexler, "Her taste could sometimes be very mainstream. That's part of her genius too. When it went off a bit, it went off in its own way."

"She picked those songs. I didn't like those songs for her. We also had 'Fool on the Hill,' which we never completed, and I was against that too. We have damn near a finished record on it," Wexler reveals. Along with almost a dozen other unreleased cut from this era, "I've got enough for an album," he said in 1988. "But the masters don't exist anymore, because they were destroyed in a fire. I do, however, have a seven-and-a-half [inches per second] tape of the sessions, which Atlantic is considering using to put out an album, which I still think they should do."

Soul '69 was recorded in sessions held in April 1968 and September 1968. This was the first Aretha album on which Jerry Wexler shared the production credits. His co-producer on this LP was Tom Dowd, and Arif Mardin arranged and conducted the material it contained. If Aretha wanted to do jazz, Wexler was determined to assemble the best jazz musicians he could find to accompany her. The songs "Ramblin'," "Pitiful," "Crazy He Calls Me," and Sam Cooke's "Bring It On Home to Me" featured Ron Carter on bass, Junior Mance on piano, and Kenny Burrell on guitar. Joe Zawinal (of the group Weather Report) played the Hammond organ on "Crazy He Calls Me" and the electric piano on "Bring It On Home to Me."

Since her success with "Respect," Aretha was almost universally known. In addition to her records being played on the radio, she appeared on magazine covers and she was a sought-after guest on prime-time television. She appeared on some of the most middle-of-the-road variety shows hosted by Bob Hope, Jonathan Winters, and Andy Williams. On May 4, 1969, she was one of the guest stars on the TV special *Andy Williams' Magic Lantern Show*, on NBC-TV. Also featured on the show were Williams' wife at the time, Claudine Longet, and country & western star Roger Miller.

Between the September 1968 recording sessions for *Soul '69* and the 1969 sessions for *This Girl's in Love with You*, Aretha took a long break in her recording career. "There were times when we were out of material and it was difficult to get her in the studio," Jerry Wexler recalls. Anxious to not lose any of the momentum built by her first four albums for the label, in July 1969 Atlantic quickly compiled and released the "greatest hits" package *Aretha's Gold*.

The one song that was totally unique to the *Aretha's Gold* album was her excitingly fun 1968 hit single "The House That Jack Built," which made it to Number Six on the pop chart in *Billboard*. The rest of the tracks were taken from her first four Atlantic Records albums. In 1969 Aretha had released two Top Twenty albums: *Soul '69* (Number Fifteen), and *Aretha's Gold* (Number Eighteen), both of which kept her active on the charts. Both albums hit Number One on the R&B album charts in the U.S.

Aretha's last two singles of the 1960s were very indicative of her personal life at the time: "Share Your Love with Me" and "Eleanor Rigby."

Both songs dealt with loneliness and unrequited love. These were two emotions that Aretha was reacquainting herself with on a day-to-day basis. At this point, her relationship with Ted White was in its last months.

Aretha had begun her mainstream recording career in 1960 as an insecure, eighteen-year-old singer with a pocketful of dreams, and she closed the decade as the undisputed Queen of Soul. Since signing with Atlantic Records, she had logged eight Gold singles, three Gold albums, fourteen Top Ten R&B smashes, and seventeen Top Forty pop hits. Aretha had truly arrived on the music scene in the late 1960s. Now all she had to do was piece her private life together, and she would be able to sail into the 1970s with a whole new sense of creative confidence.

CHAPTER FIVE

YOUNG, GIFTED AND BLACK

Toward the end of 1969, Aretha's marriage to Ted White ended. In a deep depression, she canceled more engagements than she kept. There was a large gap between her recording sessions for *Soul '69* and work on her eighth Atlantic album, *This Girl's in Love with You*. Fortunately there were enough cuts "in the can" from her last sessions for *Aretha Now* and *Soul '69* to provide Atlantic with single releases to carry them through the middle of the year. *Aretha's Gold* bought the company some additional time, while Aretha maintained a low profile and sorted out her personal life.

Muscle Shoals musician Jimmy Johnson recalls the problems Ted White caused in the studio, and Aretha's mental state at that time. "When we started working with her," says Johnson, "of course Ted was there. And I always felt that he was pretty much jealous of anybody that would get close to her except for him and her immediate family members. I remember when she went through breakups with him. The final break-up—I remember she was highly depressed and we'd come up to New York for the session, and maybe she wouldn't show for the session. 'Call Me' is the perfect example, I think, of some of the feelings she was having. I think she may have cried doing the lyrics of that song—because she definitely had us crying."

In addition to missed recording sessions, her string of canceled commitments included a concert booking at Caesar's Palace in Las Vegas. Frank Sinatra had to substitute for her when she suddenly bowed out of that engagement. Canceling concerts at times of stress was to become a career-long problem for Aretha.

The anxiety that she felt over her split with Ted White caused her to overeat, and she appeared bloated in the cover photo of her *This Girl's In Love with You* album. Her battles with Ted White that year caused her to become more insecure and fearful than ever before. During this period she tended to stoop, rather than stand confident and tall. On-stage, in tight-fitting gowns and flowing capes, she looked uncomfortable.

When she finally came out of her depression, Aretha was to explain, "I don't know whether you can call them real fears. Maybe, whatever it was, it stemmed from the fact that I had no confidence in my natural self. I suppose I wanted to look more glamorous, you know, so I came off looking starched, acting very starched. At the root of it was a thing I had for years about wanting to be a little shorter, so I tried to shorten myself by sort of stooping over when I walked. That developed improper posture, which is something I really had to work on."

Why on Earth would an overweight woman who was only five feet five inches tall want to be shorter? Was she so insecure that she wanted to hide from life by shrinking? Like an ostrich, Aretha has spent much of her life with her head buried in the sand, rather than confronting her problems head-on.

Throughout her career, her music has often been the gauge of her personal life. In regard to this matter, Aretha admitted, "It's hard to laugh when you want to cry."

What exactly caused Aretha's divorce from Ted White? Was he physically abusive as Clyde Otis and so many others claim? Or is that "untrue" like Ted insists? When asked point blank about their divorce. Ted replies, "I wouldn't touch that [question] with a ten-foot pole. We just decided to go our separate ways."

Since Aretha still refuses to address inquiries about her marriage to Ted, several questions about their life together remain unanswered. The enigma of Aretha's personal life during this era is in many ways more mysterious than ever. All that is certain is that her home life was frustrating and that she turned to her music for solace.

Clyde Otis confirms that it was Aretha who left Ted, and how it was done with her father's encouragement. Clyde also made it clear that Ted White did not want to let Aretha Franklin out of his life, and how it led to several ugly scenes. According to Otis, allegedly Ted came to stake his claim on his wife one night in Detroit, and Reverend C. L. Franklin met him at the door and threatened him with a gun, telling him to leave his daughter alone—or else there would be trouble. Eventually he got the message: it was over.

Ted White once told reporters, "What Aretha projects is honestly what she feels." This was never truer than when she left him. In 1970 she was to release two of her most personal albums, *Spirit in the Dark* and *This Girl's in Love with You.*

Jerry Wexler recalls that during this era in Aretha's career, she always seemed to be facing one trauma or another. "Sometimes she'd call me at four in the morning and we would talk—*long* talks," he explains. "If the call came then it would usually be about her troubles. We were close in that respect."

Wexler's biggest challenge in 1969 centered around getting Aretha back into the recording studio. "Aretha was always going through crises in her life," he recalls. "Once she was in the studio we never had any bad times, but sometimes it would be hard getting her *into* the studio."

Aretha's two 1970 albums are among the most exciting and powerful LPs of her Atlantic career. Free of Ted's influence, she finally "let loose" in the way Clyde Otis had begged her to do when she was at Columbia. They also represented a new production arrangement with Jerry Wexler, Tom Dowd, and Arif Mardin all sharing production credits. In addition, half of *This Girl's in Love with You* and all of *Spirit in the Dark* were recorded in a fresh new setting: Criteria Studios in Miami, Florida.

Some of Aretha's most outrageous adventures took place in Miami, right after she had gotten Ted White out of her life. "She was at the Fontainebleau, and they gave her the suite that Sinatra always uses; it's got a kitchen," says Wexler. "She loves to cook. She'd bring food into the studio in covered dishes. It got to be a pain in the ass sometimes, because I'd want to start the session at a reasonable hour, and she'd be busy cooking while I had the band waiting in the studio. She'd fix ham hocks, black-eyed peas, spaghetti, fried chicken. Sometimes the food would be all over the control room.

"Aretha loves to get down and go into the heart of Miami—across the tracks, to shop for food. She came back to the Fontainebleau one day with a paper bag full of pig's feet. The bag broke, and there were pig's feet all over the lobby. She just kept walking and left them there!" Wexler recalls, laughing.

Jerry was present for a lot of good times with Aretha during this era. However, he was also a devoted friend to her when she was in need. Wexler recounts that, "She got sick in Miami once when we were doing a session, and I took her to the hospital. I wheeled her through the bowels of St. Francis Hospital in Miami Beach, took her to the x-ray rooms, all of that. I was the only one around. With her big entourage, there was nobody but me. I couldn't understand it. She had pancreatitis; she was dehydrated. But she came out of it."

Four of the most electrifying cuts on *This Girl's in Love with You* were from her sessions in Miami: "Dark End of the Street," "Eleanor Rigby," "Call Me," and the title cut. On all ten cuts on this album, the strong gospel chorus of the Sweet Inspirations can be heard at full intensity. The Beatles' "Let It Be" became an inspirational treat, "Son of a Preacher Man" a declaration, and "This Girl's in Love with You" an obvious ode to the husband who had caused her so much pain. "Eleanor Rigby" was one of the most emotional songs on this album; it was clear that one of the "lonely people" she sang of in the song was Aretha herself.

One of the album's most intense performances came on the Clyde Otis composition "Sit Down and Cry." The lyrics deal with being "sold down the river," and being lied to. Aretha's singing begins slowly and then builds into a wailing lament, delivered like an emotional exorcism.

According to Jerry Wexler, during his working association with Aretha, he would "submit" material for her approval. If she insisted that she didn't like a song, he would concede. One of the songs Aretha passed on turned out to be a huge Top Ten hit for another Atlantic artist, and Aretha ended up regretting her original decision. "'Son of a Preacher Man' was written for her," says Wexler. "I brought it to her, and she said, 'I'm not gonna do this song.' And I think, 'Well, it's got to be something to do with the church,' and I always will respect that. So I gave the song to Dusty Springfield and we had a million-seller. A year later Aretha says, 'I think I want to do it.' But, by that time, all we could do was put it on an album. What a single that would have been for her!"

"Son of a Preacher Man" undoubtedly would have been a huge hit for Aretha, especially the way her rendition sounds on this album. Her delivery is so extraordinary that you believe Aretha really has been seduced by a preacher's son. "Dark End of the Street" likewise dealt with a taboo love affair and clandestine meetings after dark.

Another highlight of the album was the poignant confession of love, "Call Me," which Aretha wrote. "There is a story behind that song," she explains. "There were two people on Park Avenue and they were just getting ready to leave each other, going in different directions. As he got across the street and she was on the other side, he turned around and said, 'I love yooouu!' And she said, 'And I love you tooo!' He said, 'Call me the moment you get there.' And she said, 'I will!' And they just stopped traffic on Park Avenue and everybody was checking that out."

Inspired by those two lovers' parting comments on the street corner, Aretha sat down at the piano and wrote one of the most memorable songs of her career. In Aretha's song, she is pleading with the man she loves to pick up the telephone and call her the minute he arrives at his destination. The lines that she repeats over and over again, begging him not to forget to call, suggest that this is an exciting new love affair that is blossoming and that the singer of the song is obsessed with passion. This was Aretha's first really big record that was a beautiful and simple love ballad. The majority of her hits to this point had been up-tempo songs, and it was exciting to hear Aretha sing about the beginnings of a love affair, as opposed to her many songs about being wronged by someone she cares about.

The album also included her version of "The Weight." It had been a 1968 hit for the rock group the Band, and was written by one of the group's lead singers, Robbie Robertson. It was one of Jerry Wexler's several attempts to gain Aretha a rock & roll audience. He liked the results when Aretha recorded Elton John's "Border Song," and the Beatles' "Long and Winding Road" (both contained on 1972's *Young, Gifted and Black* album), but he wasn't happy with the recording of "The Weight" (although it hit Number Nineteen pop and Number Three R&B as a single).

"The Weight" is an odd choice to begin with. If she was going to record a rock & roll song from the Band, she may have done better with "The Night They Drove Old Dixie Down." "The Weight" is a rambling song about rolling into Nazareth and having an oppressive burden removed. Regardless of the biblical references, neither the Band's rendition nor Aretha's recording of the song was all that impressive.

"I was trying to make a bridge over to the 'flower children,' and it was a mistake," Wexler says in retrospect. "I bitterly regret having done 'The Weight' with her. I regret having submitted that song to her. The song is totally incomprehensible to her basic rhythm & blues constituency. Aretha cannot have a big hit unless it is also a hit with her black audience. It's got to be both, so this is where commercial stupidity and greed got the upper hand in me."

With regard to the original purpose for recording material like "The Weight" and "The Long and Winding Road," he admits that crossing over to the pop chart was also an ever-present goal. "We didn't want to keep Aretha as an R&B artifact. We wanted her to have a general market," says Wexler.

This Girl's in Love with You contained two of the three Beatles songs that Aretha recorded and released during this era: "Let it Be" and "Eleanor Rigby." According to her, "The Beatles, to say the least, were a phenomenon in this business. They wrote some very interesting, unique-type songs, and they were very exotic, I think, to the U.S.A." Aretha is also something of a Rolling Stones fan. Her versions of rock & roll classics are amongst her best recordings. Oddly, neither the Beatles' version of "Eleanor Rigby" nor Aretha's made it into the pop Top Ten. The Beatles' 1966 version peaked at Number Eleven, and Aretha's hit Number Seventeen.

If *This Girl's in Love with You* was Aretha's personal catharsis, then *Spirit in the Dark* surely represented her rebirth. She was ready to erase the past. The songs on this album spoke of Aretha's own disillusionment with love. She expressed herself with the exclamatory "Don't Play That Song," the telling "The Thrill Is Gone (From Yesterday's Kiss)," and the sassy "Why I Sing the Blues," which reflected her strong and confident new mood. Even more revealing were the five Franklin compositions contained on the LP: "Pullin'," "You and Me," "One Way Ticket," "Try Matty's," and the testifying classic "Spirit in the Dark." This album has the greatest number of songs written solely by Aretha. She obviously had a lot on her mind when she went into Criteria Studio to record this LP.

It seemed as if she was finally free from the chains that bound her to Ted White, and she wanted to sing about it. In the album's most famous song, she commands "Don't Play That Song (For Me)," for fear that it will rekindle memories—you know who she's trying desperately to forget. There were also hints that there was someone new in her life, especially on the title cut.

The arrangements are punchier, the singing livelier than she'd sounded in the last year-and-a-half. "We went back to funk on that album. There are no strings on that. It's all horns and really, really basic," says Jerry Wexler.

Although it was not one of her biggest hits as a single recording, "Spirit in the Dark" has become one of Aretha's signature songs. Is the "spirit" spiritual, or is it physical? When a reporter from *Ebony* magazine asked Aretha what the song meant, she answered evasively, "Well, it's true that I have to really *feel* a song before I'll deal with it, and just about every song I do is based either on an experience I've had or an experience that someone I know has gone through. 'Spirit in the Dark?' . . . Hmmmmm . . . that's one I'd rather not talk about. It's very, very personal and I don't want to get into it right now." It makes one wonder exactly what—or who—inspired the revival-meeting-type rejoicing that the song celebrates.

The song starts out slow, like a grinding seduction, and then the pace begins to pick up as Aretha urges everyone who feels "the spirit" to get up and "move" and "groove." There are four different places in the song where the pace accelerates, and Aretha's delivery becomes more and more frenzied. By the end of the song, the tambourines are shaking, the Sweet Inspirations are quaking, and Aretha is joyfully testifying about the virtues of putting your hands on your hips and getting "The Spirit in the Dark." This song is either about an uplifting religious revelation, or an incredible sexual experience.

"The Thrill is Gone (From Yesterday's Kiss)" is Aretha's obvious "kiss off" song to Ted White. While Franklin sings the lead vocal about leaving an unworthy lover, her background singers (Almeda Lattimore, Margaret Branch, and Brenda Bryant on this cut) sing, "Free at last . . . thank God Almighty . . . free at last."

Jerry Wexler explains, "*Spirit in the Dark* was an album that had its own cohesion, because we did it all together with a certain approach, but most of her other albums were collations of individual sessions. In other words, most of the time, we didn't go in and 'cut an album.' Aretha would come to New York and stay maybe a week, and we'd cut as many sides as we could—maybe four or five—and put them away. Then the next time she could come back—or maybe it might be in Miami—we'd do some more sides, and then, when we had ten sides, we'd put out an album. Of course, we tried to maintain the homogeneity of sound if we could. But *Soul '69* and *Spirit in the Dark* were really what you would call 'concept albums.'"

There were four Aretha Franklin singles released in 1970. All four of them became Top Ten hits on the R&B charts, but none of them hit the Top Ten on the pop charts. They were "Call Me" (Number One R&B / Number Thirteen pop), "Spirit in the Dark" (Number Three R&B / Number Twenty-three pop), "Don't Play That Song (For Me)" (Number One R&B / Number Eleven pop), and "Border Song (Holy Moses)" (Number Five R&B / Number Thirty-seven pop).

There was suddenly a concentrated effort centered around producing an Aretha Franklin hit record that would not only become an R&B smash, but would cross over to the pop charts as well. Although "Don't Play That Song (For Me)" had been certified Gold, Aretha was losing ground on the pop and rock radio stations. *This Girl's in Love with You* and *Spirit in the Dark* only reached Number Seventeen and Number Twenty-five on the LP charts, respectively. She hadn't had a Top Ten album in two years. Something had to be done about this situation before she lost any more ground.

"To me, *Spirit in the Dark* is a great album," says Jerry Wexler. "The fact that it couldn't sell up to the standards of the other albums was maybe that we didn't have a hit single in there. You have to remember one thing: the success of an album almost invariably was hooked into a hit single. But you're talking about 'The Thrill is Gone'—the B. B. King song—and 'That's Why I Sing the Blues.' . . . This album is a fabulous album! To me, it's only a value judgment. The ultimate confirmation is sales, I suppose. We just didn't have any luck with singles. I still think it's one of her best albums."

Fortunately, Aretha's subsequent releases in 1971 put her right back in top form. Wexler and Franklin created three consecutive Top Ten, million-selling hit singles, and a Top Ten Gold album that would firmly establish her as rock & roll's top diva: *Aretha Live at Fillmore West*.

Although Aretha's record sales had lagged a bit during 1969 and 1970, the respect of her peers remained strong. In 1970 and 1971 she continued to win Grammy Awards from the National Academy of Recording Arts and Sciences in the category of "Best R&B Recording, Female." In 1970 she was awarded a Grammy for "Share Your Love with Me," and in 1971 she took the trophy for "Don't Play That Song (For Me)."

At the Grammy Awards presentation, held in March of that year, the show marked the first time the awards were telecast. One of the songs that was nominated as "Song of the Year" was Simon & Garfunkel's "Bridge over Troubled Water." As part of the telecast, five different performers delivered their own renditions of the songs nominated in this category. The performers who sang the "Best Song" nominees were different from the performers who had been nominated for the awards. In line with this interesting programming concept, Aretha was chosen to sing "Bridge over Troubled Water." Her soulful interpretation brought down the house. That night the song won Simon & Garfunkel the Grammy Award for "Best Song of the Year," and served as the national debut of Aretha's version. Several days later, her recording of "Bridge over Troubled Water," which featured Aretha on piano and Donny Hathaway playing organ, ended up hitting Number Six on the pop charts and Number One on the R&B charts. It was certified Gold, and the following year the recording won Aretha her seventh Grammy Award. Here she was—chosen to perform the song on the awards telecast—and she eventually walked away with the prize! The Queen of Soul was definitely back on the roll!

"About the arrangement done of 'Bridge,'" explains Jerry Wexler, "instead of having her sing the first verse, I had her do it instrumentally, trading licks with Donny Hathaway. In other words [Aretha] was playing the keyboard—a piano—while [Donny] was playing the organ. When

I spoke to Paul Simon, I said, 'Paul, I hope you're not gonna be mad at me, but I left out some of your words.' But of course, to me, it gives the record a fantastic character. That was my idea, to beef up the arrangement, because Donny Hathaway also was a genius."

During the summer of 1971, Aretha flew to Europe for a full tour of concert dates. Unfortunately, the trip was not without problems. On June 28, Aretha was taken into police custody in Rome, as she attempted to board a flight bound for Paris. An Italian concert organizer had filed a "breach of contract" complaint against her, and she was temporarily detained by the authorities.

A later statement Aretha made regarding the matter, revealed that she had done one of her infamous last-minute concert cancellations, and tried to leave Italy before it was resolved. According to Franklin, "The only reason I can think of why they did this was because I had to cancel my last concert in Rome, but I played a series of nine one-nighters, and I was tired." The suit was somehow resolved, and after Aretha's luggage was searched, she was released.

Meanwhile, back in America, on July 9, 1971, Aretha's version of Ben E. King's 1961 hit, "Spanish Harlem," was released. On her recording, she changed the chorus lyrics a bit to read "*black* and Spanish Harlem." The single proved to be an even bigger hit than "Bridge over Troubled Water." "Spanish Harlem" sold a million copies, hitting Number Two pop and Number One R&B. In September 1971 the album *Aretha's Greatest Hits* was released, marking the LP debut of "You're All I Need to Get By," "Bridge over Troubled Water," and "Spanish Harlem."

However, it was the May 1971 release of *Aretha Live at Fillmore West* that was responsible for changing the demographics of her audience. The project represented a daringly different approach for presenting Aretha and her music. It marked a dramatic break from her past and presented her in a youthful, more contemporary light.

When "Respect" hit Number One in 1967, Aretha was suddenly in such great demand that she found herself playing huge concert halls and theaters. She began to travel with a full orchestra and a vocal background group, often the Sweet Inspirations. Her orchestra was Donald Townes, and the arrangements she used were overly orchestrated interpretations of her sassiest hits. Her show was more suited to places like the Olympia Theater in Paris, or Caesar's Palace in Las Vegas, than to a rock & roll venue. Aretha dressed in a spangled gown or in flowing chiffon, and her hairstyle usually consisted of a large and elaborate wig of the sort that the Supremes and Martha & the Vandellas wore in the late sixties.

The "à go-go" giddiness of the mid-sixties was replaced by the end of that decade by protest marches, political assassinations, the hippie movement, and the Vietnam War. While all of this was going on in the world around her, Aretha was busy dealing with her personal life, and her music was becoming part of the soundtrack of the era. "I've had a lot of guys—Vietnam vets—come up to me now and tell me how much my music meant to them over there," she admits.

When Aretha came out of her self-imposed seclusion in 1970, she was still rooted in the stiff style of 1968. While she had been presenting her concert act in prestigious halls around the globe, the look, the feeling, the audience interaction, and (thanks to marijuana) the smell of rock concerts had changed. When she was playing to crowded Vegas casinos and expensive concert halls, she was missing direct contact with the prime record-buying audience, twelve- to thirty-year-olds who buy rock & roll. Although she had packed a lifetime of show-business experience into her career already, she was only 28 years old when she recorded *Aretha Live at Fillmore West*.

The Fillmore West was a concert hall in San Francisco that was run by famed rock & roll impresario Bill Graham. It was the showplace of the Bay Area rock scene, and it drew its reputation from having played host to such top acts as Donovan, Sly & the Family Stone, Joe Cocker, Joan Baez, the Grateful Dead, and Santana. There were no chairs or bleachers at Fillmore West; the audience sat cross-legged on the floor, or stood up and grooved to the music being performed on-stage. People in the audience freely passed around joints during shows, and the atmosphere exemplified the whole "love-in" mentality of the late 1960s and early 1970s.

The audiences that gathered to see Aretha Franklin at Fillmore West had a chance to see the Queen of Soul in an atmosphere that was unlike any other—before or since—in her entire career. She may have missed performing at Woodstock, but for her and her fans, this was Aretha Franklin's "love-in."

The Fillmore West engagement was the brainchild of Jerry Wexler. He was determined that Aretha was not going to recede into being pegged as a soul star who occasionally sang a rock & roll song. He was determined to turn her into a full-fledged rock star with a total crossover audience. "We want these longhairs to listen to this lady. After that there'll be no problems," Wexler promised at the time. He and Bill Graham had negotiated all of the details for the engagement, and presented the package to Aretha.

One of her business advisors was Ruth Bowen, who headed up a company called Queen Booking. Ruth had been booking Aretha for $20,000 a show. Since Bill Graham could not fit enough people in Fillmore West to guarantee a box-office gross totaling that amount, Atlantic Records agreed to underwrite the engagement and produce a "live" album from the event. Eventually all parties came to an agreement, and the Queen of Soul headed for Haight-Ashbury.

Aretha discarded her staid Donald Townes arrangements, and a new show was constructed out of contemporary rock & roll tunes and rocking versions of several of her classics. The music for this engagement was provided by an all-star assembly of musicians: King Curtis & the Kingpins, the brass of the fabulous Memphis Horns (led by Wayne Jackson), Billy Preston on the organ, Aretha herself playing electric piano (on five songs), Cornell Dupree on guitar, Bernard Purdie on drums, background vocals by the Sweethearts of Soul, and—on one song—special guest star Ray Charles.

The event at Fillmore West was an entire weekend engagement, held on March 5, 6, and 7, 1971. Bill Graham stepped onto the stage and announced, "For all of us here at the Fillmore West, this is a long-awaited privilege and a great pleasure, to bring on the Number One lady . . . Miss Aretha . . . Franklin!" From that moment to the end of the show, the energy level on-stage was enough to achieve "warp speed" on *Star Trek*.

Opening with an atomic-powered version of "Respect," Aretha had the audience eating out of her hand from the very beginning. Gone were the wigs and sequins. Her hair was groomed in a short and attractive Afro, and she wore a simple and casual floor-length white dress accented with gold. Four of her strongest performances were culled from the contemporary rock classics: Stephen Stills' "Love the One You're With," Simon & Garfunkel's "Bridge over Troubled Water," the Beatles' "Eleanor Rigby," and the David Gates & Bread hit "Make it with You." The crowd loved her.

"It was a nice little cabal between me and Bill Graham to pull this off," Jerry Wexler remembers, "and we did it! I was never so delighted and surprised in my life to see the highly evolved, intelligent response of the San Francisco longhairs to every nuance and subtlety of Aretha's music. I couldn't believe it. But the response was as evolved and as well defined as though it had been an entire black audience. All of the Fillmore kids, the Haight-Ashbury acid brigade. I thought the music would never really resonate. But we took a gamble, and I think it helped a lot."

Aretha's third and final show at Fillmore West was on a Sunday night, and was highlighted with the guest appearance of Ray Charles. Aretha had just finished singing a five-and-a-half-minute version of her recent hit "Spirit in the Dark," and she walked off the stage to thunderous applause. When she returned for an encore, she walked back on-stage with Ray on her arm. "I just discovered Ray Charles!" she announced, as though she had just located a guest at a house party. Together, Aretha and Ray sang a reprised eight-minute version of "Spirit in the Dark," complete with several bars of ad-libbed lyrics from Charles. At one point he took over the keyboard of her electric piano, which was positioned at the edge of "stage right."

It was a historic moment—Aretha Franklin and Ray Charles together on the same stage—and Jerry Wexler had captured it on audio tape. According to Wexler, the whole duet was kind of a chance pairing, and was totally unrehearsed and excitingly spontaneous. "Ray was embarrassed because he had missed some of the words, and I had a hell of a job getting him to approve the release of the record, because he thought it made him look bad. I used all of my businessman's con on him. I wasn't fooling him. But I was just trying to say, 'Ray, this is too good to keep 'in the can,' you and Aretha—even if it's not a model of musical perfection.' He finally went along with it. My two idols together!" Wexler exclaims. "Boy, if I only could have gotten them to do a duet album."

Aretha once explained to *Time* magazine that she had finally overcome her stage fright by pretending she was "just at a party, and the audience is just my friends." If ever there was such a party, it was truly the one that Aretha threw in San Francisco that night. She closed the show with her version of Ashford & Simpson's "Reach Out and Touch (Somebody's Hand)," while walking out into the audience seated at her feet.

The three concerts and the resulting album all became the across-the-board smashes that Jerry Wexler had hoped for. The LP was released in May 1971, hit Number Seven on the album charts, and was certified Gold. Aretha reached a whole new audience with that particular album, and it encouraged her to take a new stance on her life. Stripping away the Las Vegas trappings of her first golden era, the Aretha Franklin of 1971–1973 was the back-to-basics, hippie / black pride version of herself. It was an era of "natural" black hairstyles and a rediscovery of African roots for many black people in America. It was during this same period that Aretha recorded her next milestone album, *Young, Gifted and Black.*

Her fresh new outlook on life in the early 1970s was partially due to her romantic feelings toward the new man in her life: Ken Cunningham. He had served as her road manager in the late sixties and after her breakup with Ted White she began what was to be a six-year relationship with him. In 1970 she gave birth to her fourth son, whom she and Ken named Kecalf (pronounced "Kalf.") The name is an acronym composed of the initials of the boy's parents: Kenneth E. Cunningham and Aretha Louise Franklin.

Together Aretha and Ken set up housekeeping in a high-rise duplex apartment off Fifth Avenue, on the chic Upper East Side of Manhattan. Although they never married, this was to become one of the most lasting and satisfying personal relationships in Aretha's life. Ken helped center her in a way that Ted never had been able to do. When she was breaking up with Ted, Aretha not only over-ate, but she would also drown her sorrows with liquor. In the early 1970s, Ken Cunningham helped her to drink less, and at one point, to shed some of the excess weight she had put on in the late 1960s.

At the time of the Fillmore West concerts, Jerry Wexler spoke to journalists in his room at the Huntington Hotel in San Francisco. When asked about Aretha's reported drinking, he stated, "She's got it under control now, I think." For the time being her life generally seeemed to be "under control" as well, and she was free to explore some new directions with her music.

In August 1971, Aretha lost another one of her friends. King Curtis had been playing saxophone on her recordings since the *Aretha Arrives* LP in 1967. He often went out on tour with her, and he conducted the band for Aretha's historic *Fillmore West* album. He owned a building on East 68th Street in New York City. He was outside on the sidewalk, talking with some of the tenants, when a junkie reportedly started an argument with him and stabbed him to death. Aretha sang at his funeral, and the Kingpins and the Memphis Horns all played in his honor. In addition to his instrumentals on Aretha's albums, King Curtis had several Atlantic albums of his own, which stand as a testament to his vast musical talent.

In November 1971, Aretha agreed to appear on the syndicated television program *The David Frost Show*, as the starring guest for an entire 90-minute program. The show was to be structured as a salute to the Queen of Soul. A large portion of the show was to be taken up by musical numbers, but here were several interim segments that would consist of David Frost interviewing Aretha.

Word had gotten to Frost's producers that Aretha was a difficult television interviewee, and that she was notorious for giving one-word answers to expansive questions. Just to make sure everything went smoothly, a member of the production crew was sent to Ruth Bowen's office at Queen Booking to conduct a preliminary interview with Aretha, to see how conversational she was in person.

At the time, Ken Reynolds was working on the show as the assistant music talent coordinator. On that particular show, Reynolds recalls, "One of my responsibilities was putting together the pre-interview notes, which is to give David notes on what Aretha would be singing, what she wanted to talk about, and what the highlighted conversations should be. This was put together after you spent a certain amount of time just talking to the artist and getting the information."

"I went up to Queen Booking," he continues, "and it was a very informal meeting. In fact, Ruth Bowen and I sat on the floor, and Aretha sat on the floor as well! I told Aretha specifically what I was doing, that I was there to talk to her to put together notes so that when she came on the show that night, the conversation would go smoothly. When I spoke to Aretha that afternoon on the floor of Ruth Bowen's office, it was like I was talking to an old friend. I'd ask her, 'How many kids do you have?' and she would say, 'I've got four boys, and this one, he does this . . . and that one, he does that' . . . I'd ask, 'Where do you live?' and Aretha would go into great detail . . . Everything I asked, I got very expansive answers for. So I put in my notes, 'Aretha is a great talker. She's like talking to an old friend. She has all these great stories, and they just flow off of the tip of her tongue—it's going to be a great interview.'

"I knew that Aretha was going to be the guest for the entire show, and to me, the worst thing that could happen was that the host would run out of things to talk about. So, knowing that Aretha was scheduled to sing thirteen songs, I did a little bit of mathematical calculation: 13 songs, at an average of three minutes each, is 39 minutes. An hour-and-a-half show—90 minutes—has only 71 minutes of tape time, and the remainder of the show is spent on commercials. Now, 39 from 71 leaves about 32 minutes devoted to talking, so I had listed twenty-five areas of conversation in my report to David Frost.

"I returned to the show and gave my report to David, and he said, 'Oh wow! This is great!' The evening arrived, and the show started out smoothly. As soon as she came out on-stage she sang two songs back-to-back: 'Since You've Been Gone' and 'Soul Serenade,' and she just blows everybody away. After the first two songs, she comes over to David and she sits down, and David goes, 'Aretha! Aretha, we're so glad to have you here, blah, blah, blah . . . Tell me, how many kids do you have?' And she turns to David and says, 'Four.' 'What are their names?' 'Clarence, Edward, Teddy, and Kecalf.' 'Where do you live?' 'New York.'

"And within the first segment of talking to her, he had gone through all of my twenty-five areas of suggested conversation! She was obviously totally intimidated by the presence of the audience and the television cameras. All of a sudden she wasn't talkative—she froze, and she gave one-word answers to every question.

"I had written all of these great notes—'She's talkative. She's so loquacious.' And then, when David asked her the same questions, she answered with one word! I remember, at one point, David just looked at the camera and put the notes aside and talked. He was determined to make her talk, and at some point he did get sentences out of her. He didn't get stories out of her like he got out of Diahann Carroll, or like he got out of Sophia Loren, but he did get her to talk. David called me up to his office after the show, and I thought, 'Oh shit! This is it—I'm getting fired!' I got up there and he said, 'Ken, I want her back on the show!' I nearly went into shock, but he meant it, because he was so in love with her musical talent."

Reynolds also remembers another amusing episode that occurred in the middle of the taping of that particular show. While the video tape was still rolling, Aretha suddenly excused herself, got up, and left the stage, leaving Frost to fill in with a monologue. "In the middle of one of the interview segments," Reynolds remembers, "Aretha says, 'Could you excuse me?' Which threw everybody off for a shock—you're on TV, what do you mean, 'Can I be excused?' If you're the only guest, and then there'll be nothing! So David is in shock, but he says, 'Of course,' and this was not cut out of the tape. She gets up, goes offstage, and she walks back on-stage smoking a Kool cigarette! She had gotten up in the middle of a live television taping to get a cigarette—I couldn't believe it! But that's Aretha."

At the time Aretha appeared on *The David Frost Show* that fall, she was at the height of her love affair with Ken Cunningham. Reynolds remembers that "one of the things we talked about in our interview was that she and Ken were opening a boutique and it was called Do It to Me, and it was going to be up in Harlem at 125th Street, but it never opened. She was real excited about that. But I tended to think that she always got very excited about anything that her man did, that she's been involved with. She's one of those women who believes in the Tammy Wynette philosophy of: 'Stand By Your Man.'"

Reynolds' main contact with Ken Cunningham came at the camera-blocking rehearsal that afternoon for *The David Frost Show*. He recalls that "Ken Cunningham was a tall, nice-looking man. He didn't have a whole lot to say, and stayed pretty much in the background. Again, Aretha paid a lot of attention to him, asking him lots of questions about his opinion. But he was very unobtrusive. He wasn't a showbiz husband, he wasn't butting in, or demanding anything of the crew."

Young, Gifted and Black is Aretha's most highly acclaimed studio album of the 1970s. The songs on it showed her off with such strength, confidence, and vocal dexterity that it was no wonder it sold so phenomenally well, and it contained five different hit singles. Its release coincided with the whole "black pride" phase of her career, which she reflected in her personal style, her public statements, and her music.

According to her at the time, "Well, I believe that the black revolution certainly forced me and the majority of black people to begin taking a second look at ourselves. It wasn't that we were all that ashamed of ourselves, we merely started appreciating our *natural* selves . . . sort of, you know, falling in love with ourselves *just as we are*. We found that we had far more to be proud of. So I suppose the revolution influenced me a great deal, but I must say that mine was a very *personal* evolution—an evolution of the *me* in myself. But then I suppose that the whole meaning of the revolution is very much tied up with that sort of thing, so it certainly must have helped what I was trying to do for myself. I know I've improved my overall look and sound, they're much better. And I've gained a great deal of confidence in myself."

One of the most autobiographical performances contained on *Young, Gifted and Black* was her version of "A Brand New Me." Looking back, Franklin recalls, "'A Brand New Me' was written by Kenny Gamble, and that's one of my favorite songs. Dusty Springfield recorded that first, and I recorded it after her. 'It's too bad we couldn't get these songs first!' I'd say. Gee, I wish, when I hear something like that, and I hear another artist do that, I wished that I could have gotten that first. But, thanks to them, and their performance, it's brought to my attention. Kenny Gamble, I think, is one of the best writers and producers in this business, and he's done some great things—'A Brand New Me' was one of them."

Most of the songs on *Young, Gifted and Black* were songs that she had heard elsewhere, taken a liking to, and decided to record. She had been listening to a lot of rock & roll, and the material on this album reflects the kind of things she was listening to at the time. Among the songs she recorded were own distinctive versions of the Beatles' "The Long and Winding Road," Elton John's "Border Song (Holy Moses)," Dionne Warwick's "April Fools," the Delphonics' "Didn't I (Blow Your Mind This Time)," Lulu's "Oh Me Oh My (I'm a Fool for You Baby)," and Nina Simone's "Young, Gifted and Black."

It was the era of the female troubadour in America. Female singer / songwriters were suddenly the rage, as witnessed by the strong emergence in 1971 of Carole King, Carly Simon, and Roberta Flack. All of these women sat down at the piano and sang about their life experiences, and record buyers were getting into their autobiographical compositions. Aretha's singing and playing were the unifying force that made this particular album so exciting. Her performance on the title cut and on her own compositions "First Snow in Kokomo," "Day Dreaming," "Rock Steady," and "All the King's Horses" help to make this album an emotion-charged classic.

The whole "female troubadour" image dominates this album. It placed Aretha in a bright new light. Her performance on the song "Young, Gifted and Black" is of the same quality, intensity, and purity as Carole King's song "Tapestry," Roberta Flack's interpretation of "The First Time Ever I Saw Your Face," and Carly Simon singing "That's the Way I Always Heard It Should Be." On this album, Aretha had become the true embodiment of the "natural woman" she once sang about. Unfortunately, this quality was not to repeat itself on any of her subsequent albums, which makes this LP all the more special.

At the time, Aretha felt that she had discovered a whole new inner self. She explained that the song "A Brand New Me" was precisely how she perceived herself: "That [song] expresses exactly how I felt when I recorded it, and actually how I feel right now—like a brand-new woman, a brand new me. I'm feeling much better these days. I'm a far gayer person.

I'm coming up with a lot of fresh new material, and I'm putting a lot more into working on my act. I've gotten rid of a lot of things that were weighing me down and I'm, well . . . like a new person right now."

She was later to admit that the song "Day Dreaming" was quite autobiographical and dealt with someone in show business with whom she was infatuated. "'Day Dreaming' was rather personal," Aretha told me when I pried. "And I was thinking about someone who used to be a friend of mine. I'll give you a hint. Used to be with one of the hottest groups in the country, tall, dark and fine. 'OOOOwwww wooo wooo wheee!'" she exclaims. "I said 'tall and fine'—he could sing! My my my my my!" (Although it sounds suspiciously as though the mystery man might be Dennis Edwards of the Temptations, Aretha wouldn't reveal his identity.)

Oddly enough, *Young, Gifted and Black* was recorded in a piecemeal fashion. Some of the cuts were recorded in Miami, at Criteria Studios, and some at Atlantic Recording Studios in New York City. "Oh Me Oh My (I'm a Fool for You Baby)" and "A Brand New Me" were produced by Jerry Wexler and Arif Mardin; the rest of the cuts were co-produced by the trio of Wexler, Mardin, and Tom Dowd.

The album also featured an impressive list of all-star musicians and singers. Jerry Wexler's newest discovery, Donny Hathaway, played the electric organ and piano on several of the cuts, behind Aretha's lead piano work. Also on the album were Billy Preston, Hubert Laws, Mac "Dr. John" Rebennack, Hugh McCracken, Eric Gale, Chuck Rainey, and Cornell Dupree. The Memphis Horns are heard on "Rock Steady" and "I've Been Loving You Too Long," and the background vocals are divided between the Sweet Inspirations and the trio of Carolyn and Erma Franklin, and Margaret Branch.

The album was released on January 1972, climbed up to Number Eleven on the charts, and was certified Gold. Its immediate acceptance was directly related to the across-the-board success of the exciting smash single "Rock Steady." The song which had been released as a single on October 11, 1972, hit Number Nine pop Number Two R&B, and became her third Gold single of the year. The B-side of the sing, "Oh Me Oh My (I'm a Fool for You Baby)" also charted. "Day Dreaming" was the next single, and it too hit the pop Top Ten and went Gold. It also became her twelfth

Number One R&B smash. The following year, *Young, Gifted and Black* was to win Aretha her sixth consecutive Grammy Award in the category of "Best R&B Performance, Female," which by now was being dubbed "The Aretha Franklin Award."

Aretha Live at Fillmore West and *Young, Gifted and Black* were critical masterpieces for Aretha. Her career was at an all-time high, and she was enjoying her life for the first time in years. She was coming to grips with her past, and she was moving forward with a new-found sense of self-confidence. Her next album project was one that was very important to her, as it would take her back to the church.

According to her brother, Reverend Cecil Franklin, "You listen to [Aretha] and it's just like being in church. She does with her voice exactly what a preacher does with his when he moans to a congregation. That moan strikes a responsive chord in the congregation and somebody answers you back with their own moan, which means, 'I know what you're moaning about, because I feel the same way.' So you have something sort of like a thread spinning out and touching and tying everybody together in a shared experience, just like getting happy and shouting together in church."

"I don't want to sound phony about this," Aretha told *Ebony* magazine in 1971, "for I feel a real kinship with God, and that's what has helped me pull out of the problems I've faced. Anybody who has kept up with my career knows that I've had my share of problems and trouble, but look at me today. I'm here. I have my health, I'm strong, I have my career and my family and plenty of friends everywhere, and the reason why is that, through the years, no matter how much success I achieved, I never lost my faith in God.

"I go back to New Bethel Baptist Church," she explained, "and I'm just Aretha to the people, and they are 'Brother' this and 'Sister' that to me. I really believe that people have become more and more broadminded about entertainers. They've come to realize that you can be an entertainer and still be someone who is trying to do the right thing by everyone, which is what I always try to do."

Her next move was to prove more than "right," it was going to crystallize her gospel-singing background into an overwhelmingly successful album; in fact, it was to become the most successful gospel album ever recorded! *Amazing Grace* was a project that brought Aretha's past, present and future all together in a two-record set. It had long been Jerry Wexler's dream to take Sister Franklin back to church to rediscover her roots, and to take the record-buying audience along with her.

"It's going to be done with James Cleveland, and we'll record it in church with a real good choir," she announced in the fall of 1971. When the project came together, it not only reunited her with Cleveland, but with several other important people from her past, including Clara Ward, Reverend C. L. Franklin, and John Hammond.

The album was recorded on two consecutive nights in January of 1972 at the New Temple Missionary Baptist Church in Los Angeles. Aretha was the lead vocalist on all of the songs, and she was joined in song by her childhood mentor, Reverend James Cleveland, on the traditional gospel hymn "Precious Memories." On all of the songs contained on the album, Aretha was backed by the Southern California Community Choir, which Cleveland directed. Highlights of the album include a version of Inez Andrews' "Mary, Don't You Weep" that raises goosebumps, a powerful rendition of Clara Ward's "How I Got Over," and a glorious, ten-minute version of "Amazing Grace."

Three of the songs on the album are inspirational versions of two contemporary songs from the 1970s (Carole King's "You've Got a Friend" and Marvin Gaye's "Wholly Holy,") and a gospel version of Rodgers and Hammerstein's "You'll Never Walk Alone." Aretha also reprised the song "Never Grow Old," which she had recorded at her father's church in 1956, on her historic debut album.

As he had done for *Young, Gifted and Black*, and *Aretha's Greatest Hits*, Ken Cunningham was responsible for all of the photography used on this album package. On the *Amazing Grace* and *Young, Gifted and Black* album covers, Aretha was depicted as a 1970s version of an African woman, swathed in a traditional dashiki-style gown and a tall head-wrap of the same colorful cloth. This was all part of the African fashion trend that was sweeping through black America at the time.

In the audience during the *Amazing Grace* recording session sat two of the most important people in her life: her father, and her idol Clara

Ward. According to John Hammond's liner notes, Clara and her mother, Gertrude, can be heard "moaning in the background" along with the choir.

In the middle of the procession, Reverend C. L. Franklin took the pulpit and spoke to the congregation. Following a moving version of "Climbing Higher Mountains," Reverend Franklin, his voice full of emotion, remarked, "That took me all the way back to the living room at home, when she was six and seven years of age. I saw you crying, and I saw you respond. But I was about to bust wide open. You talk about being moved! Not only because Aretha is my daughter—Aretha is just a stone singer! Reverend James Cleveland knows about those days, when James came to prepare our choir for a gospel broadcast—which is still in existence. And he and Aretha used to go in the living room and spend hours in there singing different songs. She's influenced greatly by James, greatly by Clara Ward. If you want to know the truth, she has never left the church!"

According to Arif Mardin, "It was so incredible. Aretha got extremely emotional doing some of the songs and she had to sit, you know, and kind of reflect."

In addition to her awe-inspiring singing on this album, Aretha also delivered a bit of scripture in the "Sister Franklin" style. As part of the song "Give Yourself to Jesus," she slowly and effectively began reciting from the Twenty-third Psalm.

The recording of *Amazing Grace* was such a historic event that a camera crew was also present for both evenings at the New Temple Baptist Church. It wasn't just filmed by a news crew; Academy Award-winning director Sydney Pollack was brought in to capture on film the whole monumental proceeding. Although the material is the property of Warner Brothers, the film was never edited or released. It remains "in the can" on a shelf somewhere, still waiting for the right moment when it will surface as a theatrical release, or as a DVD.

The very concept of Aretha Franklin returning to the church to record *Amazing Grace* sounds like a natural move for her, and seems as if it must surely have been her own idea. However, according to Jerry Wexler, she had to be talked into it. Originally, she was terrified that members of the Baptist religion would take offense. "The album that I really had to coax her to do was the gospel album," he explains. "I was after her for years to do that. Coming from a church family—her father and all—she had a lot of qualms about doing it, and I could understand them. There was a great feeling at this time about people who left the church and were singing the devil's music. There was shame and guilt, and you couldn't go back. When Sam Cooke went 'pop,' he never went back and did another note of gospel."

Wexler claims, "She didn't want opprobrium from the church. After all, she's a deeply religious person, and she's been brought up in the ministry, and there's been all the gospel people around her, the Clara Wards and the James Clevelands. She had a lot of qualms about going in and doing church music, when here she'd been singing blues and jazz—'profaning,' so to speak."

The arrangements and the interaction of Aretha with the choir and the congregation are sheer magic. "Those arrangements were between her and James Cleveland," explains Wexler. "I had virtually nothing to do with the arrangements. My contribution was getting that rhythm section in there, a secular rhythm section, and bringing them to the church to rehearse with the choir for days before we made the album, and with Aretha and James Cleveland both playing keyboards. Those arrangements, and some of them were things that she and James Cleveland put together. But my contribution to that would have to be in the area of good supervision and production. But musically, the balancing and everything else, whatever, it just fell that way. We had a truck [with recording equipment] outside. Since it was a live session—actually, it was a service on a Friday night, with the congregation there—it was not the kind of thing where you stop a tape and go in and say, 'Let's change the third bar of the bridge.'"

During the recording of the album, the spirit moved several of the members of the congregation. Several of the women at the service went into dramatic "testifying" trances and fits of rejoicing. "I remember Gertrude pitched one of her regular 'hissies,'" Wexler recalls of Clara Ward's mother. "I mean where they go into a gospel trance, and the ladies with the white coats with the Red Cross on them lead them to the ambulance, and they go into rigor and they speak in tongues."

Released in June of 1972, *Amazing Grace* was a calculated risk. Would the members of the "me generation" flock together and follow Sister Franklin to church? The answer was an astonishing "yes!" The album not only went Gold, but made it to Number Seven on the LP charts alongside such unlikely company as the Rolling Stones' *Exile on Main Street* and Jethro Tull's *Thick as a Brick*. In addition to the success of the album, the single version of "Wholly Holy" logged four weeks on the pop singles chart. *The New York Times* was to refer to Aretha's *Amazing Grace* as "among her finest achievements," and it ended up winning Aretha her eighth Grammy Award, in the category of "Best Soul Gospel."

"I think the record was so successful because the choir was great, we had a good audience, and we had the preparation," Jerry Wexler recalls. "If we had the tenacity to bring 'the devil's rhythm section' into church, you understand there had to be a hell of a payoff for it, because it could have been dangerous. Of course, it is not like there isn't a tradition of all kinds of instruments in the sanctified church. Again, *Amazing Grace* has spontaneity and a soulful feeling too."

Aretha changed her formula slightly for her next album, by changing producers for the first time since she had joined Atlantic Records in 1966. As she has done at Columbia with Clyde Otis, Aretha was taken by the idea of recording an album with another of Dinah Washington's producers, Quincy Jones. (On *Amazing Grace*, Aretha had shared co-producing credit with Jerry Wexler and Arif Mardin.) On 1973's *Hey Now Hey (The Other Side of the Sky)*, Aretha shared producing credit with Quincy Jones. It was her most inconsistent album since her days at Columbia.

Jones once proclaimed that "Aretha always had a fire in her; music's been her ticket to freedom." Although their album together contained one of her hottest hit singles, "Angel," the rest of *Hey Now Hey* turned out to be a real fire extinguisher. Peaking at Number Thirty on the LP charts, it was her first Atlantic album not to crack the Top Twenty-five, and began a seven year cycle of career tailspin.

First of all, *Hey Now Hey (The Other Side of the Sky)* sported one of the worst album covers of the entire decade. A rudimentary pencil-sketch portrait of Aretha featured a double-image sketch of her superimposed—upside down—in the middle of her face. Although she was again depicted wearing an African headwrap, this particular sketch looked like an entry in a junior-high-school art contest. The interior of the gatefold LP cover contained cartoon versions of Franklin, Jones, and several inner-city street characters. Aretha herself was drawn as a reed-thin Egyptian princess with enormous wings, a fully exposed breast, and a microphone in her hand. Another of the cartoon characters on the LP's interior is a black matador who is bullfighting. However, instead of fighting a bull, he is waving his cape at a giant syringe. The album design is credited to Aretha Franklin, Ken Cunningham, and artist Jim Dunn. The concept might have sounded great during a late-night conversation, but in its ultimate execution it was an instant visual turn-off.

This album is most significant for yielding the hit single "Angel," which was written by Carolyn Franklin. It peaked at Number Twenty on the pop chart, but on the R&B chart it went right to the top, becoming her thirteenth Number One soul hit. It is still one of the most-requested hits in Aretha's repertoire.

Three of the cuts on the album were great jazz numbers. A slow and beautiful version of Leonard Bernstein and Stephen Sondheim's "Somewhere" is especially moving, and the be-bopping "Moody's Mood" provided the album with its high points. (Together with "Just Right Tonight," those two cuts were included on the 1984 Atlantic release called *Aretha's Jazz*. The other side of the *Aretha's Jazz* LP was culled from *Soul '69*.) What Aretha and Quincy should have done at the time was to go all the way, and produce the ultimate Aretha Franklin jazz LP. Instead, they filled it up with one great ballad ("Angel") and a bunch of rambling grade-B songs.

Jerry Wexler confirms that *Hey Now Hey (The Other Side of the Sky)* was the product of a complete shift away from the original blueprints. "Quincy's album started out to be a jazz album," he says, "and then it just started to drag on and on and on, and they changed their approach in the middle, and they went to make a regular commercial pop / soul album. Frankly, that [album] was a disappointment to me."

One of the songs that Aretha and Quincy produced together was "Master of Eyes (The Deepness of Your Eyes)." It has a sort of psychedelic-narcotic feeling, with echoing vocal tracks, and someone blowing a set of

Middle Eastern pipes, like those of a snake charmer. The song was released as a single and made it to Number Thirty-three on the pop chart. However the song was not included on *Hey Now Hey*.

[In 1994, when *Hey Now Hey (The Other Side of the Sky)* was released on CD for the first time, the song "Master of Eyes (The Deepness of Your Eyes)" was added as the last track of the album, which makes perfect sense. When the 2007 album *Rare & Unreleased Recordings from the Golden Reign of The Queen of Soul* was released by Atlantic Records, it included eight tracks from the sessions for *Hey Now Hey* that were never released. Perhaps a full album that gathers together all of these tracks produced with Quincy Jones would be the ultimate way this material should be heard.

The year 1973 was one of high exposure for Aretha. She was seen singing and performing in comedy skits on *The Flip Wilson Show*, and she even showed up on an all-star tribute to big-band jazz great Duke Ellington. The extravagant January 13 television special was called *Duke Ellington . . . We Love You Madly*, and the producer and musical director was Quincy Jones. Also on the 90-minute CBS program were Count Basie, Ray Charles, Peggy Lee, Sarah Vaughn, Billy Eckstine, Sammy Davis, Jr., Joe Williams, James Cleveland, Quincy Jones, and the ever-sophisticated Duke Ellington.

Aretha's personal appearances that year found her playing three of the largest venues in America: the Houston Astrodome, the Boston Garden, and the Los Angeles Forum. In September 1973, Aretha was one of several black entertainers who appeared in a benefit concert at the Cathedral of St. John the Divine in New York City, held to raise money to aid drought victims in West Africa. She also played a series of concerts in South Africa that year, of which she clearly stated, "I made them give me a contract in which I specify that I won't sing before any segregated audiences. They'll either have to be totally integrated or all-black. I won't sing for an all-white audience. Black people must be able to come and hear me sing."

That same year, Aretha had the sad task of singing at Clara Ward's funeral, which was held in Philadelphia. She sang one of the songs that made Clara famous, "The Day Is Past and Gone," which Aretha had recorded at the age of fourteen. In 1972 she had sung at Mahalia Jackson's funeral, performing another selection from the *Songs of Faith* album, "Precious

Lord," Suddenly, all of the great ladies that Aretha had known and looked up to as a child were gone: Dinah Washington, Mahalia Jackson, and now Clara Ward. It was up to her to carry on in their tradition.

In 1973 Aretha went back in the studio with Jerry Wexler to produce what was to be remembered as their last great album together, *Let Me in Your Life.* Whatever momentum she lost with the lackluster *Hey Now Hey,* she temporarily regained with this album. As a total album package, *Let Me in Your Life* is one of Aretha's most beautiful, sophisticated and classy LPs. It showed her off as a mature and focused performer, weaving songs of love and devotion. None of the songs on this album are soul shouting sprees, rock & roll, or dance tunes. A majority of the songs contain her signature piano playing and Arif Mardin's horn and string arrangements. It is as pleasant and unified as Billie Holiday's *Lady in Satin* or Barbra Streisand's *People*—yet it is 100-percent Aretha.

The songwriters whose material was utilized on this album give one an idea of the caliber of the songs: Bobby Goldsboro, Leon Russell, Stevie Wonder, Bill Withers, and Ashford & Simpson. The musicians, likewise, were all top-notch: Cornell Dupree, Bob James, Richard Tee, David Spinoza, Rick Morotta, Ralph MacDonald, Donny Hathaway, Willie Weeks, and the background vocals of Cissy Houston.

The album was released in February 1974, and made it to Number Fourteen on the LP Charts. There were two singles released from *Let Me in Your Life*: "Until You Come Back to Me (That's What I'm Gonna Do)" and "I'm in Love." Aretha especially remembers recording "Until You Come Back to Me." "Stevie Wonder wrote that," she recalls. "I was staying in New York at the time, up on 88th Street between Fifth and Madison, right down the street from the Guggenheim Museum. And, let's see—I think we had a dry spell there, and that was a resurgence of hits. Thank you, Stevie!"

"Until You Come Back to Me" went Gold, hit Number Three on the pop charts, and became her last Top Ten hit of the decade. "I'm in Love," which Bobby Womack composed, hit Number Nineteen on the pop charts. However, on the R&B charts, both songs hit the top, becoming her fourteenth and fifteenth Number One R&B smashes since signing with Atlantic.

All of the songs on *Let Me in Your Life* were produced by Jerry Wexler, Arif Mardin, and Aretha Franklin, except for four cuts ("With Pen in Hand," "Oh Baby," "If You Don't Think," and "A Song for You") that added Tom Dowd to the production lineup. A remake of the Marvin Gaye and Tammi Terrell hit "Ain't Nothing Like the Real Thing" was also released as a single and went on to win Aretha another Grammy Award the following year.

In 1974, Aretha won a Grammy Award for the little-known single, "Master of Eyes (The Deepness of Your Eyes)." "Ain't Nothing Like the Real Thing" brought her number of Grammys to an astonishing total of ten. For eight years in a row she had captured the title of "Best R&B Performance, Female." She had won in that category every year since its creation in 1967. During the beginning of 1974, the Queen of Soul was comfortably seated on her throne, at the top of the record world. Unfortunately, when things began to go awry later that year, she had much farther to fall.

CHAPTER SIX

TROUBLE IN MIND

Aretha once commented, "I cannot imagine an artist—or anyone creative—who does not have a lull from time to time." For her, the lull began in 1974 and lasted for five years. It would be easy to point a finger at any one of several possible reasons why her creative success began to slip away. These factors included a change in musical styles, the advent of disco music, poor song selections, and several exceedingly ill-chosen career moves.

Her next pair of album releases, *With Everything I Feel in Me* (1974) and *You* (1975), are among the five most disappointing albums of her entire career. The most bewildering aspect of these two albums is the fact that they represent Aretha's final recordings with Jerry Wexler as producer. Actually, the production credits on both of those albums list Jerry Wexler and Aretha Franklin as its producers, so she has to share the blame.

Jerry Wexler comes to a dead stop when our conversation comes around to his 1974 and 1975 LPs with Aretha. "I don't want to talk about those albums," he says flatly. "I'm not happy with them, except for an occasional, isolated song such as 'Until You Come Back to Me.' There were some good songs, you know, lurking somewhere in those albums. I'm not saying that they're bad albums, but I'd rather not talk about them."

According to him, the last Aretha album that he really put his heart in was *Let Me in Your Life*. "That album was the beginning of things winding down," he recalls. "There would be some great individual songs on the subsequent albums, like 'Until You Come Back to Me,' for example, which I think should have been a smash. Stevie Wonder wrote that song, and I think it's one of the greatest things she ever did. But somehow we didn't get lucky with it."

When *With Everything I Feel in Me* was released in December of 1974, "luck" took a holiday. The disc was Aretha's first Atlantic LP to fail to make the Top Forty on the album chart. It comprised a disappointing mixture of mid-tempo songs and ballads that never seemed to get off the ground. It is also the first Aretha album to utilize synthesizers and echo effects. Somehow the Queen of Soul was lost in the mix, and she failed to find an audience this time around.

As for Wexler's statement that these last two collaborations contained a flash or two of brilliance, there are indeed a couple of songs that start to cook—but the recipe is seriously deficient. *With Everything I Feel in Me* contained one single release, "Without Love," which only made it to Number Forty-five on the pop chart. The song itself finds Aretha utilizing some of the shrillest notes in her range, amid a performance that sounds as though she is bored. Her version of Burt Bacharach's "Don't Go Breaking My Heart" starts out like an up-tempo ballad, but ends with a weak attempt at replicating the snapping snare sounds of Gloria Gaynor's first disco hit, "Never Can Say Goodbye" (1974). At the end of her remake of Dionne Warwick's hit "You'll Never Get to Heaven," Aretha does nearly two minutes of scat "la-la-la's" that seem to go on forever. Her rendition of Stevie Wonder's "I Love Every Little Thing About You" is a lackluster attempt to reproduce Stevie's zesty, synthesizer-dominated original. The best numbers on the album include the sassy Carolyn Franklin composition "Sing It Again—Say It Again" and the gospel sound of James Cleveland's "All of These Things." However, neither of these tunes were up to the high standards she set for herself on *Young, Gifted and Black*.

Regardless of the music on *With Everything I Feel in Me*, the startling cover photo of Aretha caught everyone's attention. She had been wanting to surprise her fans and to project a more youthful image, but this was a real eye-opener: a svelte Aretha provocatively wrapped in a white fur coat—and apparently nothing else. This was in direct contrast to the plump Aretha photographed in a black fur coat that same year for the cover of *Let Me in Your Life*—which resembled a Blackglama fur coat advertisement from their famed "What Becomes a Legend Most?" campaign. This, however, was the cheesecake shot to end them all, with Aretha showing ample amounts of cleavage, a much thinner face and a shapely thigh.

After two years of wrapping herself in weight-concealing African robes and headgear, Aretha was anxious to change her look. The loose-fitting African clothes that she had been wearing had effectively masked her heaviness, but in 1974 she was ready to shed her "earth mother" image—and forty unwanted pounds. She dropped from 165 to 125 pounds. On a medium-height woman, the loss of forty pounds is quite dramatic—and for a while, Aretha reveled in the change.

At the time, she proclaimed that she was "feeling better now—not just physically, but also about myself—than I have in a long, long time." She and Ken Cunningham had moved to a six-story brownstone from the high-rise duplex apartment they had been sharing in New York City.

"All the girls will understand the change in attitude and self-appreciation when they hear that I dropped from a size fifteen dress down to a size nine [or] ten, and I can even wear size eight in some things. Any woman knows that kind of thing makes you feel mighty good," she said. "Actually, I didn't do anything really all that dramatic in order to lose weight. I followed some common sense rules about overeating and I just avoided all those wrong things that everybody knows about, such as cakes, pastries, ice cream, and soda pop. It all started when I went into a dress shop and the saleslady started showing me things in *size fifteen!* With my height—I'm only five foot, five inches—I couldn't stand being that size. Size fourteen was bad enough, but when she said the magic words 'size fifteen,' I started saying some magic words to myself, and they were, 'Oh-oh, girl. You've gotta start backing up—*way back!* I made up my mind then and there to lose weight, and I did. First thing I did was go to a place in New York where they have a special table with devices that knead you in all the spots where you're bulging and need toning up. They suggested a diet for me, but I confess that I didn't stick to it very long. I read enough diets to know what I was doing wrong, so I sat down and worked out my own weigh-losing plan. I wanted one that I could be comfortable with, and I didn't want to have to take pills—no medicine at all."

According to her the only substances that she utilized were vinegar and honey. "A lot of people know about the vinegar-and-honey thing," she explained, "but here's the way I used it. As soon as I got up in the morning, I'd take one teaspoon of honey and two teaspoons of apple-cider vinegar and stir them in about one-third glass of water. I'd drink this before having any breakfast at all. Then I'd have a small glass of orange or grapefruit juice and half a slice of dry toast and sometimes an egg. Later in the day I'd have some clear soup and a small amount of vegetables or fruit. I followed this routine for a week or so, just to clean out my system and prepare it for dieting. When I started eating more solid foods, I'd go to the kitchen and do my 'corners' thing. That means taking spoons and dipping just the 'corners' out of pots. I'd have a tablespoon or so of whatever I liked, then I'd go back upstairs, telling myself I'd had a marvelous meal. It didn't take long for my eating habits to change completely. I began losing interest in food and I stopped thinking about eating all the time as I once did.

"I didn't want to lose too much weight too fast, so I paced myself and weighed every day and took off no more than three or four pounds a week. The important thing for me was the vinegar and honey, which kept my stomach feeling okay as my system adapted to the change. I didn't get ill or nervous as some do," she said. Following her own regimen, she lost the forty pounds in a matter of four and a half months. This was, however, to be a once-in-a-lifetime occurrence for Aretha. Any slim and trim photographs of Aretha clearly define this one particular year of her life. The weight would return by the end of the decade.

"Foxy" was an adjective that was used quite freely during the 1970s to describe someone sexy-looking. If 1972–1973 was Aretha's dowdy "African matron" period, then 1974–1975 was surely her "foxy lady" era.

The svelte new figure that she sported during this period encouraged Aretha to take some of her most daring fashion risks. Throughout the seventies, more often than not, Aretha's choices in clothes, on-stage and off, proved misguided. Although she had indeed pulled off with amazing aplomb the cheesecake shot on the cover of *With Everything I Feel in Me*, her fashion whims were, more often than not, total disasters.

Her concert engagements that year showed total inconsistency with her reputation as the Queen of Soul. When she bounded onto the stage of Harlem's Apollo Theater in a sequined lavender outfit with a lavender top hat, singing "Rock-A-Bye Your Baby with a Dixie Melody," she really threw her soul fans for a loop. However, she reserved her most ridiculous outfit for Radio City Music Hall in October of 1974. It was here that she came on-stage in a clown costume—complete with a red plastic bulb nose and a silly hat—singing "That's Entertainment." What *did* she have in mind when she dreamed up these routines?

"I thought it was a nice change of pace," she explained when the press questioned her choice of material. "As for people accusing me of not being myself—well, who else am I? I am always myself. Maybe the public just doesn't know me?"

She lost further ground when she released her *You* album in November 1975. It was her last album with Jerry Wexler producing, and neither of them will discuss it to this day. There were fewer flashes of brilliance on this album than there were on *With Everything I Feel in Me*. The one highlight was Aretha's composition "Mr. D.J. (5 for the D.J.)," but even that funky cut is substandard. The single release of that song peaked at Number Fifty-three pop, and the album only made it as far as Number Eighty-three on the LP chart. She recorded songs by some of her favorite writers, but not even Van McCoy ("Walk Softly,") Ronnie Shannon ("You Got All the Aces,") and her sister Carolyn ("As Long as You Are There") could help her out of the quicksand she was sinking in this time around.

The cover photo of *You* is embarrassingly sloppy and undignified. Aretha is depicted lounging on a lawn in a bare-midriffed halter top, her sandals off, with a pair of crazy sunglasses on her head. Who on Earth chose this photo?

Billboard claimed that on *You*, Aretha was "back doing what she does best, raucous yet controlled singing. [She] fits into today's disco mold well on several cuts." Who were they kidding? If only she was doing good disco music, it would have been better than the material that is on this album. As it was, she was missing the boat on all counts. *Interview* magazine was more on target in 1986 when it described *You* as "a listless album . . . deserves the cut-out bin."

After producing *You* with Aretha Franklin, Jerry Wexler left Atlantic Records in 1975, and became a vice-president at Warner Brothers Records.

This ended an incredible era in Aretha's musical life. Together, Wexler and Franklin had created an amazing total of eighteen albums (including the four "greatest hits" packages).

Aretha appeared on several television programs in 1975. In addition to being seen on *The Academy Awards* telecast and *The Grammy Awards* show, she was a guest star on *The Muhammad Ali Special* and a special called *Bob Hope on Campus*. She also taped *The Tonight Show* and the late-night rock & roll series *Midnight Special*. The *Midnight Special* segment was a tribute to Aretha, which presented several film clips and a special performance.

"She was on *Midnight Special* at her thinnest, and she looked great," recalls Tisha Fein, who was the producer of the special salute to Lady Soul. "It was very difficult to get her to agree to do it, but once she agreed, she was real charming. We opened the segment with a film montage and cut to 'Respect,' and just wonderful footage of her in church with Reverend James Cleveland, with Mick Jagger in the audience. It was wonderful. She started playing the piano, and she said, "I was never very good on the piano, and see—it's like that again tonight, isn't it?' She did some spirituals and talked about growing up. I asked her some of her favorite moments, and she said, 'That would have to be at the 20 Grand, working with my sisters. And working with my dad in church. And singing with Ray Charles—he's my hero, an inspiration to me.' She came to the studio in a beautiful pink dress, and taped the show. She was still very shy, but she was real charming."

Although her latest recordings were failing to find an audience, Aretha retained her star stature. In fact, she gleaned several honors during this period, including an Honorary Doctor of Laws degree from Bethune-Cookman College in Daytona Beach, Florida. Suddenly she had a new title to add to her list: "Dr. Aretha Franklin." A few nights after receiving her honorary degree, she played a concert date at the Westchester Premier Theater, north of Manhattan. When she came on-stage that night, an enthusiastic fan stood up and shouted, "All right, Miss Ph.D.!"

In 1975, a new female R&B singer literally burst onto the music charts, and ended up cracking the Top Ten with her debut single. She proceeded to rack up six consecutive Gold albums and two Platinum albums from 1975 to 1979. Her style was hot and sassy, and the public gravitated to her not only for her fresh singing style, but also because her father had been a beloved 1950s singing star. For lack of a better way to describe her vocal style, the press consistently referred to this singer as "the new Aretha Franklin."

Her name was Natalie Cole, and she appeared on the scene at the exact time that Aretha's record sales were dropping off. At first, Aretha and Natalie developed a warm friendship. In 1976, when the Grammy nominations were announced, it was the first time in eight years that Aretha wasn't up for any awards. When the winners were announced, Natalie was presented with two of the trophies. The night of the presentation, Cole was named "Best New Artist," and her song "This Will Be" became the first non-Aretha recording to win in the category of "Best R&B Performance, Female." Backstage at *The Grammy Awards* ceremony, it was clear to Natalie that her friendship with Aretha had ended.

"Aretha Franklin does not like me," Cole proclaimed after the incident. Explaining her short-lived friendship with Aretha, Natalie said, "I sang at a banquet that was given in Aretha's honor at the Waldorf-Astoria in New York, and all we did was shake hands, and she said, 'I'm hearing a lot about you,' and I said, 'Really? You're one of my favorite, favorite people.' She sent me flowers when I opened at different places, and then she called me up to wish me 'Merry Christmas,' and invite me out to lunch sometime the next month.

"I don't know what happened, but someone told her I went around bragging about the fact that she called me, and that she must have been scared of me or something, trying to feel me out. Then I'm calling her, and she wasn't returning my calls, and the next thing was the Grammys. I went up to her and she 'broke my face.'* I mean, she really hurt me. I said, 'How come you haven't called or anything?' And she said, 'How come I haven't called? Huh!'" With that Aretha turned and headed in the opposite direction. Natalie was crushed.

[*Seventies slang for a devastating remark or insult, delivered face-to-face.]

"That night I'd won two Grammys and I was almost in tears," Natalie recalls. "I felt so bad, I really wished I hadn't won. And that's awful. No one is trying to take anything away from her."

There is a marked tendency on the part of the press and public to build up a star to the point of superhuman proportions, and then tear him or her down. *Rolling Stone* magazine fanned the flames of the Franklin / Cole feud by reporting: "Reviewers have pointed to Cole's reliance on numerous Franklin trademarks . . . The comparisons are all the more dramatic because Aretha is being characterized in the media as the aging Queen of Soul, in decline . . . Aretha has not responded well to it. At Atlantic Records, it is said, she was jealous of Roberta Flack's success and the attention she was getting from Atlantic executives. Aretha's morale was kept up only by such token honors as Grammy Awards; she won for "Best Female R&B Vocalist" each year as if she owned the category. And then last year—along came Natalie Cole."

Suddenly, Aretha found herself receiving some of the most unkind press of her career. How could she be happy after stories like this one hit the newsstands? Desperate times called for desperate measures, and something dramatic had to be done to get her singing career back on course.

What "Dr. Aretha" needed now was a bit of musical healing, and it was producer Curtis Mayfield who was called in. In 1976 there was a movie in production called *Sparkle*. It was the story of three black teenage girls growing up in Harlem with dreams of becoming a world-famous signing trio (loosely reminiscent of the Supremes' story). The movie starred several talented black actors who were then unknown and who went on to become stars in the 1980s. The cast included Irene Cara, Lonette McKee, and Philip Michael Thomas. Cara became a star in the 1980 film *Fame*, McKee starred in the films *Cotton Club* and *'Round Midnight*, and Thomas became a sensation on TV's *Miami Vice*.

However, when it came time to record the soundtrack album for *Sparkle*, Curtis Mayfield decided that instead of using the voices of the film's stars, he would produce an album of the eight original songs used in the movie, as recorded by an established singing star. The resulting album, *Sparkle*, recorded by Aretha, went on to become her first Gold album in three years, and it produced three hit singles for her.

When asked whose idea it was to use Aretha's vocals instead of the cast's, Lonette McKee replied, "Believe me, it wasn't ours. This was going to be our big break. For all of us. But we were all so green and none of us had very good representation, and the deal they came to us with was very strange. I think I would have made about eight dollars after one billion copies had sold. I didn't know much, but I knew enough not to sign. But they [Warner Brothers] never came to us with another offer. The next thing I knew, Curtis Mayfield was giving an interview in one of the major black publications saying he couldn't understand how they could cast unknowns like Irene and Lonette, when they should have gone with black stars like Diana [Ross] and Aretha. He didn't want any of us. He made it hard, deliberately setting the keys of the songs in uncomfortable registers for all of us. And I guess his spite, coupled with Warner's lack of faith, brought about the soundtrack arrangement with Aretha. It was seen as a chance to appease everybody, and possibly to help the film. I don't think she [Aretha] was aware of the politics."

When the *Sparkle* project was presented, Aretha was in the mood for a change-of-pace album. "Musically, I am just looking for 'up' things. Who wants to be 'down?' I'm just looking for happy things," she said at the time *You* was being readied for release. *Sparkle* was the perfect album. There were no options for changing the arrangements, and there was no pressure for finding new material, as it was a "concept album."

Curtis had made a name for himself in the movie business when he composed the score to the 1972 film *Superfly*. Although the movie was a slick "black exploitation film" about drug dealers in the big city, Mayfield elevated it to another level by creating some exciting music to underscore the action in it. The album *Superfly* had become a Number One Gold hit, and had created two Top Ten hit singles with the songs "Superfly" and "Freddie's Dead."

The eight distinct and exciting songs Mayfield wrote for *Sparkle* crackled with emotion and crisp production. The *Sparkle* album was a departure for Aretha, and it was totally different than the music that was on the charts at the time.

In 1976 a danceable new electronic beat began to infiltrate the music scene with pulsing sounds. It was the beginning of the disco era, and several stars who had been creating hits alongside Aretha, jumped on the bandwagon and scored with disco records. Diana Ross' "Love Hangover," the Bee Gees' "You Should Be Dancing," and the Supremes' "I'm Gonna Let My Heart Do the Walking" became popular disco hits, and crossed over to the pop charts. Instead of following the pack to the dance clubs, *Sparkle* took Aretha on a brilliant return to soul.

Since the film *Sparkle* took place in the early 1960s, the songs that Curtis Mayfield crafted had a rhythmic feeling reminiscent of early Motown, with the added dimension of a Philadelphia-style R&B horn section. The music had a gritty urban beat, and the finished product was aimed directly at the R&B marketplace that Aretha had been losing touch with. "(Giving Him) Something He Can Feel" was sung with gutsy conviction, "Look into Your Heart" was a rich ballad with strings, and "Rock with Me" had a red-hot soul sound that was danceable without utilizing a disco formula.

The first single from the album, "(Giving Him) Something He Can Feel," became an instant Number One hit on the R&B charts, while peaking at Number Twenty-eight pop. The cuts "Jump" and "Look into Your Heart" also went on to become hits during the year. In December 1976, Atlantic released the greatest-hits album *Aretha Franklin: Ten Years of Gold*, tracing her hits from "I Never Loved a Man (The Way I Love You)" to "(Giving Him) Something He Can Feel." A month later "(Giving Him) Something He Can Feel" was nominated for a Grammy.

During the summer of 1976 there were rumors that Aretha was going to make her movie debut, working for the producers of *Sparkle*. An item in *Soul* magazine claimed that she was reading scripts for Warner Brothers. The project that was reportedly being discussed was a musical version of the 1933 Katharine Hepburn film *Morning Glory*. Aretha Franklin in Katharine Hepburn's role of stage struck actress Eva Lovelace? It was an interesting idea, but it was never to materialize.

Following her work with Curtis Mayfield on the *Sparkle* album, Aretha was to drift from record producer to record producer, looking for someone to continue the limitless magic that her career had once possessed. The 1960s musical approach on *Sparkle* was fine for one album, but she needed to find a viable contemporary sound.

Her next three albums for Atlantic saw her slipping to the lowest point in her career since she became known as the Queen of Soul. Each of these albums had worse sales figures than the one preceding it, and Aretha's career was beginning to slip into oblivion.

To produce her next single, Aretha turned in a completely different direction, teaming with Marvin Hamlish, Carole Bayer Sager, and co-producers Marty and David Paich of the rock group Toto. All four of those producers combined to create one song, "Break It to Me Gently." The resulting single only made it to Number Eighty-five on the pop chart. The song was included on the 1977 album *Sweet Passion*, and the rest of the album was produced by Lamont Dozier of the famed trio Holland / Dozier / Holland—who put Motown Records on the map in the 1960s by producing the Supremes, Martha & the Vandellas, and the Four Tops. Unfortunately, this album was a disaster. Aretha's scat version of "I Got the Music in Me" is one of her all-time worst recordings. Not even Marvin Hamlisch's "What I Did for Love," from *A Chorus Line*, had enough passion to carry this dull album.

At some point in 1976 Aretha had broken up with Ken Cunningham and found herself free and single. In typically "guarded" Aretha fashion, she never gave a public explanation as to why she had suddenly ended the affair. While she was trying to find a new direction on the music charts in 1977, Aretha's personal life took an upward turn. In January 1977 she was scheduled to appear at a benefit for underprivileged children in the Los Angeles area. The charity event was organized by Roosevelt Grier, as part of his Giant Step program. Aretha shared the bill with Ben Vereen that evening. Ben introduced Aretha's son Clarence to a friend of his, actor Glynn Turman. "My mother just loves you," Clarence told Glynn. "Who's your mother?" Turman asked. "Aretha Franklin," Clarence replied. With that, Clarence took Glynn to his mother's dressing room and introduced him. Almost instantly, Aretha and Glynn fell madly in love with each other.

Aretha invited Glynn to her upcoming thirty-fifth birthday party, and he invited her to come and visit one of the acting classes he was teaching. He came to her party, she went to his class, and the sparks continued to fly.

Four years younger than Aretha, he was twelve when he made his stage debut in Lorraine Hansberry's powerful play *A Raisin in the Sun*, with Sidney Poitier. He was one of the stars of the 1975 film *Cooley High*, Ingmar Bergman's 1978 *The Serpent's Egg*, and the TV miniseries

Centennial. Glynn had been married twice before he met Aretha, and he had three children from his previous marriages.

According to Aretha at the time, "There was something about him that was very gentle, but also very strong, and I was attracted to that. We began seeing each other, and I discovered a certain warmth about him—a real comforting kind of warmth that a woman feels for the right man. He was polite to me, a real gentleman all the time, and intelligent, articulate—all the things I really like in a man. I never told him this, but I used to kind of holler every time I saw him, because I thought he was so fine! Maybe it was his Aquarian personality that I liked so much. I read a lot about astrology, but I can tell you what caused me to fall in love with Glynn Turman had very little to do with the moon and stars!"

Although there was only four years' difference in their ages, *Ebony* magazine in 1977 included Aretha and Glynn in an article that was headlined "Older Women / Younger Men: A Growing Trend in Love Affairs." Aretha retorted, "What is this business about me being an 'older woman?' I want everyone to know that I'm a *young* woman with nothing but young ideas. There's *nothing* 'older' about Aretha!"

Glynn proposed marriage late in 1977, and Aretha accepted. They were married on April 11, 1978, in Detroit at her father's church. Aretha's gown was made of eggshell-colored silk, with a seven-foot train. It was trimmed in mink, covered with lace appliqués, and embroidered with 17,500 seed pearls. Glynn had a dozen groomsmen and Aretha had a dozen bridesmaids. The Four Tops sang the Stevie Wonder song "Isn't She Lovely" as Aretha walked down the aisle. Naturally, the ceremony was performed by Reverend C. L. Franklin. Aretha's four sons and Glynn's three children were in attendance. Aretha's sister Carolyn and her cousin Brenda each sang a solo at the wedding. Their wedding cake was a four-tiered work of art that stood several feet tall.

Actor Lou Gossett, who is a good friend of Glynn's, said at the time, "Glynn and Aretha are two halves of a circle. She's got guts and soul and he's got a disciplined, artistic temperament. They're very close buddies too, and that's an indication of a long-term relationship."

They definitely had their differences as well. Glynn didn't smoke, and Aretha was up to two packs of Kools a day. He was a vegetarian, while she exclaimed carnivorously in *People* magazine, "Give me a piece of meat every time!" However, for the time being this was just what Aretha needed in her life—romance.

At the time of their marriage, their children outnumbered them, three and a half to one. Her four sons, Clarence, Edward, Teddy, and Kecalf, combined with his children, Stephanie, Darryl, and Russell, made their household something like a black show-business version of *The Brady Bunch*.

When it was suggested to Aretha that the marriage might not work out, she replied defensively, "It's really hard for me to believe that anyone would be sitting around predicting all kinds of problems for us when they don't even know what Glynn and I are all about. Glynn is my husband, and we're not only very much in love, but we're very, very good friends. We both love and *like* each other, and the *like* part is very important, too. There will be no 'family problems,' because *my* family and *his* family have become *our* family—just one big, happy, loving family. And everyone should understand that."

Aretha and Glynn had already gotten involved in several projects together. They had filmed a French television special together in 1977, in which they sang a duet of "You Can't Take That Away From Me," and dramatically performed the balcony scene from *Cyrano de Bergerac*, and he was encouraging her to make her acting debut in a film about the life story of Bessie Smith—which never came about.

Aretha's brother and manager, Cecil, said at the time, "She's as happy as she's ever been. She's not singing the blues!"

Unfortunately, what she was singing on record was very disappointing to her fans. Theoretically, Aretha's reunion with producer Curtis Mayfield on her next album sounded like a good idea. However, the resulting LP, *Almighty Fire*, was a complete mess. Although there were echoes of several of the songs from *Sparkle*, this album had none of the spark, and none of the fire.

The title cut, "Almighty Fire (Woman of the Future)," was characterized by Aretha shrieking on multiple tracks some nonsense about the year 2001. The music of this album all sounds very muddy and overproduced. Aretha sings most of the songs in a very shrill fashion, and none of the material is the least bit interesting. The only song that makes any attempt at expressing true emotion, is "I'm Your Speed," which Aretha wrote with Glynn. The only reason that it is interesting is that it is obviously their love poem to each other. The song is just Aretha—on multiple tracks—and a piano. Unfortunately, there is no hook and no chorus, so the song is directionless. This album did not turn out to be the sound of the future, at least not here on Earth. It was simply in a galaxy of its own.

Almighty Fire only made it to Number Sixty-three on the LP chart, and contained no hit singles. Somehow it garnered a Grammy Award nomination in the category of "Best R&B Performance, Female." However, Donna Summer's sexy disco anthem "Last Dance" took the trophy.

Aretha's penchant for eccentric fashions reached new peaks in the mid-seventies. For a while she outfitted herself in silver lamé, to emulate the outrageous metallic costumes of Patti LaBelle's group, LaBelle—with Nona Hendryx and Sarah Dash. When "halter tops" and supportless "tube tops" were the rage, Aretha chose several for stage wear. No one seems to have told her that she shouldn't wear them. Around the time that the treasures of King Tut's tomb were making the rounds of the major American museums, Aretha was suddenly stricken with a bad case of "Egyptomania." She was seen on one television special as if dressed for a barge ride down the ancient Nile.

"I remember her being carried out on-stage on a sedan chair like Cleopatra," recalls Greg Porto, the designer of several Atlantic Records album covers. "She stood there in a multicolored outfit singing 'You Light Up My Life.' She was trying to look like an Egyptian princess, but she just looked silly. When she hit the last note of the song, she lifted her arms up over her head to reveal gold lamé wings attached to the dress. She was trying to look like Nefertiti, but it was just an exercise in bad taste."

One famous appearance on TV's *Midnight Special* found her exposing much too much flesh. She looked ridiculous in a bare-midriff halter top and see-through mesh pants. It was painfully obvious that she was surrounded by people who were giving nods of approval to her most inappropriate selections in clothing and musical material.

Years later, Aretha was able to admit, "I've had a couple of real disasters with stuff I've designed for the stage. Oh wow, they were bad!" She still remembers one particular creation. She had purchased several yards of velvet that she had fallen in love with. However, she recalls, laughing, 'When it was made into a dress, I decided it would look better on a sofa!'"

In June 1978 Aretha played Carnegie Hall in New York City, and drew an all-star crowd. She was visited backstage by Dionne Warwick, Patti LaBelle, Stephanie Mills, and Andrew Young, U.S. Ambassador to the UN. Interest in Aretha's career as a performer was still strong, which made her albums from this era even more frustrating to listen to. They were so far below her capacity that it was disappointment for her longtime fans.

Aretha's final album of the 1970s was also her last full album for Atlantic Records. In 1979, disco had grown to become the hottest sound around. It was the year that Cher sold a million copies of her disco smash "Take Me Home," Donna Summer and Barbra Streisand teamed up to produce the disco duet of all times "No More Tears (Enough is Enough)," and even Rod Stewart created a disco classic with "Da Ya Think I'm Sexy." It seemed like a logical move and an assured bet that Aretha could go into the studio and create the hottest disco record of the year. What could the Queen of Soul come up with if she decided to make her bid at the dance craze that was sweeping the globe? When she went into the recording studio with producer Van McCoy, who created the Number One dance hit "The Hustle," a hot dance-floor smash was anticipated.

What they produced together, was a complete mess titled *La Diva*. It was a mixture of grade-C numbers and rambling ballads that were torture to listen to. The closest Aretha came to disco was the song "Only Star," which was an embarrassing bilingual debacle in English and Spanish. The album was a complete bomb, and has the distinction of becoming the lowest-charting new studio LP of her post-Columbia career. It contained no hit singles, and is acknowledged as the worst album of her entire Atlantic Records catalogue. It was a sad way to end a business arrangement that had brought Aretha her greatest commercial successes.

La Diva represented her all-time career nadir. The sound of her proclaiming in song, "I'm a disco queen" signaled the end of her reign. The Queen of Soul had clearly lost her once-tight grip on her royal scepter.

The cover photo of *La Diva* depicted Aretha lounging on a long red sofa in a pair of cowboy boots and a very unflattering, low-cut leather dress. She may as well have sat this dance out; there was nothing on the album worth hitting the dance floor for. *Rolling Stone*, in its review of *La Diva*, lamented that "Aretha Franklin has regressed from being one of our most powerful R&B performers into a mere purveyor of over-arranged pap."

As though ending the decade on a career low point weren't bad enough, Aretha's life was once again struck by tragedy. In June 1979, burglars broke into her father's Detroit home. Reverend Franklin was shot twice. He eventually lapsed into a coma from which he never recovered, and died five years later. Aretha began flying to Detroit at least twice a month to visit her bedridden father.

Her brother Cecil said at the time, "It's been a very disconcerting, tragic year for her. She did several benefits to help offset his medical bills, and spent a great deal of time personally taking care of him."

In late summer of 1979, Aretha headlined a concert at the Greek Theater in Los Angeles. The review that appeared in *Soul* magazine commented that Aretha seemed to be "preoccupied" throughout the concert, which included her versions of Earth, Wind and Fire's "September" and "Boogie Wonderland." For the encore, Aretha came on-stage and said, "For those of you who would like to know, my dad is much better tonight." When she attempted to say more, tears prevented her from continuing to speak. She regained her composure and dove into the George Benson hit, "The Greatest Love of All," a song that is an anthem for survivors—which is exactly what Aretha Franklin is.

The 1970s had been a decade of extreme contrasts for Aretha. She scored some of her greatest successes with albums like *Amazing Grace*, *Aretha Live at Fillmore West*, and *Young, Gifted and Black*. However her final trio of Atlantic albums marked a creative low point, and her father's tragic shooting had cast a new shadow over her life. Although she was happily married to Glynn Turman, her dad's health was always in the back of her mind. As she had done so many times before, Aretha looked to her music for solace. The only direction that her life could take from this point was a sharp turn upward.

CHAPTER SEVEN

ARETHA JUMPS TO IT

In 1980, Aretha's contract at Atlantic Records lapsed and it was time for her to shop for a new record label. As in her situation fourteen years before, she needed to find the right company, one that would get behind her and totally revamp her career. When she left Atlantic, she felt that she had been neglected by the company.

"I had some great years there and I'm appreciative for the launching pad with which they provided me after being with Columbia for five years," she said at the time. "However, sometimes you stay with a situation just a little too long, and there were things that left quite a bit to be desired, especially toward the end. I guess around 1975 I began to notice a change in their general approach. We weren't hitting. I felt it was because of lack of promotion more than anything. No airplay. It doesn't make any difference how good your product is; if people don't hear it, what does it mean? How can they buy it if they can't hear it?"

In 1967 she had been amazed at the personal attention that she received from Jerry Wexler, Tom Dowd, Arif Mardin, and Ahmet Ertegun. "They didn't just sit in a big office and go through the paperwork and count the money," Aretha recalled of her golden era at Atlantic. "They really got involved with the projects, which was rather out of the ordinary. Particularly in the sixties, that was unheard of, with the chairman of the board down in the studio with his sleeves rolled up, dealing with what was going on." She longed to find herself in that kind of nurturing situation again.

Since her last three albums had landed on the marketplace with a resounding thud, she needed some serious help if she was going to pull her sagging recording career out of the danger zone. Her new saviors turned out to be Clive Davis and the small but heavy-hitting label he ran—Arista Records.

Arista was born in 1974, when Davis took over a small operation called Bell Records. When he started with Bell, he inherited two unknown singer / songwriters who were under option to the label. Dropping everyone else's options, he decided to retain the pair of songwriters, who had released only one album apiece.

Davis, who had made his mark in the recording business at Columbia by discovering, signing, and developing stars like Janis Joplin and Sly & the Family Stone, was out to prove that he still had the Midas touch. He changed Bell's name to Arista, and proceeded to turn the company into a major hit-making force. He also turned the two unknown singer / songwriters into major-league stars. Their names were Barry Manilow and Melissa Manchester.

Throughout the 1970s, Arista scored one hit after another with its varied roster of stars that included Patti Smith, Ray Parker Jr., Alan Parsons, Air Supply, Phyllis Hyman, and Angela Bofill. While he was interested in developing new talent, Clive Davis has also been credited with reviving the careers of several singing stars of the sixties and seventies, such as Melanie (*Sunset and Other Beginnings*, 1975), Martha Reeves (*The Rest of My Life*, 1976), and Eddie Kendricks (*Vintage '78*). However, he really perfected his craft when he totally revamped the careers of Dionne Warwick, Aretha Franklin, and Carly Simon.

Dionne had one of the most commercially successful recording careers in the music industry from 1963 to 1972. With Burt Bacharach writing and producing her songs, she had one of the longest-running hot streaks in the business. As in Aretha's situation with Jerry Wexler, when Dionne and Bacharach parted company, her career hit a six-year low point. Also echoing Aretha's dilemma, Warwick spent most of the seventies going from producer to producer, looking for the magic that was somehow lost.

In 1979, Dionne signed with Arista Records, and with her debut album on the label, *Dionne*, she scored the biggest-selling album of her career.

Produced by Barry Manilow at the height of his fame, the LP became the first Platinum album of Warwick's career. She won two Grammy Awards and scored on the music charts with the million-selling single "I'll Never Love This Way Again" and the hit "Déjà Vu." By matching the right artist with the right producer, Clive Davis virtually resurrected Dionne's career at a point when it was floundering.

When Aretha's contract lapsed with Atlantic, Davis was taken with the idea of doing for Aretha what he had just done for Dionne, by bringing her back bigger than ever. Aretha, likewise was interested to see what Arista could do for her. "I was reading the trade papers," she explained in 1980, "looking at where they [Arista] were on the charts, how they promoted their records, the product released, and how they ran their company. I liked what I saw."

Clive Davis distinctly recalls the negotiations with Aretha in early 1980. "Her New York attorney called me to find out if we were interested," says Davis, "and I was interested! We discussed the business arrangements. When that had been resolved, then the two of us decided it would be good to have a face-to-face meeting, and I went to her home in Los Angeles, for a meal.

"She was interested in joining Arista, based upon what she knew of me over the years. I've been very friendly with a number of people she knows well—Stevie Wonder and a whole group of people. I'm certain she noted what happened with Dionne. She was very aware, she reads the trades very carefully.

"She was just as gracious as could be," Clive recalls of their initial meeting. "She was very aware of my career, and what I was doing at Arista. She was very much looking forward to it, and we said that we would work as a partnership, and as a team. That's what she had missed since the Jerry Wexler days. Basically, the only one she had worked with as a partner was Jerry."

At the time, Aretha was being considered by everyone in the business as a phenomenal talent who was wasting her voice on unworthy material. With regard to song choices, Davis claims, "Material is like a pitcher on a baseball team. The vocalist could be enormous, and without hit songs, you could just wait there, as you know from many other artists who could still sing as well as they ever did, but without the right material, they can't do it."

Performing in concert on April 25, 1980, at Avery Fisher Hall in New York City's Lincoln Center, Aretha turned to the audience and introduced Davis as "the eloquent president of my new record company." She was at a turning point in her career, and she was about to enter a new phase.

She had begun the year at the bottom of her popularity, but the Avery Fisher Hall performance marked her official low point. *Rolling Stone* magazine ripped into her with its review of the concert: "Franklin obviously craves the kind of comeback that Dionne Warwick enjoyed this past year. But to judge from her sloppy distracted performance at Lincoln Center, the road back won't be easy." The reviewer found her show to be "a particularly excruciating exercise in masochism as Franklin and the band lost each other in a lumbering sludge." Her singing of Michael Jackson's "Don't Stop 'Til You Get Enough" with two male dancers, and Peter Allen's "I Go to Rio" while twirling a beach umbrella, caused the magazine to describe her show as having "the trappings of a tacky burlesque show."

It had to be uphill from this point. Her career couldn't slip much further. Thanks to her movie debut and a carefully planned new album, by the end of the year, the resurrection of Aretha would officially be in full swing.

In June 1980, the outrageous comedy film *The Blues Brothers* debuted, and became a box-office smash. The integration of Aretha into the project was an inspired idea. In fact, she was one of several R&B stars who had featured roles in the film. Each of them had a segment of the movie in which to shine. Aretha was seen as a waitress in a greasy coffee shop, singing her Number One hit song "Think." Also in the film was Ray Charles as the owner of Ray's Music Exchange, James Brown as a Baptist preacher, and Cab Calloway as the handyman in the orphanage where the Blues Brothers were raised.

The Blues Brothers starred John Belushi and Dan Aykroyd in the title roles as Jake and Elwood Blues. The whole premise started out as a skit on the television show *Saturday Night Live*. It blossomed into a recording career for the Blues Brothers on Atlantic Records, and ultimately the movie, which was directed by John Landis.

The story involves Jake and Elwood trying to raise $5,000 to pay the taxes owed on the orphanage where they grew up. To raise the money, they decided to reunite their once-great blues band. The core of their band is now a combo act in a cheesy hotel lounge. Another band member, Alan Rubin, is the maître d' in a posh restaurant, and Matt "Guitar" Murphy is working in his wife's soul food restaurant. Aretha's role as the owner / operator of the Maxwell Street soul kitchen became one of the highlights of the film.

Jake and Elwood show up at Aretha's establishment to lure her man, Murphy, into rejoining the band. Franklin, in a soiled pink waitress outfit and scuffy bedroom slippers, proved herself a born scene-stealer. When Murphy informs her that he is leaving her to play with the Blues Brothers, she warns him that he had better "think" before he leaps. She jumps into an accusatory version of her hit "Think," with a trio of background singers (Carolyn Franklin, Brenda Corbett, and Margaret Branch) recruited from their stools at the restaurant's dining counter.

Aretha recorded a new, longer, and slightly faster version of "Think" for the film. Also, the horns are much more dominant than on the original 1968 hit. All of the songs on *The Blues Brothers* soundtrack album were produced by Bob Tischler. Aretha's revised rendition of "Think" was her last recorded song for Atlantic Records.

In the film, when she loses her man to the Blues Brothers' band, Aretha scuffles back toward the kitchen, glances toward the camera, rolls her eyes, and with resignation deadpans the one word that summed up the way she felt: "Shit!" Her scene, and her acting, were among the best elements of the movie. *The Blues Brothers* ended with the biggest car-chase scene ever filmed—especially in terms of the amount of automotive carnage strewn about the screen. Reviews were mixed about the broad, slapstick way in which the film unfolded. But Aretha drew across-the-board raves. There was even talk of her being considered for a "Best Supporting Actress" Academy Award nomination.

The soundtrack album was certified Gold, and made it to Number Thirteen on the LP chart. The last song she released on Atlantic found the Queen of Soul back on her throne, singing one of the songs that made her famous. Now it was time for her to make her move into the contemporary music scene.

After panning the movie's silliness, film critic Pauline Keal commented that "the film, however, brings Aretha Franklin to the screen, and she's so completely there and so funny as she sings 'Think' that she transcends the film's incompetence."

"*The Blues Brothers*, I enjoyed making tremendously," Aretha exclaimed. "It was my debut in film. The only thing I really didn't like about it was the hours. I had to get up at seven o'clock in the morning to get ready to be on the set. But once you got there, and once you started rolling, then everything fell into place. I had a lot of fun with Belushi, and Dan Akyroyd—great guys—big sense of humor, and very, very professional and astute. So I had a good time. It makes everything so much easier when you're having fun and you're enjoying what you're doing."

According to her, the filming of the movie came "at a time when I was ending up my contract with Atlantic Records and deciding what other company I wanted to join, at a time when I had no hit record out there. And that was different. You can imagine my thrill at making a hit in my first movie!

"I confess that I would like to do another film," she said at the time. "Maybe something like the Bessie Smith story. I truly empathize with Bessie Smith, and would love to play her life. She was a singer, a great singer. I'm a singer. People have said I'm great. And I can come mighty close to simulating Bessie's size, too!"

In October 1980, Franklin's first Arista album, *Aretha*, was released. Unlike what Arista accomplished with Warwick's 1979 *Dionne* album, *Aretha* didn't singlehandedly revive Aretha's career. It was to take five years and four albums before Aretha hit the Platinum mark. It was going to be a slow rebuilding process to take her from the awful *La Diva* album to the triumph of 1985's *Who's Zoomin' Who?*

Each of the first three albums on the label sold progressively better than its predecessor, regaining lost ground with each release. The 1980 *Aretha* album (also the title of Franklin's 1986 Arista LP) was, nonetheless, an important step in her redevelopment. Although it did not represent an exciting breakthrough, it did provide Aretha with a classy musical setting. It gave her the opportunity to sing songs of her golden era such as Otis Redding's "Can't Turn You Loose," and presented her with her first cover version of a rock & roll tune since 1973—on the Doobie Brothers' "What a Fool Believes."

Clive Davis recalls that the *Aretha* album set the tone for all of the albums they have worked on together. "The game plan always was for me to locate the material, and to send it on to her," he explains. "If she did not care for it, and if I didn't love it, I would not push it. If she liked it, that would end it right then and there. If she did not like it, I would only insist if I loved it, but I rarely had to go to that extreme. There was once or twice that she wavered a little, and I asked her to listen to it again. She would call me back and she'd say, 'You know, I listened once or twice more, and I really like it now.' There were times where she didn't care for a few of the songs, but we really did work as a team, and in a few instances she came up with her own material."

In many ways, *Aretha* was a back-to-basics project for her. Four of the songs were produced by Arif Mardin, and four cuts were produced by Chuck Jackson. The last song on the album was Aretha's composition "School Days," which she and Jackson produced together.

Some of the most important decisions Aretha and Clive made together involved the selection of producers for her albums. Finding the right people to work with on her debut LP for Arista was a crucial concern. According to Clive Davis, "Chuck Jackson sent me two songs, which included 'United Together.' I liked the material so much that I said that she should meet with him, and he at least would produce those two songs. Then she liked working with him, so it grew into four songs. Arif was the other half of it, because we felt that there was a background there—an awareness."

Aretha enjoyed recording with Chuck Jackson. Discussing their relationship in the studio, she explained that, "He kind of listened the first day, and then, from there on in, he got right into it. Naturally, on his own songs, he was more particular about exactly what he wanted, but it was more about me putting in the trimmings. Being a writer myself, I respect writers and how they want their songs to sound, so I always bear that in mind when I'm working with a producer who also writes."

Jackson's main claim to fame is that he co-produced all of Natalie Cole's biggest hits in the 1970s, with his partner Marvin Yancy. "I've known

Chuck for years," Aretha said in 1980. "He brought me a whole bunch of songs way back, around twelve years ago, songs he'd written with Marvin Yancy. Chuck's the brother of the Reverend Jesse Jackson, who's a friend of the family. At the time I didn't select anything, although we did do one tune a couple of years back: 'You.' When it was suggested that Chuck might produce some of the album, we talked and I felt that some magic might happen. I liked some of the things he'd done with Marvin on Natalie Cole. And when we did get together, it all worked out like peaches and cream!"

On the album sessions, Aretha worked with several of the musicians and singers from her most productive period at Atlantic. In fact, Cissy Houston and the Sweet Inspirations reunited especially for this album. "We got the old gang back together," Aretha said enthusiastically. "Cornell Dupree, Richard Tee, the Sweet Inspirations, and so on, and we had a ball! We were really happy with the results."

With regard to the reasoning behind having half of the album produced by Chuck and half by Arif Mardin, she explained, "It's just that we wanted a contrast. So Clive talked with Arif. In fact, he talked to him even before we started working with Chuck, but his commitments prevented him from doing the whole album. Naturally he's a good friend. Before, when we worked together, Arif was almost always in the arranging seat—he did such great arrangements on horns and strings—and this time he was in the producing seat, and it was great! We worked very well together. I had picked the tunes with Clive, so it was just about putting the tracks together and going from there."

Originally, the autobiographical song "School Days" was to be the centerpiece of the album, and it was Aretha's idea that the cover of the album was to be a photo of her sitting in the middle of the classroom, surrounded by children, and eating an ice cream cone. Arista talked her out of the concept, reasoning that it was too "busy" a shot to prove effective. The cover photo ultimately was a pleasant-looking close-up of Aretha in a white blazer and a navy blue silk blouse. The whole ice cream idea was relegated to an inner-sleeve photo of Aretha in a straw hat, eating an enormous, triple-dip cone.

The hottest song on the album was her version of Otis Redding's "Can't Turn You Loose." It was a perfect choice to show off the feeling and the excitement of the old Aretha, singing material from her most glittering era. "As far as the Otis tune goes," she explained, "we talked about it at Atlantic a lot, but never got around to doing it. I feel the timing for the song is good, since there's a definite revival of interest in the tunes of the sixties—'Midnight Hour,' 'Soul Man,' and so on. The movie [*The Blues Brothers*] is a witness to that interest."

"I feel we're getting back to good music—back to music that will move you," Aretha claimed in 1980. With her new album, the public and the press responded to her return to soulful basics. "A knock-out album!" is what *Stereo Review* called *Aretha*. "A potent, punchy and phenomenal assortment of great performances . . . an album to be reckoned with," raved *The Chicago Sun-Times*. And *Blues and Soul* magazine heralded the fact that "after a slow spell, Queen Aretha makes a spectacular debut on Arista."

The album went on to become her most popular album since *Sparkle* in 1976. Peaking at Number Forty-seven on the LP charts, *Aretha* contained two hit singles, "United Together" and "Come to Me."

On November 17, 1980, the Queen of Soul performed for the Queen of England at a gala command performance in London. Aretha's performance was part of a variety show for the Royal Family. "Sammy Davis hosted," Aretha recalls, "and Sheena Easton was there, and Cleo Laine, and James Cagney, and J. R. Ewing [actor Larry Hagman]. It was wonderful. After the performance, the Royal Family came down on-stage. Lady Di wasn't married to Prince Charles yet, but she was there, and the Queen Mum, and I found them to be warm, genuine kind of people. It certainly was a milestone for me. Then, right after performing for the Royal Family, I performed six nights at the Royal Victoria, two shows a night." The two songs Aretha sang for the Royal Family were "Amazing Grace" and "The Shining Hour."

When her debut album on Arista was released in the fall of 1980, Aretha was quite pleased with the way the company handled everything. She especially liked the personalized attention Clive Davis gave her, which was similar to the care that Jerry Wexler had provided her with during her heyday at Atlantic.

"I liked the way the company did their thing," she said of Arista, following the release of the 1980 *Aretha* LP. "They've always appeared to be creative, progressive, and a company that's making great strides. And Clive has great expertise and experience in the business. We met briefly while I was with CBS, and then again around 1973, when we were negotiating with Atlantic, and I was looking at some other situations. But I'm really happy to be working with him and I am thrilled at the enthusiasm and excitement that the company has for the album. It's exactly what I've been looking for—the kind of support that you need when you've put energy and creativity into a project."

When Aretha signed with Arista Records, there was unanimous excitement that the company had tapped the talent of a genuine music industry superstar. However, at the same time, there was also a sense of apprehension that they might be dealing with a real prima donna. There were extreme fears that she wouldn't cooperate with the company executives when it came time to give press interviews.

At the time of her signing, Dennis Fine was the head of the publicity department at Arista. Everyone in the industry was aware of the stories that Aretha and the press were long-running adversaries. Her reluctance to grant interviews dated back to the infamous 1968 *Time* cover story. Fine was worried that Aretha wasn't going to be at all cooperative.

"There was this great fear when she came in. Not by Clive, or anything, but there was this fear from everybody else that she was very difficult," Fine recalls. "The big fear was that this was going to be a diva. All I kept hearing was stories about how difficult she was—that she's going to be impossible to work with, and she doesn't do this, and she doesn't do that."

Fine, however, was pleasantly surprised at how easy she was to deal with. "She was terrific!" he claims. "She did her interviews when she was asked to. I mean, she didn't want to do very many. She didn't feel that she should go plaster herself around, but on the first record, which was a ballad, we had a hit. She did interviews, and she was always willing to do things. She'd do television if you really asked her to do it. Everything was involved in what kind of deal it was."

Working for Dennis at Arista at the time was a high-powered music industry publicist named Barbara Shelley. Dennis would plot out a publicity course for Franklin to pursue, and Shelley would make certain it was implemented. According to Fine, "Aretha had this guy who was supposedly her press agent—never paid him—he was a character—maybe she did pay him, but it was one of those trade-off deals. But this guy was always around for something. My instructions to Barbara were, 'Snowplow through this guy. Push him out of the way, and do what you have to do.' That's how she got the working relationship with Aretha, because Barbara just got right in there. Aretha did all sorts of things, she was very gracious, and she always used to send 'Thank You' cards. She was much more of a surprise. I really liked her.

"We had funny times with her," Dennis recalls. Citing one of his favorite visions of Aretha, he tells of one particular afternoon when Franklin taped *The Tonight Show* in Los Angeles. "Barbara and I took her to do the [Johnny] Carson show, and I remember she was heavy. Not that she's not heavy, but she was having her heavier phase, and she was rehearsing in hot pants, and a sweatshirt."

Following her dramatic weight loss in 1974, Aretha gradually put on all the weight she had shed, and by the 1980s the words "diet" and "slim" were simply not in her vocabulary. Aretha is the first to admit that she always loved good food. According to her, dieting became a problem when she married Glynn Turman, and suddenly she found herself in the kitchen, cooking for seven hungry kids—most of them with voracious teenage appetites. In that atmosphere, Aretha simply gave up watching her weight.

Using her favorite term for cooking, Aretha admits, "Yes, I like 'switchin' in the kitchen.' It's relaxing and it's creative. I have my own special dishes—banana pudding, homemade ice cream, barbecued ribs, hams, quiche. And we've been growing our own fresh vegetables in the garden. I've been learning the art of French cooking and I've already done some Indonesian and Viennese dishes—so I'm not doing bad. I do it all: New Orleans gumbo, greens, ham hocks, chitlins, ribs, and a great hickory-smoked barbecue sauce.

"I couldn't bear to deny myself all my life all the good foods I like to eat, just to keep a slim, bird-like figure. I love to eat fried chicken, greens, soul food. And I like banana splits, malts, plenty of ice cream. Anything fattening I seem to like. I don't want to go back to being quite as thin as

I got a few years back. It was great from some perspectives—like going to dress stores and buying exactly what I wanted off the rack—but to me, it wasn't quite the weight I wanted. However, now I'm on the other side of it and I do want to lose a few pounds!

"I remember one time when I appeared on an NAACP Image Awards show in Hollywood," Franklin recalls. "I weighed little or nothing! But it made me feel weak, irritable, all that keeping away from food. I'll never knock off that much weight again in my life. One day I can eat anything. Everything I crave. Then the very next day I'll start out like a calorie executioner—one half grapefruit, and couple of eggs, some bran toast. I balance it off like that. Starvation diets are a sin, and deadly."

Ever since the mid-1970s, Aretha has been talking about writing her own cookbook, which she wants to title *Switchin' in the Kitchen*. According to Dennis Fine, "Aretha Franklin's cookbook could be interesting. We tried to talk her into doing it when we were at Arista; we thought it would be kind of fun. And then Clive didn't think it was such a good idea. I think that he didn't want to keep calling attention to her size. You know Clive, he's very fussy about those things."

Fine recalls arriving at Franklin's house one morning to accompany her to an afternoon outdoor stadium concert. "She was packing a big lunch," he remembers. "Everybody was there—the three backup singers, the makeup people, and she was packing chicken and Aretha's famous 'Blackout Cake,' and they were just going to town! I've got to tell you—it's delicious—it's good stuff!"

The one recipe that Franklin has shared is the one she calls "Aretha's Chicken Italiano." According to her, "Take six or eight pieces of chicken, all types: breasts, legs, thighs, wings, whatever you like. Get a couple of sticks of butter, and melt your butter. Brown your chicken on both sides lightly. Now you have this butter base and you put about—I would say—a teaspoonful of rosemary in it and let it simmer. That's it. And you're talking about finger-lickin' good. The Colonel never had it so good!" she exclaims.

The real "proof in the pudding" in Aretha's recording career came the following January when the Grammy Award nominations were released. Franklin's version of "Can't Turn You Loose" was nominated in her signature category, "Best R&B Vocal Performance, Female." Inspired by such a symbol of artistic victory, Clive Davis decided that Arista would host a gala party in Aretha's honor to celebrate the Grammy she was destined to win.

It was going to be a busy evening for Aretha, as she was not only scheduled to appear on *The Grammy Awards* telecast, but also to perform a concert in New York's City Center. Her evening's itinerary was as follows: She was to be backstage at Radio City Music Hall for *The Grammy Awards* presentation. Early in the show she was to perform "Can't Turn You Loose" and stand by for the announcement of the winner of the category. Next she was to dash over to City Center on West 55th Street and give her full concert performance. Finally, she was to head five blocks down the Avenue of the Americas to the Time / Life Building, take two elevators to the Tower Suite on the forty-eighth floor, and be the guest of honor at the party Arista was throwing for her.

It was Dennis Fine's task to put together the arrangements for the party. He had heard rumors of Aretha's apprehension about heights, but he didn't realize how serious her fear was. Specifically, she was afraid of being trapped in a burning skyscraper. She had never been in a burning building; she simply had been traumatized by watching the movie *The Towering Inferno* one too many times, surmises Fine. Unsuspecting of the consequences, he proceeded to make plans for the fête.

This was the first time since 1975 that *The Grammy Awards* were presented in New York City, and all of the record companies were scurrying around to reserve the most prestigious party sites in Manhattan. According to Dennis Fine, "This was going to be a post-Grammy party, and it was geared to Aretha. Clive wanted the Tower Suite, so we took the Tower Suite. We went ahead and we made the whole deal. We got the band, the disco sound guys, and the big buffet."

As the plans were being formulated, Dennis called Aretha and asked for her approval of their party arrangements. He recalls that her first comment should have been his clue that there were going to be problems. "Couldn't you make this in the basement?" she said to Fine when he outlined Arista's plan for the party.

"It was like, 'Here's the party, this is what we're doing,' and she said, 'Oh well, you know, really . . . well, yeah, I'll do it.' I mean, nobody thought she wouldn't do it," he recalls. When it came time for the big evening, things did not go exactly as planned.

The Grammy Awards segment of the evening went without a hitch. Aretha, looking great in a bright red dress, performed her nominated song at Radio City Music Hall, while millions of television viewers watched. Also nominated for the prize were Minnie Ripperton, Roberta Flack, Diana Ross, and Stephanie Mills. After all of the attention paid to Aretha, Stephanie Mills' song "Never Know Love Like This Before" won.

"When we left *The Grammy Awards*," recalls Barbara Shelley, "we got into the limo to rush over to City Center, to just make her curtain, and the limo driver made all the wrong turns of the one-way streets in Manhattan, so we barely got her on the stage at City Center in time. She really lost her cool. It was the first time I really ever heard Aretha scream. She absolutely yelled at the limo driver at the top of her lungs. She really was a nervous wreck. It takes a lot for Aretha Franklin to get nervous, because she is a very calm person. But she was afraid she wasn't going to make it over in time for her curtain." She arrived in time, and the show was a huge success.

With the concert over, Aretha and her entourage got back in the limo and went down to the Time / Life Building. When she arrived at the building, the party was in full swing. There was an electric sense of excitement that night in Rockefeller Center, following *The Grammy Awards*. The fact that Aretha didn't win wasn't going to put a damper on the evening. The crowd that gathered at the Tower Suite to honor her was star-studded, and filled with anticipation of her arrival. The guests that night included Dionne Warwick, Christopher Reeve, Nicholas Ashford, Valerie Simpson, Jane Seymour, Rex Smith, Donna Summer, and Teddy Pendergrass. They all arrived at the after-midnight soirée specifically to salute the Queen of Soul. But Aretha never made it to the party, even though she made it to the building.

All of the music industry media were there too—including me—celebrity journalist Mark Bego. Speaking from personal experience, Aretha missed a great party that was thrown to celebrate her nomination. I can still remember the full buffet and the open bar that Arista and Clive had waiting for her, in her honor!

Those of us who were upstairs, waiting for the arrival of the guest of honor, kept wandering around the party with our drinks in our hands, asking each other, "Is Aretha here yet? Where is Aretha?" Finally, word spread around the party that she was in the building. What we didn't realize was that she was never going to make it up to the top of the building.

Dennis Fine remembers that Aretha made it as far as the first elevator, but when she found out she had to take a second one, she lost her courage. According to him, "The first elevator went up about twenty stories, and she had to make the crossover. When she saw there was a second elevator, she went right back down."

The story was big news the next day. "It was in all the papers that Aretha Franklin couldn't make it up to her own party because of her fear of heights," Fine laughs.

The following morning *The New York Daily News* ran a story about the party, headlining the fact that "she couldn't rise to the occasion." The story ran with a photo of Teddy Pendergrass, Nick Ashford, and Clive Davis. In the story, Davis was quoted as saying, "The problem is that she has acrophobia and couldn't make it up the elevator. She's working on it."

Clive was later to explain, "She was so upset she sent me flowers and a letter. She was very apologetic."

The publicity generated by her "no show" at her own party only helped to build up the excitement about her week-long engagement at City Center. The press loved her performance, and found it refreshingly uncluttered. Though there were no clown outfits in this show, Aretha did make one of her entrances in a rickshaw, clad in a Japanese kimono. She kept her costume changes simple, removing the kimono to reveal a beautiful gown, or slipping on a full-length white fur coat for the encore.

Ira Mayer, in *The New York Post*, found that "Aretha's still the soul queen . . . giving one of the better shows of her recent performing years— heavy on the soul and light on the Las Vegas pop schlock." Robert Palmer, in his review in *The New York Times*, claimed that while "she has often showed an unerring instinct for picking the most inappropriate material and for sabotaging the pacing of her sets with gimmicky, utterly banal stage routines . . . for the most part she just sang—magnificently."

In addition to appearing on *The Grammy Awards* telecast, and on-stage at City Center, Aretha rounded out the week by appearing on TV's *Saturday Night Live*, singing "Can't Turn You Loose." She may not have gotten a Grammy Award that week, but she certainly let New York City—and the rest of America—know that the Queen of Soul had returned to the scene.

At this same time, there was a hot Top Ten hit by the jazz / rock group Steely Dan called "Hey Nineteen." In the lyrics of the song, lead singer Donald Fagen sings about his love affair with a nineteen-year-old girl, and their age differences. In the song he laments that he grew up in the sixties, and his teenage lover knows a different set of dances, and more distressing than that—she doesn't even know who the "Queen of Soul" is! It was a fact that Aretha hadn't had a Top Forty pop hit since 1974, and a whole generation of record buyers had arrived on the scene without an awareness of her music. Her next two Arista albums set out to solve the problem.

Because the most popular material from her *Aretha* album was produced by Arif Mardin—including "Can't Turn You Loose"—it was mutually decided that he should be the producer of her next album. The reunion resulted in one of the classiest albums of Aretha's entire recording career, *Love All the Hurt Away*. Leaving nothing to chance on this disc, the undisputed best people were brought in to work on it—from the musicians to the album cover photographer.

The album kicked off with the title cut, which was a lush duet with Aretha and George Benson. The song became the LP's big hit single, peaking at Number Forty-six on the pop chart. Aretha really rocked out on her exciting interpretation of the Rolling Stones' "You Can't Always Get What You Want," and she sizzled with her version of Sam & Dave's 1966 hit "Hold On I'm Comin'." She also revamped the song "It's My Turn," which had been a hit for Diana Ross. The Franklin rendition bristled with new-found feeling. The pace of the song was slowed down a bit, with Aretha's own emotion-guided piano-playing highlighted.

Two of the songs on the album, "Whole Lot of Me" and "Kind of Man," were written by Aretha. She also co-produced a trio of songs with Mardin including "Truth and Honesty," which was penned by Burt Bacharach, Carole Bayer Sager, and Peter Allen. The balance between the up-tempo songs and the ballads was maintained by the consistent high quality of the music. The crisp and distinctive sound of this album is miles ahead of its predecessor. *Love All the Hurt Away* ended up hitting Number Thirty-six on the *Billboard* album charts, becoming her first LP to crack the Top Forty in six years.

Among the musicians on the album were Jeff Porcaro, Steve Lukather, and David Paich of the group Toto; Louis Johnson of the funk duo the Brothers Johnson; keyboard master Greg Phillinganes, and percussionist Paulinho Da Costa. Reverend James Cleveland directed the background choir on "You Can't Always Get What You Want." The singers backing Aretha included Cissy Houston; Darlene Love; and Linda Lawrence, a former member of the Supremes.

The album cover alone was worth the cost of the LP. Aretha was depicted like a Hollywood star of the 1930s, sitting atop a stack of suitcases, showing off her shapely legs to full advantage. The effect was wonderful, with Aretha striking a Marlene Dietrich-like pose. The photographer was the legendary George Hurrell, whose portraits of Jean Harlow, Joan Crawford, Bette Davis, Veronica Lake, Marlene Dietrich, and all of the great ladies of the movies had made him a star in his own right. The suitcase-pose concept was credited to Aretha.

"George Hurrell photographed many of the great ladies of the screen, in what was called 'Hollywood's Golden Era,' and of course he had to photograph *moi*!" she laughs. "So we gave it the 'total' look, and we did a little takeoff on the Hollywood glamour-girl-type thing where the girl is sitting on all of the suitcases, and the photographers are all running all over the place, and flashes are going off everywhere. I thought it turned out quite nice."

According to her, the most fun she had during the recording of this album was doing her duet with George Benson. "I love George Benson, love to hear him sing," Aretha proclaims. "We got in the studio late one night. I was doing my session, and he was doing his session, and then he had to leave his session to come over to mine, and we put it on. There was a lot of atmosphere there that night. The lights were down low, and we just kind of got into a groove, and had a good time. 'Love All the Hurt Away'—we did!"

In many ways, *Love All the Hurt Away* was just what the doctor ordered to cure Aretha's record-sales ills. The title-cut single received plenty of airplay, and she was sounding more focused, centered, and happy with her life.

This was the height of her life in the lap of luxury, Hollywood-style. She and Glynn Turman and their combined family lived together in a large mansion in Encino, California, not far from Michael Jackson and his family. The house sat on a three-acre lot with many trees and beautifully landscaped gardens. The plush San Fernando Valley setting was befitting of a star of the stature that Aretha had attained.

Dennis Fine recalls Aretha's West Coast home with awe. It was decorated in pink, with a huge swimming pool in the backyard. "I was amazed when I saw the house in Encino—the pink house. It looked like something out of the forties or the thirties. You could see the bedrooms upstairs when you came in from the hallway. And there were two curved staircases that flowed downward."

Aretha's son Edward had gotten married in mid-1980, and the wedding was held at the "pink house." The ceremony was performed by Reverend James Cleveland, alongside the swimming pool. Three hundred guests attended, and were served hors d'oeuvres afterward. That evening a formal, sit-down dinner was held at the Beverly Wilshire Hotel.

She had a lovely home and a devoted husband, and she had reached a nice plateau in her life. With the exception of her father being in a coma in Detroit those past few years, it looked as though her personal life was all in order.

According to her at the time, "When I come home, I'm one of the family—I'm a mother and wife. No there *aren't* two Arethas. One part of me is the singer, and the other part is the family person—but we're all the *same*! I like to stay home and I like to go out too. But it's important for me to be with my family, so I spend as much time as I can with them."

Speaking about his wife's devotion to her craft, Glynn pointed out that "people just don't realize how hard Aretha works at what she does. Sure, she has a natural gift, but she's always practicing, always keeping in shape vocally."

Glowing about her marriage, Aretha said, "He does his acting thing, and I do my singing thing. We do a lot of things together. We have a lot of laughs together." Their favorite restaurants were the unglamorous spots with great food, like "that South Town soul food place in Hollywood," Aretha said. "Their fried chicken is the greatest. But that doesn't take away from the delicious soul food my uncle serves at his place out on Adams. Greens, corn pone—his is the best. Glynn and I go over there all the time. Uncle Vernon used to have a place in Chicago, then he opened up out here, Chef Rose's Eat Shop and Soul Food. And Glynn and I go to church together. Always a Baptist one, though."

Elaborating on the "two Arethas," public and private, she was to explain, "There are people in all my audiences who can relate to me just like I am. There may have been some emotional conflicts in my life that have played upon my stage work, but there again, what woman does not have those same problems? They say I drank a lot. Well, I don't drink now. Not at all. I have no emotional hang-ups. No problems. Just those of everyday nature that all people have. Oh there are some, but I always solve them, if they concern me, whether I created them or not. Above all, I am happy. Thank God for that. I read a lot, newspapers, magazines, and books. I love biographies, stories of how other people made it in the world. I watch television news and even the normal escapist shows. I love musicals. Glynn and I make TV commercials together for the NAACP."

Aretha was very content in her life with Glynn Turman, and she felt fulfilled and secure. These days were among her happiest. They both benefited from their marriage: he had given her the confidence in her acting ability when she appeared in *The Blues Brothers*, and he was encouraging her to pursue further acting roles. She loved talking about him in interviews, and she drew him into her spotlight. Often they were the subject of "couples" articles in magazines, including *People*. He would frequently accompany her to public appearances, press conferences, and special events. When he appeared out of town in theatrical productions, she would fly across the country to be by his side.

In the fall of 1981, Aretha was asked to cut the ribbon that officially opened the Los Angeles Street Scene Festival, presented by the mayor's office, and Glynn went along with her. The festival was held in downtown Los Angeles, as a multiethnic cultural event, complete with live entertainment, food, and displays. Barbara Shelley decided that she would surprise Aretha by serving her a complete soul food breakfast in the back of her limousine on their way from Encino to downtown L.A. Barbara thought that the breakfast would add a wonderful touch to the morning, since Aretha was not an "A.M. person." The event became a comedy of errors.

"We had to be downtown at something like seven or eight o'clock in the morning, which was outrageously early," explains Barbara. "The press conference was at nine in the morning, but I had to have Aretha there at 8:30. She had agreed to do it, but she hates to do anything before noon. The record company provided us with a limousine, and I bought a hot plate, and I went to the automotive store and got an attachment that would plug into the cigarette lighter of the limo. We stopped at the soul food restaurant on Sunset Boulevard, and we picked up grits, biscuits, and gravy, and I kept everything heating on the hot plate on our way out to Encino to pick up Aretha and Glynn. Of course, when she got into the limousine, she laughed. She thought that was very funny and sweet. We had our little soul food breakfast on our way downtown to the Mayor's Office. When we arrived there, Mayor Tom Bradley was extremely grateful that a big star like Aretha Franklin would come down for the Street Scene." The ribbon-cutting went without a hitch. The morning was a huge success—until they attempted to leave.

When Aretha, Glynn, and Barbara returned to the limousine, the battery was dead. Barbara had forgotten to turn off the hot plate. She felt terrible, but she claims that Aretha kept her cool while they were stuck in the middle of the Street Scene without transportation. "You try to do everything right, and thanks to me, nobody could leave until the limo company sent another limo downtown," Barbara recalls. "There we sat, Aretha, Glynn, and me. We started sampling the various food displays at the Street Scene. It must have been 90 degrees, it was so damn hot! Of course, during that time, fans were coming over for autographs, and she was being imposed upon in every possible way that you don't want to happen at these events. Exactly what you try to avoid. Aretha was a total lady through the whole thing. She was so polite about it. She said, 'You know, when it comes to things like this, I've learned the only thing you can do is just wait and relax.'

"A *not-fun* morning was had by all," Barbara recalls. "But Aretha was delightful through the whole thing. You know, I was a nervous wreck. Of course, the limo company finally did send another limo, and we did send Aretha and Glynn back to Encino. By the time I got back home to Hollywood, I wanted to commit suicide!"

In December of 1981, Aretha played three nights at the Roxy in Los Angeles. Performing at the intimate rock & roll club on Sunset Strip the week before Christmas, she won the praise of audiences and critics alike. *The Los Angeles Times* found that the shows were "a treat for those of us who wished she would go back to what she does best: pure unadulterated soul music . . . Franklin—once plagued by much-publicized personal problems—concentrated on songs that stressed the healing and triumphant powers of love." *The Los Angeles Herald-Examiner* called her a "do right woman who can do no wrong."

Finally, after a six-year cold spell, Aretha was officially back in the winner's circle. In January of 1982, when the Grammy Award nominations were released, Aretha's recording of "Hold On I'm Comin'" was up for honors in the "Best R&B Vocal Performance, Female" category. The following month, she won her eleventh Grammy Award.

Aretha's third Arista album, the ultra-hot *Jump to It*, returned her to the Gold standard. It was years since she had had a bona fide hit, and this was considered her big comeback album. It was also the first of two impressive back-to-back albums with Luther Vandross producing.

Luther Vandross became an overnight success as a singer / songwriter / producer in 1981, when he released his Gold album *Never Too Much*. However, like so many entertainers who suddenly find commercial fame, Luther's emergence on the music scene came after many years of working in the business. In the 1970s he sang on several Gold and Platinum albums, including David Bowie's *Young Americans*, Chic's *C'est Chic*, Quincy Jones' *Sounds . . . and Stuff Like That*, and the soundtrack to the film *The Wiz*. He also sang background vocals on albums by Bette Midler, Cat Stevens, and Carly Simon. In 1976 he formed his own group called Luther, and released two critically acclaimed albums: *Luther* (1976) and *This Close to You* (1977).

Vandross grew up in Manhattan, in the Alfred E. Smith housing project near Chinatown, and in the Bronx, where he attended high school. He was destined to find his way into the record business. According to him, his mother was instrumental in developing his musical taste from an early age. "Her influence was incredible," he recalls. "But in a subliminal way. My brother would get a bicycle for Christmas. I would get records by Aretha Franklin. She knew instinctively that I would spend my life surrounded by music." He studied every nuance of Aretha's albums, and was later to profess to *The New York Times*, "I'm an Arethacologist!"

Remembering the most traumatic event of his high school years, Luther tells of his feeling of sincere devastation, and how it affected his schoolwork. "I couldn't study," he says in dead seriousness, "Diana Ross left the Supremes!" He grew up idolizing Dionne Warwick, Diana Ross, and Aretha Franklin.

In the 1970s, Luther began to build a reputation as a background singer, vocal arranger, and a songwriter. His song "Funky Music (Is a Part of Me)" went through a slight rewrite to become the David Bowie song "Fascination," from the *Young Americans* album. When a song was needed for the Broadway show *The Wiz*, it was Luther's composition "Everybody Rejoice" that supplanted "Ding Dong! The Witch is Dead," in the soulful musical version of *The Wizard of Oz*.

In the late seventies, Luther began lending his voice to radio and television jingles, and in 1980 he was one of the lead vocalists on the album *The Glow of Love*, by the "studio group" Change. Based on his track record on all of these projects, in 1981 he signed a recording contract with Epic Records. His debut album, *Never Too Much*, was released, and everything came together for Vandross; the vocal prowess, the choice of songs, and the crisp production work yielded spectacular results.

His recordings were charged with passionate energy, and sung in an emotionally intense style. Although Vandross was exceedingly rotund, his vocal delivery suggested charismatic sex appeal. He suddenly found himself cast as an unlikely, yet musically convincing, sex symbol.

In 1982, two of Luther's wildest dreams came true when his debut solo album was certified Gold and he was asked to produce Aretha's next album. Being at the helm of Franklin's LP was a job that he'd been spending his entire life in preparation for. In an issue of *Rolling Stone* magazine, he had proclaimed his desire to produce albums by his three favorite singers: Aretha, Dionne, and Diana.

According to Aretha, "I was looking for a producer to do my next album, just prior to *Jump to It*, and I had heard *Never Too Much*. I liked the record, and I liked what I heard. It's a funny thing, but he did something on that particular recording that I was working on at home: 'A House Is Not a Home.' I said, 'Aha, he beat you to the punch!' But I still hadn't quite settled on Luther producing me. I had been thinking about him as well as some other people. And then my cousin Brenda, who sings with me, mentioned his name again. 'Why don't you let Luther Vandross produce your next album, he is really hot!' she said. Coupled with the fact that there was a relatedness and a similarity in stylings, I said, 'Why not? He obviously knows what he's doing!'"

Clive Davis recalls reading the Vandross interview: "I had read an article that he had done in *Rolling Stone*, where he said that his three favorite artists in the world were Aretha Franklin, Dionne Warwick, and Diana Ross. It's not easy coming up with not only hit songs, but also songs that would stretch Aretha musically, and also provide her with a black base that she of course so naturally has. Having read that interview that Luther gave to *Rolling Stone*, and with his success at the time as a producer, and as an artist, I thought that it would be a good association. I arranged for the two of them to meet, and that's how it came about."

In addition to the albums that he produced for himself in 1982 and 1983, Luther also produced four albums for three top divas. His outside productions those two years included Aretha's *Jump to It* and *Get It Right*, Dionne Warwick's *How Many Times Can We Say Goodbye*, and Cheryl Lynn's *Instant Love*. All of the albums have a unifying thread. All contain eight songs, up to six minutes each. Several of the songs on each of the four albums were Vandross compositions, and at least one would be a new version of a classic R&B hit from the 1960s. The up-tempo songs would all snap with excitement, led by Marcus Miller's thumping bass. Paul Riser's lush string and horn arrangements made for a full and sensuous sound on all of the tracks. Although each of these four albums are masterfully crafted, Aretha's pair of Luther-produced discs sound the best.

Jump to It and *Get It Right* were recorded in both New York City and in L. A. When Aretha and Luther got together in the recording studio in Los Angeles, they found that they not only shared a love for music, but also a hearty appetite. "When I first met Luther," Franklin recalls, "he had me laughing like *crazy*! He's a great guy, and on some of those sessions, boy, we had us some fried chicken . . . wow! We had a lot of fun together, I can tell you."

Randy Jones, the original cowboy in the group Village People, was working on his first solo recordings in the early 1980s, for John Hammond's record label Zoo York Records. He recalls a surprise encounter with Aretha and Luther in New York City. According to Jones, "I was just leaving Media Sound recording studio on West 57th Street, when a limousine pulled up out front. The doors swung open and out stepped Luther Vandross. Luther was carrying a purse, and I knew it wasn't his own—because it didn't match his outfit! Following him, out stepped Aretha—who was dressed in full-length fur coat. She stepped out of the car carrying an entire bucket of Kentucky Fried Chicken! It was quite a sight to behold, and the two of them were obviously having a great time together."

A production assistant who was present during the *Jump to It* sessions recalls the night of Aretha and Luther's fried chicken extravaganza. The source claims that it was a wonder the recording was completed, there was so much food in the studio: "You know how you walk into a recording studio, and you walk down long corridors, and it's always kind of dark? As I approached the back studio, where they were recording, it was really dark, and it was really warm, unlike most studios, which are cold—everybody keeps the temperature cool to keep them awake. It must have been up to 95 degrees in there! I walked into this tropical environment, with the lights dimmed. I opened the door to the studio, and the smell of chicken was just overwhelming! There were these industrial-size buckets of Kentucky Fried Chicken! The buckets were probably three feet tall by two feet in diameter. I never saw anything like this. There were bones everywhere, and these gigantic cans of Wild Bee Honey. In the middle of all of this hot tea and honey and chicken bones were Aretha and Luther. I never saw anything like this in my life!"

"I dealt with her as one singer to another," Vandross says of his sessions with Franklin. "I sang her everything the way I heard it, and she took most of my suggestions. The vocals were put down in one take. Aretha is the one take queen."

Their crowning creation together was the title cut of her 1982 album *Jump to It*. "It's one of the best pieces of material that came along for me in a good little while. Vandross and I very uniquely happened," explains Aretha. "*Jump to It* started a new pace in recording for me, a different sound. It's perhaps a bit more teen-oriented than some of my earlier things. I like to record what feels good and sound good to me."

The most exciting part of that particular hit comes at the point where Aretha delivers several lines of the lyrics as though she is on the telephone, gossiping to a girlfriend named Kitty. Among the hot street phrases that she uses in her repartee are lines about getting "the 4-1-1" about "who drop kicked who" (in other words, receiving the information about who has broken up with whom in someone's personal relationship). Mid-conversation, Aretha announces to Kitty that she has to hang up the phone, because it is 3:59 p.m., and her boyfriend is due to call at four o'clock sharp.

Barbara Shelley remembers bringing in a film crew from *The Today Show*, and watching while the tracks for *Jump to It* were being created. "It was a terrific segment," she recalls of the television footage. "Aretha sat at the piano with Boyd Matteson, and they did a wonderful segment for *The Today Show* together. Aretha sat at the piano with Boyd, and they tested each other on Christian gospel songs, and it was rather fun."

After the TV taping was over, Barbara hung out at the studio and watched Aretha and Luther get down to work. "When they were working on *Jump to It*," she recalls "Aretha ad-libbed that whole little rap, that '4-1-1 . . .' I remember sitting in the studio watching her write that segment of the song. She had so much fun. It was like watching a little kid play a game that she loved, for the first time. Aretha in the studio is a sparkling, fun experience. The two of them working on that particular song was great fun, and you knew that song was going to be a success. It was just too much fun and everyone was having too much of a good time for anything less than fantastic to happen as a result of that session."

Jump to It was an inspired bit of recording. As *Rolling Stone* raved, "Aretha's back and Luther's got her!" The rest of the album contained special additional gems that generated the same fresh excitement as the title track. The song "If She Don't Want Your Lovin'" is a sassy bit of storytelling, with Aretha telling a man to whom she is attracted to that he had better give up his current love, and check out "Sugar Ray Aretha." "I Wanna Make It Up to You" is an inspired duet between Aretha and Levi Stubbs of the Four Tops, with the rest of the Tops providing their classic Motown-styled backgrounds along with Erma Franklin. The album also contains an electrifying version of the Isley Brothers' 1969 million-seller "It's Your Thing," and an ethereal ballad by Smokey Robinson called "Just My Daydream."

As she had done on all of her first three Arista albums, Aretha eased herself into the producer's chair. The songs "It's Your Thing" and "I Wanna Make It Up to You" were co-produced by Aretha and Luther, and bespoke her growing desire to begin to take more creative responsibility for her musical destiny.

The critical raves for *Jump to It* were numerous. "The 'Queen of Soul' makes a comeback!" exclaimed *The Chicago Tribune.* "There isn't a false move anywhere, and Franklin has never sounded cockier or more confident . . . *Jump to It* really is the best soul album so far this year," heralded *The Los Angeles Times. Billboard* announced that "Aretha Franklin's *Jump to It* is her best dance record in ages, a tribute to Luther Vandross' spirited writing and producing." And *The New York Post* extolled "her best recording in years," featuring "a contemporary sound that is both appropriate and exciting."

The song "Jump to It" leapt up the charts, hitting Number One on the R&B singles chart. The album was certified Gold, and on the pop chart the song "Jump to It" (Number Twenty-four) became her biggest smash since "I'm in Love" in 1974. Aretha was definitely back on top.

To reciprocate for Levi Stubbs and the Four Tops' appearance on the *Jump to It* album, Aretha sang a duet with the group on their 1983 Motown album, *Back Where I Belong.* The song was an exciting ballad called "What Have We Got to Lose," written by Willie Hutch and Berry Gordy, Jr. It had been twenty-six years since Gordy had come to the

Franklin home in Detroit, Michigan, and tried to sign Aretha and her sister Erma to a production contract with him and his then-partner, Billy Davis. At long last, Aretha had recorded a song for Gordy's dynasty-like company, Motown Records.

Aretha had been friends with Levi Stubbs and his singing partners, Abdul "Duke" Fakir, Lawrence Payton, and Obie Benson, since her growing up days back in Detroit. Levi's deep and soulful voice worked well with Aretha's singing on "I Wanna Make It Up to You" and "What Have We Got to Lose." Following the release of the *Jump to It* album, Franklin and the Four Tops headlined a concert engagement at Radio City Music Hall in New York City. Aretha was in peak form for the concert, and the Four Tops were also experiencing a resurgence in their career. They had just scored their first Top Twenty pop hit in eight years, with "When She Was My Girl." Teaming Aretha with the Four Tops was an inspired move—live and on record.

It had been over ten years since Kenneth Reynolds had first met Aretha, while working on *The David Frost Show*. In 1982 he was working for Polygram Records and their subsidiary label, Casablanca, which the Four Tops recorded for—prior to their return to Motown. His next encounter with Aretha was backstage at Radio City Music Hall, when he was in charge of media relations for the Four Tops.

It was that evening, right before the show, when Aretha made a surprise visit to the Four Tops' dressing room. "I was in the dressing room with Levi and Abdul and all the guys, and Gunther Hensler, who was then the president of Polygram," Reynolds recalls. "When all of a sudden Aretha Franklin walks in. She has a fur coat on, and she has this walk—like you expect Aretha to walk. It was almost as if she was walking on her toes or something. I can remember that so specifically, because I just froze in my tracks when she walked in.

"She walks in and says 'Hello!' to everybody. She's got this little garment bag draped over her arm, and she walks up to Levi and says, 'You know that song that I do with George Benson—"Love All the Hurt Away?" I want you to do that with me tonight.' And Levi says, 'Aretha, I don't know the song.' And she says, 'Oh don't worry baby, it goes like this: "Dah, dah, dah-da-da dah . . ."' She says, 'I'll see you out there, it'll be okay,' She turns and she walks out of the dressing room. Everybody just stood there with their mouths open. Well, obviously Levi was used to this, and he sort of just laughed.

"I turned to Levi and said, 'What are you going to do? Aretha Franklin just told you to come and sing a song with her. You told her you don't know the song. She says, "It goes like this . . ." and she sings it to you. And now of course you're supposed to know it because she sang it, and you're supposed to sing it like she sang it!'

"I don't know how he learned all of the words that quickly, maybe it's just the singer's instinct," Reynolds says. "But I'll tell you something, Levi came out and he sang 'Love All the Hurt Away' to the point where George Benson should have been ashamed. If I hadn't seen it with my own eyes, I never would have believed it. It sounded like they had rehearsed it all day. That's what happens when you put two pros like that together!"

In addition to her recordings, in 1982 Aretha used her voice to raise funds for cultural support and to benefit her favorite charities. On June 14 she starred in a benefit concert at Carnegie Hall for the Joffrey Ballet. Nancy Reagan was the honorary national chairwoman.

"She put on a great show, it was absolutely dynamite!" recalls Roger Max Barrow, who was the director of development for the Joffrey Ballet at the time. "It was called *No Dancing Allowed!* That was sort of a clever way to prepare people that they were coming to a Joffrey concert—with no dancing. As these galas go, especially for classical companies, people are used to seeing full-length ballets, and it's a little staid. This was really unique in that it got the Joffrey really rocking."

According to Barrow, there were few performers in 1982 who were popular enough to draw a sell-out crowd—when the tickets were a thousand dollars apiece. Aretha Franklin, however, was. "We really went through a lag there, where there were very few single artists that could carry off a thousand-dollar ticket. Today we have Cher, we have Madonna, in addition to Barbra Streisand and Bette Midler, that could do it. But they weren't doing concerts for other people at that time, so this was really a one-time thing.

"Lesley Ann Warren acted as the emcee, and the two special guests were Ben Vereen and Marvin Hamlisch. They were the opening act, and then Aretha Franklin did her thing after that. There was an intermission, then she performed for an hour. I think she was really quite honored to be there, and she put on a hell of a show. With those other three people [on the bill], she really could have walked out and done twenty minutes. I think everybody was quite surprised that she performed that long, and that she belted it out—she wasn't holding back. She gave a 102-percent!" exclaimed Barrow.

The Joffrey Ballet has honored Aretha by presenting a ballet that was choreographed using her music. "There is a ballet in our repertoire called 'Love Songs,' and it's a ballet to recordings by Aretha and Dionne Warwick," explains Marlyn Baum, publicist for the Joffrey. "William Forsythe, who was trained at the Joffrey Ballet School, is now the Artistic Director of the Frankfurt Ballet, and he is the choreographer of 'Love Songs.' The ballet 'Love Songs' is in the repertory of the Frankfurt Ballet, and it's also in our repertory." It debuted in Munich in 1979.

Franklin's recordings of "If You Gotta Make a Fool of Somebody," "You're All I Need of Get By," and "Baby, I Love You" were used in the American version of the ballet. In addition to having been performed live, "Love Songs" has also been filmed as part of the PBS-TV series *Dance in America*. In Germany, "Love Songs" has not only been performed in Munich and Frankfurt, but the Stuttgart Ballet also mounted a production of it. In Stuttgart an additional Aretha classic song was added as its finale— "(You Make Me Feel Like) A Natural Woman."

Aretha was so pleased with the outcome of the Joffrey Ballet benefit that she decided to organize her own annual charity event. The original concept was to host a dinner show every year, in a different city, to raise money for worthy causes. She solidified her plans for the first event, and began lining up musical guests. She called her project "The Artis't Ball." The first was held on September 14, 1982, at the Beverly Hilton Hotel, starring herself, the Four Tops, and Lulu. The evening's proceeds were split between the Sickle Cell Anemia Foundation and the Arthritis Foundation. According to insiders, the event failed to raise a substantial amount of money for either of the charities, because it was completely disorganized.

In defense of Aretha, this fiasco has to be viewed within the context of what was happening in her personal life. In addition to the financial and emotional pressures of her father's illness, and her growing boredom with the Hollywood lifestyle, her storybook marriage suddenly and mysteriously ended. Something happened between her and Glynn that was so traumatic that it left no chance of reconciliation.

The most widely circulated rumor stated that Aretha—allegedly—discovered Glynn having an affair with someone who was quite close to her, and that it instantly marked the end of their relationship. A neighbor, who lived down the street from the couple, commented that she was surprised the marriage had lasted as long as it did, because Franklin and Turman had such "opposite lifestyles." One of Aretha's business associates claims that this was not the first of Glynn's extramarital activities. According to the source, "He was just messing around with everything that moved."

Whatever happened, the breakup had a devastating effect on Aretha. In one dramatic sweep, she left him and her movie-star-style mansion, and moved to suburban Detroit. This marked the beginning of her reclusive existence in Michigan.

Aretha was never to explain to the press or her co-workers why she left Glynn. She spoke only of her move back to Detroit. According to her, "The main reason that I moved back was my dad's illness. It was a lot easier for me to just come back instead of trying to fly back every two weeks, every month, with my schedule. So it made it a lot easier for me."

"I love being back home," she said of Detroit, during this era. "I've had the opportunity to see old friends of mine, like fifteen-, twenty-year friends. People that I haven't seen since I was a teenager: girlfriends and dishing up the dirt and the 'tee' [gossip] and 'who drop kicked who?' and all that sort of thing . . . a little dirt now and then!" she laughs, mimicking her "Jump to It" ad-libs.

"There's one guy who I had a crush on when I was all of twelve years old, and he cracks up whenever I tell him that," she continued. "It's great being back home. Had I known that Detroit had to offer what it has to offer, before I moved to Los Angeles from New York, I would have moved back to Detroit then."

In 1983, based on the overwhelming success of *Jump to It*, Aretha went back in the recording studio, with Luther Vandross producing. Although their follow-up album together sold less well than *Jump to It* had, it was just as finely crafted an album as its predecessor. The title cut, "Get It Right" made for a thumping, snapping Number One hit single on the R&B charts, and a second single, "Every Girl (Wants My Guy)," hit the R&B Top Ten.

Cut from the same eight-song album formula of all of Luther's 1981–83 productions, *Get It Right* reunited Franklin with the same musical professionals she had worked with on *Jump to It*, including Cissy Houston and Darlene Love singing background vocals, Paul Riser's string and horn arrangements, and all of Luther's favorite musicians.

The song "Every Girl (Wants My Guy)" featured Aretha gossiping to her girlfriend Kitty again on the telephone, as a continuation to "Jump to It." She also sang an elongated version of the Temptations' 1968 hit "I Wish It Would Rain," complete with the thunder crackling in the background. One of the songs on the album, "Giving In" was written by Aretha's oldest son, Clarence Franklin, and another of her sons, Teddy F. White, Jr., played the "fill guitar" on the song.

The press reviews for *Get It Right* were mixed. While some critics thought that this album was even more successful than *Jump to It*, others thought it was less inspired. *The Washington Post* claimed that "Vandross and Franklin have extended their collaboration into an even more consistent, more rewarding album: *Get It Right*." On the other hand *The Buffalo Evening News* said, "This album is not as good as last year's *Jump to It* . . . but that merely means that this is the second best thing Lady Soul has done in years."

While producers Luther Vandross, Arif Mardin, and Chuck Jackson had been laboring to come up with the right musical setting to shape Aretha's 1980s image, the Creative Services Department at Arista was struggling to give her sense of visual focus as well. The album cover for *Get It Right* presented Aretha at her most glamorous. She was photographed by Francesco Scavullo, famed for his *Cosmopolitan* magazine covers, and she was made up by Way Bandy. The resulting photos that grace this album are exquisite examples of high fashion photography at its best. For *Jump to It*, Harry Langdon had done a fine job of photographing Aretha, but her outfit—a tuxedo jacket and a supportless glitter tube top—was atrocious. Definitely the wrong look for her ample figure. On the back cover photo, drastic retouching on her cleavage is obvious in an attempt to soften the unflattering look the outfit created.

Aretha's penchant for inappropriate low-cut gowns has often been a cause of controversy. What she perceives as "sexy" often gets her into trouble. In the late 1970s, Aretha appeared on *The Tonight Show* in a dress that was cut so low it was considered risqué by the show's producers. The talk show's host, Johnny Carson, was reportedly embarrassed at the sight of Aretha's dress. Camera crews on that particular show were forced to shoot her from the neck up.

When Barbara Shelley started working with Aretha in the early 1980s, she "pitched" Franklin as a potential guest on *The Tonight Show*. She was completely unaware of the problems that Aretha's low-cut gown had caused. "Gini Fosdick was the talent coordinator at *The Tonight Show*," Shelley explains. "She was the one who told me that Johnny Carson would love to use Aretha Franklin on *The Tonight Show* because she is the Queen of Soul, and how could they say 'no' to Aretha Franklin? But I was asked very confidentially, 'Could you please do something about her cleavage?'"

According to Barbara, the whole event became a running gag between her and Aretha. "It became an 'in-joke' with us that she had to wear turtleneck evening gowns on *The Tonight Show*!'"

One ex-member of Arista's Creative Services Department reveals that several of Aretha's photographs were extensively retouched to cut away excess pounds. On the inside of Aretha's *Love All the Hurt Away* album, there is this photo of Franklin peering out from behind a door. "Aretha was enormous," says the source. "Between her boobs and her stomach, there were two tremendous rolls going past the border of the door. Ria Lewerke [Arista's art director] had them do plastic surgery on her. The 'before' looked like this fat mama, with her belly sticking out to 'here,' like she was pregnant, and the other one was this woman in this really slinky dress. It was great."

According to the source, Aretha herself was in love with the results of the retouching, and was so taken by the slimming illusion that she never wanted to go on a diet again; she simply wanted retouching: "She looked so svelte in the picture. She was shaped up perfectly and she loved it. I mean, she looked great. It was exactly the way she wanted to look, and it was the easiest diet in the world!

"We really worked like dogs to make those album covers correct," the former Arista employee explains. "We had to fight against her—the outfits that she came to some of the photo sessions in! The things that she wanted for album covers, the things she picked—oh my God! Probably every one of us from the Creative Services Department lost ten years from our lives thanks to Aretha Franklin, and the torture that she put us through over those album covers. We stuck to our guns, that we were going to have beautiful and classic album covers befitting her position in the marketplace as the Queen of Soul. We respected her as the Queen of Soul, and we were going to force her to respect herself—no matter what!"

With her first four albums on Arista, Aretha was successfully brought out of her late-1970s doldrums. Since she had lost a bit of sales momentum with *Get It Right*, it was going to take another dramatic leap forward with her next release to reestablish the strong crossover appeal she once had. There were a couple more obstacles that she had to navigate over before her path back to the top was clear. But Aretha was well on her way, and heading in the right direction.

CHAPTER EIGHT

THE FREEWAY BACK TO THE TOP

Although Aretha's *Jump to It* album had done wonders to revive her career, her acknowledged comeback disc was 1985's brilliant *Who's Zoomin' Who?* It not only brought her back to the forefront of the record-buying marketplace, but it served as the vehicle that blasted her into the million-selling Platinum galaxy. Scoring an album with sales in excess of a million copies is a distinction that even her biggest-selling LPs at Atlantic Records had never attained.

In the interim, however, between 1983's *Get It Right* and the crossover brilliance of *Who's Zoomin' Who?*, Aretha was to encounter several setbacks and false starts. Lawsuits, canceled engagements, and death of her father put a temporary halt to her immediate career plans.

After the completion of *Get it Right*, Aretha sued Arista Records for breach of contract. The suit claimed that Arista had violated her agreement with them allegedly failing to credit her royalty account for the combined sales of 600,000 copies of her albums *Aretha* (1980) and *Love All the Hurt Away*. She also claimed that the record company had made charges against her recording fund account, as opposed to drawing money out of her royalty account. The suit further alleged that Arista had contracted Luther Vandross to produce their two albums together "for substantial cash advances and royalties," without Aretha's express consent.

According to Barbara Shelley, "She asked to have the books reviewed, which is not unusual. That's done periodically. I don't know exactly why she did it. I don't know if it was to stall for a record, or because she really needed the money. She had asked for a loan or an advance, and they [Arista] turned her down. As a result, she placed this action."

In retrospect, Clive Davis says of the incident, "I think that she had been verbally told one thing by some advisor of hers, and it never amounted to an actual lawsuit, or maybe it is just a paper filed. I don't know. She and I never talked about it. I never got involved."

Ever since her film debut in *The Blues Brothers* in 1980, Aretha had been toying with the idea of further acting assignments. There had been talk of a *Blues Brothers II* being filmed. John Belushi had gone so far as to ask Aretha to appear in the sequel, but his untimely death by drug overdose in 1982 had ended the possibility of that. "I'd like to do at least five more roles," she told *Women's Wear Daily*. "I'm not an actress, but I can do a good part. I think I can excel in a good part."

In early 1984 a stage role presented itself that was too perfect to turn down. Aretha agreed to accept the title role in a Broadway show called *Sing, Mahalia, Sing*, about Mahalia Jackson, and she began to prepare to bring to life the role of Jackson, who had been an inspiration to her when she was growing up.

"She and my dad were great friends, and she would come over to the house when she was in town," Aretha reminisced admiringly when the play was announced. "Of course, she would come to my father's church, and he would not let her get out without singing. [She was] an absolutely great lady, a devout Christian, who was warm and had a great sense of humor."

Aretha studied Mahalia's recordings, and spent time talking to several of the gospel legend's friends to gain insight. The production schedule called for three weeks of rehearsals in New York City, beginning on May 2, 1984. Performances were booked, and a full itinerary of dates was announced. The show's run would encompass the entire summer of 1984 and include engagements at the Palace in Columbus, Ohio; the State Theater in Cleveland, Ohio; Aire Crown in Chicago, Illinois; The Masonic Temple in Detroit, Michigan; and City Center in New York City. The dates were scheduled so that Aretha wouldn't ever be any farther than a twelve-hour drive away from Detroit, where her father remained in a coma.

Another reason all of her *Sing, Mahalia, Sing* dates had to be close enough to reach by car from Detroit was that she had suddenly developed an extreme fear of flying. Her latest and most dreaded phobia began that year on a midnight plane from Georgia. It seems that on a flight from Atlanta to Detroit late one night, the aircraft she was riding in encountered some extreme turbulence. As Aretha describes it, the plane "did one of those dipsy-doodles." According to her, "I was on one of those little numbers where, if the man across the aisle breathed too loud, you could hear that—the plane was so tiny. I guess after twenty-two, twenty-three years of flying, I can have a bad flight—and I did!"

When the time came to begin rehearsals in New York, she reportedly got as far as the Detroit Metropolitan Airport and got cold feet. She never made it to Manhattan to start work on the play, so the project was aborted before it began. The show's producer, Aston Springer, sued Aretha for breach of contract for suddenly dropping out of the production. In February of 1989 it was determined in federal court in New York that although no contract had been breached, Springer was entitled to recover his preproduction costs. A separate trial was scheduled to determine the amount that Aretha was required to pay Springer to compensate for his losses. Whitman Knapp, the judge who ruled on the case, found that Franklin's self-professed fear of flying was no excuse for backing out of the show. According to him, "If she could not bring herself to fly, she should have traveled by way of ground transportation."

She had no sooner abandoned *Sing, Mahalia, Sing* than her father's health suddenly took a turn for the worse. After living for several years in a coma, on July 24, 1984, Reverend C. L. Franklin died at the age of 69. Aretha was devastated by his death, even though he had been lingering between life and the hereafter for several years.

According to Erma Franklin, Aretha "spent over a half million dollars on him—$1,500 a week just for nurses. But she still can't talk about it, not even to her own family. You can't even say the word 'death' around her. You have to say 'passed away' or some other expression. She and my dad were very, very, very close."

In early 1985 the State of New York sued Aretha for what it claimed were unpaid back taxes on recording sessions dating back to the 1970s. The suit claimed that, as a nonresident of the state, Aretha had received payment for recording sessions done in New York City between 1972 and 1977, for which she had failed to pay $46,000 in taxes. The suit also claimed that she owed an additional $56,000 in interest and penalties. With regard to the $102,000 suit, Aretha's lawyer, Andrew Feinman, explained that "there was and is, a law in New York State that says when a non-resident performs services here, taxes must be paid to the state." He also claimed that the suit was completely "discriminatory" in that "they can pick and choose who they will sue. Thousands of recording artists come to New York studios to record, and they are only enforcing the law against very few."

Things became especially sticky when Aretha announced concert dates for June 12–15, 1985, at Carnegie Hall. The tickets went on sale, and all four nights sold out almost immediately. Less than two weeks before the concert dates, Aretha canceled the engagement when she was advised that she was going to be served with papers if she set foot in New York State, and that there was going to be a lien against the money. Her brother and manager, Cecil, claimed that the cancellation was due to her fear of flying, when it may have been her fear of the New York State Income Tax Department. (In 1986 the suit was finally settled out of court.)

The two concert engagements Aretha did complete in 1985 were in Detroit and Chicago. In February she appeared at the Premier Center, in the Detroit suburb of Sterling Heights. In April she was driven by car to Chicago, where she headlined several nights at Park West. One of the Park West shows was taped for the syndicated television program, *Soundstage*. Both engagements were met with lukewarm reviews. *The Detroit News* claimed that she ignored several of her trademark songs and relied on medley versions of "See Saw," "Ain't No Way," and "Rock Steady." The review's headline read, "Aretha Ignores Her Big Hits—And the Show Suffers." A review in *The Chicago Sun-Times* likewise claimed that "Aretha hits and misses . . . her magic is momentary."

The Premier Center engagement was amid one of her heavier phases. At the end of the show, when Aretha removed her breakaway skirt to finish the show in a creation resembling a skintight one-piece bathing suit, the audience was startled. *The Detroit News* reviewer complained, "Regrettably, Miss Franklin didn't help matters with her choice of costuming . . . I don't know who her couturiers are, but somebody should have a long talk with them."

Being overweight was only one of her problems. Another one was plain and simple: Aretha needed a hit record! She had to have a song that would not only recapture the interest of her old fans, but would also give her career a fresh new focus. Fortunately, that magical album was in the works while all of these mishaps were taking place. Aretha had begun recording her next album in October 1984, and it was to make all the difference in the world.

Owing to her fear of flying, and her lawsuit with New York State, *Who's Zoomin' Who?* set a precedent: if anyone wanted to work with Aretha Franklin, they had to come to Detroit, because she wasn't leaving town. Although the instrumental tracks on most of the cuts on Aretha's 1985 and 1986 albums were done in New York and California, all of Franklin's vocals were recorded at United Sound in Detroit.

Prior to her fiftieth consecutive album release, Aretha had taken over a year off from the recording studio. In addition to contemplating the *Sing, Mahalia, Sing* project, she had spent her time taking French lessons and investing in real estate. She not only purchased a large home in the chic suburb of Bloomfield Hills, but she also bought a new luxury apartment in downtown Detroit, in one of the expensive residential complexes along the Detroit River.

"I hadn't had a vacation, really, in about eight or nine years," she explained, "just constantly working—being off some days, and just kind of laying around, taking it easy. But that is not an actual and real vacation, where you pick your spot, and you want to go someplace exotic, and you and your friend . . . you know, that sort of thing. So last year it gave me the opportunity to kind of get into some things, and some other interests that I have. Like the money market I got into, and I've been studying real estate as well. I'm interested in real estate for resale profit, that kind of thing, and investments and things. It gave me the opportunity and the time to investigate and do things that I would not otherwise have had the time to do. So, being off last year could have been a blessing in disguise."

She had also been listening to the latest hits on the radio, and she had been formulating some ideas about what she would like to do on her next album. "I've been listening to the radio," Aretha said at the time, "and I like some of the music I heard—songs by Van Halen, John Waite, Luther Vandross. I said to myself, 'Hey, let me get out here and do something serious!' Till now, a lot of my music's been adult-oriented. I wanted something kids could really get into. Besides, I like to bop too!"

Before he became a record producer, Narada Michael Walden was the drummer with John McLaughlin's Mahavishnu Orchestra. In the late 1970s he had been recording his own albums, as well as producing and writing. He came to the attention of Clive Davis at Arista Records, and two of the first people he produced records for were Phyllis Hyman and Angela Bofill. However, his greatest triumphs were to come from producing two of Arista Records' other ladies, Aretha Franklin and Whitney Houston.

"Clive Davis knew that I really wanted to do this project with Aretha," Walden said of his involvement with *Who's Zoomin' Who?* "When he told me I could take a stab at it, I was thrilled, especially since I had the chance to do more than just two songs."

Walden began sending demos of suggested songs to Clive Davis. Davis, in turn, would submit them to Aretha. "She was delighted with what she heard," Walden recalls. "I sent her roughs on 'Push,' 'Freeway,' and 'Zoomin'.' It was funny because 'Freeway of Love' was originally going to be on one of my albums—but *without* the line about wearing your pants tight! I revamped the lyrics for Aretha. I'm glad it worked out this way. That record would have been a bigger hit for her than for me."

After Aretha approved of several of Walden's tunes, they began a long-distance dialogue. "I really came up with a lot of the ideas lyrically from talking with Aretha on the phone," he reveals. "I'd ask her about what she'd do at home, how did she spend her time. She told me that one of the things she liked to do on occasion was go to a club and maybe she'd be checking out some guy who'd be checking her out, too—that's where I got a lot of the ideas for the song 'Who's Zoomin' Who.' I discovered that Aretha has this great sense of humor, something I had no idea about before we began working together. In fact, I was real surprised when we first met; I didn't expect her to be so young and so vibrant! I mean, she's been making records for such a long time that I was surprised to find her so open, so into what's happening *today*."

According to Walden, the album was in the planning stages when Aretha's lawsuit with Arista got in the way. "They had to renegotiate, and she refused to sing until it was cleared up. So there was a layoff. It was like going back to old friends in a way, the music being an old friend." Aretha and Arista ironed out their problems, and she returned to the recording studio.

Professionally, Narada and Aretha hit it off in the studio immediately. "He knows his music very well," she said. "He knows what he's going to do when he gets there, and yet it's not a straight-ahead work kind of thing. It's very relaxed. We kid around a lot, we talk about a lot of different things between takes. And then, after one of those good takes, I get the best ribs in town!" First it was fried chicken with Luther; now she was on to barbecued spareribs with Narada!

"She sounds real comfortable," Walden explained, prior to the album's release. "I think it worked out well to go to Detroit where she's at home. Everywhere she goes, she has a security guard. She pulls up in her limousine and gets out with a fur coat on. She takes her fur coat off, and she's got jeans and a sweatshirt on underneath. Hip class, you know what I mean? She'd come in and do a rough take of a song just to get an idea how she wanted to sing it, and about three or four takes later, we'd have it. And each time she got better and better. The good thing about her is that she knows when it's a record and when it's not. She'll sing it down once or twice, and me, I'm excited. She says, 'No, now I'm ready to go for it.' And, sure enough, just when you think you've heard it all, here it comes—boom! Because her style of singing is not just flat-out singing, she plays with it. She can be very gritty and then also very ladylike at the same time. She has a way of singing and talking, singing to you and talking to you. She's very subtle.

"She has great ideas about herself and what she wants to say. Like on 'Jump to It' she goes, 'Kitty, give me the 4-1-1: who drop-kicked who this week?' And that's the way she talks, man. On 'Freeway of Love,' on the new album, she has this little rap that goes, 'With the wind and your fingers in my hair, makes me feel like we're going for an extended throw-down. So drop the top, baby, and let's cruise into It's-Better-Than-Ever Street!' She's a real slickster. It's the Queen. It's the Queen's lingo in the high court."

Walden claims that "She would call Luther Vandross just to say, 'Baby, Narada's throwin' down!'" Indeed, the songs that came out of their sessions together nearly melted the vinyl they were pressed on.

"She brings to the studio incredible wisdom, incredible savvy, incredible humor. She's like a black Mae West!" says Narada, who was especially impressed with her musical intuition. "She's like a walking cloud. She looks down and sees things how she wants to see them, and says it how she wants to say it. It's not like it's all church to me. In the voice you feel a lot of gospel roots, it's true. But her expression of the church is very streetwise."

According to him, she always knows what is best for her, and what shows off her voice the best. "If I would want her to do one line over in a verse, I had to have a real good excuse to make her want to sing it again. She'd say, 'Just the way I like it.' And I would say, 'That's great, but there's one line that could have been a little better or had a little more expression . . . or something.' Nope. That's it, buddy. I would have to tell her the tape machine blew up and get it again."

Likewise, recording engineer Dave Frazer found Aretha totally professional. "She knew, when she came in, what she wanted to do. She knew the song, she knew the licks, she knew everything ahead of time, which is somewhat unusual to a certain extent. She came in like she had already sung the song over and over, which I guess she did. She doesn't give you the impression she would do that, but she comes in and knows it."

"Narada was fabulous to work with," says Aretha. "I'm an Aries, he's an Aries-Taurus—on the cusp. Ditto with Luther—Aries-Taurus. Aries and Aries don't do so well sometimes. Because we are so professional, we overcome the Aries stigma. So Narada was really fabulous to work with. When I think about his experience in the business, and my experience, and the fact that he is so professional and so am I—it is no surprise that things came out the way they did! I am delighted with it."

Ultimately, six of the songs on *Who's Zoomin' Who?* were produced by Narada Michael Walden, one song was produced by Dave Stewart of the group Eurythmics, and two of the cuts were produced by Aretha alone. She had dabbled in co-producing songs before, but this time around she dove right in and took control of two of the sessions.

The album's title cut was a collaborative effort. Aretha had heard the phrase "Who's zoomin' who?" from a couple of acquaintances, and she discussed it with Walden. He and a writing partner took Aretha's concept of making the phrase into a song, and it is credited to Walden, Preston Glass, and Aretha.

Aretha explained of the song's origin, "'Who's Zoomin' Who' came from a group of gentlemen out of New York who called themselves the New Breeders. They were a very productive, creative group who made things like dashikis, earrings, shoes, material items for sale. They used to use the term 'This guy really zoomed me,' or 'This chick really zoomed me.' And I really loved the cliché. Then there was some relationship I was involved in at the time with this gentleman. I think he rather thought he was zooming me, but I didn't think so. In fact, I knew that he wasn't. So it was a question of 'who's zoomin' who?'"

The song "Another Night" was written by Beppe Cantorelli and Roy Freeland. Clive Davis originally found it for Aretha. "Clive Davis called me about that song," remembers Franklin, "and he said, 'I've got a great song, you've got to hear it. I'm gonna Federal Express it to you!' And I got it the next day, and I quite agreed: this is a smashing song! And I called him back and I told him, 'We've got one! This is a great song, I love it.'"

The song "Ain't Nobody Ever Loved You" was another song that Narada Michael Walden and Preston Glass came up with. "The calypso song," says Aretha, "I loved, because I love the atmosphere it creates when one is listening. It puts you right in the islands. Anyone who's been to the islands, to Nassau, to Martinique, to Jamaica, and so on, just for those three or four minutes, I think I puts you right back in the islands, and it reminds you of the good times and trade winds, and things like that."

That song gave Aretha another chance to do some of her famous ad-libbing—however, this time she put her foreign language lessons to work by ad-libbing in French. "I loved doing the bit of French that I did," she says, "I like French very much. I went on vacation to Martinique and Martinique is a French island, and *'Oui, je parle Français!'* ['Yes, I speak French!']"

The music for the six songs that Narada produced for this album were recorded in the San Francisco Bay area, so Aretha wasn't in the studio with any of the musicians. She simply laid down her vocal tracks in Detroit with Walden and his recording engineer, Dave Frazer. In fact, she didn't even know that some of the musicians who played on the tracks were included on her album until it was released. With regard to the medium-paced song "Until You Say You Love Me," Aretha commented, "I noticed on the liner notes that Randy Jackson of the J-5 [Jackson Five] played on that song, and also [disco star] Sylvester, whom I like very much. It's a great song, I like the sound. It rather reminded me of the period in the sixties—early Motown."

The really revolutionary thing about *Who's Zoomin' Who?* was the fact that it not only recaptured the exciting, soulful side of Aretha, but also brought out the rock & roll side of her as well. The song "Freeway of Love" featured Clarence Clemons of Bruce Springsteen's band; "Sisters Are Doin' It For Themselves" was a collaboration with Eurythmics, and "Push" was a duet with Peter Wolf of the J. Giles Band.

Originally, the concept was to have David Bowie sing "Push" with Aretha, but when scheduling conflicts occurred, Peter Wolf was brought in, and Carlos Santana played the guitar solo on the cut. "There again, Narada Walden wrote 'Push,'" Aretha explained. "The gentleman that you hear doing the duet vocal is Peter Wolf. Peter Wolf used to record for Atlantic during the years that I was there. Of course, at that time we had not met. We had the pleasure of meeting to do 'Push.' He was a very nice man—quiet, rather unassuming, I would say. I thought it turned out really hot!"

According to Wolf, recording in the Detroit studio was exciting, especially since they had both recorded for Atlantic in the early 1970s. "Every one of her takes is a unique performance, it's on such a high level!"

The hottest song on the album was without a doubt the duet between Aretha and Annie Lennox of the duo Eurythmics. Annie's partner, writer /

producer / guitarist Dave Stewart, produced the track, which is a real rock scorcher, bristling with energy. "'Sisters Are Doin' It for Themselves,'" Aretha says, "there again Clive called me and told me, 'I've got a great song!' Annie had sent it over to Clive at the record company, and he sent it out to me. My schedule was pretty tight, and I kept saying, 'I don't think I can do that. I just came out of the studio.' I had been in there, prior to his calling, I guess for a month. And he said, 'You've just gotta . . . you just gotta. We have to cut this!' I went back to the studio and Annie and Dave were there. Great group of people, they came in from New York. She likes baked potatoes, so we called one of my favorite places, which is Wendy's. And we got baked potatoes for Annie and a slab of ribs for me and Dave—great guy. I found them to be very professional and technical in the studio, and very relaxed and fun. We had a good time!"

When Aretha was preparing to go to the recording studio, she decided that since she was about to make music with the duo of rock & roll heavyweights, she had better dress in a rock outfit. However, when she got to the studio, she found that Annie Lennox had second-guessed what the Queen of Soul would be wearing, "I think we had a role-reversal there," Aretha laughs. "Because I showed up wearing the 'punk' look, and the Levi's jacket and the rhinestones—that look. And she showed up very chic, with a black pantsuit, and spectator shoes. I thought it was kind of cute."

After the session, Annie Lennox raved, "Watching her sing with such effortless power, I realized why the Queen of Soul still holds the crown!" (The song was also included on the Eurythmics' 1985 album *Be Yourself Tonight*.)

The song "Sisters Are Doin' It for Themselves" is very much a feminist anthem. "Well, I think it rather reflects what is happening today in the ERA and the women's-lib movement," Aretha says. "They're coming out of the kitchen. All women are not geared to domesticity, I guess you might say. Some woman are more business- and career-oriented than being domestic, and being at home, and in the kitchen. I rather feel, if a woman feels like she can handle the job, then why not equal pay? And of course today we're seeing women in jobs, and in areas that we have not seen them in, like firefighters. I have seen them in the streets doing construction and directing traffic and just doing things that they haven't been doing. I think if a woman has enough heart to get out there and deal with that, then she should get equal pay."

Another exciting career progression came on this album, with the two cuts Aretha produced for herself: "Integrity" and "Sweet Bitter Love." Several of the musicians on those two songs were from the sessions she had done with Luther Vandross—namely keyboard player Nat Adderly, Jr., drummer Yogi Horton, and arranger Paul Riser.

"Well, it's about those male-female relationships," said Aretha of the song "Integrity." "I wrote that and I produced it, and my group did the background vocals on that particular song: Brenda, Margaret, and Sandra. It's kind of like those sweet beginnings and all of that sort of thing—when you meet somebody that you really dig, and they get you on the hook, and then they switch up and they have another program. As much as I have to say about it, I guess, is, everybody was not meant to be with each other, and if it's meant to work it's gonna work. And if it doesn't work, at least use a little integrity." Although she did not confirm or deny it, the song sounds suspiciously as though it is about her relationship with Glynn Turman. When I asked her if they were still on speaking terms, she replied, "Glynn and I are still good friends."

"I had a lot of fun doing 'Integrity,'" she continues. "I think it came out just as I wanted it to be. There again, it's reminiscent a bit of the sixties, and some of the things that Curtis Mayfield did. I really enjoyed doing it. I've got to write more, and I've got to produce more.

"'Sweet Bitter Love' is a remake of something that I recorded on Columbia Records in the sixties. And I always loved the song, the first time I did it. Van McCoy wrote that song, and he also [with Clyde Otis] produced it for me on Columbia, and periodically I would say, "I like that so much I'm gonna recut it. But I never quite seemed to get around to it. And then, I have a friend who kept saying, 'Aretha, why don't cut "Sweet Bitter Love?"' And finally, with his prodding, I said, 'Okay, I think the time is right to do this.' And it was one ultra-pleasure for me to produce 'Sweet Bitter Love.' I had a great time—I loved producing."

She also said, in our 1985 interview, that "Clive Davis, the president of Arista, has given me a production deal to produce two other artists of my naming." There was also talk about Aretha having her own record label, but nothing ever came of the proposed projects at Arista.

"In the past, I've co-produced on some of my Atlantic albums," she continued. "I worked with Jerry Wexler, Arif Mardin, and Tom Dowd. But this was the first time I did it all by myself. And I really liked wearing that producer's hat. For the first time I didn't have any outside influences, so I found it very freeing."

As for the reason it took her so long to become more involved in producing, she said, "I just wasn't as experienced. I learned a whole lot from doing this—a lot about the more technical aspects of recording—so I definitely want to be producing myself more in the future. I'd even like to produce a couple of other acts—maybe a group like the Four Tops and another female artist."

The album cover was quite a pleasing concept. It depicted a city street scene, with a large portrait drawing of Aretha plastered on a wall, like a poster advertising a concert. The color sketch of Aretha, done mainly in reds and browns, is very flattering. "About the album cover for *Who's Zoomin' Who?*," Aretha explained, "a young lady named Artis Lane did the cover portrait. I was very surprised and delighted to find that she was from Detroit. We were trying to get in touch with her, because I had seen her work in *People* magazine. And a friend of mine, the lady who does my makeup, Regina Lynch, told me, 'I know Artis Lane.' She put me in touch with her, and we talked. It was kind of a metaphysical cover. She did it just by talking to me on the phone, and by listening to various works of mine. She's a very talented and gifted lady, and I was very pleased with it."

Not only did the sound of this particular album move Aretha back into the forefront of contemporary music, but it also introduced her to the world of music videos. "I think that videos are a very, very necessary promotional tool," she admits. "I think, as opposed to yesterday, new artists coming in the business will be in people's homes a lot quicker than they would have been, had they have come in prior to video. I have seen some great ones, and I have seen some other videos that, as a friend of mine described—'it looked like someone's bad dream.'"

Aretha's debut video, for the song "Freeway of Love," was a sheer cinematic delight. She looked fantastic, with her hair coiffed in a short-cropped and youthful style. The automotive theme of the song, and the lines about taking a ride in a pink Cadillac, were highlighted by the presence of the famous tail-finned automobile. The classic sound of Aretha Franklin in rocking fine form, made this one of the most exciting videos ever filmed.

According to Ken Reynolds, the video was not without its last-minute changes. By 1985 Reynolds had moved to Arista Records, and he recalls that "Brian Grant, who did Donna Summer's 'She Works Hard for the Money' video, also directed Aretha's 'Freeway of Love' video. He had sent proposals over, and we had gone over it with Aretha. She wanted *this* changed, and we'd send it back to him, and he would send it back with the revisions made, and she wanted *that* changed. The director kept accommodating the changes, but there was no problem—he made whatever changes she wanted made in the script.

"The crew was assembled in New York, London, and Los Angeles, and they were all flown into Detroit to shoot this great 'Freeway of Love' video, that was encompassing the Ford Motor factory in Detroit, with Aretha on the assembly line. The treatment looked great, it was fast-moving, with Aretha doing all of these different things. Well, the day that the crew arrived, Aretha suddenly announced, 'Well, I've changed my mind. I don't want to go to the Ford Motor Company, we gonna do it a little differently. My friend has a club, I'm gonna sing at my friend's club, and you can intercut all of the other things.

"So, if you notice in the 'Freeway of Love' video," Reynolds points out, "Aretha's only visuals are done in the club. The outtakes and everything else was done elsewhere. The original script called for Aretha to be in all these places, but at the last minute she changed her mind. But did it effect the video? No. In fact it won several awards, so she obviously knows what she's doing."

"The video was filmed at Doug's Body Shop in Detroit," said Aretha. "It's a very quaint place. Everything in there is a car. The booths where you eat are like semi-cars. They have all the luxuries that the cars originally had in them: the push-button windows, the steering wheel, the radio, everything is there. Because Doug's was car-oriented, and the song was about this pink Cadillac on the freeway, we selected Doug's. In the video, you can see that they passed the General Motors Building, and Detroit being the 'Motor City,' I thought it was quite apropos."

According to Franklin, "The car we used in the video, the pink Cadillac, was Jayne Mansfield's old Cadillac. Mickey Hargitay's name was all over the glove compartment. There is an antique car club here in Detroit, and they gave us the use of the car for the afternoon. They were very, very particular about it: Who was gonna drive it? Who was gonna do this? Who was gonna do that? Of course, being such an investment, I can understand their being cautious about those things. Great car though!"

One of the most exciting aspects of the video was the way Aretha looked in it. She sported a drastically short haircut that looked youthful and hip. "I wore a little punk haircut. I thought it was cute, and, interestingly, I got a lot of compliments from men and women on that particular hairstyle. When I first looked in the mirror I went, 'AAAAHHHH! [a shocked shriek]. I don't know whether I want to go out with this!' But I kind of got used to it, and the more I looked at it, the more I liked it. Then I played with it, and I kind of made it 'me.' So it was cute, it was punk, it was fun.'"

In addition to her fear of air travel, music videos gave Aretha a further reason not to go on concert tours. According to her, "Now [performers] have a chance to be right there in your living room without all those years out on the road. Not that they won't have to face audiences live at some point, but I think videos are a great way for recording artists to be exposed to a lot of people at one time." Her own videos have helped make it possible for her not to leave Detroit.

"Don't say Aretha is making a comeback," she insisted when *Who's Zoomin' Who?* was released, "because I've never been away!" However, on a sales, airplay, and chart-action basis, that is exactly what it represented. It became her biggest-selling album ever. It yielded five Top Forty singles, and gleaned the first Platinum certification of her entire career.

Not only did the disc serve as a treat for the legion of her fans from the 1960s, but its hot, fresh, sassy sound also captured a new audience of young record buyers who had previously considered her a nostalgic legend of days gone by. In many ways, *Who's Zoomin' Who?* performed the same career-revitalizing magic that Tina Turner's *Private Dancer* had done the year before. *Private Dancer* had won Tina her first pair of Grammy Awards as a solo artist, and had likewise brought her to an all-time peak in the music business.

"I'm very happy for Tina and what she accomplished," said Aretha of the obvious parallel, "but we are totally different, so there's no comparison.

"I felt good about what Narada came up with," she explained, "because it was quality music, right into what's happening today, and I wanted to come up with something for the kids. After all, I like to bop too! I really like this stuff. In fact, I think it's some of the best material I've done since the mid-sixties. Don't get me wrong, I really liked *Jump to It* and *Get It Right* and 'Every Girl Wants My Guy' from the sessions with Luther, and some of the other things I've done with Arista—the duet with George Benson, and 'It's My Turn'—but this new album: phew!"

Vince Aletti proclaimed in *Rolling Stone* that "this is an album full of unexpected moves—and from nearly every angle, Aretha is at the top of her form . . . There's enough vocal brilliance here to stun any listener within range." Brian Chin wrote in *The New York Post* that the album marked "the beginning of a new career awakening for her," and Ralph Novak exclaimed in *People* magazine, "Franklin has never sounded better than she does on this album!"

Who's Zoomin' Who? was released in July 1985, and logged fifty-one weeks on *Billboard's* album chart, peaking at Number Thirteen. It was her highest-charting album since *Amazing Grace* in 1972. By September of that year it was certified Gold, and in December it went Platinum in the United States.

The first single released from it, "Freeway of Love," became one of the biggest smashes of the entire summer. In August 1985 it hit Number One on the R&B chart, and Number Three on the pop chart, making it her twentieth Number One R&B hit and her fifteenth Top Ten pop hit. It also marked a career distinction, when the "dance remix" version of the song reached Number One on the "dance music" chart.

The song "Who's Zoomin' Who" was the next single release, peaking at Number Two R&B, Number Seven pop, and Number One on the "dance music" chart. The single became her first back-to-back Top Ten pop smash since the early seventies, and her sixteenth Top Ten pop hit—which tied her with Connie Francis for that distinction.

Three subsequent singles from this LP made it into the Top Thirty, making this the most hit-filled studio album of her career. The singles and their highest chart figures are as follows, "Sisters Are Doin' It for Themselves" (Number Eighteen pop), "Another Night" (Number Nine R&B), and "Ain't Nobody Ever Loved You" (Number Thirty R&B). This was also Aretha's first album to be released simultaneously on compact disc.

According to Clive Davis, the success of the *Who's Zoomin' Who?* album was the result of a constant building process that had begun in 1980. "It was a growing familiarity as to what we were doing together," he explains. "We had a nice hit with 'United Together.' We tried duets with George Benson with 'Love All the Hurt Away.' 'Jump to It" was a giant hit [that] went Number One on the dance charts. We won Grammys, we got up to the Gold, and then we took the big step. After Luther and the two albums we did with him, I then introduced her to Narada. She didn't know who Narada was, and it led to the successful albums we've had with him. The material kept getting better, and the association with Narada worked beautifully. So it built up to that—her first Platinum album ever in her career."

In addition to her multiple triumphs on the record charts, it was also a year of accolades and awards for "Dr. Aretha." The succession of laudatory festivities kicked into high gear when the State of Michigan saluted her twenty-fifth year in show business by declaring her voice a "natural resource." In a ceremony on the steps of the Michigan State Capitol in Lansing, May 23, 1985, was officially proclaimed Aretha Franklin Appreciation Day.

Dressed in a wide-brimmed red hat, a very smart white suit, and a red fox fur piece draped over her shoulder, Aretha looked every inch an elegant international superstar. "I'm especially delighted with the idea of making my voice a Natural Resource of Michigan—being that I am a Michigan girl at heart," Aretha announced to the huge crowd of officials, fans, and press gathered at the capitol.

Presiding over the event, Governor James J. Blanchard spoke of Franklin's attributes: "Anyone who has had a radio on, or a record player, or followed entertainment, or lived in Michigan, or cares about soul, knows the name Aretha Franklin," he said. "She has more awards and Grammys than anyone we know who has won elections."

Earlier in the day, Aretha was present at ceremonies held in both the Michigan State Senate and House of Representatives. Both arms of the government made resolutions to enter into the record the official declaration of Franklin's "natural resource" status. The senate resolution claimed that Aretha "continued to diversify her distinctive style, and it is a mark of genius that she remains an artist's artist in a field often dominated by a lack of permanence with regard to the popularity of styles and performers."

The house resolution stated that, "We look forward to her future hits and are very proud to count her as Michigan's envoy in the music entertainment world."

Representative Nelson Saunders saluted Aretha's distinctive talents: "In recognition for her tremendous performing talents, the Michigan House of Representatives is grateful for the opportunity to honor Aretha Franklin in recognition of her outstanding career as the Queen of Soul. It is only fitting that the Governor and the Michigan State Legislature honor a Michigan citizen who has had such an impact on Detroit, Michigan, the national and international music scenes, the way Aretha Franklin has."

On July 24, 1985, a section of Washington Boulevard, at State Street in Detroit, was officially renamed "Aretha Franklin's Freeway of Love." The ceremony took place at 12:30 at the intersection, and several city officials presided over the event. Arista Records gave away 200 automobile license plates that read "Zoomin'—Aretha Franklin's Freeway of Love." Exactly at 12:30, several radio stations played the song "Freeway of Love" in her honor.

An article in *The Detroit News* lamented that "about the only thing missing will be Aretha, who has a previous engagement." Indeed she was absent.

In an interview conducted at her Bloomfield Hills home that afternoon, Aretha told this author, "Today, yes, the Mayor and the City Council have changed Washington Boulevard, which is one of our better streets in Detroit, to the Freeway of Love. And I *must* get in a pink Cadillac and ride down the Freeway of Love!" she said, laughing.

She also explained that "August the tenth there is gong to be a ceremony. There is going to be another renaming of a street in Detroit, in honor of my dad, the Reverend C. L. Franklin. They are changing Linwood partially to 'C. L. Franklin Boulevard.' We will be at those ceremonies August the tenth. And that is with very much appreciation, and many thanks to Mayor Young, and Miss Erma Henderson of the City Council."

When I asked if there was a current romance in her life, Aretha replied, "Oh absolutely, absolutely. What would life be without romance? And what is romance without the one you love? Right? There's someone that I'm seeing, yes. I prefer not to say who. I think sometimes it's advantageous for people not to know you're dating. At least ladies in the business. Because sometimes the flak that the gentleman gets is really not fair, and it has to be a very, very strong man, and a man who is very secure in who he is—as opposed to who you are, and how the two relate to each other. But sometimes the guys don't get a fair shake, the ones who escort the ladies—the Arethas, the Dianas, the Dionnes, and so on—in the business. So I think it can be very advantageous for people not to know who it is. And I really think it's up to the two of you whether or not you want to say, and whether or not he feels that he can deal with that and 'Hey, that's no sweat, 'cause I'm into you.'"

Obviously, Aretha and her mystery man were still checking each other out before they decided to make their relationship public. She had previously stated that "I've met my share of guys between the ages of thirty and forty-five who have insulted and assaulted my intelligence with their stories and games. When I meet those kind of guys, I say, 'Hello and good-bye!' Now, there are some men who have come through with flying colors!"

The beau who passed the test was later revealed to be Willie Wilkerson, a Detroit fireman whom she'd met quite by accident. Aretha was in downtown Detroit, by the waterfront, when a handsome man who had broken his leg hobbled over to her and asked if she would sign his cast. According to her, "At that time, *Jump to It* had just gone Gold. He'd jumped off a firetruck and broken his leg, so I wrote on his cast, 'Next time don't "Jump to It!"'" It was kind of love at first sight."

Tall and good-looking, Wilkerson is just the kind of man who appealed to Aretha. She proclaimed, "I'm glad that he could make the distinction between the lady and the artist, because a lot of men can't."

Describing him, Franklin says that he's "a real gentleman, and he's *hot!* I get on the phone with my girlfriends and tell them all the details! But I'm not ready to make any major commitments right now in that area. Of course, I never say 'never,' but for now I'm not thinking about getting married again.

"What do I find attractive in a man?" Aretha asks. "To begin with, obviously, physical appearance. The way he carries himself. Confidence. Intellect. His conversation. How he treats me. Good men are scarce as hen's teeth for sure. *Mature* good men are particularly hard to find. But I found one. I like him very much. He likes my cooking very much, and he likes me!"

Since he began dating Aretha, Willie has left the Detroit Fire Department. He is now the owner of his own fleet of taxicabs. Willie says of Aretha, "I know who she is, and I have all the respect in the world for what she's accomplished. But it's still the lady that counts. She's a very warm, very loving woman."

According to a cover story about the couple in *Jet* magazine, "her relationship with Wilkerson had flourished because he is able to separate the celebrity from the earthy woman propped up in front of the television watching soap operas."

Aretha, who believes very strongly in astrology, claims that her Aries birthday and his Capricorn sun sign make for "a fiery match—we're very compatible." She further explains that their relationship is a complete role reversal of his occupation as a firefighter: "[He's] not putting out the fire, he's starting it!"

In January 1986, Aretha made some additions to her list of accolades as the Grammy nominations were announced. She was nominated in two categories: "Freeway of Love" was up for "Best R&B Performance, Female," and "Sisters Are Doin' It for Themselves" with Eurythmics was nominated as "Best R&B Vocal by a Duo, Group or Chorus." The Commodores' "Night Shift" ended up taking the latter award, while Aretha's "Freeway of Love" brought her the twelfth Grammy Award of her career.

In addition to being heard on the radio via her hit records, Aretha also lent her voice to several commercials. In 1985 alone she sang the "Coke Is It" jingle for Coca-Cola, and the "Aren't You Glad" song for Dial soap. For the Dial account, Aretha was signed to a one-year contract for a confidential amount of money. The commercial was produced by Needham Harper Worldwide of Chicago. As was usual for Aretha after 1984, the music tracks were completed in Chicago and her vocals were added in Detroit. In the campaign, Aretha was not identified by name, but the voice was unmistakable. According to Aretha, she was not opposed to doing endorsements. She explained, "Frito-Lay we were going to do, but the negotiations fell through. I didn't turn it down. I certainly eat lots of Frito-Lay corn chips!"

During the summer of 1985, Aretha was talking about starring in a Broadway musical about the life of Bessie Smith. "That is a very real possibility," she said at the time. "Well, it's pro and con. I have the script for *Bessie*, and the producers have flown out for talks with me. The only thing about Broadway that I really don't care for is the night-after-night kind of thing. It's hard work and if you're gonna do it, you have to get in shape, and you have to really stay in shape. I like variety, and I like to move around. So that would be the only drawback I think that I would have there: the monotony of the night-after-night appearance, which I don't particularly care for, unless I'm having a *whole lot* of fun!

"About Bessie Smith—I just saw a very interesting piece of film on her a couple of days ago. I can certainly see what it was that everybody enjoyed about Bessie Smith. And, as I said, I have the script and I'm reading it. It is cracking me up, I must tell you! I'm laying on the floor some nights! It's a beautiful, beautiful script," she claimed. Because of her fear of flying and her disdain for monotony, she never pursued the theatrical offer.

If there were ever tailor-made roles for Aretha to portray on-stage, they are Mahalia Jackson and Bessie Smith. Why Aretha can't discipline herself or challenge herself enough to tackle musicals, or more films is beyond everyone. She is not only cheating her public, but she is cheating herself by not seizing the opportunities that are presented to her. Is she afraid of failure, or is she afraid of success? Everyone seemed to hope that one of her friends in the movie business, like Quincy Jones, Oprah Winfrey, or Whoopie Goldberg, would one day coax her back in front of the movie cameras.

Her first year of not flying cost her several other public appearances as well. "I missed some things that I really wanted to do," Aretha explained.

"Like the Kennedy Center: they honored Lena Horne last year, and she requested that I sing, and I wasn't able to make that. And the Democratic Convention—Reverend Jesse Jackson—when he spoke, I missed that, and of course the *Mahalia* play on Broadway. But look out—the girl is coming!" she promised in 1985.

The year 1986 was slated to mark Franklin's return to the concert halls of America. "The truth is, I missed that special exchange that happened between me and my audience," she claimed as concert dates were announced. She also said that she had conquered her fear of flying, and that she planned to jet from city-to-city for the summer-long tour. She didn't keep either promise.

She was also planning a series of fund-raising concerts to help offset Jesse Jackson's 1984 presidential campaign debt. The concerts were to star Aretha along with Stevie Wonder, Luther Vandross, and Smokey Robinson.

Although the proposed Jesse Jackson fund-raising "megaconcert" never transpired, several solo concert dates were set up for Aretha, and the tickets quickly sold out. On the itinerary was a prestigious return to Radio City Music Hall in New York City. Unfortunately, her fear of flying was far from conquered, and she backed out of most of the dates at the last minute, leaving irate promoters and several thousand disappointed ticket-holders. As the *Boston Herald* later noted, "She canceled her heavily advertised New York dates, and has only appeared at a handful of Midwest halls."

It seemed that if she had to venture more than a couple of miles away from Detroit, the bookings would surely be canceled. Instead of leaving town, she agreed to do a television special for the Showtime cable network. The resulting program, *Aretha!*, was her very first headlining television special. Naturally, the hour-long TV special supplanted the aborted tour of the United States that summer. According to Allen Sabinson, Showtime's senior vice-president in charge of programming, "We are trying to bring to our subscribers the classic vocalists of our time . . . Certainly, Aretha belongs in this category . . . And the fact that she does not do any national concert tours will make it even more special for our viewers."

The special was taped on May 2 and 3, 1986, at Detroit's Music Hall Center for the Performing Arts. The 60-year-old art deco Music Hall was chosen by Aretha. It was her way of thanking the venue for having dedicated two performances of the gospel production *Your Arms Too Short to Box with God*, in 1979 and 1981, as benefits to raise money for her father's hospitalization.

"We gave her creative approval of all elements of the show," says Bonnie Burns, the special's supervising producer. "She picked the songs, the wardrobe, the musicians and she [wanted] to do it in Detroit, because that's her home base. Aretha had been approached for years about doing her own television special, but she declined all offers. I think if they put on an Aretha Franklin special ten years ago, it would have been a big event. Aretha is right at any time."

Aretha's supporting cast included her background group, the Prima Donnas, Clarence Clemons, the sixty-five member Saint James Baptist Church Choir, her brother Cecil Franklin, and her sister Carolyn. The songs she chose to perform in concert truly ran the gamut of her entire career, and included a three song-gospel fest with Carolyn, Cecil, and the choir, three songs from her Columbia days, five of her Atlantic hits, and "Freeway of Love" and "Who's Zoomin' Who."

Aretha looked "hot" for her entrance—in a beautiful, backless, beaded red dress, and wrapped in a full-length feather coat. She began the show with a peppy version of "Can't Turn You Loose," which crackled with excitement. Especially memorable were three rarely performed songs taken from her early-1960s Columbia albums: "Won't Be Long," "Try a Little Tenderness," and "Rock-A-Bye Your Baby with a Dixie Melody." The classics from her Atlantic days, however, succeeded in varying degrees. While "(You Make Me Feel Like) A Natural Woman" received a smolderingly soulful rendition, "Respect" and "Chain of Fools" suffered from uninspiringly dull over-orchestration. "Who's Zoomin' Who" lacked punch, but "Freeway of Love" benefited from Clarence Clemons' guest instrumental and inspired Aretha to deliver a full-throttle version of the hit song. The show finished off with the gospel segment, which rounded out the hour, and helped to display another facet of Franklin's talent.

An especially touching moment in the show came when Aretha spoke to the audience about a song that her father used to sing to her when she was a child. The song was "Look to the Rainbow," and before she delivered the beautiful ballad, she dedicated the song to her four sons. She had her son Teddy stand up and take a bow, explaining, "He's graduating this June from college—so you know I'm a proud mama."

The obvious problem with an Aretha Franklin concert performance is that it is impossible for her to sing every one of her hits. While "Respect" and "I Never Love a Man (The Way I Love You)" are mandatory inclusions, several hits are inevitably omitted. Considering the limitations of a single hour, this special at least touched on as many sides of her music as possible.

Executives from Showtime were reportedly disappointed with her performance on the special. One production assistant with the cable network reveals, "After it was all over, the word around Showtime was not good. We kept saying, 'Aretha phoned it [her performance] in.' It's like she'd committed [herself] to doing this, but she was really not interested in doing it. Her costumes were especially bad. She was wearing this costume that kept falling off her shoulder, and it was embarrassing. What she was wearing—it was like this tank-top thing, and [her breasts were] falling out. I realize she is a big lady, but she shouldn't be wearing tank tops!" Aretha still had not given up those tops designed for smaller woman.

"The people around her are afraid to tell her that she looks horrible in some of the outfits that she chooses," claims one of her business associates from Detroit. "It is really a shame, because she is such a wonderful woman. People are scared to tell her anything critical, even though it is for her own good. It is sad, because she ends up looking silly instead of sophisticated or fashionable."

That same summer, Aretha appeared on another television special, *Motown on Showtime: The Temptations and The Four Tops*. Franklin was seen sitting at the piano in a Detroit sound stage, harmonizing with Levi Stubbs and the Four Tops. Together they reminisced candidly about the Tops' performance at Aretha's wedding in the late seventies, and they harmonized on the song "Isn't She Lovely." In many ways this brief segment with the Four Tops revealed more about Aretha—the private person—than her entire hour on-stage at the Music Hall. Surrounded by her old friends, she appeared much more relaxed and informal. It was also a pleasure to see her as the accomplished pianist that she is, displaying her talents at the keyboards with the casual ease of a living room sing-along.

Who's Zoomin' Who? was such an enormous success that when the time came for her next release, the logical plan was to return to the same winning formula. Again, the album was made up of nine songs, with the production duties divided in the same way: six cuts produced by Narada Michael Walden, two produced by Aretha, and one by a big-name rock & roll star—Keith Richards of the Rolling Stones. Adhering to the winning format, her 1986 album also contained two superstar duets. This time around it was George Michael and Larry Graham who each shared the microphone on one song apiece with her.

Confusingly, the album was titled *Aretha*, as had been the title of her 1980 Arista debut LP. However, the results were far better. Although distinctly different from *Zoomin'*, the *Aretha* 1986 album was a continuation of the high-quality music that *Who's Zoomin' Who?* had contained, while breaking some new ground.

The first single released from *Aretha* was a remake of one of the Rolling Stones' greatest hits, "Jumpin' Jack Flash." This hard-rocking version of the song was produced by Keith Richards, with the group's guitarist, Ron Wood, playing guitar on the cut. According to Aretha, when the pair of Stones came to Detroit to work on the song, it was the first time she had met either one of them. "I'd met Mick [Jagger]," she explained. "When I was in London, he came backstage and we had a nice little chat. He's very down-to-earth. And then Mick and Ahmet [Ertegun] are very close, so of course I'd run into him now and then."

Although Mick had pursued solo projects away from the Rolling Stones, Keith had taken longer to find his confidence away from the group. He claims that producing the cut for Franklin's album was just the assignment that he was looking for. "Before the Aretha thing, I think I was terrified of doing something myself. Now I know I can," says Richards.

Not only was the song used on Aretha's album, but it was also used as the title track for the Whoopie Goldberg film of the same name. In fact, Goldberg, Richards, and Wood all came to Detroit to film the music video that accompanied the song. In it Aretha wore an outrageous, tiger-striped, knicker-length jumpsuit, a leather jacket, and a wild punk hair do—complete with an askew ponytail hanging off the right side.

According to Clive Davis, this project was one that he and Aretha had a difference of opinion on. "I saw the movie—without the music—and they had asked for Aretha to do the title song," he recalls. "I was not that impressed with the movie. I liked it a little bit, but I had more misgivings about the film. So I told her, 'I think it's a mediocre film.' But she was intrigued with working with Whoopie. So, she said, 'Look, I understand what you're saying, but I'll do it.' So then I came up with the Keith Richards idea, proposed it to Keith [as producer], and he said yes."

When "Jumpin' Jack Flash" was released, it peaked at Number Twenty-two on the pop charts and Number Twenty on the R&B chart. The next single, "Jimmy Lee," produced by Narada Michael Walden hit Number Twenty-eight on the pop chart, and Number Two on the R&B chart, in February 1987. However, it was the third single that performed the magic trick of hitting Number One not only on the American pop and R&B charts, but internationally.

The song was the superstar duet to end them all—Aretha Franklin and George Michael. Michael, fresh from a hot streak as half of the vocal duet Wham!, had begun doing guest appearances on other people's albums, while he was planning his debut solo LP. The duet performance of Aretha and George was a perfect vehicle for both singers. It exposed Aretha to the young record buyers that Michael was attracting, and Aretha lent the kind of legitimacy to George's career that the pop star lacked. Beyond the demographics of the single's marketing, the song "I Knew You Were Waiting (For Me)" was simply an excellent performance by all parties involved.

In April 1987, exactly twenty years after the release of her first Number One pop smash, "Respect," Aretha was back where she belonged—on top of the charts around the world. With "I Knew You Were Waiting (For Me)," Lady Soul scored her seventeenth Top Ten pop hit, breaking the previous record of sixteen which was set by Connie Francis and her 1962 hit, "Vacation." But then, hit-making and record breaking were becoming a way of life for Aretha.

"The George Michael project, I put together," says Clive Davis. "He called me after he left Wham! He called me for the sole and explicit purpose of my finding a song, picking the producer, and him working with Aretha—and that's what I did. I called her up and recommended it—I explained to her who George was. In contemporizing her, and keeping her contemporary, it was beneficial, really, for both artists. For him, he was looking to establish individual credibility, and that he was not just a pop artist. And, for her, she was able to reach a teenage audience that was important for her to be known by. So the difficulty was finding a song. As luck would have it, Tom Sturgess of Chrysalis Music got 'I Knew You Were Waiting (For Me),' and sent it to me. I just thought it would be perfect as a duet, and I sent it to both artists, and they loved it. And that's how it happened."

For George Michael, recording with Aretha was a dream come true. According to him, "Quite simply, she's the best! As much as I love a lot of other female artists, there's no one who touches her."

In addition to containing the Number One smash "I Knew You Were Waiting (For Me)," the 1986 album *Aretha* was certified Gold, and also yielded several more solid performances. It included a song that she and Larry Graham had originally recorded as a duet for *Who's Zoomin' Who?*, called "If You Need My Love Tonight," which was saved for this album. There was also the rocking Top Forty R&B hit "Rock-A-Lott," and the beautiful Aretha-produced ballad "Look to the Rainbow." (The latter was written in the 1940s by E. Y. "Yip" Harburg and Burton Lane. It was Harburg's follow-up song to his *Wizard of Oz* signature song, "Over the Rainbow," which he had written in the 1930s with Harold Arlen. These are two of Aretha's all-time favorite songs from her childhood. Since she had recorded "Over the Rainbow" on her first Columbia album in 1960, it was only fitting that she should come full circle to record the sequel in 1986.)

To complete the package, the album cover was a portrait of Aretha by Andy Warhol. It was one of his last pieces of artwork, as he suddenly died in early 1987. Warhol had once done a series of four portraits called "Reigning Queens," which included Queen Elizabeth of England and Queen Beatrix of the Netherlands. How fitting that he should add the Queen of Soul to his gallery of masterpieces before he died.

To fully underscore Aretha's 1980s resurgence, in 1987 her first video cassette, *Aretha: Ridin' on the Freeway*, was released by RCA / Columbia Home Video. It contained her video performances of "Freeway of Love,"

"Another Night," "Jimmy Lee," "Jumpin' Jack Flash," and "I Knew You Were Waiting (For Me)." The supporting cast naturally included George Michael, Keith Richards, Whoopie Goldberg, Ron Wood, and Clarence Clemons.

Arif Mardin, who worked with Aretha at Atlantic and at Arista, was especially pleased with her career comeback. "She was extremely successful with Atlantic, but then, like many good marriages, sometimes things get stale," he points out. "So Clive Davis, obviously, is a very astute record man. He should get an award for the job he did with the acts he has—especially the ladies like Aretha, Dionne, and, of course, Whitney [Houston]. He developed the artists to the right point."

Jerry Wexler likewise claims, "I'm just overjoyed that she came back with such a tremendous blast, and returned as a big artist again, after being dormant for so long."

Adding to Aretha's growing list of awards, in January 1987 she became the first woman to be inducted into the Rock & Roll Hall of Fame. "Well, the doors are open, girls!" Aretha laughed with delight at the distinction. "Seriously, I thought it was fabulous, and I'm delighted to be held in that esteem." Although she didn't get into a plane (or train, for that matter) to pick up her citation, she sent her brother Cecil, and was thrilled with the honor.

The Rock & Roll Hall of Fame Foundation was formed in 1984 by a group of music industry executives, to salute the achievements of singers, groups, and musicians who have shaped rock history. A group of 200 rock and pop music experts—including critics and producers—nominate and then vote on the Hall of Fame's annual inductees. To be eligible for consideration, a recording artist must have released his or her first record twenty-five years ago. The first awards ceremony took place in 1986, and the likes of Elvis Presley, Buddy Holly, Chuck Berry, James Brown, and Sam Cooke were honored.

Aretha was indicated into the Rock & Roll Hall of Fame the second year. Also honored at the black-tie gala that January at the Waldorf-Astoria Hotel in New York City were a stellar list of co-inductees, including Marvin Gaye, Fats Domino, Ray Charles, Little Richard, B. B. King, Jackie Wilson, Bo Diddley, the Coasters, Joe Turner, Muddy Waters,

Clyde McPhatter, and Aretha's childhood friend Smokey Robinson. "It was certainly a milestone in my career!" she exclaimed.

In March 1988, Aretha had to start making more trophy space in her living room. When the thirtieth annual Grammy Awards were presented at Radio City Music Hall in New York City, she took her thirteenth and fourteenth Grammys, to become the female artist with the greatest number of the awards in any category. The song "I Knew You Were Waiting (For Me)" won as the "Best R&B Performance by a Duo, Group or Chorus," and her 1986 album *Aretha* won as the "Best R&B Vocal Performance, Female." Her thirteenth award beat Ella Fitzgerald's number of Grammys, and Aretha's fourteenth surpassed the record previously held by opera singer Leontyne Price.

Again, Aretha remained in Detroit for the awards. She hadn't traveled any farther than Chicago or Cleveland in several years, and she wasn't about to break her self-imposed exile for a couple more trophies—especially since she already had a dozen of them in her home.

Did Aretha celebrate that triumphant Grammy night by partying all night long in Detroit? No, she stayed in her Bloomfield Hills home with her boyfriend, Willie Wilkerson, and viewed the show on television. According to her, "I had a nice pot of Great Northern beans on and some cornbread, and we just enjoyed eating and watching the show." That's Aretha Franklin—living legend, and undisputed queen of the house!

CHAPTER NINE

THE SPIRIT OF DETROIT

Most Detroiters in show business have to venture out of Los Angeles or New York City to find work—but if you're the Queen of Soul, the work comes to you. Since Aretha generally refuses to leave the Motor City, the producers of all of her projects now have to work around her geographic demands. That suits Aretha just fine; not only does she get to enjoy the constant comfort of her two Detroit residences, but she is actively promoting the facilities of her hometown. Her travel boycott has focused more music-industry attention on Detroit than has anything else since the ascendancy of Motown Records in the 1960s.

"Detroit has, and the suburban areas have, everything that any other metropolitan major city has today," said Aretha in 1985. "And I've just about seen it all! Beautiful suburban areas: Bloomfield, Birmingham, Wabeek—it's gorgeous. The fishing is great if you like to fish. There are lakes everywhere. Gee, there must be at least seven lakes in this area. And Mayor [Coleman] Young has just done a fabulous, fabulous job with the waterfront downtown. You have River Front [a downtown apartment complex], which is just gorgeous, and there are a number of new constructions going up along the waterfront. Honey, listen, Detroit is coming into its own, and absolutely arriving in a big, big way!"

By moving to Detroit in the eighties, did Aretha miss the so-called fast lane of the show-business whirl in Los Angeles? According to her at the time, "I guess what I miss the most about L.A. is the convenience of running over to *The Tonight Show* or to *Merv Griffin* or to *Solid Gold*, and the convenience of doing those [television] shows—and Fat Burgers!" she exclaimed, plugging L.A.'s most famous hamburger joint.

She was quite happy with her uncomplicated life in the Detroit suburbs. Her white, six-bedroom Colonial house stands on a three-acre lot with a swimming pool and a vegetable garden. "I'm the lady next door, I'm a neighborly type of person," she explained. "I have a garden, and we're eating fresh out of the garden with no additives and preservatives, and all of that sort of thing. I had greens a couple of weeks ago, just prior to going to see Luther Vandross' show, and I must tell you, between the greens and Vandross, I had a great evening! What one of my friends would call 'a leading evening.' In the garden I've got mustards [mustard greens] and turnips mixed, and I have green tomatoes . . . green tomatoes? What other color would they be before they get red?" she laughed. "I have corn on the cob, I have squash, I have string beans, I have almost everything that any good garden should have, and I have a bit of a green thumb."

Although this statement might sound as though she has cut down on her favorite high-calorie food to concentrate on fresh vegetables, that is hardly the case. The second half of the 1980s witnessed Aretha at one of her heaviest phases. While she grows her own greens and tomatoes, they merely garnish plates of spareribs, ham hocks, and her butter-rich Chicken Italiano.

What was her life like in the suburbs, circa 1985? "I get up about 11:00, 11:30 a.m. Then it's the soaps: *The Young and the Restless* first. Soap operas until three-o'clock and what I call 'kitchen talk.' I'm in the living room and my housekeeper, Katherine, is in the kitchen, and we're screaming back and forth, 'Did you see that?' I like the nighttime soaps too."

"[I] play tennis—I've got a mean backhand, a two-fisted one like Chris Evert's. I swim a little. I like to go to the driving range. I crochet. I've made a number of skirts, berets, various articles. I like to cook and I like to boogie down at L'Esprit or Club Taboo here in town. I love ballet, studied it in New York and in L.A. And I love the fights. I used to watch them as a child, with my dad. I go way back with them," she says.

In spite of her constantly remaining overweight, Aretha keeps socially active. She has become known around town as quite a hostess, and she enjoys giving elaborate parties at her home. "I have some pretty good ones," she admitted. "One of the last ones was a Hawaiian luau. We had white sand shipped in—put it everywhere, three, four feet deep around the pool, so it felt like you were actually on the beach. And we had Hawaiian dancers, the pig on the spit."

In addition to parties, soap operas, gardening, and French lessons, fashion is high on Aretha's list of interests. Ever since she moved to New York City in 1960, she has always been crazy for clothes. "When I first started, I wore Ceil Chapman gowns," she recalls. "I've been wondering for years what happened to the Ceil Chapman line of clothing. My manager took me to her place on Park Avenue right at the beginning, to pick out things that I liked, or that she thought I looked well in. So I was wearing designers right in the beginning."

Although she was still in love with the current fashion scene, she was also frustrated that the major designers only cut their lines up to size twelve, when she—at the time—wore a 14. Calvin Klein especially frustrated her, because she would love to wear his designs. "Valentino is another one who will only cut up to 12, I guess," she sighed, exhaling a lungful of smoke from her Kool cigarette. "And Valentino has some of the most chic clothing that I have ever laid eyes on. I became enraged every time I see the Valentino line. Every once in a while I can get a De La Renta, depending on how it's cut. Then again, he's like Valentino."

Her fashion dilemma frustrated her so much that she made a public plea, in the mid-eighties, in the fashion bible *Women's Wear Daily*, addressed to Calvin Klein. "Please," she implored, "if you won't do a 14—and you're making the girls who wear 14 very unhappy—please do a special order!"

One fashion industry insider reveals that Aretha has gone so far as to contact Calvin Klein to try to place a personal order to her specifications. Often celebrities will do that, and then negotiate a special rate of payment for wearing a designer's fashions. Unfortunately, Aretha's request was met with a crisp refusal.

According to this inside source, "She contacted Paul Wilmot, who is the vice president in charge of public relations at Calvin Klein. He's the one who handles all the personal orders for people like Joan Rivers and Bianca Jagger and [socialite] Mercedes Kellogg. Well, Aretha called twice, like two seasons—once in the fall, and once in the spring. She was interested in looking at the collection and possibly buying things from it. Calvin doesn't do personal 'custom orders,' but people will call and he'll have them in, and they'll look at the collection, and they'll pick things out, and then they work it out. Paul Wilmot decided that Aretha was *not* the Calvin Klein image, so they were not interested in dressing her.

"The two things that Aretha was interested in—one of them was a shearling miniskirt that made the *W* [magazine] 'Fashion Disasters' section, and the other was a stretch lace, floor-length evening gown. I don't know if she wanted it in black or white, but either was totally inappropriate— stretch lace that Paulina [Porzikova—a svelte fashion model] could barely get into—let alone Aretha! He just said [to her], 'We're sorry, but I don't think we're gonna have time.'"

Throughout her entire career, Aretha's fashion sense has paralleled the tale of *The Emperor's New Clothes*. Like the Emperor's subjects, who were afraid to inform their leader that he was stark naked, the Queen of Soul's confidantes are either unaware of her status as a "fashion victim," or they are afraid to hurt her feelings. Someone that she trusts ought to have nerve enough to tell her that she looks foolish squeezed into outfits designed for women half her size.

In the early 1980s, fascinated with the idea of creating her own line of clothes, Aretha went so far as to design several outfits. Before her fear of flying occurred, she set up meetings with a couple of top designers in the business, and planned to discuss marketing ideas. The designers were not impressed. "I was supposed to come out with a line of clothing, and I made a couple of trips to New York to talk to various designers and their managers there. I talked to Willi Smith. I put in calls to Stephen Burrows, but nothing really came of the meeting. I don't quite understand—in a way I do, and in a way I don't. They rather seem to be apprehensive about the coupling for some reason. Didn't sound very secure in who they were. I'm really not sure, so I'd really rather not say. But I have these illustrations drawn up. I had a young lady in Los Angeles do them for me, and of course they're dated now. But I might do some new sketches. I designed a T-shirt dress, long before Norma Kamali came out with it. And I saw a number of other things in *Vogue* and *Bazaar* that I had sketched, and they had no way of seeing my sketches, but I know, prior to their coming out with them, my sketches were first. So I think I would have been in front of them. And, hey—a second career? Why not design?" she laughs.

Regardless of her confidence in her own fashion sense, the press continues to question her taste in clothes. Showing a photo of Tina Turner wearing a miniskirt and Aretha in a minidress, *USA Today* ran an article on the 1987 mini-craze. While the article claimed that Turner could wear anything she wanted and still look fantastic, underneath Aretha's photo the caption read, "Would the first lady of soul flunk our mini test?" Apparently, the answer was "yes."

Another of her passions is horses. When she was married to Glynn Turman, some of his equestrian enthusiasm rubbed off on her. He had enjoyed raising and riding Arabian horses. When she was asked at the time if she was a horseback rider, she quipped, "I ride, all right—limos, my Alfa Romeo, anything with four wheels!"

When she moved to Detroit, she found that she had the time to develop an interest in horses. The only other person in show business that Aretha knew who was really into horses was Wayne Newton. According to her, "I was interested in buying some thoroughbred horses to run. Not for the big stakes like Belmont or anything, but to run at DRC (Detroit Race Course) or Hazel Park. I knew he had horses, so I called him about that." Aretha and Wayne became quite good friends due to their shared interest in horses.

Aretha's stable was started with a male, whom she named Don Juan. "He is a beautiful horse, Don Juan," she explained, "Very well-mannered; he struts his stuff, he sidesteps, he curtseys, and he prances backwards. He is an equestrian horse. So now I'm buying a female brood mare, Arabian, and a couple of little foals, boy and girl. A couple of thoroughbreds too. I'm into siring horses now."

In addition to recording all of her post-1983 albums in Detroit, Aretha does all of her television tapings there as well. In 1986, when Dick Clark wanted Aretha to appear on his annual *American Music Awards* telecast, he had to arrange for a special satellite hookup to present her live from her hometown. Between the single and video versions of "Freeway of Love," Franklin was nominated for four of the awards, and she ultimately won in two different categories: "Favorite Soul / R&B Video, Female" and "Favorite Soul / R&B Single, Female." Accepting the first award, she was shown on camera in Detroit, in a dressing room at the Premier Center, wearing a minidress and a sculptured New Wave hairdo. "I'd like to thank the record buyers and all of you for getting out on the 'Freeway of Love' with me. I love you—you know I do!" she said accepting the first award. The second time around, she was fighting back tears when she said, "I would like to accept it in memory of my dad, Reverend C. L. Franklin."

Also live from the Premier Center, Aretha performed her hit "Another Night," wearing one of her more bizarre outfits. She began the number wrapped in a full-length black velvet coat with half-sleeves and an enormous collar that came up from behind her, forming a glittering shell of rhinestones that surrounded her entire head. It looked like something that Darth Vader would wear to Mardi Gras. When she removed the coat mid-song, she revealed a backless, bare-shouldered dress with an elaborately designed pattern of silver, copper, and brown sequins. Jumping around on-stage during the bouncy up-tempo song, she gave the satellite audience of millions of rock and soul fans an ample view of the Queen of Soul in action. Aretha's performance was wonderful. She was animated and alive, and her outfit only added to the outrageous quality of the production number.

The show was produced the year that "We Are the World" was eligible for awards, and it was used to close the telecast. For the finale of the show, hostess Diana Ross invited members of the Los Angeles Shrine Theater audience to join her on-stage, to sing a mega-version of the all-star choral song. On-stage with Ross were Whitney Houston, Stevie Wonder, Smokey Robinson, Kim Carnes, Harry Belafonte, Julian Lennon, Huey Lewis, and a sea of singing superstars. Also on-stage with her was Michael Jackson (and his date of the evening, Elizabeth Taylor). Since there were several simultaneous satellite hookups around the world, the song "We Are the World" was also sung by Aretha in Detroit, by Johnny Cash in Tucson, and by Paul McCartney in London. It was quite a feat to mount this global sing-along. Unfortunately, because of the several seconds of satellite delay, Aretha, Cash and McCartney were all singing out of sync—but the very idea of Aretha harmonizing with Paul McCartney, Michael Jackson, and Elizabeth Taylor made for the most amazing television appearances of her entire career.

In January 1987, TV cameras captured a historic and soulful event, when Aretha Franklin and James Brown appeared together for the very first time in their long and glorious careers. The event was a television salute to Brown with several glittering superstars of soul, titled *A Soul Session: James Brown and Friends*, and it was shown on the Cinemax cable network. Although the resulting special is an awesome display of several soulful legends in action, the taping was not without its problems—namely a rift between Aretha and James.

When Tisha Fein was asked by Cinemax to produce the special, she was thrilled by the prospect of fashioning a tribute to James Brown. The most "special" guest she could think of having on the program was Aretha. Fein had been friendly with Aretha and her brother Cecil since she had produced the *Midnight Special* tribute to her in the 1970s. Tisha had subsequently worked with Aretha on several of *The Grammy Awards* telecasts.

"*The Soul Session* was something I was hired to produce with James Brown," Fein explains, "but it was my idea, putting Aretha in it and moving it to Detroit. It seemed like a good way to combine soul with the place it came from, with a couple of people who had never worked together before."

The taping took place at Club Taboo in downtown Detroit, which Aretha reportedly co-owns with a group of local friends. "She suggested it," says Fein of the location, "and it was a great club. Since she is part-owner of it, she was like the queen of the club. The audiences just went crazy for her. I used her club, and all of her sisters as background singers." Also on the bill for the taping were Wilson Pickett, Joe Cocker, Billy Vera, and Robert Palmer.

Fein's only comment about the reported battle between the Queen of Soul and the Godfather or Soul was: "James and Aretha had never sung together, and I don't think they'd ever sing together again. She was terrific, and wonderful, but there was no love lost between them. He wasn't really the gentleman that he could have been."

However, a behind-the-scenes production assistant says that the "4-1-1" on "the Godfather vs. the Queen" was one of competitiveness on Brown's part. Everything had gone without a hitch during rehearsals on Friday afternoon, January 9.

"It was like a friendly competition," musical director Dan Hartman recalls of the rehearsals. "I think they happened to really love each other, because of what they both stand for, even though James needed his bit of the spotlight. And, certainly, Aretha deserves and got her part of the spotlight. They just think the world of each other, because they sort of created this thing—this 'soul' image. I saw [that] at the rehearsals, when James Brown came on-stage, he was there first, just moments before she stepped up on-stage. Then she stepped up, and it was just the neatest feeling to see the two of them together. It was a special moment."

According to Hartman, Aretha kept the conversation to a minimum. "She said maybe two words the whole time, like 'Ummm-hmmm, okay.' That kind of thing. We were saying, 'Well, we'll do this song here,' going over the work, and she said, 'Ummm-hmmm, ummm-hmmm, okay.' And I said, 'Why don't you run through your numbers?' And she said, 'Okay.' Then, when she sings—her rehearsals were as astonishing as any of her greatest performances on record. She just came up on-stage in street clothes, and no big 'do' or anything, you know, and just walked up and said 'hello' and was introduced to everybody. She was very cool, and very smooth. When she sang at the sound check I was amazed, Aretha is a smooth pro—she's the quintessential soul singer."

The Friday-night taping featured only Brown and Wilson Pickett. Together they presented a sixteen-song, one hour-and-forty-minute show for an enthusiastic crowd. On Saturday, Franklin, Palmer, Cocker, and Vera were added to the lineup to tape their solos, and duets with James. Although their rehearsals had proceeded smoothly, some sort of friction apparently developed between James and Aretha.

According to the production assistant, "James was definitely intimidated by Aretha—absolutely. Especially because it was her club and it was her town. He turned her monitors down when she was singing, which is a really shitty thing to do to a singer. It was really a mean thing for him to have done. It was apparent to people in the audience—[that there was a] rift between them. However, after careful editing, it was still magic what they did together on-stage."

"The only thing that upsets Aretha on-stage is if she can't hear herself," says Barbara Shelley. She recalls that "the sound check was great, but by the time Aretha got on-stage—and the sound was completely off—she went crazy! She kept signaling me and Cecil to come on over. So we walked out of our seats and went right up to the stage. Cecil said she was threatening to leave the stage if the sound wasn't fixed. Quite honestly, there were a hundred people in the crew, hovering all over the place, so there was no way that any one of us had any control over anything. She was extremely upset when she came off the stage."

To watch the television special, one would never guess that there were any major problems between the two soul stars. What ultimately did appear on the TV screen was Aretha's red-hot performance of "Do Right Woman, Do Right Man." In fact, her delivery was far more soulful than it had been on her overly orchestrated 1986 Showtime special. It's no wonder Brown was threatened by Franklin. He was supposed to return to center stage to do a medley of that song with his hit "It's a Man's World," just as they had done in rehearsal. Without informing anyone, he decided to cut the song, and instead asked a startled Aretha to slow-dance with him while the band vamped the music to "It's a Man's World."

Gary Graff of *The Detroit Free Press* recalls being very disappointed by what he witnessed at the TV taping. "They looked like they weren't enjoying being with each other," he says of the James-and-Aretha segment. "You've got to remember, James is the consummate showman, he'll put a smiling face on anything, and he did not look happy. If you watch the special, it doesn't look like there is any chemistry there, or any communication. They barely look at each other. It was kind of nasty."

Whatever the problem was between Brown and Franklin, it seemed to be dispelled after Aretha sang a solo version of her then-current hit, "Jimmy Lee." James came on-stage again, and the pair sang a duet version of his 1964 hit "Please, Please, Please," without a major conflict. For the finale, James and Aretha were joined by Wilson Pickett, Billy Vera, Robert Palmer, Joe Cocker, and Dan Hartman. The cast of rock and soul stars proceeded to tear into an exciting version of James Brown's 1980s hit "Living in America."

ARETHA
Through the Years

By the mid-eighties Aretha was back to making hits in a continuous winning streak, including: "Another Night," "Who's Zoomin' Who," "Sisters Are Doin' It For Themselves," "Rock-A-Lott," and "Jimmy Lee." *(Photo: Arista Records / MJB Photo Archives)*

Aretha Franklin has had an amazing recording career that has lasted over fifty years. She grew up in a household where singing stars like Dinah Washington and Sam Cooke would visit. She began singing in the choir of her father's church in Detroit, Michigan, and recorded her first album, *Songs of Faith*, when she was just fourteen years old. *(Photo: James J. Kriegsmann / Rhino Records / MJB Photo Archives)*

In 1960, when Aretha was eighteen years old, she was signed to Columbia Records, where she started her long career as the singer of pop standards and jazz. The man who signed her to the record label was legendary jazz producer John Hammond. *(Photo: Columbia Records / MJB Photo Archives)*

While Columbia was promoting her records, they carefully kept facts about Aretha's personal life out of the public's eye. Her fans had no idea that she had already given birth to two children by the time she was eighteen. *(Photo: Columbia Records / MJB Photo Archives)*

Aretha's father, Reverend C. L. Franklin, in 1963. He was not only famous for the fiery sermons he delivered in his downtown Detroit church, but he was also quite a controversial character as well. He fathered the baby of a thirteen-year-old girl in his congregation while he was married to Aretha's mother. *(Photo: AP / Wide World)*

By 1967, Aretha Franklin had earned her right to sing the blues. She spent most of her young life dominated by the men in her life, including her father, and her first husband Ted White. Several sources claim that White physically abused her during their marriage. *(Photo: Atlantic Records / Vince Aletti Collection)*

Once signed to Atlantic Records, Aretha unleashed the power of her voice that she had been holding inside during her jazz-singing years at Columbia. Starting with the songs "I Never Loved a Man the Way I Love You" and "Respect" she became a huge overnight sensation on the record charts. *(Photo: James J. Kriegsmann / Atlantic Records / MJB Photo Archives)*

Starting in 1967, Aretha's initial recordings at Atlantic Records yielded one Top Ten hit after another, including: "(You Make Me Feel Like) A Natural Woman," "Chain of Fools," "Think," "Baby I Love You," and "The House That Jack Built." *(Photo: Rhino Records / MJB Photo Archives)*

In the late sixties Aretha seemed to be at her most focused and carefree when she was in the recording studio in New York City. Once she was there she could concentrate on her music, and temporarily forget about her physically and mentally abusive marriage to Ted White. *(Photo: Chuck Stewart)*

When she was appearing in Chicago in 1968 a local disc jockey by the name of Purvis Spann walked on-stage, placed a crown on her head, and declared that Aretha was the "Queen of Soul." That name has stuck ever since. *(Photo: Charles Moniz Collection)*

Jerry Wexler (left), Aretha, and her brother Cecil Franklin (right). It was Wexler who was responsible for giving Aretha's career a new direction and focus. He wanted to make sure that she not only had relevance on the R&B charts, but was also embraced by the rock & roll audience as well. *(Photo: Vince Aletti Collection)*

Aretha Franklin has always been fascinated with ancient Egypt. She was in her Queen Nefertiti phase on October 9, 1970, when she appeared on the *This is Tom Jones* television series. Together, Aretha and Tom sang hot duet versions of her hit "See Saw," and his signature song "It's Not Unusual" on the show. *(Photo: ABC-TV / MJB Photo Archives)*

On March 14, 1972, Aretha won a Grammy Award for her recording of "Bridge over Troubled Water." Backstage she was surrounded by The Righteous Brothers: Bill Medley (left) and Bobby Hatfield (right). *(Photo: AP / Wide World)*

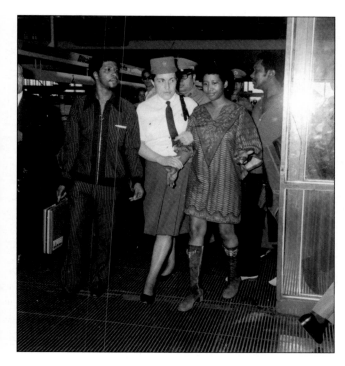

Aretha was taken into custody at the airport in Rome, Italy, June 28, 1971. She was accused of breach of contract when she suddenly cancelled a concert appearance. Franklin has a career-long reputation for cancelling engagements at the last minute.
(Photo: AP / Wide World)

In the early 1970s Aretha produced two of the most successful albums of her career at Atlantic Records: *Young, Gifted and Black*, and her return to gospel with *Amazing Grace*. Both albums won her Grammy Awards.
(Photo: Atlantic Records / MJB Photo Archives)

<< Aretha Franklin was at her thinnest phase in the early seventies, as this photo from Radio City Music Hall in 1973 illustrates. She was paying close attention to her diet, and her live-in boyfriend at the time, Ken Cunningham, encouraged her to stay in shape. *(Photo: Chuck Pulin / Star File)*

After Jerry Wexler left Atlantic Records in 1975, Aretha's recording career had fallen into a slump. Her 1976 *Sparkle* album paired the diva with producer Curtis Mayfield. Together they created a fresh-sounding concept record that contained Franklin's most successful music of the late 1970s. *(Photo: Atlantic Records / MJB Photo Archives)* >>

<< In the late seventies Aretha starting putting on extra weight, and took to wearing unflattering tube tops, like this one she wore on the cover of her 1977 *Sweet Passion* album. While the sound of disco dominated the record charts, Aretha seemed to lose her musical direction. *(Photo: Atlantic Records / Mark Bego Collection)*

On April 12, 1978, Aretha walked down the aisle with her second husband, actor Glynn Turman. The ceremony took place at New Bethel Baptist Church in Detroit, where they were married by her father, Reverend C. L. Franklin. *(Photo: AP / Wide World)*

Five days after their wedding in Detroit, on April 17, 1978, Aretha and Glynn had a reception at a hotel in Los Angeles. Aretha's youngest son, eight-year-old Kecalf (left), looks on in awe. *(Photo: AP / Wide World)*

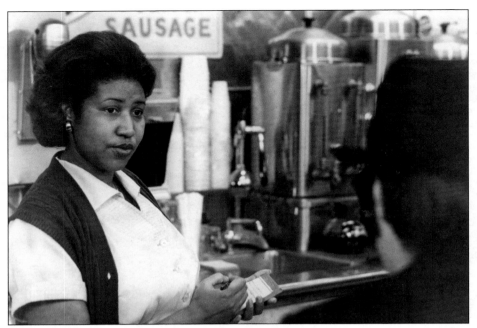

In the 1980 film *The Blues Brothers*, Aretha Franklin made her screen acting debut. She played a sassy waitress in a diner, who warns her man that he had better "Think" before he considers walking out on her!
(Photo: Universal Studios / Mark Bego Collection)

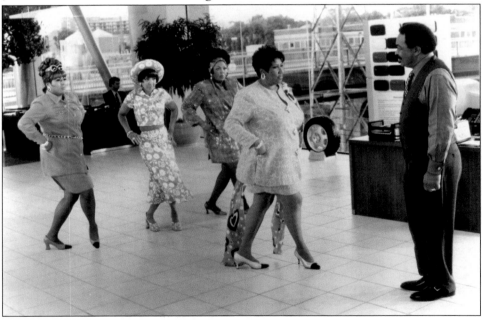

In the 1998 film *The Blues Brothers 2000*, Aretha reprised her role of "Mrs. Murphy." However, this time around her character had traded in her diner, and now she was the owner of a high-profile car dealership. Here she sings a revamped version of one of her trademark hits, which was rewritten to become: "R-E-S-P-E-C-T."
(Photo: Universal Studios / MJB Photo Archives)

Aretha's love of low-cut gowns caused her problems throughout the years with television producers, and with the art directors at Arista Records. To retaliate, Franklin showed up at one public event in a men's tuxedo, and a fur coat. *(Photo: Charles Moniz Collection)*

Once Aretha signed with Arista Records, Clive Davis made it his game plan to find the right songs, as well as record producers who understood Franklin's strengths, and who knew the changing music scene of the 1980s. *(Photo: Arista Records / MJB Photo Archives)*

Arista Records president Clive Davis, and Atlantic Records producer Jerry Wexler, at the 1981 party held in Aretha's honor at the Time / Life Building in New York City. Struck by a fear of heights, Franklin refused to take a second elevator to her forty-eighth-floor event. She missed a wonderfully lavish star-studded party that night. *(Photo: Arista Records / MJB Photo Archives)*

Luther Vandross and Aretha Franklin performing together at Madison Square Garden. Aretha had been one of Luther's idols when he was growing up, and working with her was a dream come true. *(Photo: Epic Records / Mark Bego Collection)*

Record producer Narada Michael Walden is responsible for some of Aretha's most electrifying music of the 1980s and 1990s. For Franklin's *Through the Storm* album, Walden (left) teamed Aretha (center) with that era's hottest new diva, Whitney Houston (right), to create the 1989 hit song "It Isn't, It Wasn't, It Ain't Never Gonna Be." *(Photo: Arista Records / MJB Photo Archives)*

Peter Max not only designed the cover for Aretha's 1989 album, he also painted this rare photo sleeve for the album's title track: "Through the Storm," which was a hit duet with Elton John. *(Illustration: Peter Max / Arista Records / Mark Bego Collection)*

Aretha Franklin in white gloves and one of her trademark low-cut gowns. She hit high notes and had eyes popping when she performed at the White House before President and Mrs. Clinton in 1994. When she leaned forward to take a bow, she reportedly exposed an inappropriate amount of herself. *(Photo: Lisa Berg / PBS Productions / MJB Photo Archives)*

VH1's 1998 Divas Live concert, broadcast from The Beacon Theater in New York City, was a prestigious event that placed Aretha in the center of the action. The star "divas" of that night were (left to right): Gloria Estefan, Mariah Carey, Aretha Franklin, Carole King, Celine Dion, and Shania Twain.
(Photo: Mark Bryan Brown / Epic Records / MJB Photo Archives)

The Queen of Soul at B. B. King's nightclub in Times Square in New York City, June 25, 2004. Even after years of chain smoking, at the age of sixty-two Aretha proved that she still had the vocal power to belt out a song.
(Photo: Derek Storm)

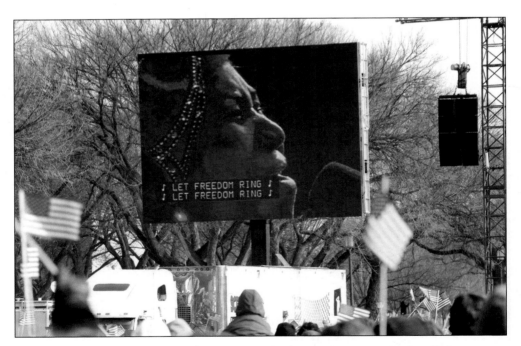

Without a doubt, one of Aretha's crowning achievements was singing "My Country 'Tis of Thee" at President Barack Obama's inauguration in Washington D. C., on January 20, 2009. Aretha's performance was broadcast on giant screens all over the Mall in the nation's capitol, and on television around the world.
(Photo: Walter McBride / Retna)

Without a major record label behind her, in 2006 Franklin had recorded and "executive produced" her own album entitled *A Woman Falling Out of Love*, which she expected to release in 2007. It took her five years to find a distributor for it. When it finally came out in 2011, it failed to find an audience.
(Photo: Derek Storm)

Franklin at a Sony BMG Records party following the Grammy Awards, on February 10, 2008. That evening Aretha started a feud in the press with Tina Turner. On the telecast Beyoncé had introduced Turner as "the Queen" of rock divas. The Queen of Soul let everyone know she was not happy— because she was the only "Queen."
(Photo: Smith / Retna)

Aretha loves to wrap herself in fur, and she adores dressing in décolletage-exposing form-fitting gowns like this one she wore in Los Angeles on February 8, 2008. That evening she was saluted as the MusiCares organization's Person of the Year.
(Photo: Sara de Boer / Retna)

Aretha lost eighty-five pounds in a month and a half due to her mysterious 2010 surgery. Determined to show the world that she was healthy, she made several public appearances like this one on TV's *The Oprah Winfrey Show*. A slimmer Queen of Soul (left), waves to the audience with Oprah (right) in Chicago, May 17, 2011. *(Photo: Grabowski / Retna)*

Aretha Franklin attends the Elton John AIDS Foundation's 25th Anniversary Gala at The Cathedral of St. John the Divine on Tuesday, Nov. 7, 2017, in New York. *(Photo: Andy Kropa / Invision / AP)*

Although Aretha was ticked off at James, she maintained her cool. According to Barbara Shelley, "I will say she was a lady about the whole thing. When she got off the stage, she still agreed to do various interviews that she had commitments to do, to promote the special, in spite of the problems she encountered."

Later that year, Aretha returned to the church for an inspired event. After fifteen years, Aretha was ready to record a new album of gospel music. "I never left gospel," she proclaims. "It's an integral part of myself. I carry the gospel with me regardless of what I am singing. Gospel is my background, my roots."

With that in mind, in July 1987, Aretha mounted one of the most challenging and fulfilling albums projects of her career: *One Lord, One Faith, One Baptism*. The resulting two-record set is much more than a mere recording of gospel singing and inspirational performances—it is an all-star revival meeting captured on tape during three hot and steamy nights at the New Bethel Baptist Church in Detroit. More than an Aretha Franklin solo album, the package is a deeply inspired church service in which the music is only part of the program. Over thirty minutes of spoken word, contained in six separate invocations or speeches, makes up a large portion of this album, interleaved into over fifty minutes of music. (On the original compact disc, two of the six spoken segments—totaling fourteen minutes—were deleted so the program would fit onto a single disc.)

There are only three solo Aretha Franklin performances on *One Lore, One Faith, One Baptism*: "Walk in the Light," "Ave Maria," and "The Lord's Prayer." The other seven songs are duets with Mavis Staples, Joe Ligon, Reverend Jaspar Williams, and the Franklin Sisters (Carolyn and Erma Franklin, and their cousin Brenda Corbett). The speakers on the album are equally notable: Reverend Jesse Jackson; Aretha's brother, Reverend Cecil Franklin; Reverend Jaspar Williams; and Reverend Donald Parsons of the Mount Calvary Baptist Church in Chicago.

"This was by popular demand!" Aretha proclaimed. "It's commonly known I came from gospel, and I can't tell you how many people have been asking for this since *Amazing Grace*. I wanted to do it sooner, but there were always prior commitments. I wanted to do a new gospel collection, because gospel made the most significant contributions to my musical training and singing, since I grew up in the church."

Not only was the project an historic one in that it reunited Aretha, Erma, and Carolyn with the music of their childhood, in their father's church, but it also marked the first album that Aretha ever produced entirely by herself. "I spoke to Clive Davis about it, and he loved it—he even made me the producer," she explained. "That's great, because I wanted to record many of the songs I loved as a child in the church—my own gospel favorites. No one could produce it like I could.

"I like producing, mainly because it gives me all of the freedom that I would like to have in recording," she explains. "Everything is me. There are no outside influences; from the background, to the track, to the selection of the material, to the performance, it's my thing. That's what I like most about producing. That is not to say that I don't like being produced by other producers, and good producers—and there are many of them. But I very much like doing my own thing too.

"This was my baby, my labor of love," Aretha said, glowing after the three nights of recording at the New Bethel Baptist Church. "I wanted to produce this album, because I didn't think anyone was better qualified than myself. Those ladies in this business that want to produce, should. It wasn't that difficult for me."

The album was recorded on July 27, 28, and 30 in the middle of a heat wave. It was 105 degrees outside those three days, and the evenings at New Bethel were every bit as hot—musically as well as on the thermometer. The crowds of four thousand people in church those nights were handed fans to cool themselves. The fans were printed with full-color advertisements for one of three local funeral homes: McCall, Swanson, or Cole. Outside the church, signs reading "Funeral in Progress" kept people from parking in the way of the crowds, the press, and the recording engineers. Although the music that was made at the altar those nights in downtown Detroit was indeed "to die for," it was a celebration of life and of eternity, not of death or mourning. They were presented with all the fervor of an old-time Baptist revival meeting, with the Queen of Soul herself leading the procession.

"It was exciting," Rita Griffin recalls of those three hot summer nights. "Anytime Detroit does something, or anything musical is done that pertains to Aretha or Motown, it is quite a family reunion. Everybody was gathered there that you hadn't seen in a long time. Along with members of the church, of course, it was filled with people. I like this about her: Reverend Franklin had a thing where the doors of the church were never closed. There was no such thing as a 'private' anything going on at New Bethel. It's very much open to the public. I like the way Aretha handled it—pretty much the same way. Naturally, tickets had to be issued, but there was no charge for them. So there was a cross-section of people—friends and fans and family, and the church family."

In 1972, when *Amazing Grace* was recorded, the tickets to attend the gospel session at the New Temple Missionary Baptist Church in Los Angeles were sold for ten dollars apiece. For the 1987 sessions, tickets were given away through the church, and in giveaways on two local radio stations, WGPR and WCHB. The collection plate was passed and several thousand dollars were raised for the Detroit Children's Hospital and to feed the needy.

In addition to the established gospel stars who sang with Aretha, she was also backed by a 100-voice choir comprising the choir of the New Bethel Baptist Church and the Thomas Whitfield Group. Minister Thomas A. Whitfield supervised the music and choral arrangements, and the choir director was Michael E. Fletcher. However, the entire event was coordinated and produced by Aretha herself. Not only did she choose the songs, the musicians, her singing partners, the speakers, the choir director, and the church, but she also decided how the finished package should be presented."

"It's a concept album," she explained. "We had church as well as recorded [songs]. There are spoken-word pieces leading from cut to cut. For the opening cut, 'Jesus Is the Light of the World,' the choir marched in holding candles. It was beautiful."

One of the most exciting moments in the three nights of recording came on Monday, July 27, when Aretha's longtime friend, Reverend Jesse Jackson, was on hand to speak and to introduce segments of that evening's program. Jackson referred to Aretha as "our sister beloved, who wears the coat of many colors—Sister Aretha Franklin."

There were several awe-inspiring performances. Aretha's slow, sincere versions of "The Lord's Prayer" and "Ave Maria" were performed with an almost operatic quality. Listening to them is like eavesdropping on a thankful woman who is praying to God.

The two duets by Aretha and Mavis Staples are worth the entire purchase of the album. Introducing Staples to the microphone, Aretha explained to the congregation, "Mavis and I grew up, as teenagers, traveling with our families—she and the Staple Singers, and myself and my dad, and Lucy Branch and Sammy Bryant. And we met on a Mississippi road one evening. And we're going back to our roots tonight."

"Sho' nuff!" shouted Staples in reply. With that, the pair launched into a version of "Oh Happy Day" that shook the rafters of the church.

The two-hour program ended with a soul-stirring rendition of "Packing Up, Getting Ready to Go," which teamed Aretha with Mavis Staples, Joe Ligon of the gospel group the Mighty Clouds of Joy, and the Franklin Sisters. Detroit newspapers called the event "The Gospel Songfest." Indeed it was.

"It's a great album, and I'm proud of it," said Aretha, when the sessions were completed. "[It] brought back so many good memories. Gospel just has the inspiration that rock doesn't have."

"My schedule is really pretty busy," explained Thomas Whitfield of his surprise involvement in *One Lord, One Faith, One Baptism*. "I produce a lot of primary gospel artists, but [Aretha] called me and said she wanted to have a meeting on a Tuesday night. I said, 'Well shoot—I'm not going to miss that evening!' So, I went over and she started to tell me what songs she wanted to do, what keys they were in, and the things she wanted me to arrange. That it was going to be on July 27, 28, and 30. From the time we started to put those songs together, there was a feeling in the room that you wouldn't believe. We couldn't hardly have a rehearsal for having 'church.' People were crying and shouting!"

According to Whitfield, Aretha's desire was to recapture the feeling of the traditional revival meetings and gospel shows that she and her sisters used to witness in the 1950s. "For singers today," he says, "it is hard to replicate how they sang back then, because they didn't really sing structured at all. The parts just kind of *fell*. You had to kind of catch on. Today, gospel music has come to a place where it is a lot more structured and a lot more professional. So we updated the sound."

"It was spiritually uplifting for me," says Aretha. "I'm going to have to do this more often. It was wonderful, just wonderful. It was at least 110 degrees in the church. Packed to capacity. I thought doing it at the church was quite appropriate. I don't think I could have done it anywhere else."

Three of the songs on the album were Clara Ward compositions. Aretha especially wanted to sing the songs "Jesus Hears Every Prayer," "Surely God is Able," and "Packing Up, Getting Ready to Go" as a tribute to Sister Ward. The latter song was recorded each of the three nights. After the completion of the third take, Aretha wasn't satisfied that she had gotten the ultimate version of the song to do Ward's composition justice. With her producer's rein strongly in hand, she commanded a retake of the song. The resulting version of "Packing Up, Getting Ready to Go" was definitely worth the effort. "It was so spirited to use that as a song going out," said Carolyn Franklin. "Yes, I saw quite a few brethren jumping up for that one."

Carolyn further explained that the whole project was kept secret by her sister until the last minute. "I had known she was going to do a gospel album," Carolyn recalled, "but I didn't know we [Carolyn and Erma] were going to be involved. It was just one of those things where she said, 'Let's do those songs by the Ward Singers we did as kids.' She said she wanted to recreate her childhood, like in the church with the candlelight service. My dad did that years ago."

As producer, Aretha had to make the final decisions about editing the material. "There was so much of it," she recalls, "I had to talk to Clive about whether it should be cut back. He decided we should do the best thing: make it a double LP."

Ultimately, there were selections cut from the three hot nights in Detroit. A quiet but effective version of "God Specializes," a tribute to Aretha's father on "Father I Stretch Out My Hands to Thee," a Mavis Staples duet on "Be Grateful," and another Joe Ligon duet on "Beams of Heaven" were all left on the editing room floor.

Considering the pop, rock, and R&B success that Aretha was experiencing with *Who's Zoomin' Who?* and *Aretha*, 1987 was the perfect time to go off on a gospel tangent. From a marketing standpoint, Clive Davis claimed that there would be no question of *One Lord, One Faith, One*

Baptism finding an audience. "There was never any negative implication regarding its potential," Davis elaborated. "There was tremendous public interest in this album. I think it will become a landmark. Nobody does gospel better than Aretha. She has the ability to capture the core of a lyric, the nerve of a song, the essential soul."

Jim Crawley, national sales vice-president of Arista Records, echoed Davis' feelings about marketing. "It is a totally different piece of product," he explained. "The most important thing to remember is that music is art, but it is also business. With the gospel project, I think what we will try to do is get the album really well publicized to people who are in the demographic of who will buy the album—promote it even through the churches."

"She should continually be introduced to a new and expanding audience," Davis elaborated before the album was released. "That is what I have been doing. You have to stay contemporary and relevant. We work very closely together as a creative partnership. It has been working in a sense that almost every album [of Aretha's on Arista] has sold more than the one before."

But was *One Lord, One Faith, One Baptism* commercially viable? "Record sales, man, that is the litmus test," claims Jerry Wexler. If that is the case, Aretha's 1987 gospel album was an ambitious failure. Although the reviews were all very positive, in the end it did fail to find a record-buying audience. Critically, it was a huge, award-winning success, but in terms of albums sold, it gleaned the poorest sales figures of any of her Arista LPs. In *Billboard* magazine it peaked at Number 106.

The problems seemed to stem more from the album's edited presentation than from the lack of heart and soul on the singing tracks. In the long run, the half hour of invocations and speeches killed the intensity of the songs. Exceedingly poor editing found the song "Higher Ground" divided between side three and side four on the LP record version of the package. Only the compact-disc version of *One Lord, One Faith, One Baptism* was artistically successful—as the listener is free to delete all of the monologues, thanks to digital programming.

It is sad that such a sure-fire project, which was so highly anticipated, should fail so conclusively. Even the single version of "Oh Happy Day" failed to hit the charts. There were some high points, in spite of the lukewarm sales figures that the album met with. *One Lord, One Faith, One Baptism* ended up winning a Dove Award from the Gospel Music Association as "Best Traditional Black Album." Attention from the Grammy Awards in the gospel category, was guaranteed from the very start. (In January 1989 the album was nominated for a Grammy as the "Best Soul Gospel Performance, Female;" and the single "Oh Happy Day" by Aretha and Mavis, was nominated as the "Best Soul Gospel Performance by a Duo, Group, Choir, or Chorus.")

While *The New York Times* claimed that the album "reaches for gospel's higher ground," it also stated that the result is muted, fragmented, and unsatisfying." *The New Yorker* magazine pointed out that "Compared with *Aretha Gospel* and *Amazing Grace, One Lord, One Faith, One Baptism* is more concerned with preserving the design and momentum of a church service than with presenting a concert composed of religious songs." And although *Rolling Stone* gave the album four stars (out of a possible five), it also pointed out that, "ostensibly a record of celebration, *One Lord, One Faith, One Baptism* is weighed down by some very heavy crosses."

Arista Records did get behind the album, to a certain extent. Press members on the Arista mailing list were sent promotional Aretha Franklin handheld fans, with the album cover reproduced on the front, and stapled to wooden paint stirrers—just like the funeral-parlor fans that are handed out at New Bethel Baptist Church. However, someone should have given novice producer Aretha some solid advice as to the sequencing of the album package. Instead of thirty minutes of talking, the four missing songs should have taken the place of the speeches.

However, the behind-the-scenes story of *One Lord, One Faith, One Baptism* makes the commercial failure of the package more understandable. What the general public didn't realize was that the album was the last recording Aretha owed Arista Records on her existing contract. Her contract required her to deliver to Arista a live album. What Arista would have preferred was a dynamite pop LP, such as *Aretha Live at Fillmore West*, which would provide the label with 1980s versions of "Respect," "Think," and "(You Make Me Feel Like) A Natural Woman."

As Erma Franklin confirmed, "All she owed them was a live album, and they didn't specify what kind. I'm sure they would have been more pleased if she had done another pop album, but she was at liberty to do what she pleased."

Speaking of the album, Aretha claimed, "It's not Peggy Lee. It's quite energetic and aggressive, with a real religious fervor." She never mentioned the word "commercial" in her description of the LP.

Although *One Lord, One Faith, One Baptism* sold short of the Gold standard that her pop albums had recently attained, Clive Davis was not upset with the results or the sales figures. According to him, "We had no expectation that it would cross over. It was done purely as a gospel album, knowing that it would sell over another decade or so, and it's now close to 300,000 units [as of July 1988]. I would assume it will continue to sell, year in and year out. I think it's fine, and we didn't judge it by the normal standards. We always knew that we would, at some point in working together, do a gospel album, and I would let her take full charge of it. I think the singing is wonderful, I mean, she did it in a sort of a documentary way. It's a very personal album to Aretha—the fact that it was done in her father's church. I think it will be a mainstream catalog seller, and continue to sell over the years."

Was *One Lord, One Faith, One Baptism* merely a vanity project that she knew would be fun, and finish her exiting Arista contract in a single stroke? The album was released in November 1987, and by January 1988 the media were already buzzing about the fact that representatives from several major record labels had flown to Detroit to lure Aretha away from Arista Records. Warner Brothers Records was one of the major-league companies reportedly in the bidding.

Although Aretha's association with Clive Davis and Arista had been quite successful commercially, not everyone agreed that the relationship had been a bed of roses. According to one former Arista employee, "I wouldn't be surprised if she'd had it with Clive Davis' ego by now. I mean enough is enough. And probably Warner's is offering her a lot of money. She's been threatening to get off the label since the *Who's Zoomin' Who?* album. She got her gospel album out of Clive, and I don't know what else she's got, but she'd like to get real money. I mean, while she's got some hits, she could command much bigger money than I think they're willing to give her. I think Clive's attitude is, 'If I don't find you the songs, and

I don't put you together with the likes of Narada, you're not gonna get anywhere anyway. So you want to be that way about it, you ask for your half-million a record, or whatever.' I don't really know what she's asking. On the other hand, in Aretha's case, she doesn't work [concert tours], and the only way for her to make money is from the records; she's doing virtually no live performances anymore."

Since she received her thirteenth and fourteenth Grammy Awards, her Dove Award, and an NAACP Award as "Female Artist of the Year," all in the first half of 1988, it didn't matter that her gospel album didn't go Gold. As a pop and R&B star, she was hotter than ever. This gave her the upper hand as she began negotiations on her next album contract.

Amid her record label shopping spree, *Billboard* magazine leaked out some of the details of Aretha's demands. According to the publication, what she was asking as her new fee was a million dollars per album! If she indeed ended up commanding that price, she would be setting a new precedent in recording advances.

While she was deciding which major recording company would usher her into the 1990s, Aretha had several other projects to occupy herself with. In the spring of 1988, the Queen of Soul was busy posing for artists from Madame Tussaud's Wax Museum in London, planning a proposed Detroit Easter Parade [which didn't take place], filming an anti-DWI public-service television spot, and recording a new song with the Four Tops. She was also preoccupied with the health of her sister Carolyn— who was dying of cancer.

In retrospect, it is easy to see why *One Lord, One Faith, One Baptism* was important to Aretha when she recorded it. Although it was a closely guarded secret, she knew that Carolyn was fighting a losing battle against the ravages of cancer. The gospel album—recorded with her sisters—was to be their last project together. Little sister Carolyn had always been under Aretha's protective wing. Whenever Carolyn would get into a schoolyard fight as a child, Aretha was there to protect her. When she became a singing star, and Carolyn's own recording career floundered, Aretha recorded her sisters compositions, and made Carolyn a star in her own right. When Carolyn was stricken with cancer, Aretha was right there to help her fight her battle to live. Aretha moved Carolyn into her Bloomfield Hills home to give her younger sister round-the-clock care. Like the passing of her father, Carolyn's untimely death, on April 25, 1988, was unspeakably painful for Aretha.

Although her solo recording career had ended in the 1970s, Carolyn had remained quite active in the entertainment business in the 1980s, thanks to Aretha. She appeared in the movie *The Blues Brothers*, on Aretha's 1986 Showtime TV special, and on the 1987 *James Brown and Friends* telecast.

Having become friendly with Dan Hartman during the James Brown taping, Carolyn sang background vocals on the 1987 Paul King album *Joy*. Hartman produced the album by British singer King, and he flew Carolyn from Detroit to his Connecticut recording studio. According to Hartman, she was energetic and full of life. The title of Carolyn's debut album in the 1960s was *Baby Dynamite*, and she used to laugh, "They don't call me 'Baby Dynamite' for nothing!"

"Carolyn is fantastic!" Hartman proclaimed after working with her on the Paul King album. "She's the consummate musician, and sort of puts it all into the drive of helping people, which I think is brilliant. She's not interested in the center-stage spot for herself, as much as she's interested in helping people. She does a lot of community work in Detroit, and told me about the young talent she works with there."

One of her dreams was to obtain her college degree, and to set up a practice in the field of entertainment law. She was working on her degree when she was diagnosed as having cancer, in March 1987. Her illness did not dissuade her from pursuing her dreams, and she continued her studies while she underwent treatment.

According to Carolyn, "Kids sign their lives away [in the music business]. You have to know basic law and basic business. The young artists have so many things working against them. It's a hellified business." It was her intention to help young singers who were just starting their careers.

"We all knew she was in bad health," recalls Dan Hartman. "I knew, in fact, that she'd had an operation, a very serious operation, before Christmas. I knew from 'Retha's agents, because I was in touch with all those people, when Carolyn had gone in the hospital for a major cancer operation. Ruth [Bowen] said, 'It's pretty major, but she's pulled through it okay, and she's gonna be at Aretha's house convalescing.' So I sent her a giant bouquet of flowers at Aretha's house."

Lying on her deathbed in Aretha's house, Carolyn's last wish was granted, and she was presented her diploma. According to her sister Erma, "The president of Marygrove [College], the dean of students, and the head of the music department participated in a special bedside ceremony. It was that important to her." That was on April 15, 1988, ten days before her death."

"Her personality provided the fortitude that helped during the past year," said Erma. "She didn't complain even when she was in excruciating pain. She said she was going to fight the disease until her last breath. And in the end, it appeared that her arms were raised in battle."

Carolyn's funeral, at the New Bethel Baptist Church, was a three-hour service of song and eulogy. In addition to two thousand friends and family members, the ceremony was also attended by Detroit's mayor, Coleman Young, as well as Lawrence Payton and Levi Stubbs of the Four Tops, Martha Reeves, Ron White of The Miracles, and Cleo Staples. Flower arrangements were sent by Whitney and Cissy Houston, Dionne Warwick, Mary Wilson, Jennifer Holiday, and Berry Gordy, Jr. Several telegrams were read to the congregation, including one from Lena Horne. Carolyn was buried at Detroit's Woodlawn Cemetery.

While Carolyn was ill, Aretha had kept herself occupied with projects that she could do in Detroit. Recording her third duet with the Four Tops was a sheer pleasure and a creative distraction for her. The song, which was included on their 1988 Arista debut album, *Indestructible*, is titled "If Ever a Love There Was." "I love the Four Tops," says Aretha. "We're great friends, and they are some of my favorite people, as well as favorite artists. My brother and Levi are very close." She explains that all three of their sessions together had been a blast in the studio, "We did 'Make It Up to You,'" and we recorded here a couple of summers ago. That was one of the best summers I've ever had, being in the studio with the Tops—I mean we had a good time. Whenever Levi would start doing his vocals, the ladies would start sliding down the walls, and we couldn't get any work done!" she laughs, "But we really had a good time."

As a single, "If Ever a Love There Was" made it to Number Thirty-one on the R&B chart in America. And, it made it to Number Twenty-six on the Adult Contemporary chart in *Billboard* magazine.

On March 10, 1988, Aretha went before the television cameras to film a public-service announcement against driving under the influence of drugs and liquor. Taped before a live audience at Detroit's Music Hall, Aretha adapted her 1968 hit record "Think" for the campaign. New lyrics were written, and the video was entitled "Think . . . Don't Drive with Drugs or Drink!" The video was made into 30- and 60-second TV spots, as a public service, funded by the Chrysler Corporation. It debuted March 18 on MTV, and a radio version of the song was also produced.

The day of the videotaping, there was a luncheon in Washington, D.C., to kick off the anti-DWI campaign, which was attended by Carly Simon, Eddie Rabbit, Jermaine Jackson, and Juice Newton. Since Aretha still wouldn't leave Detroit, she appeared at the luncheon via satellite. Her image was telecast to appear on 36 TV monitors, stacked in a configuration that spelled out the word "Think."

In July 1988, Clive Davis spoke of Aretha's contractual situation with Arista. "Her status is that she's agreed to do a certain amount of additional records for us," he explained. "She recently signed to do that a few weeks ago. So at least for the time being, we're gonna be continue recording her. She just redid 'Think' for us—she updated it when Arif [Mardin] went in to record 'Think' for her commercial. He sent me the track, and I really liked it. So I asked her to do a new version of it. Plus, at some point we're going to do a greatest-hits album, and we want to do two or three new songs for that. We've got the Four Tops [duet]; that will go on their album, and it'll probably go on her album, too. She'll be working on those cuts."

How did Clive Davis view Aretha's well-known fear of flying, and her inability to leave Detroit? "I've had no trouble," he claimed. "It's not hampered our recording abilities. It's hampered touring, without a question, but it's not hampered recording."

Because he had to bring camera crews and recording crews to work with Aretha in her hometown, Davis felt that her co-workers are all understanding, and are willing to work around Aretha's geographic demands. "It's not pulling rank or anything. It's a real problem. She's not gone to any other state by plane, and she doesn't like traveling by train," he explained.

How is Aretha viewed by the local Detroit media? According to Gary Graff, "There's still warm feelings about her, but I think she's starting to be viewed as kind of freakish, reclusive, just kind of 'up there.' She just makes an appearance at the fights or the Pistons games. There's a lot of respect and a lot of warm feelings for her, but it's not the same thing that you get for [fellow Detroit native] Bob Segar—that's for sure. He's the one who's out there and active."

The producer of one Detroit television show recalls that Aretha once canceled a live TV appearance, using the excuse that she had a conflicting fingernail appointment. This sort of thing has damaged her reputation with the local media. Says the producer, "Her commitment does not mean much, so we tend to want to stay away from booking her. I don't know if it's the people around her, or it it's Aretha. Whenever I even wanted to book her, it took me a long time to get through to someone. I met her several years ago, and she could not have been lovelier. But, as far as reputation goes, nobody in Detroit really counts on Aretha showing up, or Aretha's commitment. Everybody's a little apprehensive to ask Aretha, because we don't really know if she'll be there when she's supposed to be."

Here is a perfect example of how Aretha still hurts her own career with her long-standing fear of the media. *The Detroit Free Press* and *The Detroit News* are both among the top ten most widely circulated newspapers in America, and the local TV stations reach millions of viewers. There should be no question as to Aretha's reliability as far as the media is concerned. If she is going to continue to remain in the public spotlight, she needs to focus herself a bit more. Her closest allies in the media—circa 1988— were Shirley Eder of *The Detroit Free Press* and Linda Solomon of *The Detroit News*, and she tended to stay in touch with these two columnists if she had something to announce. However, she needed to do something to dispel her reputation as an unreliable eccentric.

Every once in a while, Aretha warms up to the idea of attempting air travel again, but she has yet to take another flight. "She doesn't really like leaving home," says Tisha Fein. "It's common knowledge, and people know that she doesn't like to fly. She was just getting her courage up again, when there was that big crash at the Detroit airport." Fein refers to the tragic August 16, 1987 crash that killed 156 people only seconds after the plane took off from Detroit Metropolitan Airport. That crash made Aretha decide to stay clear of airplanes for several more years.

It is amazing how many people are willing to work around Aretha's fear of leaving Detroit. *Vogue* magazine flew in fashion photographers to capture Aretha on film for their March 1988 issue. In addition, Aretha confirmed that "the people from Madame Tussaud's are coming in to do my figure for the wax museum in London." When you're the Queen of Soul, apparently, all of your loyal subjects come to you.

When Atlantic Records celebrated its fortieth anniversary with a huge, all-day concert in New York City's Madison Square Garden, it was hoped that Aretha might at least attempt a train trip. The producers of the May 14, 1988 event had hoped to open the festivities with a duet by two of Atlantic Records' biggest stars, Aretha Franklin and Ray Charles. As it turned out, neither of them were present.

In August 1988, as part of its *American Masters* television series, PBS aired an hour-long biographical tribute to Aretha. Originally the special was produced and broadcast by BBC in England. The details of Aretha's personal life were glossed over, and what remained was basically an overview of her career. Within that framework, the TV show's strong point was its use of film and video clips that brilliantly illustrated her evolution as a performer. In addition to her 1968 performance of "Chain of Fools" on *The Jonathan Winters Show*, her 1981 appearance on *Saturday Night Live*, and her exciting 1985 video of "Sisters Are Doin' It for Themselves," several rare film clips were also utilized. The archival footage included an early-sixties TV performance of the song "Won't Be Long," Martin Luther King, Jr. joining Aretha on-stage at Cobo Hall in 1968, a black & white film of her at the Fillmore West concerts in 1971, and scenes from the recording of her *Amazing Grace* album.

The *American Masters* telecast also included videotaped comments from Aretha and several of her business associates. At one point during the program, she was seen pressed into one of her tight-fitting outfits, talking about the men in her life. Sounding like a soul version of Mae West, Aretha deadpanned to the camera, "I have always maintained that a real man is not going to be intimidated by me. Some men can *rise* to the occasion, and others cannot."

In September 1988, when George Michael was doing his highly successful American concert tour, Detroit was one of the cities he played. As a special surprise guest, Aretha showed up at the Palace and sang her duet with George. The Detroit crowd went berserk when Lady Soul hit the stage to make a one-night-only appearance.

Having been immortalized by Madame Tussaud's Wax Museum and by Andy Warhol, Aretha was next the subject of another famous artist. In the autumn of 1988, Peter Max was asked by Luther Vandross to paint portraits of Luther's three favorite subjects: Aretha Franklin, Diana Ross, and Dionne Warwick. In February of 1989, Max was commissioned by Arista Records to paint the cover portrait of Aretha for her next album, *Through the Storm*.

One afternoon, that same month, Peter Max called me tell me that he had been invited to paint the cover of *Through the Storm*, and to ask me if I could help him with the project. He knew I was writing this book, so he asked if I would bring him some copies of Aretha Franklin photos to his studio, so that he could formulate some ideas for his portrait of her. I gladly agreed. I went to Peter's studio on the Upper West Side of Manhattan, and while I was there, I asked him if he would return the favor, and do an exclusive portrait of Aretha for me that I could use in the book. He agreed. So, not only did I have a hand in the creation of the *Through the Storm* album cover, but Peter Max also contributed to the creation of this book!

How appropriate that Aretha, the most successful female singer of the 1960s, should be captured on canvas by the most successful graphic artist of that decade. According to Max, "Aretha was a fascinating subject to paint. She has a colorful voice which paints inspiring pictures with her songs. She is truly a great artist!"

When the fall television season began in October 1988, Aretha's voice was heard on two new projects: she recorded a jingle for Chevrolet, and sang the theme song for the NBC television series *A Different World*. The theme song to *A Different World* was composed by the show's producer, Bill Cosby, and its musical director, Stu Gardner. The lyrics were written by one of the show's costars, Dawnn Lewis. Ironically, one of the show's cast members was Glynn Turman. In 1989 Aretha added Diet Coke to her growing list of TV jingles. Although there doesn't seem to be an underlying theme or focus to Aretha's career choices in the late 1980s, she did manage to keep her name and her voice actively on the airwaves.

True to her unpredictable form, in the last weeks of 1988, Aretha left Michigan for the first time in three years. Suddenly, and without much publicity, she was booked to appear at Trump's Castle in Atlantic City, New Jersey, on December 2–4. Her mode of transportation however was neither car, train, nor plane. Instead, she traveled in a custom-made bus. According to her, "We've got twenty-two people with us on the bus, plus all of the new exquisite, lavish gowns I'm wearing in the show." Describing one of her new outfits, Aretha explained, "It's a gold bow coat designed for me by Jim Cape that goes with my Josephine Baker number. I take the final bows in it, and the encore song. It has four feet of white fox cuffs that drop all the way from my wrists to my knees! It's gold beaded, and has a huge stand-up white fox collar that frames the face. Cape made an all-rhinestone headdress to go with it. Before he made this gown and headdress, Jim Cape went to New York to speak to Josephine Baker's son Claude—he has a restaurant in New York City—who gave Jim some pictures of his mother's fabulous wardrobe to work from."

Aretha and her full-figured version of Baker's gown were a big hit amid the slot machines in Atlantic City. She lost several pounds for her first out-of-town engagement in years, and sported a neatly coiffed and short-cropped reddish-blonde hairdo. In a tight-fitting white-beaded gown, slit up to the thigh, Aretha performed "Freeway of Love" with a troupe of dancers. In an automotive motif, the dancers wore assembly-line jumpsuits, and rolled car tires across the stage, while Aretha sang. When the three-day engagement was over, Aretha hopped aboard her luxury bus, and headed back on the freeway to Detroit.

As 1989 began, Aretha resolved to look back on her childhood and write a book about a particular segment of her life. According to her, "I want to write about gospel music history and about the years I sang gospel and traveled with my dad from the age of fourteen to seventeen." In early 1989 she began shopping for a publisher.

In February, several publishers in New York City engaged in an auction for Aretha's "proposed" autobiography. According to one editor involved, "There wasn't a formal proposal in writing, it was just being sold on a verbal promise, and it was our [this publisher's] hope that it would actually become a cohesive book."

As it turned out, Doubleday won the "bidding war" that ensued, topping five publishers with its offer of $525,000 as an advance against royalties. However, Aretha decided that she wanted $2 million or she wasn't interested. "We couldn't reach an agreement with them over the price," explained Franklin's literary representative Debra Grayson. Was the money really the problem, or was this just Aretha's way of killing the project? It is doubtful that she ever intended on putting her tale of anguish and personal heartbreak down on paper to begin with.

At the same time she was also at work on her new album, *Through the Storm*. Although she had yet to sign a long-term contract with the company, it was recorded and released by Arista Records. While the LP was still in the planning stages, she was occupied with composing a couple of new tunes for it. "I have about four good melodies on the drawing board," Aretha explained. "Most of my songs are very romantic, because I'm very sentimental."

On February 22, 1989, Aretha added to her collection of Grammy Awards, when her album *One Lord, One Faith, One Baptism* won her the fifteenth statuette of her career. Not only did the album win her the "Best Soul Gospel Performance, Female," trophy, but the Aretha-produced cut entitled "Speech by Rev. Jesse Jackson (July 27)," won the "Best Spoken Word" Grammy.

In May of 1989, Aretha's fifty-sixth album, *Through the Storm* was released and became an instant hit. Not only did it feature a colorful cover portrait by Peter Max, but it continued her collaborative work with producer Narada Michael Walden. On the album, Aretha continued her 1980s passion for superstar duets. On the tracks of *Through the Storm* she is heard vocalizing with Elton John, Whitney Houston, and on another song she duets with James Brown. For the recording of "Gimme Your

Love," Aretha and James were not in the same recording studio for the production of the vocal tracks. This was the last recording James made before he entered prison in late 1988, on charges of drug possession and resisting arrest. Her duet with Whitney, "It Isn't, It Wasn't, It Ain't Never Gonna Be," became a campy classic as a single, and the title cut duet with Elton John became a huge pop and R&B hit.

As a single, "Gimme Your Love" made it to Number Forty-eight on the R&B chart. The Whitney Houston duet made it to Number Forty-one pop, Number Five R&B, and Number Twenty-nine in the UK. And the single version of "Through the Storm" became a Number Sixteen pop hit, Number Seventeen R&B, and Number Three on the Adult Contemporary chart. In the UK, the Elton / Aretha duet hit Number Forty-one. The album *Through the Storm* hit Number Fifty-five in the U.S., and Number Forty-six in the UK. It wasn't her biggest selling album, but it kept her on the charts and in the Top Forty on both sides of the Atlantic Ocean in 1989.

Ultimately, who makes Aretha's career decisions for her? Her brother Cecil held the official title as her "manager," at the time. But according to Barbara Shelley, Aretha makes all of her own decisions. "She is the most intelligent woman I've ever worked with in my career," Shelley claims. "She's smarter than anyone else, and she knows more about managing her own career than all of these other celebrities who have a cast of thousands of people telling them what to do and advising them. Aretha Franklin could probably be a manager for anyone in show business. She certainly keeps her own career exactly where she wants it. I don't think she wants any more fame, glory, money, or notoriety than she has. She knows when to come out of hiding. Even though everybody's yelling at her about going on tour, she knows when she really has to do something, and she does it. Much bigger stars are much more insecure about their talent and their careers than she is. They're all so neurotic about whether they're gonna be a star or not. Aretha just is a star, and she manages to maintain it, without a lot of work."

Not everyone agrees with that theory. Clyde Otis still feels that Aretha could achieve greater heights—and that she has cheated herself out of a more solid string of career achievements. "She's never achieved the greatness that I feel is due her," Otis claims. "And it has nothing to do with the amount of records she is selling. I look at how Clive is handling her now, and they've got her chasing the market. You see, Aretha Franklin *is* the market. In other words, she didn't have to cut 'Freeway of Love' or all of those things to be successful. I feel that she could very easily do what she does best, and nobody could ever touch her. And she'd sell probably a lot more records than she does. But then Clive feels, 'Well, hey, let's do what's selling.' What you must understand with an artist like [Aretha] is—that artist *is* the market. That's what I had to convince Dinah of before she agreed to record 'What a Diff'rence a Day Makes.' Aretha never has allowed herself to stand on her own and be *her* star."

According to Clyde, "With Aretha, I guarantee you that there is a market out there for her right now, if she would just be honest and true to herself. It could be any kind of song, but she's got to be herself like Barbra Streisand is. You can't get Barbra to do something that doesn't suit her. Aretha is a woman who has tremendous vitality, is tremendously talented, and has never achieved that degree of stardom."

If Clyde Otis was given the opportunity to go into a recording studio with Aretha again, what kind of material would he like to see her sing? "'(You Make Me Feel Like) A Natural Woman,'" he claims, "and I'd just go on from there—all over. I'd look for the great, great songs—there are so many of them—great songs that *should* be sung. I'd make her be herself. Any song that she felt that she could relate to is a song that we'd cut. I'd just make her sing the hell out of the song, that's all I'd want. I don't care what the tempo is, I don't care what market it's for—that's where I'd put her."

Does he feel that Aretha has the capacity to produce her recordings herself? "Not really as well as she can be produced," he says, "but I would prefer to see her produce herself than see her produced by many of the people who have been producing her. They don't really grasp the depth of her talent and bring that out, or allow it to be brought out. I think she comes closer to bringing it out than anybody."

According to Jerry Wexler, "First there was Bessie Smith. Next there was Billie Holiday. Then there was Dinah Washington. Now in our time, there is Aretha Franklin. Like her wonderful predecessors, she is for the ages."

If he had the opportunity to return to the studio with Aretha, what direction would he recommend for her? "She should make every kind of music. She should make a classic kind of Sarah Vaughn album, singing great standards, with great arrangements, with great jazz players. I would recommend that instantly—among other things. I'm talking like a beautiful thing with the strings and all. Then she should also make a 'cooking' album with a small jazz band. Not so much the standard ballads, but more of the 'Moody's Mood (For Love),' and the pure jazz," says Wexler.

"I think she's unique," says Clive Davis. "I think that she's historic—and deservedly so, and legendary—and deservedly so. She's got a natural intuitive genius that's really a privilege to work with and to find material for. Her resurgence and resumption of her rightful stature has been a joy for me. Aretha *is* the Queen of Soul. Everything about her has been a joy. I can only tell you that she's been an absolute delight and pleasure. No one is gonna categorize her. Now that she's done her gospel album, we're back to recording contemporary songs for the next few albums. She's shown that she can do great contemporary material, and I think the next album or two will be in that area."

Whatever kind of music Aretha chooses to record next, it is certain that it will garner the kind of attention that her status as a singing legend guarantees. "Watch me—I've got a million songs to sing!" she exclaims. "I sing in the shower, I sing everywhere. I'm *always* going to sing. Even if it's at the ladies' bazaar after I retire. Listen, I'll be like Perry Como. Did you see that TV show when he's in bed, with his head on the pillow and a mike just resting there? I'll be like that. They'll have to prop me up on pillows. I'll be singing until 2001." And beyond, her fans hope.

Aretha once said, "Life's a whole lot like pinochle. It's all in your hand. You got nothin' to start with, and what you can get is up to how well you can play the game." She's obviously played her cards well, and she's assuredly got several more aces up her sleeve.

"My voice is better than ever, because of experience," she says of her huskier, more expressive 1980s voice. It has been seasoned by experience and a countless number of Kool cigarettes. "At risk of sounding egotistical—it just gets better. I am my favorite vocalist." Amen.

She is also acknowledged as the favorite vocalist of other legends in show business. When Lena Horne released her highly acclaimed 1988 album *Lena: The Men in My Life*, Horne announced that she wished she could sing like Aretha. "If I had my druthers, I'd be Aretha Franklin," mused Lena. "She has the *passion* feeling, and there's nobody like her. Her passion just comes through!"

"I'm a staunch Democrat," says Aretha of her politics. Naturally, she did all that she could to assist Reverend Jesse Jackson in his bid to run for President on the Democratic ticket in 1988. "And I do community work, donating to various organizations such as sickle-cell anemia and United Negro College Fund and the NAACP. I like to do things with children and for the church. And I'm conscious of being a positive role model for children, which is even more important today than it ever was. When they can't get it together to do their homework, they can tell you one end of a rap record to the other."

"My children are maturing and becoming independent, fine young gentlemen," she says of her four sons. On the subject of her own self-image, she claims that "[I'm] just the nice lady next door. I am a mother, and I do have my home to run, and have to go to the dentist and to the doctor and all the places everybody else has to go to. So I have to balance my time."

It seems that Aretha has resolved several of her past conflicts. However, she never speaks to Ted White. "We don't correspond," White says. "We talk maybe once every ten years. The last time I talked to Aretha was when my son [Teddy, Jr.] started college. Once when he was sick. We have no contact."

Oddly enough, Aretha still owns the house on Sorrento Avenue that she shared with Ted White in the late sixties. The house, which has sat vacant for several years, was condemned by the city, and in 1989 the neighbors started taking legal action against Aretha for the eyesore. Obviously the house still holds too many painful memories for her. Instead of repairing or selling the house, she has chosen to retain it and let it decay.

According to White, after their divorce, "I managed some [singing] artists, and did some writing for a while, and then it was kind of hard to go back to those long, hard road trips, and build people all over again.

I just didn't have the heart for it." He went on to obtain his real-estate license, and today is a successful realtor in Detroit. Their son, Teddy, Jr., graduated from Michigan State University with a telecommunications degree, and in 1988 he began hosting a local Detroit television program.

Although she has not seen Glynn Turman since their divorce, Aretha claims that they have spoken on the phone from time to time. Aretha is living a comfortable and uncomplicated life in the suburbs, and that's the way she wants it to remain.

Slowly, Aretha is beginning to venture out of Detroit. In May of 1989 she returned to Atlantic City to perform at Caesar's Palace. Aretha came to New York City and headlined Radio City Music Hall on July 5, 6, and 7, 1989. Immediately afterward she rushed back to her hometown of Detroit. Aretha was scheduled to appear on the television show *Late Night with David Letterman* on July 11. However, in her own inimitable fashion, Aretha canceled at the last minute. According to the NBC-TV publicity department, "It was basically a misunderstanding as to the number of people who were going to appear with her on-stage." Obviously, her reliability hasn't improved with age. She remains the reclusive Queen of the Motor City.

It really doesn't matter if she ever leaves the Detroit city limits or not. In downtown Detroit, right where Woodward Avenue meets the waterfront, there is a gigantic copper statue of a man balancing the sun in one hand and a family in the other. It is known as "The Spirit of Detroit." With the amount of show business importance that she has focused on the city, the City Council may have to erect a statue of Aretha—and name it "The *New* Spirit of Detroit."

One of her business associates has laughingly suggested that Aretha could become one of the attractions on a guided tour of Detroit, since she so rarely leaves town. They could point out her suburban home, where she lives in lavishly eccentric seclusion, as if it were the local equivalent of Buckingham Palace. "This *is* home," Aretha proudly proclaims of Detroit. "It's a city of winners!"

DÉNOUEMENT 1989

She's been in the record business for over thirty years. She has had a career that other vocalists can only dream of matching. She is to contemporary pop and soul music what Ella Fitzgerald is to jazz singing. Aretha's vast wealth of creative achievements is staggering. As she prepares to enter the 1990s with her fame at an all-time high, is Aretha Franklin really happy with her accomplishments? Does she continue to work as an innovator in the record business because she loves her career so much, or is she obsessed with burying herself in work?

Since an in-person interview with her comes with a full list of taboo topics, to this day she is a woman of mystery. One isn't allowed to inquire about her mother or her father, unless it relates to the church or her singing career. Her relationship with them remains a puzzle, with pieces missing from it. Underneath the surface, is she still wrestling with childhood demons that continue to pursue her?

While she has amassed an incredible body of recorded music, and guaranteed herself the title of "living legend," is she fulfilled? On the one hand, she *is* the super-secure Queen of Soul, confident of her laurels and her stature in the music industry. Yet there are still several never-discussed emotional wounds that time doesn't seem to heal. As an adult, to what degree is Aretha still haunted by the pain of her unsolved childhood disappointments?

Half the time she is the soulful superwoman who commands "R-E-S-P-E-C-T," demanding that you take a ride with her on "The Freeway of Love." The other half of the time she still seems to be the timid twelve-year-old girl standing on a chair in front of her father's congregation, hoping for acceptance.

Aretha proceeds through life as though a dark cloud of tragedy still hangs overhead like an ever-present sword of Damocles. Her excessive chain-smoking, her tendency to overeat fattening food, and her avoidance of leaving Detroit are obvious devices that she used to insulate herself from her own insecurities. Whenever reality or potential confrontations come too close to her doorstep, Aretha tends to shield herself from the world. She hasn't done a concert tour in years, and when she does set dates, they are often canceled at the last minute. She has developed a reputation of questionable reliability. Instead of embarking on challenging new projects that are within her grasp, such as musical plays and movies, she remains content to surround herself with familiar low-stress endeavors.

Her fear of flying, her terror of being trapped in a burning building, and her refusal to leave Detroit for years at a time, have given her the public image of an eccentric. Is she the prisoner of her own celebrity status, or has the prospect of career expansion simply lost its appeal for her?

The biggest question is: What does the future hold for Aretha? While her singing career continues to present new challenges for her, and keeps her on the list of contemporary hit-makers, will she ever resume her movie career? She showed off such brilliant comic flair in *The Blues Brothers* that it would be a shame if that appearance alone represented her acting endeavors. She has the talent and the stature in show business to produce her own film properties. She spends her time designing a line of clothing when she should be orchestrating a movie version of *The Bessie Smith Story*, to be filmed entirely in the Detroit area.

She seems to shy away from contact with her audience—on screen and in person. She acts as if she were afraid to reveal too much of herself. She prefers the "safe distance" that her recording career affords her. She has only to record her albums, do a quick video shooting, and let her record company do the rest. There are few singing stars who could get away with such a small degree of personal exposure and still retain their popularity. However, Aretha Franklin is a star of such magnitude that she can pull off self-imposed suburban confinement.

On the personal side, why hasn't Aretha married her longtime fiancé, Willie Wilkerson? Is she afraid that wedding bells signal some sort of a jinx with the men in her life? During the summer of 1988, Aretha threw another of her famous fêtes—a costume party at her Detroit home. She dressed as Queen Nefertiti, and Willie masqueraded as a convict in a striped "jailbird" uniform. In reality, Aretha is the queen of all of her domain, and Willie is clearly the prisoner of his affections. It seems that

Lady Soul is happy with things the way they are, and she doesn't want to upset the apple cart.

Having already brought such an incredible amount of creative fire to the contemporary music scene—from the revolutionary sixties to the high-tech eighties, perhaps Aretha feels that her music alone speaks for itself. Her career accomplishments, her expressive singing voice and her devotion to the church have all made her one of the most beloved celebrities of the Twentieth Century. In person, she really is the unpretentious, homey, down-to-earth woman that one imagines her to be. One hopes her own achievements have brought her as much happiness as they have given millions of people around the world.

Is she still the "mysterious lady of sorrow," or has she found an inner strength that brings her fulfillment? Does she still carry around the insecurities that seemed to paralyze her in the early sixties, or has she resolved the regrets and losses that have delivered sadness to her doorstep? Sequestered in her Detroit home, only Aretha herself can provide the answers to these questions.

Fortunately for everyone, her recordings and videos continue to keep her career alive and vital. And if she continues to produce music of the caliber of her 1980s output—what's to complain about? Within that realm, there are still plenty of vistas for her to explore. This is not where Aretha's story ends; it continues to grow and expand with each new album. Aretha is a unique, one-of-a-kind original, and as she enters the 1990s, she still continues to find new songs to sing.

Ever since she ascended the throne in the 1960s and was crowned the Queen of Soul, there has never existed the possibility that she would consider relinquishing her scepter. She has had her absences from the Top Ten record charts, but it is clear—even if she never makes another recording—that she is still a singer of unquestioned star status. If she chooses to become the Greta Garbo of R&B music, it will not effect the impact that she has had in the entertainment business. One cannot talk about soul music without mentioning Aretha Franklin. Perhaps she will make good her promise and never consider retirement.

She has *already* amassed a list of career accomplishments to rival those of Bessie Smith, Billie Holiday, and Dinah Washington. She has clearly transcended the mere labels of hit maker, popular singer, and soul star. She is truly a legend in the music business, and the best news of all is that there is still much more music on the horizon for her.

With the hit records, the Grammy Awards, the soulful glitz of her concert act, and the visual excitement of her video performances—is Aretha Franklin's life an exciting dream come true? Or has it been a painful nightmare? In reality, it has been an unpredictable combination of both. In her career she has attained Olympian heights, yet her personal life has hit emotional shattering depths. Together they make up the bittersweet life of the incomparable Aretha Franklin, the one and only Queen of Soul.

CHAPTER TEN

A ROSE IS STILL A ROSE— THE 1990S AND BEYOND

For Aretha Franklin, the decade of the 1990s represented a uniquely creative era, highlighted by critically acclaimed solo albums, several high profile concert appearances, three lifetime achievement awards, as well as starring in three high profile television specials, and another film role. She recorded a duet with Frank Sinatra, was featured on a movie soundtrack album which sold over six million copies, and produced an entire LP of hip-hop nineties music. As if this was not enough, she also stretched her repertoire in ground-breaking new directions by performing classical opera pieces that left audiences breathless with awe. Time and time again she was acknowledged as a true music industry "diva" whose talent seems to defy all categorization.

One of the most exciting aspects of Aretha's nineties music is the fact that she has never recorded a wider variety of material, nor has she worked with a wider range of different musical producers. She tackled and excelled at everything within her ever expanding musical scope. The spectrum she covered included dance music ("Deeper Love"), Broadway ("I Dreamed a Dream"), rock & roll ("Everyday People"), gospel ("I'll Fly Away"), contemporary ballads ("It Hurts Like Hell"), holiday tunes ("O Christmas Tree"), swinging jazz ("What Now My Love"), soul ("Mary Goes Round"), hip hop ("A Rose Is Still a Rose"), and finally Italian opera ("Nussen Dorma").

243

Amid the final decade of the Twentieth Century she worked with several of the producers from her past eras, including Arif Mardin (1960s), Carole Bayer Sager (1970s), as well as Narada Michael Walden and Luther Vandross (1980s). In this same era she recorded with over a dozen new producers. Each of them has helped to bring out unique and different shadings of her incredibly expressive voice. They included Lauryn Hill, Michel Legrand, C&C Music Factory, Phil Ramone, Kenny "Babyface" Edmonds, Burt Bacharach, and Paul Shaffer. In this way, she has maintained her classic sound and made inroads into fresh new musical territory.

On the other side of the coin, this same ten year period was also one dotted with mishap, controversy, and the loss of several of her close friends. She has encountered financial disputes with the Internal Revenue Service, and has been sued by department stores, limousine services, and several others for the non-payment of bills she has racked up. In addition, her long-awaited autobiography—which was published in 1999—was a gigantically disappointing mess. Unforthcoming, vague, and rambling, it was as big a sales disaster as it was a critical "bomb."

Although she finally quit smoking cigarettes in the 1990s, she watched her weight balloon to an all-time high, and on occasion she has even had to step in and rescue her children from scrapes with the law. While she is the undisputed "Queen" of a genre of music that the mere mention of her name immediately defines, she is also equally as happy to play the role of "domestic goddess" in her comfortable suburban Detroit home.

In addition to all of her musical accomplishments, Aretha has remained in the forefront of the public's eye throughout the nineties, and into the new millennium. Gossip columns, the tabloid papers, and respected magazines and newspapers—like *Time* and *The New York Times*—all avidly report her comings and goings. Whether or not she has a record on the charts or not is immaterial at this point. Her celebrity status has become so enormous that she makes news no matter what she does creatively. Readers avidly follow her legal disputes, her ongoing love affair with food, her fluctuating weight, and her now-legendary forays into bad fashion choices. Aretha now falls in the same category as Madonna and Elizabeth Taylor, where an upcoming appearance is always preceded by the thought, "What on Earth is she going to wear this time?" And, in La Franklin's case, the results have been more often unflattering than not. While she is worshiped for her talent and her stature in the music business, she is no idle "idol" sitting on a pedestal. Fashion criticisms aside, she is a living, breathing public figure; a contemporary woman who is very much alive and active. Inargueably, she is a true character and an original creation all her own.

For Aretha, the decade of the 1980s had ended on a sad note. In 1988 and 1989 alone, her brother Cecil, sister Carolyn, and her grandmother died. Then, on April 26, 1990, New York US District Judge Whitman Knapp ordered her to pay the sum of $209,364.07 with interest, for having walked out on the Broadway-bound play *Sing, Mahalia, Sing.*

As with most creative people, Aretha chose to throw herself into her career, instead of dwelling on negative things. August 9 and 10 of 1990, she performed to packed houses at Manhattan's famed Radio City Music Hall. On December 5 of that year she was saluted by the National Association of Recording Arts & Sciences (NARAS), with a "Living Legend" Grammy award from her peers.

Always lending a hand in her hometown of Detroit, on March 23, 1991, Aretha sang at the funeral of soldier Anthony Riggs, who had only been back home from the Gulf War for several days, when he was murdered. At first, the authorities had felt that Riggs' death was due to some random violent act. However, the whole affair became a local scandal when it was discovered that he had, in fact, been killed by his wife and brother-in-law for their own financial benefit. Aretha's supportive performance took place at the Little Rock Baptist Church in Detroit.

In the summer of 1991 Aretha swung into the decade as she released her ninth Arista album, *What You See Is What You Sweat.* It is a varied offering from seven different producers or production teams, notably including Narada Michael Walden, Burt Bacharach & Carole Bayer Sager, Luther Vandross, Michel Legrand, David "Pic" Conley & David Townsend, Elliot Wolff & Oliver Leiber, and Franklin herself.

The album opens with Aretha's exciting updating of the Sly & the Family Stone classic, "Everyday People." The song begins with Franklin shouting, "Yo, gang, let's kick the ballistics," and then she proceeds to launch into a spectacular extravaganza of soulful singing, joyful cheerleading, and improvised scatting. With a lively and upbeat vocal background troupe assisting her, she turns the classic sixties song into a pulsating party of a cut. At one point, the chorus cheers her on with a rhythmic "Go, go, go, Queen of Soul."

The selections on this diverse and beautifully produced album range from the snappy and sassy "Mary Goes Round," to the classy arrangement she has on Michel Legrand's lush "What Did You Give." Soul sister Ree clearly gets even by "dissing" her man in "What You See Is What You Sweat," and has some frivolous fun with Luther Vandross on their pop duet "Doctor's Orders." One of the biggest highlights on the album is the thoughtful and beautiful ballad, "Ever Changing Times," a duet with Michael McDonald on this Burt Bacharach and Carole Bayer Sager composition.

Another memorable cut is Aretha's interpretation of the show-stopping song "I Dreamed a Dream" from Broadway's *Les Miserables*. Accompanying herself on the acoustic piano, Franklin takes this powerhouse ballad of defeat, and changes the final lyrics to make her performance an anthem of encouragement and empowerment. In the plot of the show, this song is sung by the character of Fantine, who uses it to lament that her wretched life is over and she is about to die in defeat. Whereas Fantine sings that life has "killed" her dreams, Aretha sings that life "*must not*" kill hers. It had been decades since Aretha had tackled a Broadway tune on one of her albums, and in her inimitable fashion, she made this one a signature anthem all her own.

The reviews for the album were decidedly mixed. Stephen Holden in *Rolling Stone* proclaimed, "Although the material runs the gamut of styles, Franklin infuses her personality so indelibly into every song that somehow it all holds together . . . 'I Dreamed a Dream' . . . from the Broadway musical *Les Miserables* is turned into an obstacle course of vocal challenges with Franklin tossing around saucy embellishments and shivering melismata and bearing down so convincing on the line 'Tigers tear your dreams' that you can almost feel the teeth and hear the rips . . . *What You See Is What You Sweat* stands as one of her better albums. If the songs are uneven, they don't prevent the Queen of Soul from exuberantly expressing the breadth of her musical personality, from regal pop-gospel diva to funky everyday person." (1)

However, in *Entertainment Weekly*, Amy Linden wrote, "Just because Aretha Franklin has a voice magnificent enough to sing the phone book doesn't mean she should . . . a schizoid mix of mediocre material that includes the pointless, chirpy 'Mary Goes Round' and the pop-soul fluff of the title song . . . Her duet with Luther Vandross ('Doctor's Orders') is so cluttered with synthesizers you can barely hear the two masters." (2)

"Everyday People" was released as a single from the album, complete with three different mixes of the song, two of which appear on the album. According to Aretha, it was her own idea to cover a Sly Stone number. "I've always liked his catalog," she explained at the time. "There are many things that he did in the sixties that I really liked, and 'Everyday People' just kinda grabbed me, when I started re-listening to his catalog, that was the one that I liked the best." (3)

Aretha looked trim and fit when she made a rare TV appearance on the local Detroit talk show, *Dayna*, to promote her *What You See Is What You Sweat* album on July 10, 1991. Wearing a white leather mini-skirt accented with black checks, matching jacket and a black blouse, she looked lovely, and spoke quite candidly about her life. She also performed "Everyday People" in front of her hometown studio audience.

She appeared to be very relaxed and focused on this particular show. Part of the credit goes to the talkshow hostess, Dayna, who is one of Aretha's local girlfriends. Franklin seemed much more at ease and centered than she has been on some of the network morning shows where everything is rushed, and interviews are often brief at best. When she was asked by Dayna what her advice would be to someone caught in the throes of tragedy, Aretha somberly replied, "Just a few words and that is: 'Surely, God is able.'" (3)

Fielding an inquiry from an audience member as to her secrets to staying youthful appearing, Franklin laughingly claimed that her secret was a combination of "Slim Fast and a real good man." (3)

When Dayna inquired about relationships, she asked if Aretha had encountered any problems with intimidating male suitors. Aretha snapped back in true girlfriend-to-girlfriend fashion, "I am as approachable as any other woman. Not on-stage, [but] when I come off stage. I'm not charging admission at my front door, and there won't be a concert inside. So, approach me the same way that you would any other woman. However, there are some men who—some who—I guess you could say, they are intimidated. But those are just the ones who are a little insecure within themselves, and who are not confident within themselves. What I do [as an occupation] and who I am has nothing to do with a man and a woman relationship." (3)

She also defended her convictions to continue to live in the Motor City, in spite of the crime and problems which continued to plague that urban area. According to Aretha, "I think what's happening in Detroit, is happening in most major cities today, so I don't think that Detroit should be singled out in any unique or special way having to do with crime and problems that major cities are having. And, most of my family and my friends are here, and this is home to me." (3)

Perhaps the most wonderful thing that Aretha said during the hour-long all-Aretha tribute on the chat show, came when someone in the audience asked her what her plans were for retirement. With conviction in her voice, Franklin replied, "I'm NOT gonna retire!" (3) With that, the studio audience launched into a thunderously huge round of applause.

In spite of her efforts to promote her latest album, *What You See Is What You Sweat* came and went without much fanfare. The song "Everyday People" made it to Number Thirteen on the R&B Singles charts, and spent one week on the UK charts at Number Sixty-nine. Her snappy duet with Luther Vandross was nominated for a Grammy Award, but that was the height of its success. On the American album charts, this varied LP only made it to Number 153. A sales failure, the album is now considered a forgotten gem in her Arista album catalog. Whether it just got lost in the shuffle that year, or was out of touch with what was going on amidst the record charts that season, it seemed to disappear as quickly as it was released.

Yet, she was very much in the public eye. Aretha returned to New York City, September 13 and 14 to play Radio City Music Hall once again. Back in Detroit on October 30, she was at the Westin Hotel at the Renaissance Center in downtown Detroit to sing "Happy Birthday" to her buddy, Rev. Jesse Jackson.

On November 11, 1991 Aretha made a comical guest appearance on the top-rated CBS comedy television series, *Murphy Brown*. Throughout the show's successful run, actress Candice Bergen portrayed the character of Brown as a hardboiled network newswoman who idolized classic R&B music from the 1960s—to the point where her own flat and off-key renditions of soul classics were often comedy bits amidst the series' run. In the plot of this particular episode, Murphy gets to meet her soul idol, Aretha Franklin, and at the end of the show—is invited to join her for a rendition of one of her hits at the piano. The episode went on to become one of that season's most popular half hours.

According to Bergen at the time, "Aretha Franklin is the patron saint of our show. From the beginning, she has been one of our most important trademarks. She is Murphy Brown's hero, she's my hero. And, in my life—which has not been unexciting, one of the most thrilling moments was when I got to share a piano bench with Aretha Franklin when she played and sang 'Natural Woman.'" (4)

Beginning on December 29, 1991, Aretha Franklin could be heard as the singing voice on a series of nationally run Pizza Hut television commercials. She took the Fontella Bass hit "Rescue Me," and sang it as "Deliver Me," to commemorate the fast food chain's entry into the delivery end of the pizza business. Some die-hard fans bristled at the idea that Aretha should position herself as the "Queen" of pepperoni and cheese. *The Tucson Daily Star* amusingly ran an item which classified the event as "an act that—on a scale of appalling events—rates as high as asking Picasso to design a new burrito wrapper for Taco Bell." (5)

Perhaps the biggest kept resolution of the year was the fact that Aretha had quit smoking cigarettes. "I stopped smoking in 1991. It helped my voice tremendously. The clarity and everything. The range even increased," she was later to explain. (6)

"It was messing with my voice," she finally had to admit. The good news was: "The higher notes are back." However, the bad news was that her weight increased as soon as she quit smoking. The fit look she had on the *Dayna* show was gone for the rest of the decade. "But," she had to admit, "I'd rather be overweight a few pounds and work on that, than on my way to cancer." (7)

On February 25, 1992 she was back on-stage at Radio City Music Hall in New York City. This time she was singing at the Grammy Awards. She performed the song "Ever Changing Times" with Michael McDonald that evening. The following night she was honored by the Rhythm & Blues Foundation, at their third annual Pioneer Awards. At the festivities, which were held at the Rainbow Room high atop Rockefeller Center, Aretha was saluted alongside her singing contemporaries Chuck Jackson, The Dells, The Staple Singers, Rufus Thomas, and Bobby "Blue" Bland.

That same year, an avalanche of retrospective Aretha Franklin material hit the marketplace, in the embodiment of two separate CD boxed sets, and the debut of Rhino Records beginning to issue several of the classic albums from her glory days at Atlantic Records—many of them on CD for the very first time. When the 1990s girl group En Vogue revived Aretha's "Something He Can Feel" from the 1976 *Sparkle* album, and turned it into a fresh hit, the spotlight was rightfully thrown on Franklin's original rendition of the Curtis Mayfield penned song. Aretha's long-forgotten *Sparkle* album made its CD debut in 1992, followed in 1993 by CD's of *Young, Gifted and Black*, and in 1994 by *Hey Now Hey, The Other Side of The Sky*.

The most exhaustive re-issueing of classic Aretha however, came in September 1992 with Rhino's four-CD boxed set, *Aretha Franklin: Queen of Soul—The Atlantic Recordings*. This ultimate Aretha package traces her Atlantic years in eighty-six cuts, from 1967's "I Ain't Never Loved A Man (The Way I Love You)" to 1977's "Break It To Me Gently." All of the obvious hits and favorite album cuts are here, plus some rarely heard gems including: "Dark End of The Street," "So Swell When You're Well," "Master of Eyes (The Deepness of Your Eyes)," "With Everything I Feel In Me," "Mr. D.J. (5 for The D.J.)," "Sparkle," "All The King's Men," and "Something He Can Feel." And, thanks to writer David Nathan, several quotes from the original edition of this book appear in the liner notes of the beautifully packaged eighty page booklet. The package went on to win a Grammy Award as the "Best Liner Notes" of 1992, with the award being presented to the writers of the essays included.

Not to be outdone, the Legacy division of Columbia Records

assembled a double CD album entitled *Aretha Franklin: Jazz to Soul*, including thirty-nine songs on two distinctly different discs. The first disc is dedicated to Aretha's blues and jazz sides from her Columbia days, including "What a Diff'rence a Day Makes," "Blue Holiday," and "Drinking Again." It also featured three rarities: a previously unreleased version of "Once In a While," a previously unreleased alternate version of the song "Skylark," and a previously unreleased alternate take of "Impossible." Disc Two traced Aretha's most commercial recordings for Columbia, including "Operation Heartbreak," "Soulville," "Runnin' Out of Fools," "Trouble in Mind," "Walk on By," "Every Little Bit Hurts," and "Mockingbird."

When the Record Industry Association of America (RIAA) tallied up the cumulative sales for Aretha's first gospel album, *Amazing Grace*, they found that it had exceeded sales of two million copies. So, on August 26, 1992, they certified it both Platinum, and Double Platinum.

While her fans were delving into her past recordings, for Aretha it was full steam ahead with her personal appearances, both in public and at private events. In the spring of 1992, a new Aretha song—"If I Lose"—was included on the soundtrack from the popular Woody Harleson and Wesley Snipes film *White Men Can't Jump*. It is an eclectic album featuring everything from the rap of BoyzIIMen and Queen Latifah, to gospel/pop from Bebe & Cece Winans. "If I Lose" shows off Ree on a jazzy piano led ballad. On June 12 she performed "Bridge over Troubled Water" and "Everyday People" at a gathering of New York City's Friar's Club, honoring Arista president, and Aretha mentor, Clive Davis. The event was held at the Waldorf Astoria Hotel on Park Avenue.

On July 14, 1992, Aretha Franklin made an appearance at the Democratic National Convention, singing the National Anthem. For her, this was the beginning of a strong presence throughout the decade, of being involved in political events, performing at the White House, and being honored at official Washington D.C. functions.

She was also one of the guests at the wedding of Whitney Houston and Bobby Brown in Mendham, New Jersey on July 18, 1992. Other guests included Dionne Warwick and Clive Davis. By having Aretha, Dionne, Whitney and Clive all present, it almost seemed like an Arista

Records roster meeting.

In late 1992 when the second volume of rocking Christmas music, *A Very Special Christmas 2* was released, Aretha was heard alongside such varied stars as BoyzIIMen, Sinead O'Connor, Ann & Nancy Wilson of Heart, Debbie Gibson, Frank Sinatra & Cyndi Lauper, Randy Travis, Tom Petty, Run DMC, and Michael Bolton. While Darlene Love & Ronnie Spector raucously partied their way through "Rockin' Around the Christmas Tree," and Bonnie Raitt & Charles Brown got bluesy on "Merry Christmas Baby," Aretha takes the classy route, turning "O Christmas Tree" into a lushly orchestrated ballad. Her voice—which has never sounded better—lilts above the sound of lush strings. This standout cut was produced by Marty Paich, and his brother David Paich, both of the rock group Toto.

When President Bill Clinton was inaugurated in January of 1993, it was done to a jubilant sea of parties, concerts, dinners and special events. On January 17 Aretha performed at one of the events, billed as *A Call to Reunion: A Musical Celebration* at the Lincoln Memorial. Two days later she performed "I Dreamed a Dream" at the gala entitled *An American Reunion: The Fifty Second Presidential Gala*.

The biggest gala was an all-star televised tribute concert for Clinton and his administration. There was Aretha on-stage alongside Barbra Streisand, Fleetwood Mac, Kenny G, Michael Bolton, Judy Collins, Little Richard, Michael Jackson, and the First Family. Aretha performed that night in a shoulderless spangled white gown with a tight fitting bustier gown which flowed out into a full skirt. Her hair was swept upward into a bun on top of her head.

However, it was the outdoor event at the Lincoln Memorial that gave Aretha the most publicity. Although everyone agreed that she looked and sounded fabulous, not everyone agreed that she was at all in "politically correct" 1990s fashion by wearing a full-length sable fur coat. Animal Rights activists complained loudly, and newspapers fielded heated "letters to the editor." The January 22, 1993 issue of *USA Today* pointed out the "politically IN-correct" show of fur coats at the festivities, headlined "Furs Out In Force For Inauguration." (8) Suddenly a whole controversy was stirred up, and Aretha was at the eye of the storm.

In the February 4, 1993 issue of *USA Today,* Bonnie Davis of

Rockville, Maryland wrote in to complain, "Where has Aretha Franklin been for the past five years? If she's picked up a newspaper, listened to a radio, or simply walked down the street, she'd know most people are sickened by the sight of fur. Maybe she doesn't care. Well, after seeing her prance around the steps of the Lincoln Memorial in her tacky fur, I've lost all R-E-S-P-E-C-T for her." In that same issue, Bill Outlaw of Washington D.C. came to her defense by proclaiming, "I keep wondering who determines what is politically correct. The whole idea behind our country is freedom of expression, and political correctness is actually an oxymoron. As for Aretha Franklin, she may receive some criticism from animal activist groups, but she has the R-E-S-P-E-C-T of a great majority of the American public." (9)

Finally, even Aretha had to get into the fray. She dismissed the whole affair in *Vanity Fair* magazine by arguing, "Leather comes from animals, you know what I'm saying? We're all using a lot of leather with respect to our shoes and handbags and things like that, so come on, let's be for real." (10) You go Aretha!

It was to be her first television special in years, so when it came time to tape *Aretha Franklin Duets* on April 27, 1993 at Broadway's Nederlander Theater, all of the stops were pulled out and everyone turned out to hail the Queen of Soul. The event was taped for broadcast on the Fox TV network on May 9, where it ran in an edited down hour-long version.

Not only did Bonnie Raitt, Rod Stewart, Elton John, Smokey Robinson, and Gloria Estefan come to sing with her, they also came to praise her. According to Bonnie that night, "I can never believe this is happening. You know, it doesn't get any better than Aretha Franklin. I grew up wearing out 45's of 'Respect,' 'Chain of Fools,' 'I Never Loved a Man,' and even though the music was always incredible, somehow I knew that she had to always get into the lyrics before she could record 'em. If it didn't mean a whole lot, it wouldn't get cut. 'Since You've Been Gone,' which is her song by-the-way, has always been one of my all-time favorites. And, it is the thrill of my lifetime to be here to sing it with her tonight." (4)

Even Hollywood stars like Robert De Niro and Dustin Hoffman were on hand to laud laurels on the Queen. "Tonight, all of you here tonight are fans of the female singer of our generation," said De Niro.

"We've never met, and yet I feel as though I know her, and that speaks to the power of her music. Her songs have been an important part of several of my films, most notably 'Do Right Woman' in *Cape Fear*, and 'Baby, I Love You' in *Good Fellas*. But more importantly, her music is part of the soundtrack of most our lives, and the real tribute to her tonight is that she has connected with so many of us." (4)

Dustin Hoffman opened the concert, by announcing, "Tonight we're here to celebrate Aretha Franklin. Please welcome The Aretha-Airs." (4) With that the curtain rose to reveal Smokey Robinson, Rod Stewart and Elton John singing the "chain, chain, chain" chorus line of "Chain of Fools," over and over again. Smokey was in a charcoal sharkskin suit. Rod wore a lime green tuxedo jacket, a lime green shirt, and black pants. Elton was in a flashy cutaway tuxedo with tails, over black leather pants. Moments later, they were joined on-stage by Franklin. Her hair was blown out into a large high-on-her-head wavy style. She wore a black military jacket emblazoned with crests and medals, over a black mini skirt. She was accessorized with big dangling gold and turquoise earrings. Singing her lead vocals while Smokey, Rod and Elton handled the familiar background vocals, Aretha was in her element.

Throughout the evening, she spoke very eloquently to the audience, and the proceedings were very classy and upbeat throughout. The songs were all from the "greatest hits" songbooks of Franklin's and those of her guests. Elton's "Border Song (Holy Moses)" and Aretha's "Spirit in the Dark" were presented as a pair of double grand piano duets with Franklin and John each playing and singing to each other. For the later song they were joined on-stage by Raitt, Estefan, Stewart, Robinson, and De Niro.

Introducing her number with Aretha, Gloria Estefan proclaimed, "I can't really express what a thrill it is to be here sharing the stage with Aretha Franklin. Oh yes—most definitely, she's one of my idols. And, like all you, when it comes to Aretha, I'm a huge fan. I would have done any of her songs, but when she asked me to sing 'Coming Out of the Dark,' I was especially thrilled. It's a song that means a great deal to me, and to sing it with the Queen of Soul adds a whole new meaning to it." (4) Indeed it did.

Also on this program she was united with her Detroit buddy, Smokey

Robinson. Interestingly, in all of the years they had known each other, this was the first time they had ever sung together on a television show. They performed his 1980s hit "Just To See Her." For that particular number she wore a tastefully cut mini-skirt suit, and ankle strapped high heels.

Prior to singing a duet with Aretha, Rod Stewart explained that he was going to ignore the pre-written cue cards, and instead delivered the heartfelt message: "This is the highlight of my life to be standing on the stage with this wonderful woman who has surely got one of the best voices of the Twentieth Century—in my opinion. It is truly a thrill to be up here!" (4)

Aretha Franklin is a very cultured, and artistically aware woman. Although she is on one hand known as the Queen of Soul, she has demonstrated time and time again her expertise at singing, pop, jazz, blues, Broadway show tunes, standards, and gospel music. She also has a knowledge and an deep appreciation for two other musical forms, both of which are within her grasp as a performer and as an interpreter. Those two musical forms are opera and ballet, and in the 1990s she brought them both to her repertoire. Sometimes she is incredibly successful at these new realms, and sometimes she is not. She obviously thought that the taping of the *Duets* television special represented the perfect arena for her to attempt ballet. Not everyone agreed.

For whatever reason, the one sequence that was cut out of the television special was a ballet number which, featured Aretha in a revealing bustier and a tutu. What the television audience did see, was Aretha in a bustier outfit with a skirt of diaphanous pink tulle, which she wore for her duet with Rod Stewart on "This Old Heart of Mine." She looked very chesty, and while shimmying and shaking on-stage mid-song, she appeared to be oozing out of the constraints of the tight fitting garment.

James T. Jones IV wrote of the audience reaction in *Vanity Fair*, "Others were left speechless by a surreal ballet sequence in which Aretha, in a tutu, attempted pirouettes." (10)

However, it was Liz Smith, who, in her syndicated gossip column minced no words when she wrote, "She must know she's too bosomy to wear such clothing, but clearly she just doesn't care what we think, and that attitude is what separates mere stars from true divas." (10)

Scalded by the public scolding, Aretha wrote Liz Smith back a letter which read: "How dare you be so presumptuous as to presume you could know my attitudes with respect to anything other than music . . . Obviously I have enough of what it takes to wear a bustier and I haven't had any complaints. When you get to be a noted and respected fashion editor, please let us all know . . . You are hardly in a position to determine what separates stars from divas since you are neither one or an authority on either." (10) Aretha had spoken. And, she was far from finished with her in-questionable-taste low cut dresses. In fact, she was just warming up.

Aside from the edited out ballet fiasco, the show was a huge success. The memorable music and the star duets which are contained on it is worthy of a CD release.

On April 30, Aretha was busy picking up yet another award. That night she was one of eight women honored by *Essence* magazine at the sixth annual *Essence* Awards ceremony held at the Paramount Theater at Madison Square Garden.

Without a doubt, the hottest song Aretha cut the entire decade was "Deeper Love," which teamed her with producing duo of Robert Clivillés and David Cole, better known as C&C Music Factory. The pair came to prominence when they scored a huge Number One hit with the 1990 dance cut "Gonna Make You Sweat (Everybody Dance Now)," and the radio smash "Things That Make You Go Hmmmm . . ." Putting the Queen of Soul with these mix-masters in 1993, produced her most danceable and upbeat cut in ages. Although the song did not set new sales records, the fierce cut let everyone know that Aretha was still at the top of her game.

The song "Deeper Love" was originally included on the soundtrack album for the Whoopie Goldberg movie *Sister Act 2: Back in the Habit*. However, the most exciting versions of the song appear on a five cut single version of the song from Arista Records, including the eleven+ minute "Tribesman Mix," and the twelve+ minute "C&C Music Factory Mix." Aretha proved on this cut that she would still "rock steady" with the best of them on the dancefloor. In America, the song only made it to Number Sixty-three on the Pop Singles chart, however, in Britain it became a huge Number Five hit.

In its November 5, 1993 issue, *Entertainment Weekly* magazine tallied their selections for the "100 Greatest CD's" that could be purchased to create the ultimate collection. The article was written under the assumption that every essential 1990s compact disc collection could be easily owned by purchasing key CD compilations in just about every category, and several essential "masterpieces." The gamut ran from Frank Sinatra (*Songs for Swingin' Lovers* 1956) and Barbra Streisand (*The Broadway Album* 1985) from the pop realm, the Beatles (*Abbey Road* 1969 and *The Beatles 1962–1966*) and the Rolling Stones (*Exile on Main Street* 1972) representing rock, all the way to classical (Beethoven's *Symphony No. 9*) and jazz (John Coltrane's *A Love Supreme* 1964 and Ella Fitzgerald's *The Duke Ellington Songbook* 1957).

Several performers were represented by their "Greatest Hits" compilations alone, including the Carpenters, the Police, Sly & the Family Stone, Madonna, and Patsy Cline. The entire Motown catalog of Supremes, Temptations, and Martha & the Vandellas music was represented by the excellent four CD boxed set, *Hitsville USA: The Motown Singles Collection 1959–1971* (1992). The editors of *Entertainment Weekly* wisely chose Aretha's two-CD collection *30 Greatest Hits* to represent her in an "if you can purchase only one Franklin album" fashion.

Describing *30 Greatest Hits*, the cover story claimed, "You need all her great songs—hence this collection. Follow it to the end and you'll find a few pop indulgences ('Eleanor Rigby') that don't quite catch her at her best. But Miss Franklin is so grand that her lapses are part of her charm." (11)

One of the most remarkable of Aretha's recordings of the 1990s appeared on Frank Sinatra's first of two *Duets* albums. This 1993 LP was a brilliant way to cast Sinatra in a contemporary setting by teaming up his voice with those of some of the hottest newcomers of the pop music field, as well as some of his own contemporaries. The album was also unique in that none of Sinatra's "duet" partners were in the same recording studio at the same time as Sinatra—due to his ill health at the time. Trading lyrics with the likes of Luther Vandross, Barbra Streisand, Gloria Estefan, Natalie Cole, Carly Simon, and Anita Baker, this was a tribute to thirteen of his most famous trademark songs. The song which paired the Chairman of the Board with the Queen of Soul, is a swinging version of "What Now

My Love" with the pair improvising sassy lines to each other in ultra-cool Rat Pack fashion. To hear Aretha ad-lib to Frank Sinatra, "don't even worry about it" is nothing short of "priceless."

Although—at this point—she had amassed the astonishing number of fifteen Grammy Awards for her recordings, on March 1, 1994 Aretha added another of the gramophone-shaped trophies to her collection. Being awarded a Lifetime Achievement Grammy Award put her into an exclusive category of historic recording artists. Through the years, other recipients of this honor have included: Nat "King" Cole, Ella Fitzgerald, Patsy Cline, Billie Holiday, Paul McCartney, Lena Horne, and Fred Astaire. On 1994's live telecast of *The Grammy Awards* show from Radio City Music Hall, Aretha was seen singing "(You Make Me Feel Like) A Natural Woman" for the international viewing audience of millions. To many of her fans—this one song would always be regarded as her greatest single hit.

Although it had been promised for years, finally in 1994 Arista Records released a "best of" disc comprising all of that label's most popular and most successful Aretha cuts. Entitled *Aretha Franklin Greatest Hits 1980–1994*, it has all of the big hits, including "Freeway of Love," "I Knew You Were Waiting," "Deeper Love," "Jump to It" and "Get It Right." It also contains "(You Make Me Feel Like A) Natural Woman" by the trio of Bonnie Raitt, Gloria Estefan and Aretha from her TV special, as well as "I Dreamed a Dream," complete with the Edward James Olmos introduction she received when she performed it at the Presidential Inauguration. In addition, it includes two new Franklin ballads, produced by Kenny "Babyface" Edmonds: "Honey" and "Willing to Forgive," both of which were released as singles. "Honey" made it to Number 114 in the United States, and Number Thirty on the R&B chart. "Willing to Forgive" however made it to Number Twenty-six on the US pop charts, Number Five on the R&B chart, and Number Seventeen in the UK.

Babyface had already had success producing Toni Braxton and Whitney Houston, so he seemed like a natural choice to work with Aretha. It was originally Clive Davis who orchestrated their meeting, uncertain of how they would get along in the studio.

Babyface was later to explain to Aretha—in a dialogue in *Interview* magazine, "I was a little nervous when I went into the studio with you because I didn't know what you thought of me as a producer or writer or artist. I didn't know if it was just a hook-up organized by Clive. And because of your talent, I didn't know if you would think anything of what my opinion would be. I have worked with people who don't hold a candle to your credit but have far more attitude than they should, acting like they should be Aretha. But I'm glad to say, I was very happy about how things went." (12)

She in turn said to him in the same article, "Long before we got to the studio, I knew that you were highly qualified, but I didn't have any reservations at all. I was just hoping I'd really get a good one! And I did—I love both of the songs we did." (12)

Although the album *Aretha Franklin: Greatest Hits 1980–1994* only made it to Number Eighty-five on the *Billboard* magazine album chart and Number Twenty-seven in England, it eventually sold a million copies in America, and was certified Platinum.

The year 1994 was another high profile one for Franklin. On March 12, Aretha was the musical guest on NBC-TV's *Saturday Night Live*, and on April 22 she attended and was part of the seventh annual *Essence* Awards, which were again held at the Paramount Theater in New York City. On May 1 she performed at the 25th annual Jazz & Heritage Festival in New Orleans, Louisiana.

It seemed like everything was in order in her life. She was also very happy with the quality and diversity of the music she was creating. Aretha stated at the time, "I'm very pleased with the music at this point. I'm still looking for the man, though, I've met a lot of gentlemen, and I date occasionally, but I haven't met the one I've been waiting for." (12)

What kind of man was she looking for? "I usually tend to prefer a taller gentleman. Stylish. A positive person. Ambitious. And successful," she proclaimed at the time. (13)

Like many media stars, unfortunately, Aretha finds that she has a tendency to intimidate suitors. According to her, "It has been a problem. I have even discussed it with other ladies in the business to see whether or not they were having the same problems. Some men feel like they're gonna be called 'Mr. Franklin' or something. Any *real* men can rise to the occasion with no sweat. One guy I was interested in told a friend of mine that he thought I was gonna ask him to carry my bags someday. That sounds like he doesn't think very much of himself." (12)

That same year Aretha was also one of the featured artists heard on the disc *A Tribute to Curtis Mayfield*. While Gladys Knight ripped her way through the feisty "Choice of Colors," Bruce Springsteen went rhythmic on "Gypsy Woman," and B. B. King got soulful on "Woman's Got Soul," Aretha took the ballad route—choosing "The Makings of You." It is great to hear her on this wonderful album—which is one of the best of the 1990s proliferation of all-star songwriter tribute discs.

Rhino Records that year released two excellent single disc greatest hits CDs, *The Very Best of Aretha Franklin, Volume One, The '60s*, and *The Very Best of Aretha Franklin, Volume Two, The '70s*. Essentially they represent the *30 Greatest Hits* album, divided in two, with the addition of "Border Song (Holy Moses)," "All the King's Horses," and "Something He Can Feel," and the omission of the gospel song "Wholly Holy."

On June 20, 1994, Aretha Franklin gave a historic concert, performing for the first time at the White House. Singing before 180 invited guests, plus President Bill Clinton and First Lady Hillary Clinton, Aretha dazzled the crowd which gathered in the Rose Garden. The varied program highlighted several of her classic hits—"Respect," "Freeway of Love," "I Say a Little Prayer" and "Brand New Me"—as well as several standards from her early sixties jazz past, including "I Want to Be Happy," and the ballads "Smile" and "Cottage For Sale." She was then joined on-stage by Lou Rawls for a moving version of the song "Tobacco Road." For that particular number, she dismissed her musicians with a wink: "We don't need 'em," she said. (14) With that, she sat down at the piano and accompanied herself. She and Rawls were next joined by the choir of Washington's Eastern High School, and they all closed the show with the song "I Was Born to Sing the Gospel."

That night's one-hour concert was also taped as a PBS TV special entitled *In Performance at The White House*, which was broadcast on October 12 of that year. As fabulous as her singing was that evening, no one could stop talking about the super-low cut white beaded off-the-shoulder Arnold Scaasi dress that she wore. At one point during the evening's presentation, a less-than-svelte Aretha bowed down to accept a standing ovation, and it looked like she was about to pop out of the dress. It was to become acknowledged as her most dramatic fashion *faux pas* of the decade.

The press was quick to jump on the Queen of Soul's case. According to Toriano Boynton in *USA Today*, "Low cut was the dress and mum was the word for Aretha at her post-White House concert party. Before reporters in the Ritz-Carlton ballroom could open their mouths, Franklin said, rolling her eyes, 'Thank you for not asking me any questions.'" The same article also reported that Aretha wasn't very interested in the dinner buffet "but didn't miss the chocolate-covered strawberries at desert." (15)

On November 3, 1994, Aretha performed at a benefit for the New York chapter of the National Academy of Arts and Sciences. On the 25th of that month, along with Chaka Khan and Tevin Campbell, Aretha performed at the third annual Franklin Scholarship Awards Dinner and Dance, which was held at the Cobo Hall exhibition center in downtown Detroit. This was her own pet charity, and that evening she was the "belle" of the ball. However, for Franklin, the best was yet to come.

As Aretha explained it, she was sitting at home watching television one day, when she caught President Bill Clinton on the air, saluting the National Council of Negro Women. According to her, "I was very touched to see that, and I thought maybe one day the President will give me something. And, I went on cooking . . . And the very next day, I got the call from my agent." Her agent informed her that she had been chosen as one of that year's five recipients of the Kennedy Center Lifetime Achievement Award. "I was so stunned!" she proclaimed, "because the President does bestow this honor as well. So you never know what the Lord has in store for you." (16)

It was on December 4, 1994, that Aretha Franklin received this particular honor, which is one of the biggest and most prestigious awards any American citizen can have bestowed upon them, as one of the Kennedy Center Honorees. Every year the President and First Lady present this honor on legends of the humanities, citing the person's expertise in music, dance, film, stage, directing, or producing. Along with Aretha, that year's honorees included actor Kirk Douglas, Broadway director Harold Prince, folk singer/songwriter Pete Seeger, and composer Morton Gould.

The festivities are a two night affair. The recipients were first fêted at a White House dinner reception hosted by President and Mrs. Clinton. At the White House dinner, President Clinton proclaimed, "You could say that Hillary and I went to college and law school with Aretha, because scarcely a day passed we didn't listen to her songs . . . She took the genius God gave her and applied it to earthly pain and joy." Following the dinner, President Clinton had to fly to Budapest, and was unable to attend the actual presentation ceremony which was held the next night at the Kennedy Center. That evening at the black tie White House dinner, Aretha looked stunning in a long white dress with ruffles, designed by Arnold Scaasi. (17) & (18)

At the 1994 Kennedy Center presentation, Aretha arrived twenty minutes late. She had a case of stomach flu, and was not feeling well. However, when she came sweeping in wearing a low-cut red velvet gown and a shawl framing her bare shoulders, all eyes were on her. Aretha was escorted by her new on-again-off-again beau, handsome actor Renauld White, from the television soap opera *The Guiding Light*. That evening on-stage, Aretha was saluted in song by members of New Bethel Baptist Church in Detroit, by Patti LaBelle, by the Four Tops, and treated like sheer royalty.

In addition to the prestige this award represented to Aretha, at the age of fifty-two, she was also the youngest person ever to be have it bestowed upon them. Franklin later cooed, "This award is absolutely stunning. No question that this is the *piece de resistance*." (17)

According to Aretha, during this era she had been seeing Renauld White, "on and off for years." When asked about her relationship with him by *Ebony* magazine, she revealed, "Renauld and I are close, very close . . . There's a kind of unexplainable something that happens between he and I. It's warm. I like it." (7)

What happened to her 1980s engagement to handsome fireman Willie Wilkerson? It went by the wayside, Wilkerson was later to reveal. According to him, "She's a homebody, she really is as far as I can see. She likes being around the house and likes having a man around the house.

The type of person I am, I can't sit around the house. If I could be that type of guy. I would have been there. I'm too hyper." (10)

Aretha has said in the past that she always remains friendly with the men she has dated, even when the blush of romance has faded. In 1994 Aretha asked Wilkerson, with whom she had broken up, to assist her on an upcoming concert tour. He gladly accepted, considering her to be a dear friend in need of his help. "My title is music librarian," he said at the time. "I handle sheet music. I make sure nothing is lost. I make sure music gets to her. She just asked me to do this job recently. Sounds like something small, but it's major." (10)

Years after the affair had cooled off, Aretha finally admitted that the mystery man she had talked about dating in the early 1980s was indeed Dennis Edwards, formerly of the Temptations. "Dennis Edwards was about fifteen years too late," she proclaimed. "Meaning by the time he realized the value of what he had, it was just too late. I was no longer interested. He had drop-kicked me a couple of times and I had just had enough." (7)

Edwards has since admitted, "I should have married Aretha. It was all in my court and I think I'm the one that was so scared of marrying this superstar." (10)

On January 10, 1995, Aretha performed at the Universal Amphitheater, in Universal City, California, at a tribute to Ella Fitzgerald. At that time Ella was in ill health, so it was a great honor for Franklin to lend her support to the woman whose prowess in jazz music parallels Aretha's stature in the world of pop and R&B music.

When the Grammy Awards were handed out in Los Angeles on March 1, 1995, Aretha's "A Deeper Love" was nominated as the "Best Female R&B Performance" of the year. However, it was Toni Braxton's "Breathe Again" which ultimately took that trophy.

Although Aretha was still very much "mum" about discussing her children, a 1995 article in *Vanity Fair* spoke frankly of her sons. The article, which gave a rare glimpse into her private life, reported on what they were doing with their lives by describing them as: "Edward, a theological student; Kecalf, a rapper; Teddy junior, who plays guitar and travels with his mother; and Clarence, a chronic schizophrenic." (8) Although Franklin has remained very closed-mouthed about Clarence's difficulties, the *Vanity Fair* piece brought to the public eye, the rumors about him. According to one confidential source at a suburban Detroit mental facility, "We see Clarence in and out of our programs from time to time." (19)

Speaking of motherhood, in 1995 she did state without going into any specifics, "My children have been wonderful. Times when I have been down, they have lifted me up. But once they pass a certain age, their independence begins to kick in. And as a parent you try to maintain a certain amount of control and so you have this tug-of-war between the two. You have to learn when to let go. And that's not easy." (7)

On June 20, 1995, the day that Aretha was performing at the Mud Island Amphitheater in Memphis, Tennessee, she was also being sued by Saks Fifth Avenue department store. Filing the suit on that date at the Oakland County Circuit Court in Michigan, the store claimed she owed them $262,851.15 for purchased merchandise. This event was to be the first in a series of publicly aired 1990s financial fiascos from the Franklin camp.

Aretha was on-stage in Cleveland on September 2, 1995, at the celebration for the official opening of the Rock & Roll Hall of Fame, along with Martha Reeves & the Vandellas, Chrissie Hynde, Jackson Browne, Sheryl Crow, Bruce Springsteen, Mary Wilson, Yoko Ono, Little Richard, Bob Dylan, Celine Dion, James Brown, Gregg Allman, Melissa Etheridge, Jerry Lee Lewis, and dozens of other rock legends. She performed the songs "I Can't Turn You Loose" and "(You Make Me Feel Like) A Natural Woman" on her own, and the songs "Love and Happiness" and "Freeway of Love" with Al Green.

On the 29th of that month, Aretha sang at Madison Square Garden along with Gladys Knight, Kool & The Gang, and the Isley Brothers before a sold-out crowd of 15,174 people. It was billed as the "KISS-FM Classic Soul" concert, and was one of the largest live indoor audiences Franklin has ever performed before.

That same year, in a somewhat odd move, Aretha was heard on the album *Tapestry Revisited / A Tribute to Carole King* on the song "You've Got a Friend." It is not odd that she should be included, since one of her most famous recordings is King's "Natural Woman" from this very same album of music. The strange thing is that her performance is billed as "featuring Aretha Franklin" on a Bebe and Cece Winans recording of the song. Since Aretha is a hundred times bigger in stature than this pair of talented gospel singing siblings, they should be the "featured" voices on her song. Whatever the logic, the resulting track is a beautiful affair, with all three singers taking equal turns on this inspirational classic of undying friendship.

In another "featuring Aretha Franklin" appearance, the Queen of Soul was heard on a holiday album recorded by her Detroit buddies, the Four Tops. Entitled *Christmas Here with You*, Aretha sings on three of the tracks by her quartet of famous local Detroit friends. She sparkles with "The Tops" on the songs "White Christmas," "Silent Night" and the title track. A joyously diverse album, *Christmas Here with You* marked a brief return to the Motown label which had made the Four Tops a household name in the 1960s. The album's Executive Producers were Tops' member Lawrence Payton along with Bill Dern. Each of the individual four members of the group produced their own favorite holiday cuts, giving the album a nice warm feeling throughout. According to Lawrence Payton at the time, "We couldn't have done it without her. Aretha's spirit permeated through the entire project." (20)

The biggest-selling album Aretha Franklin has ever appeared on was the soundtrack for the hit "chick flick" of 1995, *Waiting to Exhale*. The movie, which was based on Terry McMillan's best-selling book of the same name, starred Whitney Houston, Angela Bassett, Loretta Divine and Lela Rochon. The album was produced by Babyface, and it included the *creme de la creme* of the female giants of 1990s R&B music, including Patti LaBelle, Toni Braxton, Mary J. Blige, Whitney Houston, Chaka Khan, Brandy, and Aretha Franklin.

Aretha's song on the *Waiting to Exhale* album is "It Hurts Like Hell," written and produced by her new buddy, Babyface. Beautifully orchestrated, arranged and sung, it is soft and beautiful, with Franklin proving once again that she is often at her most powerful at restrained heartfelt ballads like this one. The diva simmers on this perfect ode to a love gone bad.

The reviews for the album were unanimously glowing. James T. Jones

IV in *USA Today* gave it four stars out of four, and praisingly stated, "This can't-fail 16-song soundtrack pairs the top R&B/pop female singers of the decade with Kenneth 'Babyface' Edmonds, the '90s top songwriter. The eclectic line-up automatically makes this a classic, from big-throat divas Aretha Franklin, Whitney Houston, Patti LaBelle and Chaka Khan, to 'new jills' Brandy, Mary J. Blige, Chanté Moore and Faith Evans . . . Franklin, LaBelle and Khan show they still have some of the mightiest pipes in pop." (21)

The soundtrack album was handled and marketed like an important product all its own—apart from the movie. In a very real way, it was an event unto itself. In fact, it was more successful than the movie itself as far as critical reception went. The book was fabulous, and so was Angela Bassett in this movie. Although Whitney's acting was stiffly wooden in comparison to Bassett, the film was a financial hit at the box office, and the album was a smash from the word "go."

From the very start, it was hoped that the *Waiting to Exhale* album would replicate the success Arista had with the Number One soundtrack album from Whitney's film debut in *The Bodyguard* (1992). The album was released on November 14, 1995, and the movie wasn't released until December 22. Being as, the *Waiting to Exhale* album hit Number One on both the pop and the R&B album charts, would sell in excess of six million copies, and be nominated for a Grammy as the "Album of the Year," it was obviously a case of "mission accomplished." It was also the first multi-Platinum album Aretha Franklin had ever appeared on.

According to tradition, for the 1996 Summer Olympics in Atlanta to begin, a torch had to be carried across the country to its destination, to light the main flame at the Olympic stadium, and officially begin the international games. On June 9, 1996, Aretha Franklin was one of the dignitaries on hand to meet and welcome the Olympic torch to the Motor City. According to her, "It represents so much for me to watch the torch come through here. It makes me feel proud that they're bringing the torch to Detroit." (22) By the time the torch reached its destination, it had been carried 15,000 miles and through forty-two states. Unfortunately no one thought of photographing Aretha with the torch, Statue of Liberty style.

What a photo opportunity that would have made.

Also in 1996, Aretha was one of the featured stars to appear on the album *Songs of West Side Story*. The album found a varied roster of pop, rock and soul luminaries performing as "Sharks" or "Jets," in this updating of a true Broadway gem. Michael McDonald, Little Richard, Salt-N-Pepa, Patti LaBelle, Natalie Cole, Phil Collins, Trisha Yearwood, and the late Selena are heard in this updated casting of *West Side Story*. On the album, Aretha is heard doing a nineties version of the song "Somewhere," which she had originally recorded in the 1970s.

When *The Grammy Awards* were telecast from New York City in 1997, for the first time ever, they were held in Madison Square Garden. Not only was Aretha a presenter and a performer, but she was also one of the stars nominated for album of the year on the *Waiting to Exhale* soundtrack. It had been a banner year for Kenny "Babyface" Edmonds. He also scored with the song he produced for Eric Clapton, "Change the World." Due to all of the successful projects he was involved in, he was awarded the Grammy for "Producer of the Year" that night.

To properly represent the album on the program, several of its stars, including Lady Soul herself, performed a medley of the songs from the LP. Brandy kicked it off, singing her cut from the film, "In My Room." She was followed up by Mary J. Blige and her song "I'm Not Gonna Cry." Then, the star of the film, Whitney Houston came out to sing her smash song "Exhale (Shoop Shoop)," which had entered the charts at Number One in America. She was then joined on-stage by Cece Winans, and they sang their duet from the album, "Count on Me," to be joined in song by Aretha Franklin, Chaka Khan, Brandy, and Blige. In spite of the harmonious ensemble singing that evening, ultimately the winning album of the year was *Falling into You* by Celine Dion.

At the Grammys that night Aretha looked great in a floor length, cream-colored gown with a sheer form-fitting draping of sheer silk. Her hair was short on the sides, and curly on top. According to one inside source, prior to the show Aretha was in a quandary as to what to wear. On a whim, she stepped into a bridal shop on West 57th Street, and purchased her beautiful dress right off the rack at the last minute.

Also that evening Aretha was one of the three superstar presenters to hand out the last trophy of the evening, for the "Record of the Year." On hand to do the honors with Aretha were Tony Bennett and Stevie Wonder. The winning recording was "Change the World" by Eric Clapton, with the award being presented to the performer and the producer, who in this case was Babyface.

Sony/Columbia Records in 1997 released the Aretha Franklin compilation, *Aretha Sings The Standards*, culled from her time on Columbia Records. It was quite a significant release, since none of the songs included on this excellent ten cut retrospective had ever appeared on compact disc. The rarest cut of all—from this glimpse of Aretha in her most middle-of-the-road mode from the sixties—is her jazzy version of "Moon River." It never appeared on any of her albums while she was at Columbia, and only surfaced on a rare 1969 compilation called *Once in a Lifetime*.

That same year Rhino continued to forge ahead with repackaging Aretha's Atlantic LPs, adding the new compilation *Aretha Franklin Love Songs* to her growing catalog. All but one of the songs included on this album are also included on the *Queen of Soul* boxed-set. The song "If You Don't Think," which makes its CD debut here. It was taken from her often overlooked 1974 album, *Let Me in Your Life*.

At the time, Aretha was busy working on a new movie role, and a new album, both slated for 1998 release. With regard to the LP, she told Kevin Ransom of *The Detroit News*, "It's like, 'Wow!' I just love everything on it. It's both contemporary and classic soul, because I write from a traditional-soul mode, but I used contemporary producers." (23) Indeed, it was a rose about to bloom.

She even managed to fit in a driving vacation to Canada that summer. "I love to fish, bring it home, skin it, fry it and have a ball," she laughed. "We went up to Rondeau Bay in Canada . . . The fish were small, but we had a good time. That is, until the mosquitoes ran us back into the car," she laughed. (13)

On a sad note, the Four Tops' holiday album that Aretha appeared on in 1995, *Christmas Here with You*, was to be the last one to have been recorded by all four of the Four Tops. On June 20, 1997, group member Lawrence Payton passed away. Days later, when his funeral was held, all of his Detroit friends came to pay tribute to him, and Aretha Franklin graciously sang at his funeral.

When Diana, Princess of Wales was killed in 1997, in the most infamous car crash of the century, the whole world mourned in unison. It wasn't long after her death that the record industry jumped in with their own tributes. After Elton John adopted one of his most famous songs, "Candle in the Wind" as a salute to Diana, and turned it into the biggest-selling single in recording history, a full album commemorating the loss of the beloved Princess became an inevitability. The resulting two-disc album, *Diana: Princess of Wales: Tribute* was assembled within several weeks, and featured some of the biggest names in the business.

Since time was of the essence, several international superstars donated existing songs from their catalogs which seemed fitting for this somber tribute. Barbra Streisand donated "Love Theme From *A Star Is Born* (Evergreen)," Paul McCartney is represented by "Little Willow," and Eric Clapton contributed "Tears in Heaven." Instead of representing herself with a prerecorded track, Aretha Franklin, the Queen of Soul, went into the studio and produced her own tribute to the Princess. The song, "I'll Fly Away" is especially touching. Backed by the Logos Baptist Assembly as her ethereal chorus, Franklin delivered one of the album's most heartfelt moments. She began the somber gospel number chillingly *a capella*, even announcing "We salute and pay tribute to Diana, Princess of Wales" at the beginning of the song.

On November 29, 1997, Detroit's first black mayor, Coleman Young died. He had been one of the most controversial leaders of the Motor City in all of its history. For twenty years, from 1974 to 1994, he had worked hard to turn around a city known for its economic decline. Aretha had been one of Young's strongest supporters, and at his funeral services, she raised her voice in song to praise his accomplishments. Dressed in a tasteful black dress, trimmed in white, and a black pillbox hat on her head, Franklin dedicated the song "The Impossible Dream" to Young's memory.

In February of 1998 Aretha was in New York City to attend several high profile functions. On Monday the 23rd, she was scheduled to sing an opera selection at a dinner honoring Luciano Pavarotti at a benefit for the music industry charity known as MusiCares. At the dinner, Aretha sang the aria "Nussun Dorma" from Puccini's opera, *Turnadot*. It was not an event which was open to the public, but the buzz around town was that Franklin's public operatic debut was nothing short of "awesome." The following night she repeated the performance at an Arista Records party.

The 40th Annual Grammy Awards, were held that same week, on February 25, at Radio City Music Hall. There was a lot of advance press on the event, heralding the fact that several special performances were to take place. In a very rare live television appearance, Barbra Streisand was scheduled to perform her duet with Celine Dion on the song, "Tell Him." And Luciano Pavarotti was set to sing "Nussen Dorma" as part of the classical segment of the show.

It was, however, to be a night full of unexpected surprises from the start. The rap artist who calls himself Dirty Ol' Bastard, leapt up on-stage while country music's Shawn Colvin was speaking, and went off in some sort of inane diatribe. Some bizarre man with the words "Soy Bomb" written on his bare chest, leapt up onto the stage, and danced next to an unfazed Bob Dylan—while he sang. Barbra Streisand backed out of doing her duet with Dion at the last minute, because of the flu, so Celine instead performed her dramatic "Titanic" hit, "My Heart Will Go On."

But, without a doubt the most phenomenal—and the most talked about event of the whole star-studded show, was the performance Aretha gave. Half-an-hour before Pavarotti was to go on-stage, his doctor advised him not sing, because of a throat problem. Instead, the Queen of Soul volunteered to go on in his place.

According to Aretha, "There were eight minutes to go, and they ran upstairs with the boom box and a tape of the rehearsal Mr. Pavarotti had done that afternoon, so I could hear the arrangement of the orchestra. I knew the aria because earlier in the week I had performed it for him at the Waldorf. But I had crammed for it then, and when you cram, you kind of forget it. So I had to scramble to put the pieces together." (24) Furthermore it was also not even arranged in her key.

When she sang "Nessun Dorma" that night, Aretha literally sent chills up the backs of audience members. People were in awe that she had bridged the gap between pop music into classical music, and that she had done so masterfully. When she was finished, she received a full standing ovation.

In front of a television viewing audience of an estimated 25 million in the United States alone, La Franklin had shown, once and for all, her versatility and her boundless musical talent. Rock stars and bona fide classical divas alike, were on their feet applauding for her that night.

Perfectionist that she is, Aretha was unhappy that it couldn't have been even better. "The air was blowing on me one hundred miles a minute," she later complained. "They had promised me no air on-stage. The air ended up cutting off some of my high notes. I wasn't happy with that at all." (24)

USA Today categorized it as "Commanding respect . . . delivering a soulful version of the classical opera aria." (25) *Ebony* magazine claimed that "she stunned the audience with a virtuoso performance of 'Nussun Dorma.'" (26) This impromptu moment turned into one of the crowning achievements of her career.

On a fashion note, Aretha's weight was at a high point. Yet, that particular night she wore one of the most tasteful and classy outfits of her 1990s era. She sported a red and black and gold brocade top, which was finished in mink at the wrists, and at the high necked collar. She looked stunning.

Even Aretha herself was amazed at the compliments and commendations that were being bestowed upon her. "The reaction has just been overwhelming," she said days later. "I've gotten the most beautiful, exotic floral arrangements. Eddie Murphy sent me several dozen pink roses. The house is lined with big, beautiful arrangements from one end to the other. I just can't stand it." (13)

The timing couldn't be any more perfect for Aretha. While she was being praised for her mastery of a new arena of music with her operatic performance, she was about to release her first all-new studio album in over six years, one which would mark her entry into another genre: hip hop music. With all of the excitement swirling around Aretha, it was a brilliant time to release the first single from the album, its title cut "A Rose Is Still a Rose."

Weeks before the album was released, *Rolling Stone* carried a glowing review of Aretha's new album, giving it four stars out of a possible four, with the headline: "Aretha Franklin Stakes Claim To The Nineties." Wrote reviewer James Hunter, "An extraordinary piece of work, *A Rose Is Still a Rose* immediately establishes [Lauryn] Hill as one of R&B's most gifted writer/producers. But what it does for Aretha Franklin is something trickier to bring off: It renders her legendary and contemporary all at once . . . Doing her least restricted and most comfortable singing since 1981's *Love All The Hurt Away* . . . She achieves a stunning continuity with hip-hop-sired producers . . . Aretha can rock the house, but what she really excels at is mood. This is what becomes a legend most." (27)

Although the *A Rose Is Still a Rose* album was being billed as Aretha's entry into the hip-hop urban sound, the notion that it is entirely produced by the fresh blood of the record industry, is only partially true. The first seven cuts on the album were produced by five individuals who are responsible for some of the hottest hits of the decade: one by Lauryn Hill, one by Sean "Puffy" Combs, two by Daryl Simmons, two by Jermaine Dupri, and one by Dallas Austin. For the last four cuts on the album, two are produced by Narada Michael Walden, who has worked on nearly every Aretha album since *Who's Zoomin' Who?* One is produced by Michael J. Powell, who is most notable for his 1980s work with Anita Baker, and the last song on the album, "The Woman," was written and produced by Aretha herself.

It is truly the title cut—which starts off the album—that sets the tone for the whole disc, and everything that happens on it. If one were to dissect the album, it would leave one longing for Hill to simply take the reins of a whole Franklin disk, because she was obviously—even at a young age—a master at communicating songs for, by, and about women. However, since Hill had simultaneously become the toast of the entire record business with her own Platinum album, *The Miseducation of Lauryn Hill* (1998), she did not have the time for such a task.

This is not to put down the album's other 10 cuts—it is merely to say that "A Rose Is Still a Rose" is such a complete "home run" of a song, that the rest of the cuts seem to take its lead and fit with it to create a single mood. In that, this is the most completely unified sounding non-gospel album of Aretha's two decade Arista career.

The song "A Rose Is Still a Rose" is a percolating hit from its very start. Snappy, loopy, and crackling with totally nineties excitement, it is hip-hop and young sounding while in its lyric content Aretha takes the stance of an older woman counseling a younger, heartbroken girl. The song is a masterpiece of showing off thoroughly modern Aretha at her finest.

The Sean "Puffy" Combs cut, "Never Leave You Again" is an upbeat ballad of devotion featuring Aretha's scintillating scat singing. Daryl Simmons' "In Case You Forgot" is more of a classic Aretha ballad. Jermaine Dupri's "Here We Go Again" is a crackling track which Aretha digs into with her newly restored upper register singing.

The second half of the album relaxes more into a smooth groove, with the beautiful "In the Morning" setting the tone. "I'll Dip," Dallas Austin's cut, is an infectiously slow and rhythmically sassy ballad. "Watch My Back," which Walden produced, echoes Aretha's now classic eighties sound, with her growling and playful singing making it one of the album's prime highlights. After all of the hip hop excitement of the rest of the LP, it ends with Aretha's own composition on the album, the mellow piano driven "The Woman," which she produced herself.

Justifiably, Aretha was quite proud of the finished outcome. She had broken into a whole new era of her long and glorious career. "I'm a very versatile vocalist," she proudly admitted. "That's what I think a singer should be. Whatever it is. I can sing it. I'm not a rock artist, but I've done some rocking. I love the Puffy song ["Never Leave You Again"] on my album. It's very jazzy, very cool, very easy." (6)

Although it was the whole album that was making noise, it was the song "A Rose Is Still a Rose" that was getting all the radio and print attention. Explaining the message of the song, Aretha stated, "I think what Lauryn was trying to say was regardless of what kind of relationship you had . . . you are still a flower. You are still fabulous." (13) That statement held true for Franklin herself: still fabulous after all these years.

Released in advance of the album, the title cut debuted in *Billboard* magazine at Number Eight on the R&B charts, and at Number Forty-three on the pop chart. When Arista Records president, Clive Davis telephoned Ree at home to announce the first week chart figures, she was in heaven. According to her, "I was in the kitchen when he called. What I sang at the Grammys was nothing compared to the high note I hit when he told me where my song was coming in." (13)

Said Clive at the time, 'We are not hyping anything. We're letting the music speak for itself. Yes, she is a living legend, but she is currently showing that she is relevant to youth . . . It is not a question of nostalgia and appreciation for gifts from the past." (13)

When the album hit the stores on March 24, the rave reviews just kept on coming. In *People* magazine, Steve Dougherty wrote of the *Rose* LP, "When word spreads that the Queen of Soul is coming out with an album of R&B tunes, Mariah, Whitney and the rest should take it as a cue to run and hide. Here comes Ree to show the youngsters how it's done—not just with flashy vocal technique but by plumbing the depths of feeling . . . Unfortunately, the best on this CD (the title track, written by Lauryn Hill of the Fugees) does not stand out in an unvaried landscape of sound-alike ballads. Even so, to hear Queen Aretha purr ('Oh baby') and sass ('and that's a fact!') is worth a dozen ear-boggling vocal flips by lesser royals." (28)

Giving the album four stars out of four in *USA Today*, Steve Jones wrote, "With the first note of 'A Rose Is Still a Rose,' Aretha Franklin serves notice that her 30-year reign as Queen of Soul isn't about to end . . . she shows she can still have a little fun, rocking steady with the sassy 'Watch My Back,' . . . After all this time, this rose remains in full bloom." (13)

When the album was released, it debuted at Number Thirty on the *Billboard* charts. Considering that *What You See Is What You Sweat* never even cracked the Top 100, and *Greatest Hits 1980–1994* only made it to Number Eighty-five, this was big news indeed. Arista started advertising "Rose" as "The fastest-selling album of her career!" That was the peak position it achieved on the album charts, but a career renaissance was truly on the way for the Queen of Soul, with the album being certified Gold for sales in excess of 500,000 copies sold. The single peaked at Number Five on the R&B charts, and at Number Twenty-six on the pop charts. The single version of "A Rose Is Still a Rose" was also certified Gold.

The song "Here We Go Again" was also released as a single, and became a Top Forty R&B hit. However, the most exciting aspect of the "Here We Go Again" CD single release was the inclusion of "Nessun Dorma" as a bonus track. The version of the song which is included on this release was taken from the MusicCares event, and was recorded and produced by the legendary Phil Ramone.

While she was working on the song "A Rose Is Still a Rose," Aretha became very close friends with Lauryn Hill. According to her, she even gave Hill advice. "I was ripped off here and there when I was younger," said Franklin. "So I told Lauryn, 'Nobody is going to tell you anything in the recording industry. So you have to investigate a lot, you have to surround yourself with good people—managers, agents and such who have your best interests in mind.' I also thought her generation should give our generation a big party—annually—because we put out so much information for them and they are capitalizing on it." (6) Aretha had learned a lot about the music business in the four decades in which she had been a recording star, and now she was happily speaking to, and appealing to a new generation.

After many years of anticipation, Aretha Franklin finally made it back onto the big screen in 1998 in *Blues Brothers 2000.* Reprising her role as guitar man Matt Murphy's vocally disapproving wife, Aretha again chewed the scenery as she snarled her way through a choreographed musical number, which makes this a worthy video / DVD rental.

The plot of this sequel to the original *Blues Brothers* film finds Elwood Blues leaving prison after nearly twenty years, and his quest to reunite what's left of the famed Blues Brothers Band. It is acknowledged several times in the dialogue of the movie how the character of Jake Elwood (John Belushi) died in prison. Through the loosely woven plot Elwood finds a worthy replacement in Mac (John Goodman). When Elwood and Mac arrive at a Mercedes Benz dealership in Chicago to retrieve the band's main guitar man, Mac, Murphy, and his sax playing buddy, Lou Marini, Aretha Franklin and her trio of girlfriends are on hand to lay down a soulful musical ultimatum.

In her one scene in the film Aretha looks fabulously chic in an orange mini skirt and matching jacket of orange and gold brocade. Draped over her left shoulder is a patterned orange silk scarf, held to her shoulder by a life-sized rhinestone-covered pin in the shape of frog.

"Can I speak to you privately?" an incensed Aretha asks her husband. (29) As she reads Matt Murphy the riot act, she scolds him for not giving her due "respect" for parlaying the sale of the coffee shop (depicted in the original film) into a successful automobile dealership.

"And, you know what I mean when I say respect don't you?" she inquires. (29) Suddenly right there on the floor of the car dealership, she and her trio of girlfriends (the Ridgeway Sisters) launch into a heated rendition of Aretha's signature song, "Respect," sung here in a retooled version billed as "R-E-S-P-E-C-T." It is one of the main reasons to see the film. On the soundtrack album and in the film, Aretha Franklin is heard playing piano on the track. This time around, instead of singing the chorus as her trademark "R-E-S-P-E-C-T," it has been changed to become "R-to the-S-P-E-C-T," to give it a fresh new twist.

Although the plot of this two hour plus movie is mainly far-fetched and silly, the musical numbers are wonderfully exciting. Especially prime is the Blues Brothers Band (including Steve Cropper, and Donald "Duck" Dunn) performing a sizzling "Funky Nassau" with Erykah Badu, Paul Shaffer, and Joe Morton. John Landis, who is also known for directing Michael Jackson's classic "Thriller" video, proves once again that he is excellent at staging and filming musical numbers. The "Battle of the Bands" competition at the end pits the successfully reformed Blues Brothers Band against an ensemble billed as "The Louisiana Gator Boys." As the camera pans across the two dozen musicians on-stage, it reveals the Gator Boys in fact to be a jaw-dropping all-star troupe including B. B. King, Eric Clapton, Bo Diddley, Koko Taylor, Gary "U.S." Bonds, Billy Preston, Clarence Clemons, Joshua Redman, Travis Tritt, Jeff "Skunk" Baxter (of Doobie Brothers fame), Charlie Musselwhite, Issac Hayes, Jimmy Vaughan, Steve Winwood, Grover Washington Jr., Dr. John, and Lou Rawls.

Over the credits at the end of the film, the song "New Orleans" is used to give all of the aforementioned Gator Boys, and the other stars of the film each a line of the festive Mardi Gras fête of a rock number. In it Aretha is seen and heard scatting an impromptu line of the song, as are solo lines by Badu, and the entire rest of the cast—including the group Blues Traveler, Steve Lawrence as the band's agent, and Kathleen Freeman as the mean-spirited nun who raised the orphaned Elwood Blues.

In 1998 Aretha Franklin was busily having her most high profile year of the decade. The idea of teaming up five of the hottest women in the pop and rock fields into an all-divas special, was a brilliant one which blossomed into one of the Top Ten most popular television events of the entire year. Every gamut was covered by teaming five superstars: Mariah Carey, Gloria Estefan, Shania Twain, Celine Dion, and Aretha Franklin. Adding in Carole King towards the end of the show made for an even better balance in this one-night-only New York City concert. In addition to unfolding into an unforgettable live event, *VH1 Divas Live* also yielded a great television special.

The *Divas* special itself was more than a mere concert event. It also benefited ninety-one music programs in New York City public schools. VH1 and its owner, Time Warner Cable, used it as a vehicle to raise and donate $1 million worth of musical instruments to badly needed music programs. Amid the telecast, both Mariah Carey and Shania Twain sang the program's praises for its ability to keep music students in public schools focused on their studies. It has also been proven that music students excel at mathematics, as the writing and reading of music opens up a number-based way of thinking, hearing, and calculating.

The evening also featured several female media stars introducing the five starring "divas." Aretha's segment of the show was introduced by screen actress Susan Sarandon. Aretha opened her set with "A Rose Is Still a Rose." She then introduced "my newest girlfriend," Mariah Carey, who proceeded to sing the Aretha classic, "Think," as a duet with the Queen of Soul. (30) Talkative, and obviously having a good time on the show, which was broadcast live from the Beacon Theater in New York City, Franklin announced that it was her son Teddy who was playing guitar behind her.

Although Aretha looked as large-as-ever in size, she was fabulously dressed. She had her hair up on top of her head, held in place with a gold lamé wrap. She wore a loose fitting white pant suit and a long flowing white jacket. Under the open jacket she wore a bright yellow top beaded with pearls.

At all of her events that year, Aretha sported a classy new look which made her look better than ever before. The last song she sang that evening in her three-song set was her new single, "Here We Go Again."

The way the hour-long show was structured, it gave each of the five "divas" their own brief sets, and then the end of the program was reserved for ensemble numbers. Celine Dion, who followed Aretha on the bill, brought something new to the show, by introducing singer/songwriter Carole King to sing a duet with her. The inclusion of King into the mix was an excellent choice. It blossomed into a true all-star version of "You've Got a Friend" with Estefan, Twain and Dion joining Carole, who sat and played the song on a grand piano.

What could be more fitting than to have Aretha come out and join Carole on the King composition that had become Franklin's signature tune—"(You Make Me Feel Like) A Natural Woman." For her second entrance, Aretha was very tastefully attired in a long black dress, and a black spangled cloth tied in her hair.

It was kind of amusing to see five out of six of the "divas" either in gowns or pants, and Mariah in a scene-stealing flesh-revealing mini-dress halfway up her thighs. For a refreshing change of pace, it was Aretha who was tastefully and beautifully attired, and someone else looking inappropriate in a silly outfit. According to inside sources, it was Clive Davis himself who monitored Aretha's wardrobe choices that evening. Judging by her recent past, left to her own devices, heaven knows what low-cut nightmare she may have chosen to wear.

In the finale, the other women on-stage, basically deferred to Aretha, although they all took turns on lines of the song. At the end of "Natural Woman," Aretha announced to her band, "Ok, take it on home." (30) With that, she launched into her gospel song "Testimony." Unfortunately, the other divas didn't quite know what to do, so they each got caught up in the spirit and danced on-stage, while the Queen took the proceedings to church. Mariah Carey stood stiffly by, while the other five female singing stars danced to the music and they let Franklin take over the vocal proceedings.

The show, which was already running several minutes late, rolled credits while the on-stage gospel singing was very much still underway. Fabulously, the entire concert was not only a live television special, but it was also recorded and released as a CD, and as a video cassette and DVD. However, for whatever reason, both the CD and the audio-visual versions omitted Aretha's two new songs—"A Rose Is Still a Rose" and "Here We

Go Again." Perhaps Arista Records president Clive Davis wanted everyone to go and buy Aretha's new album if they wanted to own a copy of those cuts. Regardless, the album was a huge success, which went Gold and promoted all of the "divas," who were shown off in all their glory.

Aretha was suddenly big news again, and everybody was talking about her. As Brian McCollum simply put it in *The Detroit Free Press* by proclaiming, "She stole the show from a stage full of stars at VH1's *Diva's Live.*" (24)

The *Diva's* show was such a hit that *The New York Times* even ran a story about it on the cover of its "Arts & Leisure" section, entitled "As The Categories Blur, One Diva Clearly Rules," by Albert Innuarato. Although he surveyed several "divas" from drag queen RuPaul, to bona fide operatic divas, the article proclaimed that the 1990s crown for top diva belonged to Aretha. According to Innuarato, "Time was, when divas were as innumerable as dinosaurs. They devoured one another for real, without animatronics. Today there is only one true diva, and she does not stalk opera houses. Aretha Franklin has created what can only be called gospel bel canto. Proof that Ms. Franklin is of the blood came on the *Diva's Live* telecast last month on VH1. She proceeded to eat six other female pop stars, including Mariah Carey, Gloria Estefan, Shania Twain and Celine Dion as though they were Cream of Wheat." (31)

Of her less-than-svelte physical weight, the article gasped, "Like any true diva, Ms. Franklin is huge. She wore pants, white pants. Not even Montserrat Caballé in her prime would have dared." It also pointed out that the word "diva" is from Italian, and means "goddess." Innuarato also pointed out officially, "Ms. Franklin returned the term to its true meaning on the Grammy telecast in February." (31)

Aretha's son Teddy White, Jr., whom Franklin introduced to the crowd during the *Diva's* TV taping, had been playing guitar behind his mother for the majority of the 1990s. He had also launched his own performing career, changing his name from Teddy White Jr. to Teddy Richards. His guitar work can be heard on his mother's recordings of "R-E-S-P-E-C-T," "You Can't Take Me for Granted," and "The Woman" from the *Rose* album—where he is billed as Teddy Franklin. Recently launching his own performing career in alternative rock, he was shocked one night when he arrived at a club in Port Clinton, Ohio. Speaking of the outdoor marquee he found when he arrived, he claims it read, "'Tonight: Aretha Franklin's Son,' and in little tiny letters it said, 'Teddy Richards.'" Although he was getting a boost from playing with his mother's band, Teddy was happy to find his own way in the music industry. According to him, "She's proud of what I'm doing, and proud that I'm not tugging on her skirt." (32)

In 1998 Rhino Records continued their quest to rethink and repackage the wealth of music they had in the Aretha Franklin catalog from her Atlantic years. The album *The Delta Meets Detroit: Aretha's Blues* was compiled by Norma Edwards, and offers a thoughtful smorgasbord of the best of Franklin's blues tinged-performances. Alongside such delicious songs as "Nighttime Is the Right Time," "Drown in My Own Tears," and "Going Down Slow," is a rare recording which finally makes its debut on any of Aretha's albums. The song "Takin' Another Man's Place" was originally recorded on May 26, 1969, the same week she recorded "Honest I Do" for her *This Girl's in Love With You* album. For some reason, it was never released until 1986 when it appeared on an obscure compilation called *Atlantic Blues Vocalists*. It was produced by Jerry Wexler, and was written by Detroit blues legend Mabel John.

Following suit, Columbia Legacy records released the compilation album *Aretha Franklin: This Is Jazz #34* in 1998. As part of their repackaging tribute albums to several of the label's biggest jazz legends, this sixteen cut disc explored Franklin's early '60s jazz era. Most of her best jazz cuts are here—including "Skylark," "Drinking Again," "Trouble In Mind" and "This Bitter Earth"—along with some rarely heard numbers including "Over the Rainbow" and her version of "Ain't Necessarily So." In England, Global Television & Warner Brothers Records released a two disc compilation called *Aretha Franklin: Greatest Hits*, which drew together 31 of her biggest British hits from both Atlantic Records and Arista, in non-chronological order. This album fascinatingly juxtaposes Aretha's biggest recordings from the sixties, seventies, eighties, and nineties.

That same year, another rare Aretha gem from the Columbia days, a 1964 recording of "Winter Wonderland," found its way onto the Arista album *Ultimate Christmas*. It is heard next to such Yuletide standards as Bing Crosby's "White Christmas," Nat King Cole's "The Christmas

Song," Eartha Kitt's "Santa Baby," Elvis Presley's "Blue Christmas" and Luciano Pavarotti's "Cantique De Noel (Oh Holy Night)," so she is in stellar company. Aretha sounds perky and exuberant on this holiday ode to snow arranged and conducted by Belford C. Hendricks.

In a theatrical setting, Aretha's 1993 "Inaugural Performance" of the song "I Dreamed a Dream" from *Les Miserables* was included on Arista's highly successful *Ultimate Broadway*. While the majority of the cuts were compiled from "original cast" recordings, some pop versions of songs were used in their place. Falling in this category is Judy Collin's hit recording of "Send in the Clowns" from *A Little Night Music* as opposed to using the song's original by Glynis Johns. Some theater purists balked at the idea that Aretha's optimistic version of this powerful show stopper be used on this album, instead of the one by Patti LuPone, who first recorded the song on the London cast album. It is however, a feather in Franklin's cap to be included in such outstanding company as Chita Rivera, Liza Minnelli, and Julie Andrews.

With the turn of the century approaching, in 1998 the editors of *Time* magazine tallied their list of "The 100 Most Important People Of The 20th Century." The list included several inventors and statesmen, and twenty artists and entertainers. On that list was none other than Aretha Franklin. Indeed, it was already being acknowledged that her voice and her talent have helped to shape the world of the 1900s. Also on that list of creative people were the Beatles, Bob Dylan, Lucille Ball, Frank Sinatra, James Joyce, Coco Chanel, Igor Stravinsky, Martha Graham, Pablo Picasso, Marlon Brando, Oprah Winfrey, Jim Henson, Louis Armstrong, and Charlie Chaplin.

Although it was a triumphant year for Aretha, it was not without its bumpy moments along the way. On June 11, 1998 Aretha's youngest son, Kecalf Franklin, was sentenced in Oakland County Circuit Court for the possession of cocaine. While his mother quietly looked on from her seat in the courtroom, he received eighteen months probation, narrowly escaping a jail term. Under Michigan State law, he could face up to four years in prison.

The incident which prompted this, took place on Kecalf's 28th birthday, March 4, 1998, when he was stopped by the police on Long Lake Road in Bloomfield Hills, for having a faulty brake light on his vehicle.

Come to find out, he was driving with a driver's license which had been suspended in 1996, due to violations. This made him eligible for a search. In his sock the police officers discovered "three rocks of cocaine." (33)

According to Judge Rudy Nichols at the time of his sentencing, "I told him he has family members that care for him, and that this is his chance to straighten out and avoid more legal difficulties." (33) Aretha left the courtroom through a back door to avoid the press, for whom she had no comment.

Positively the most hysterical bit of press that Aretha Franklin received in 1998 came in December, when *The Detroit Free Press* announced that All-Star Limousine service of Royal Oak, Michigan, was suing her for the non-payment of $3,651.88 in provided services, plus $1,500 in legal fees. The lawsuit wasn't a laughing matter in itself, but the list of services the limousine company provided for Aretha certainly were. According to the bill Franklin ran up, on June 15, 1998, she hired a limousine to take her to the local Jenny Craig weight-loss center at a cost of $69.00 for that ride. The following month she was dispatching the limousine driver to pick up a bucket of Kentucky Fried Chicken for her—at a cost of $126.50 for the car service alone. Apparently Aretha decided to skip out on Jenny Craig altogether, and turned her attention to some of Colonel Sanders' extra crispy drumsticks. Three days later she had the same limo service pick up one of her friends, and then swing by the drive-in window at Burger King!

According to the suit, which was before Bloomfield Hills district court judge Edward Avadenka, the bill which Aretha racked up included:

◆ June 15, 1998, drive Aretha to Jenny Craig Weight Loss Center ($69.00)

◆ July 11, 1998, pick up Aretha, take her to dinner, and to a Janet Jackson concert ($569.25)

◆ July 20, 1998, send the driver to Kentucky Fried Chicken ($126.50)

◆ July 20, 1998, pick up Aretha and take her to lunch, the dry cleaners, and the grocery store ($126.50)

◆ July 23, 1998, pick up one of Aretha's friends, take them to Burger King ($126.50)

◆ July 30, 1998, pick up Aretha from her home, take her to Columbus, Ohio ($475.00)

The list went on from there, eighteen trips in all during the months of June and July. All-Star cited some of Franklin's favorite destinations as Cobo Cleaners, a Coney Island hot dog restaurant, and Kroger's supermarket. The limousine service was also used to pick up newspapers for Aretha, and provide various other services. According to All-Star's lawyer, Scott Yaldo of Birmingham, all of the invoices were sent to Ms. Franklin very respectfully addressed to "Dear Aretha." Said Yaldo of his clients, "They don't want to be the bad guys, but they're a small company that relies on people paying their accounts." (34) When *The Star* tabloid newspaper got hold of the story, they had a field day with it, publishing it with the headline, "When Queen Of Soul Wants Take-Out, She Pays Big Time." (35) Divas do need their limousines, it goes with the territory!

This echoes the same problem that Sak's Fifth Avenue had with Aretha, when they filed a similar suit against her in 1995, also for the non-payment of her bills, suing for the clothing and accessory bill that she amassed at Sak's totaling $262,851.15. By 1998 the department store had dismissed the charges, and had written off the loss. The Internal Revenue Service was not so forgiving when they issued liens against her for declining to pay $500,000 in owed taxes.

In 1998, according to ABC News, Aretha's estimated worth was in the vicinity of $20 million. While Aretha is without peer in the singing department, apparently she is not so good with arithmetic or business sense when it comes time to pay her bills.

While being "dissed" publicly for her sloppy business practices, Aretha still had one more triumph to add to her list of 1998 accomplishments before the year was up. Aretha was booked at the Detroit Orchestra Hall to play a date with the highly revered Detroit Symphony Orchestra, on November 28, 1998. She had performed in the past with the Boston Symphony, and the Philadelphia Orchestra. However she had never performed with an orchestra in her own hometown. She explained at the time, "So I figured, 'Since I'm going to sing with the symphony anyway, why not do a few more of the arias?'" (24)

Could her die-hard fans handle the Queen of Soul going classical? "Absolutely!" she exclaimed, days before the concert took place, "Many times over. There are different kinds of soul. This is symphonic soul . . . I have very sophisticated fans, They like good music, just like I do." (24)

While the rest of the world was astonished at Aretha's seemingly sudden interest in classical music, she was quick to point out that her sister Erma had studied classical piano as a child. Recalls Aretha, "She used to play 'Flight of the Bumblebee' just fabulously. I moved into classical music naturally. The appearance at the Grammys kind of piqued it. But I had been aware of the music long before that." (24)

According to her, 'I've always heard it—never performed it, but I've always heard it. It's always been somewhere right there in the background. It's certainly a stretch from 'Dr. Feelgood' to 'Nessun Dorma,' but I love it, anyway, from one end of the spectrum to another." (36)

It was a classy and celebrity filled audience who came to witness the diva's Detroit operatic debut. Motown diva Martha Reeves was there, as well as Detroit Mayor Dennis Archer, and State of Michigan Representative John Conyers. Tickets for the event went for up to $150.00 each.

The show was divided into two distinctive halves. First the Detroit Symphony Orchestra played a program of instrumental classics, and then Aretha joined the ensemble. The orchestra's classical pieces included: Leonard Bernstein's "Candide" overture, William Grant Still's "African-American Symphony Scherzo," Duke Ellington's "Solitude" and "Giggling Rapids" from *The River*, Dizzy Gillespie's "Manteca," and Ralph Hermann's "Ellington Fantasy."

Franklin's half of the show found her being preceded on-stage by an overture of classical pieces that were meant to bridge the classical into the pop realm. It included "Also Sprach Zarathustra (Theme from *2001*)," and the themes from *Jesus Christ Superstar* and *Chariots of Fire*.

Aretha's repertoire included a slow version of "Angel" with an on-stage ballet being performed while she sang. Other performed songs included "Freeway of Love," "Why Do Fools Fall In Love?," "Think," and "It Hurts

Like Hell." However, the most anticipated performance of the evening was Aretha's singing "Vissi d'arte" from Puccini's *Tosca*.

Brian McCollum of *The Detroit Free Press* found her "sparkling in a brown, beaded silk gown—it was about immersing in the sort of glamorous and high art that has long magnetized her. The result was a frisky blend of sass and class, as when she paused—for just for a second—to subtly shake her rear while exiting the stage, just minutes before belting out an aria from Puccini's *Tosca*." (37)

Even *The Wall Street Journal* devoted a quarter page to Aretha. Writer Greg Sandow had both critical things to say, and glowing praises. "So, we'd better just ignore her overture," he said in his review, "and also look away from the corps de ballet she brought on-stage while she sang 'Angel,' one of her older hits, even though the choreography looked like it came from the really bad junior high school Christmas play. What matters is that she really is the Queen of Soul. Look at her, and you see a large woman with a disarmingly shy and eager baby face." (38)

Pointing out her phenomenal voice, Sandow claimed, "That's why she triumphs even with Puccini. She sang 'Nussen Dorma,' from *Turnadot*, at this year's Grammy Awards; in Detroit she sang 'Vissi d'arte,' from *Tosca*. You could say, with perfect truth, that her Italian could hardly sound more naïvely American, and that her style is heartily classical. But she makes the music go, like an innocent who finds wonders that scholars overlook, and her high note at the end could have brought the dead to life." He also said that he wished there had been more jazz tunes in Aretha's repertoire. However he was quick to admit, "It's pointless to complain. She does what she does." (38) That's Aretha!

Is singing an operatic aria any more difficult than singing any other kind of song? "I don't think so, no," says Aretha. "You just have to be conscientious about certain things. But you have to do that with anything." (36)

Aretha also announced at the time, that she was considering doing an all-opera album called *My Favorite Arias*. The Detroit show was also taped for a possible live album. "It's certainly been enlightening," she said at the time. "It's a broadening of my repertoire, and a growth experience, for sure." (24)

Right after her triumphant concert date in Detroit, news surfaced that Aretha had been sued again. This time around it was Chicago songwriter William "Sunny" Sanders, who was seeking royalty money amounting to $500,000 for having co-written the song "Angel" with her late sister Carolyn. A spokesperson representing Aretha, told *The Detroit Free Press* that the claim was in error, and that Saunders had in fact been paid $116,000, when he claimed to only have received $45,000.

In its December 31, 1998 issue, *The Chicago Tribune* reported that All-Star Limousine had been paid by Aretha Franklin, with two personal checks. The owner of the company grumbled, "I just think it is a shame to go to these measures to get paid what we were due." (39) That same day Aretha was out spreading good cheer for the less fortunate, by singing for hundreds of patients at Ford Hospital in Detroit. Aretha announced to the crowd, "Because some of you weren't able to get out for Christmas and the holidays, we wanted to bring a little Christmas to you." (40)

At the end of the year, the album *A Rose Is Still a Rose* was included on many publications' lists tallying the best recordings of 1998. The critics in *USA Today* found it to be one of the year's Top Ten R&B Albums, in which they also counted the year's Top Ten Country and Pop albums as well. She was even farther up the list in *Time* magazine, which christened the LP one of their Top Ten album picks of any genre, tallying it at Number Four. According to that magazine's editors, "On her latest album, Franklin teams up with some of the hottest producers in pop . . . The rejuvenating cross-generational collaborations are more than a marketing move: this is Franklin's most rewarding album in more than two decades. The queen's long reign continues." (41)

On January 5, 1999, when the Grammy Award nominations were announced, Aretha was up for two of the trophies. In the "Best R&B Female Vocal" category, the nominees were (in alphabetical order): "Are You That Somebody?" by Aaliyah, "Tyrone" by Erykah Badu, "A Rose Is Still a Rose" by Aretha Franklin, "Do Wop (That Thing)" by Lauryn Hill, and "I Get Lonely" by Janet Jackson. In the "Best R&B Album" category it was: *Live* by Erykah Badu, *Never Say Never* by Brandy, *A Rose Is Still a Rose* by Aretha Franklin, *The Miseducation of Lauryn Hill* by Lauryn Hill, and *Embrya* by Maxwell. It is interesting to note that of all the nominees, only she and Janet Jackson were stars prior to the 1990s. The rest mentioned were relative newcomers. While other divas from the past were struggling to keep up with the pack, Aretha seems to always endure.

In addition, two of her songs also received Grammy nominations. Lauryn Hill was nominated as the writer of the "Best R&B Song," for having penned "A Rose Is Still a Rose." And, the arranger of the track "Nussen Dorma," which was included on Aretha's "Here We Go Again" single, Rob Mounsey, was nominated for "Best Instrumental Arrangement with Accompanying Vocals."

Speaking of her own star status in the 1990s, Franklin has said, "I like my celebrity where it is, because I can do most things that anyone else does. I can do my own grocery shopping. I can get out and shop . . . I am a woman, and I am a lady. Farmer Jack [grocery store], on 12th Street, is exactly where I get my meat . . . They have very quick turnover of meat down there, and that's where the best meat is in the city. It's not out here [in Bloomfield Hills], it's down on 12th [in downtown Detroit]." (10)

Continuing her quest for new projects, in 1999 Aretha was once again heard lending her voice—and image—to television commercials. This time around it was Pepsi-Cola of which she was heard singing the praises. As part of the soft drink's "Joy of Pepsi" campaign, in the context of the one-minute ad, the viewer hears the distinctively rich voice of Aretha coming out of tiny moppet-like actress Hallie Kate Eisenberg in a luncheonette. At the end of the commercial, the real life Aretha is seen in one of the diner's seating booths making a snappy comment.

Although it seems she is a benevolent, and very confident superstar, she is not always gracious towards her peers. At times she seems insecure and somewhat competitive. In *Vanity Fair* in 1994, her old friend Mavis Staples revealed that she and Aretha almost came to blows over the cut "Oh Happy Day" from Aretha's 1980s gospel album. According to Mavis, after a phenomenal live duet between Staples and Franklin on the song "Oh Happy Day," Aretha insisted on re-doing the vocals in the recording studio. Aretha was apparently in fear that Mavis had stolen the song from her, and she was not going to release that version of the number. Recalled Staples, "I made a vocal run in the studio, and the engineer, you saw his hair still on his head. Aretha would say, 'Take that out. We're going to do another.' And he said, 'You wanna take that one out?' Aretha says, 'What did I say?' He said, 'Mavis, don't say a damn thing.' . . . That's when I gave up. I said, 'She just ain't going to do right, because she thinks I'm going to upstage her and she can't take nothing from me, but she don't realize that, you know. What she did to that record!" (10)

Diana Ross, who is legendary for not getting along with anyone, made a half-hearted attempt at befriending Aretha. According to Ross, "I ran into her at the inauguration [President Bill Clinton's, January 1993]. I said, 'You know what, girl? We just really need to know each other. I just think it's ridiculous that we've never taken time to know each other.' [Aretha] said, 'Well, you *say* that, but what are you going to do?'" (10) That was the end of that. Can you think of two more opposite "divas?" Let's face it, they could never be close friends. Diana's track record as a devoted friend is "nonsense," while Aretha is totally "no nonsense."

There is also her long-running feud with Patti LaBelle. Inside sources reveal that Patti and Aretha refuse to be on-stage with each other. Although they both appeared on the *Waiting to Exhale* soundtrack, they can't stand to be in the same room together. Like *The New York Times* so eloquently pointed out, true diva behavior calls for devouring the competition like the ancient dinosaurs once did.

Although the decade of the 1990s was one of great and stunningly successful Aretha Franklin accomplishments, she has also announced all sorts of projects which have never materialized. There was talk about her releasing a live album, to be recorded in Carnegie Hall, and also a new gospel album. She had dabbled in launching her own gospel record label, known as World Class Records. She was to have released a gospel Christmas album as well as an album featuring herself, Vanessa Bell Armstrong and Bobby Jones. There was also talk about Aretha doing a movie with Ann Margaret. The century ended without any of these things happening.

Since Detroit in the 1990s legalized gambling casinos within the city limits, everyone in town was clambering to get into the act. In the Motor City—which for thirty years had needed a financial shot-in-the-arm, the new casinos were looked at as a way to lure people to the once-bustling riverfront area. Franklin proposed that she open her own "Aretha's Fried Chicken & Waffles" restaurants in each of them. Aretha Franklin restaurants? It sounds like a "natural" link. As Aretha says of her own prowess in the kitchen: "I can wear some chitlins out." (7) Given her love of fattening foods, if her restaurant dream ever does come true—one can bet that the menu will be devoid of anything even remotely approaching low-calorie fare.

According to Aretha, when she isn't creating at the piano or in the recording studio, she prefers to do her creating in the kitchen. "I'm very domestic," she claims. "I like to cook and do my own cleaning. I don't like for the lady that helps me to bother my things." (13)

Describing her own relaxed at-home routine, Franklin says, "I usually get up around noon . . . Nothing gets done until three." (7)

Also on the list of 1990s projects for Aretha, was her much-talked-about autobiography. The writing of this book had been on-again / off-again for over a decade. Finally, in the later half of the decade it was back "on" again. Speaking in 1998 about it, she proclaimed, "There've been a few tears, but all in all, I'm enjoying it. I'll be 'dissing' a little bit—and 'dishing' a little bit. I'm going to be deep-dish Aretha." (13)

According to *The Detroit Free Press*, in 1995 she "signed a $1.2 million contract with Villard books for an autobiography," however the book suffered one delay after another. (42)

In September of 1999, it hit the stores. As emotion-filled as Franklin's music has been, the 1999 book, *Aretha: From These Roots*, is devoid of details, feelings, insight, and warmth. It seems that either the Queen of Soul has been sleepwalking through one of the most interesting lives of the Twentieth Century, or she simply isn't willing to share it with the world. And, apparently, not even a million dollars was enough of an allurement to convince her to do that.

Even her co-writer, David Ritz, uses his "Introduction" to shamelessly plug his other books, and to distance himself from this one by writing, "In this book, which she has waited a lifetime to write, Aretha speaks for herself." (43)

In *Aretha: From These Roots*, Franklin does not reveal the name of the father(s) of her first two children. She discusses her stormy marriage to Ted White in mere sentences. She mentions her friendship with some to the greatest musicians of her lifetime—like Dinah Washington, Sam Cooke, and Clara Ward—but never once tells the reader how they touched her life, or what it was like to be in their presence. Reading this inconsistent autobiography is infuriatingly frustrating—to say the least.

With regard to revealing the identity of who fathered her two illegitimate children she had when she was a young teenager, she was far less than forthcoming. She only states that it was some "Romeo of the roller rink." Furthermore, after giving birth to her first son, she returns to the same roller rink and ends up pregnant again. Was she scared? Was she hurt? Was she heartbroken? Did she feel any emotion at all? Did she EVER keep her roller skates on? Who knows? It certainly isn't on the pages of her sketchy autobiography.

Time after time, in her book she will detail an obscure event, like a particularly memorable dinner she ate, yet years of her career and personal life will be spanned without mention. Amidst her storytelling she has a habit of bouncing from decade to decade. While narrating the sixties, she jumps ahead to the seventies, then she makes references to the nineties, then it is back to the sixties. Whole decades are inaccurately identified. Often, when she is at a loss for details, she sums up an event by saying "we threw down." She uses the phrase so many times, one has no idea what on earth she is describing.

Apparently one of the great loves of her life is another hugely successful star. Instead of revealing his identity, she simply calls him "Mr. Mystique." She then describes a quarrel with another female star, but claims to be too lady-like to reveal her identity. Other important characters in her life story are mentioned, but are passed over in a few undescriptive sentences. She barely discusses producer Jerry Wexler's contribution to her glorious recording career at Atlantic Records, preferring instead to complain how she should have been credited as the producer of her sound.

What she does remember with detail and clarity is "food." She writes very fondly about a great hot dog, ham hocks and beans, some fried chicken or candied sweet potatoes someone made forty years ago. However, the people in her life—even her own children—are barely described. If Aretha's life story is to be told in remembrances of food—then it is safe to say that *Aretha: From These Roots* has more holes in it than ten pounds of Swiss cheese.

Given these parameters, it was easy to understand why critics instantly panned the book's vagueness and inconsistency. Lisa R. Manns in *The Detroit Free Press* pointed out in her review, "The excitement readers might expect get lost in generalizations. And if fans are expecting Franklin to bear her soul, they will be disappointed." (44) Tom Sinclair called it "surprisingly tame" in his review in *Entertainment Weekly*. He also pointed out, "Throughout the strangely prim book, Franklin glosses over unpleasant events, accentuating the positive to a degree that's almost risible . . . [her] greatest music will undoubtedly stand the test of time. Her oddly unrevealing autobiography, however, should have a decidedly shorter shelf life." (45) In the book business, a celebrity gets but one shot at penning their autobiography. Aretha sadly squandered hers.

As concert promoters began to get ready for New Year's Eve 1999, several of them had come up with such high ticket priced events, they were bound to fail to find an audience. One such event was to have taken place in New York City at the Jacob Javits Convention Center, starring Aretha Franklin, Sting, Chuck Berry, Kool & the Gang, Joan Rivers, Andrea Boccelli, and Enrique Iglesias. The lowest priced tickets began at $1,000. Unfortunately poor ticket sales caused a cancellation of the event.

However, once the new year began, Aretha was actively involved in taking her music to her fans. Aretha was one of the stars featured on the May 15, 2000 TV special, *25 Years of Number One Hits: Arista Records' Anniversary Celebration.* The special was taped on April 10 at the Shrine Auditorium in Los Angeles, and was headlined by such musical giants as Carlos Santana, Toni Braxton, Barry Manilow, Alan Jackson, Dionne Warwick, Patti Smith, Sarah McLaughlin, Puff Daddy and Whitney Houston. The program was most noted for Houston's spotty performance in which she appeared to be "on" something. She tripped over her own dress only seconds after taking the stage, kept grabbing at her sequined gown so many times it was missing huge patches of its sparkling beads, and the young diva looked dazed. Bringing her headed-for-jail husband, Bobby Brown, on-stage only underscored the craziness of her appearance.

Franklin's once warm and friendly attitude towards Houston had long ago reached the Ice Age. Their problems stemmed back to around the time of their 1989 duet recording of "It Isn't, It Wasn't, It Ain't Never

Gonna Be." One of the most pointed things that Aretha had written in her 1999 autobiography had been aimed squarely at Whitney. Ree basically announced that the problematic Ms. Houston could call her anytime she dropped the stuck-up haughty diva attitude, and not a minute beforehand.

For this particular TV special, Aretha characteristically refused to fly, drive OR take the train all the way to Los Angeles, but agreed to appear via satellite from New York City. She was in good voice and looked sharp in a black pantsuit and black tunic top. She completed the look with one of her kookier hairstyles, which was part corn-row braids, part cascading *I Dream of Jeannie* do, with a mixed in bright-orange fall.

Aretha's medley of hits that evening included a solo version of her George Michael hit "I Knew You Were Waiting (For Me)," "It Hurts Like Hell," and "Freeway of Love." For the final song, she was joined on-stage by the vocal quartet Boyz II Men. Although she was on the opposite coast in front of a New York studio audience, Franklin spoke warmly about the day Clive Davis played the demo of "I Knew You Were Waiting (For Me)," with an obvious amount of warmth for the man who had kept her recording career fresh and alive since 1980. The show was such a successful program when broadcast, that it was quickly released as a DVD, which included several special segments which were not seen on television.

In June of 2000, Aretha was one of the headliners to perform at New York City's annual JVC Jazz Festival. With the Stanley Turrentine Quintet warming up the stage, she performed at Lincoln Center's Avery Fisher Hall.

On September 6, 2000, Aretha Franklin was back in Manhattan, this time to be one of the presenters at the eleventh Rhythm & Blues Foundation's Pioneer Awards presentation. She was on hand to induct Atlantic Records founder Ahmet Ertegun with a Founders Award. Ertegun was not present, due to illness. When Aretha took the podium, she also announced that she was donating $50,000 to the Foundation. It is the Foundation's cause to honor R&B stars with money and medical care when necessary.

Although she is still acknowledged as a contemporary recording artist, it seems like it is impossible to mention her name without speaking about her status as a living legend. *Vanity Fair* in their November 2000 "Music Issue" claimed: "The 'Queen of Soul' is perhaps the one 'title' in popular music that has not grown ill-fitting with age." (46) It is assuredly a moniker she has neither outgrown, worn-out, nor strayed away from.

In the year 2000, it seemed that the whole world was transfixed by TV's "real life" experiences of a group of stranded people on an island called *Survivor*. Looking back at the career of diva Franklin, it is she who might very well be the "ultimate" show business survivor. According to Aretha, whenever she is faced with an obstacle she simply can't get over, she remembers what her grandmother would say to her. Franklin recalls, "She used to say 'Can you do anything about it?' If you can, you will. But if you can't, don't worry about it. If you can't then just let it go." (7)

One of the stumbling blocks that is still in her way, is her on-going fear of flying. Although she has announced time and time again that she has an upcoming flight planned, she never did just jump in and do it. Resigned to living without airplanes, she simply purchased a "custom bus," and like so many country music stars, she travels from city-to-city in her house on wheels. Instead of looking at it as a hindrance, she sees it as a plus. "I get to see America, just get off the bus and go into Wal-Mart and have a ball," she proclaims. (13)

"I travel by custom bus now and we cook on it, we have videos, we have games, and it's a lot of fun. And, actually, it's very refreshing from flying, to get to see some of the country side—to get out, walk around." (3) She has everything she needs on her bus: "It's beautiful. We have cooking facilities, movies, fax, phones, and a fun driver." (12)

She has tried classes, she has gone to the airport for safety instructions, she has done everything but take an airplane ride. "I did a lot of things that have not worked yet," she laughs, "because I am still not flying. So I set it to the side—I enjoy my custom bus. You can pull over, go to Red Lobster. You can't pull over at 30,000 feet." (6) The Queen of Soul must cause quite the fun tornado of commotion when she pulls up at a highway-side Red Lobster!

Her compatriots in the music business have lent their support towards her flight phobia. Luciano Pavarotti once looked her in the eye and said, "You are scared of the plane. I come to pick you up." (13)

Finding a third husband is another goal which also eludes her. If she found the right guy, would she consider it? "Sure, if I found the right man. *WHEN* I have found the right man, if we're both amenable, absolutely," she claims. (7) And, what is it that she looks for in a man: "I want romance!" she proclaims. "I like men who are thoughtful." (10)

Probably the most significant statement Aretha made during the 1990s is her declaration that she is never going to retire from her most consistent creative outlet—making music. Who knows where music is about to go in the Twenty-First Century. The only thing that we can be assured of, is that Aretha Franklin is going to be part of it.

As the new "millennium" approached, all sorts of new ideas and concepts were bantered about for the future. One Canadian official went so far as to suggest that his British Commonwealth country go "monarch free" beginning in the year 2000. However the opinion polls were so unanimously against such a concept, he quickly shut up and withdrew his thoughts. Even in an era of democracy, we still need our royalty to look up to. How comforting it is to know that as long as there is an England, and a British Commonwealth, there will always be either a King or a Queen. And, as long as there is recorded music, Aretha Franklin will always be the Queen of Soul.

CHAPTER ELEVEN

SO DAMN HAPPY

Since the year 2001, Aretha Franklin's life has been something of a seesaw of good and bad news. On the negative side of the coin, it has been an era that has seen her sons in legal trouble, her once-hot recording career slowing down, the death of several of her longtime friends, her alarmingly steady weight gain, and finally—life threatening health problems to deal with. However, on the positive side of things, it has been a time of many accolades and honors. One American president presented her with a huge award, another American president invited her to sing at his inaugural ceremony, and she added more Grammy Awards to her collection. In addition, mysterious health issues have drawn international attention to the woman who is universally acknowledged as the Queen of Soul.

Since Aretha has owned several Oakland County, Michigan, high-profile residences, one of them was reportedly used strictly for storage. At 6:00 a.m. on October 25, 2002, while Aretha was in Houston, Texas, for a performing engagement, the Bloomfield Township police and fire department were dispatched to her house near Long Lake Road and Telegraph to put out a blaze in the luxury house. Unfortunately, by the time firefighters arrived, the house was deemed to be a "total loss."

Reportedly, the home was valued at $1.8 million, yet the insurance policy Aretha had on the house was for under a million dollars. It was further determined that the fire was the work of an alleged arsonist. Incendiary materials—including what appeared to be lighter fluid—were found in the house. It was also reported in several places—including

The New York Times—that the police found similar lighter fluid on the clothing of their prime suspect, Aretha's own son, Eddie.

When Aretha returned to Michigan, she refused to cooperate with the police or the authorities. The following January, Aretha was subpoenaed to testify in the case but again refused. *Entertainment Weekly* reported that the authorities "subpoenaed the Queen of Soul, her son Edward Franklin, his roommate Dr. Edward West, and security guard Tyrone Jarrett Sr." (1)

Aretha refused to testify in the case, although she pressed her insurance company to reimburse her for the full amount of the value of the house and its belongings. The case was never solved, although one press report claimed, "The person police think sparked the blaze—according to documents obtained by the defenders—is forty-five-year-old Edward Franklin, Aretha's son. He was found hiding in the trees the morning of the fire." (2)

Since the singer refused to address the matter, it made it seem that she was protecting her son Eddie from having torched the house either accidentally or intentionally for some unknown reason. According to Oakland County Prosecutor David Gorcyca, "We need to definitively establish what facts Ms. Franklin possesses about this case and not what her lawyer wishes us to know. All of this could have been avoided with Ms. Franklin's voluntary cooperation." (1)

In 2002 Aretha Franklin lost her last female sibling when her sister Erma died at the age of sixty-four. Erma had married Thomas Garrett, and together they had two children. She had been diagnosed with lung cancer in the spring of that year and passed away on September 7. Publicly, Erma will be remembered for her biggest hit, "A Piece of My Heart," and privately she will be remembered as one of Aretha's lifelong champions. Like sister Carolyn, Erma's last major recorded performance was as part of the Franklin Sisters on Aretha's *One Lord, One Faith, One Baptism* album.

Aretha's first album to be released in 2003 was a revised reissue of her 1987 Grammy Award-winning Arista gospel disc, *One Lord, One Faith, One Baptism*. Unlike the first time it was issued, this time around it featured three never-before-released tracks, including the Mavis Staples duet, "Father I Stretch My Hands to Thee," and the song "Beams of Heaven."

The third previously unreleased song on this album is an alternate version of "Packing Up Getting Ready to Go" with Erma and Carolyn Franklin.

On June 17, 2003, Arista Records released the twelve-track album *Aretha Franklin: Gold and Platinum Collection.* A package with ten of Aretha's biggest Arista hits, the set kicks off with her two biggest singles at Atlantic: "Respect" and "Think." It is a lively and entertaining collection that includes "Jumpin' Jack Flash," "Jimmy Lee," and "Jump To It," as well as "A Rose is Still a Rose," making this album's time span from 1967 to 1998—a full thirty-one years of Aretha's hits.

In September of 2003, Aretha released her thirteenth and last new album on Arista Records, entitled *So Damn Happy.* A slow paced "quiet storm" type of album of eleven tracks by ten different producers, it found the diva in strong voice. However, the resulting album lacked in sparkle and in musical excitement. At the time, Aretha's great mentor, Clive Davis, had left Arista in the hands of L.A. Reid, and Clive's deft touch with Franklin's musical direction is sorely missing. The overall tone of the album was one of smoothly orchestrated soul tunes featuring hip-hop accents. A decade ago she released a lively album called *What You See is What You Sweat,* however on *So Damn Happy* she never once breaks a sweat.

This isn't to say that Aretha didn't enlist some top-notch people to work on the album. Two of the tracks—"Holdin' On" and "No Matter What"—were co-written by Mary J. Blige, and Blige provided all of the background vocals for those tracks. And Burt Bacharach teamed up with Elvis Presley's songwriter, Jerry Leiber, and Jerry's son, Jed, to create the slow ballad of a love affair gone wrong, "Falling Out of Love."

Describing the musical atmosphere of the album, Aretha claimed, "Some of it is hip-hop, some of it is traditional, and it just works." Comparing classic "soul" of yesterday with the "hip-hop" beat of the 2000's, she explained, "Soul is the ability to make people feel what you're feeling. Something that hip-hop artists are saying now, 'Are you feeling it?' There's a vibe that goes with a song or a performance. A vibe. It's just that simple, just a happening between the artist and the audience." (3)

According to Antonio (L.A.) Reid, the new president of Arista at that time, "There was no attempt to make a pop record. This one was personal for Aretha. We said, 'Let's have an album that feels like a soulful record.' I wanted it to be like the old days." (3)

When the album was released in 2003, Burt Bacharach claimed to the press, "I'm just most comfortable working with the female voice. It's a good song—the first I've ever written with Jerry after years of talking about it—and she provided a great vocal. We might even have a shot at getting a single out of this one." (4)

One of the songs, written by Gordon Chambers and Barry J. Eastmond, makes a blatant attempt to conjure up memories of another Aretha song with the same title: "Ain't No Way." Even though the song cannibalizes the phrase "Ain't No Way," as well as stealing the "R-E-S-P-E-C-T" line from "Respect," it merely stands as a reminder of Franklin hits gone-by, yet creates nothing new or exciting.

Without a doubt, the most effervescent song on the album is the single hit, "Wonderful." Written by Ron Lawrence, Philip "Silky" White, Katrina Willis and Aleese Simmons, it has a catchy chorus line and Aretha sounds comfortable and upbeat on her vocals.

Two of the tracks—"You Are My Joy" and "So Damn Happy"—were written and produced by Aretha herself. "You Are My Joy" is especially fulfilling, because it is one of those rare moments when adult Aretha Franklin just sits at the piano and plays the lead part of her accompanying music.

Internationally, the *So Damn Happy* album drew mixed reviews and it didn't become a huge seller, but it was to bring her acclaim amongst her fans and her peers. Some people found it dull; others loved it.

Rolling Stone magazine's Barry Walters claimed, "The Queen of Soul is still the Queen. But that doesn't mean the material on Aretha Franklin's latest album is deserving of her crown . . . on 1998's *A Rose Is Still a Rose*, Lauryn Hill, Puff Daddy and other hot hitmakers plied fresh beats and old-school samples to aim Aretha's R&B at young ears . . . Ten different producers replace *Rose's* hip-hop energy with an adult-contemporary slickness that sometimes makes the sixty-one-year-old legend's voice seem shrill. Her Highness deserves more R-E-S-P-E-C-T than this." (5)

Betty Clarke, in England's *The Guardian*, bluntly claimed, "Aretha Franklin is demanding that everyone swallow a hefty dose of positivity.

And she has chosen the homogenized mediocrity of modern R&B to do it . . . In this misconceived and—judging by the strained high notes— dangerous attempt to impress the kids, she limits herself to shooby-do-ing and sounding bemused. It's a depressing departure. During 'The Only Thing Missin',' her once-steely control turns to mush, and notes fly at us like blunt knives. Burt Bacharach's 'Falling Out of Love' sounds like a Barbra Streisand cast-off, with Franklin serving up cold karaoke . . . even the feisty words and voice of Mary J. Blige can't stop Franklin ultimately floundering and scatting into nothingness." (6)

John Bush, in *The All Music Guide* rather liked the new album. He claimed, "During the five years that separated *So Damn Happy* from her previous album, *A Rose Is Still a Rose*, Aretha Franklin made the celebrity-gossip pages many more times than she earned airplay on the radio . . . Most of the songs, led by 'The Only Thing Missin',' the title track, and 'Holdin' On,' are up to a high level, catchy and easy to understand . . . a song called 'Wonderful' that evokes the glory days of '70s soul more than any other song here. Aretha shouldn't need to resort to overkill to proclaim her joy at making music; the songs on *So Damn Happy* are all the proof her fans need to understand that her talent remains undiminished nearly fifty years after her debut as a secular act." (7)

Likewise, Jack Smith glowingly wrote in his British *BBC* review, "This, her first studio album in five years since *A Rose Is Still a Rose* . . . she again reaffirms why today's pretenders to her crown can only look up and marvel at her boundless talent . . . in *So Damn Happy* her legion of fans have a slick and superior album of depth, vision and soul that's truly one to savour." (8)

On the record charts, *So Damn Happy* made it to Number Thirty-three in the United States on *Billboard*'s album chart, and to Number Eleven on the R&B Albums chart. Unlike its predecessor, it was not certified *Gold*, meaning it sold less than 500,000 copies. However, two of the songs charted on the American R&B Singles chart: "The Only Thing Missin'" (Number Fifty-three) and "Wonderful" (Number Forty-six).

Aretha has long been the darling of the Grammy Awards, so it was little surprise when the song "Wonderful" received a nomination in the category of "Best Traditional R&B Vocal Performance." The other songs nominated in that category were "Hold Me" by Earth, Wind and Fire, "Comin' from Where I'm From" by Anthony Hamilton, "Way Up There" by Patti LaBelle, and "He Proposed" by Kelly Price.

It came as a nice surprise when Aretha won the award on February 8, 2004, which was her eighteenth Grammy Award. It signaled the fact that she was still around and still very impressively making music that people loved to hear, forty-three years since her first single release.

So Damn Happy signaled the end of an era for Aretha Franklin. It was time for her to sign a new recording contract, and she and the newly aligned Arista Records began negotiations. However, Aretha wanted more money than Arista wanted to pay to continue to release her music. After a career dispute with Arista Records, her musical home for twenty-three years, she found herself without a recording contract. Although everyone seems to look at her fourteen years at Atlantic Records as her heyday, while she was on Arista Records she won just as many Grammys (ten additional trophies), and had her longest run on the charts.

In 2004, the accolades continued to pour in for Aretha as *Rolling Stone* magazine declared Aretha artist Number Nine on their list of "The 100 Greatest Artists of All Time." The following year, in 2005, the Queen of Soul announced she was starting her own private recording label, Aretha's Records.

The music world was taken by surprise when one of Aretha's strongest supporters, Luther Vandross, suddenly died on July 1, 2005. He had suffered from a stroke on April 16, 2003, and he never fully recovered. He won two Grammy Awards for his final album, *Dance with My Father*, in 2004, and his career was basically on "hold" in anticipation of him regaining his strength. It was not to happen.

Over the years, Luther's adoring public had watched in awe as his weight drastically went up and down in time. He started out his career dramatically overweight, then he would lose weight, then he would gain it back, and then he would lose it again. Whether or not that played a factor in his sudden death at the age of fifty-four of heart failure, it certainly didn't help matters.

When his funeral took place on July 8, 2005 in New York City, several of his music industry friends were there to say "goodbye" to Luther.

Amongst them were Cissy Houston, Dionne Warwick, Patti LaBelle, Alicia Keys, Valerie Simpson, Usher, Stevie Wonder, and Aretha Franklin. Luther's body was on view at Frank E. Campbell on the Upper East Side of Manhattan, which is the funeral home that has played host to so many celebrities, including Judy Garland. The two day wake included services at Riverside Church in Harlem. Dressed in a tasteful beige coat and matching beige hat, Aretha bid "farewell" to Luther in song, by singing "Amazing Grace."

On September 20, 2005, Clive Davis' new label, J Records, released the album *Luther Vandross: An All-Star Tribute*. It included performances by many of Luther's friends and admirers, covering some of his greatest hits, including Beyoncé and Stevie Wonder ("So Amazing,") Donna Summer ("Power of Love,") Elton John ("Anyone Who Had a Heart" duet with Luther,) Fantasia ("'Til My Baby Comes Home,") Patti LaBelle ("Here and Now,") and Aretha Franklin ("A House is Not a Home.") The album was made utilizing several different producers. In Aretha's case, she turned to her old friend from Atlantic Records, Arif Mardin. As per her habit, Miss Franklin's vocals were recorded in Detroit. In other words, the musicians still journeyed to the queen.

The year 2005 was quite a winning one for Aretha. She became the second woman to be inducted into the UK Music Hall of Fame. The first woman to have received that honor was Madonna, who was also a founding member of that organization. Closer to home, Franklin was inducted into the Michigan Rock & Roll Legends Hall of Fame.

However, the year's crowning achievement came on November 9, when Aretha went to the White House in Washington D.C., to receive the Medal of Freedom lifetime achievement award from President George W. Bush. There were fourteen different recipients that year, including: actress Carol Burnett, golf pro Arnold Palmer, boxer Muhammad Ali, and broadcasting legend Paul Harvey.

To increase her visibility even further, on February 5, 2006 Aretha performed "The Star-Spangled Banner" with Aaron Neville at *Super Bowl XL*, which is traditionally the year's biggest sports event. That year the game was viewed by a televised audience of 90.7 million people.

When the 2006 Grammy nominations were announced, Aretha was again nominated in the category of "Best Traditional R&B Vocal Performance," this time around for her Luther tribute version of "A House is Not a Home." Aretha won her nineteenth Grammy Award on February 8, 2006, competing against Mariah Carey's "Mine Again," Fantasia's "Summertime," Alicia Keys' "If I Was Your Woman," and John Legend's "Stay with You."

Although she never studied music in college, Aretha continued to rack up honorary degrees from different colleges around the country. On May 13, 2006 Aretha was presented with an honorary Doctor of Music degree by the Berklee College of Music in Boston, Massachusetts.

Also that year, Aretha announced the upcoming release of her next album, *A Woman Falling Out of Love,* which was intended to be on her own label, Aretha's Records. Although Franklin announced that she had recorded duets for the album with gospel singer Karen Clark-Sheard, pop-rock star Richard Marx, and country artist Faith Hill, the recordings sat in the can for the rest of the decade.

The only Aretha Franklin album to be released in 2006 was one issued by Sony / BMG Music entitled *Joy to the World.* Now that Sony Music owned all of Aretha's Columbia catalog from the 1960s and all of her Arista recordings from the 1980s to 2003, they had the ability to put together their own compilations combining both eras of her career. The *Joy to the World* album contains her three Columbia Christmas singles, "Kissin' By the Mistletoe," "Winter Wonderland," and "The Christmas Song (Chestnuts Roasting On An Open Fire)." It took her Arista version of "Joy to the World" from 1994 and combined these four actual Christmas songs with gospel songs from her *One Faith, One Lord, One Baptism* album and a couple of standards from her days at Columbia ("Over the Rainbow" and "Ac-cent-tu-ate the Positive"). What it did more than anything else, was to make the public long for a true Christmas album from Aretha, not a stitched-together one like this.

Aretha filled much of 2007 with personal appearances at benefits and other high profile events. She also did several concert dates across America. Some of the events she participated in were outrageously commercial, and other events were classy and sophisticated. On April 1, 2007, Aretha sang "America the Beautiful" at *WrestleMania 23*. On May 14, 2007, Franklin was presented with an honorary Doctor of Music degree from the University of Pennsylvania.

Reviewing her at the Wolf Trap music venue in Vienna, Virginia, on July 5 of 2007, J. Freedom du Lac of *The Washington Post* claimed, "Franklin remains a force of nature, even after all these years of brilliant belting. She burrows into a lyric until she finds its emotional core. And her voice is still an astonishing instrument. Yes, she's lost some of her power and range (it has, after all, been some forty years since she ascended to the throne as the Queen of Soul). But Franklin continues to sing with incredible intensity and command while working mostly in her lower and middle registers." (9)

The reviewer got a particular charge out of Aretha's love of eccentrically lavish fashion statements. According to du Lac, "Franklin sashayed onto the stage in a robin's-egg blue evening gown—a satiny fishtail affair that exploded into a puff of feathers around the knees. With a matching satin wrap weaved around her shoulders and arms and a double strand of pearls hugging her bosom, Franklin wasted no time in getting down to business." (9)

The review also pointed out that Aretha was still gamely exploring new material in her concert appearances. According to the article, "Franklin also performed a playful, properly swinging version of 'Beyond the Sea,' which featured a knockout vocal complete with authoritative scatting. It was a reminder that . . . Franklin is the female soul singer against whom all others are measured." (9)

As another accolade, in 2007 Aretha Franklin's recording of "Respect" was voted a Legendary Michigan Song by MichiganRockAndRollLegends. com. And in August of that year, when Aretha attended the opening of the US Open Tennis Match with her former boyfriend, Willie Wilkerson, rumors began circulate that she was finally planning to marry him. Wherever she showed up, the Queen of Soul was making headlines.

During this era, Aretha's physical size continued to grow. She was carrying around a lot of extra weight, and people were starting to talk publicly about her obvious disregard for her health. It had been nearly ten years since she had finally quit smoking, and she had steadily been gaining weight since then. Some very unflattering photographs of her started to appear in magazines and tabloid newspapers.

However, the public's interest in Aretha continued unabated. She wasn't actively recording and releasing albums like she used to, so in 2007, two of her former record labels compiled new releases out of material they had in their vaults. Atlantic Records, via its subsidiary label, Rhino Records, issued a two-disc recording of *Aretha Franklin: Rare & Unreleased Recordings from the Golden Reign of The Queen of Soul*. The album of "previously unreleased" Aretha recordings was one of the last projects that Jerry Wexler worked on. He not only served as the album's "compilation producer," but he also used several of his recollections about working with Aretha, in the liner notes booklet.

When he was interviewed for the original edition of this book, Jerry Wexler spoke of all the recordings that he had produced with Aretha, which were still "in the can," and unreleased. He spoke with fondness about Aretha being adventurous musically, like she had been on the Beatles' psychedelic "Fool on the Hill." He also recalled always wanting to get Aretha and Ray Charles in the recording studio together and how he could never make it happen. However, it was Quincy Jones who held the honor by recording the only studio duet by Franklin and Charles. It was recorded for a Duke Ellington TV special in 1973, and the song was one of Ellington's compositions: "Ain't But the One." Thanks to Wexler's 2007 compilation, both "Fool on the Hill" and "Ain't But the One" were heard by the public for the first time.

The album also contains eight never-before-released tracks that Quincy Jones had recorded with Aretha for *Hey Now Hey (The Other Side of the Sky)*. One of the most interesting tracks from those sessions is her interpretation of Leonard Cohen's "Suzanne." In earlier material found on this album, Aretha does her version of the Supremes ("You Keep Me Hanging On"), covers Bill Withers ("Lean on Me"), and tackles the Frank Sinatra songbook ("My Way.")

While this was going on, Arista Records jumped to it with their own special Queen of Soul package: *Jewels in the Crown: All Star Duets with the Queen*. In her twenty-three years at Arista, Aretha had recorded her share of duet recordings, with the *crème de la crème* of popular singers including

George Benson ("Love All the Hurt Away"), Euthrymics ("Sisters Are Doin' It For Themselves"), Elton John ("Through the Storm"), George Michael ("I Knew You Were Waiting"), Luther Vandross ("Doctor's Orders"), and Frank Sinatra ("What Now My Love"). Producer Clive Davis—who had by now returned to Arista—added these tracks to songs she recorded with some of the newest raft of recording stars including John Legend ("What Y'All Come To Do"), Mariah Carey ("Chain of Fools"), and Mary J. Blige ("Never Gonna Break My Faith").

The *Jewels in the Crown* album featured a duet with Fantasia, "Put You Up on Game," which was released as a single, and became a hit on Urban AC radio, hitting Number Forty-one on the R&B charts. Even more exciting than that, the song she recorded with Mary J. Blige, "Never Gonna Break My Faith," was nominated for a Grammy Award in the category of "Best Gospel-Soul Vocal Performance by a Duo or Group."

Jewels in the Crown sold well and made it to Number Fifty-four on the *Billboard* album chart in America. On the R&B album chart, it peaked at Number Seven.

The 2008 tributes to the Queen of Soul began on February 8, when Franklin was honored as MusiCares "Person of the Year." The MusiCares annual event is a record industry salute to a recording artist superstar who has lent their talents to charitable causes. As a charity itself, the MusiCares organization is one which provides a place for musicians to go for health or monetary assistance. And, at this particular event, Aretha Franklin was fêted in a grand fashion at the Los Angeles Convention Center. Amongst the people there to honor her were Dan Aykroyd and Jim Belushi as the latter day "Blues Brothers," Quincy Jones, Dave Stewart of Eurythmics, Bill Cosby, Corinne Bailey Rae, John Stamos, Sarah Brightman, Tony Bennett, Blair Underwood, Natalie Cole, Chris Daughtry, Beach Boys' star Mike Love, and legendary Motown producer and former Aretha producer Lamont Dozier.

Two days later, at the 50th Annual *Grammy Awards*, Aretha was awarded her twentieth Grammy Award, for the song "Never Gonna Break My Faith," from the *Jewels in the Crown* album, her duet with Mary J. Blige. [This was her eighteenth Grammy Award for a specific song or album, but including her two "honorary" Grammys, it makes a full total of twenty Grammys for Franklin.]

Knowing that she was in the "winner's circle" that evening, and knowing that she was going to perform a special gospel number with a full choir amidst *The Grammy Awards* telecast, Aretha dressed to dazzle that evening. She wore a low-cut décolletage exposing yellow gown with spaghetti straps, draped with a long yellow / lime green / olive green flowing wrap of several yards of gauze.

She won her Grammy that evening of February 10, 2008, and was saluted as a huge star on the telecast. However, she got into a huge public "diva-like" feud with Beyoncé Knowles and Tina Turner over something that occurred during *The Grammy Awards* telecast.

What happened was that Beyoncé—in a short silver skirt—took the stage at the Staples Center in Los Angeles and named several female superstars—including Aretha Franklin, and then announced, "There is one legend who has the essence of all of those things: the glamour, the soul, the passion, the strength, the talent. Ladies and gentlemen: stand on your feet and give it up for 'The Queen.'" (10) With that, Tina Turner took the stage to receive a delighted gasp of recognition and a huge ovation from the crowd.

Beaming a huge smile, Tina Turner looked incredibly hot that evening in skin-tight silver lamé pants, and a low-cut silver halter top as she performed a song with Beyoncé. Apparently Aretha fumed from the audience. Although Tina at the time was sixty-eight, two years older than Aretha, Turner never lost her figure, or her ability to strut across the stage with the vigor of a thirty-year-old.

Aretha was seated in the audience while all of this transpired, dressed in countless yards of chiffon, waiting to do her gospel number later in the show. However, when she heard Beyoncé introducing Turner in the middle of the show as "The Queen," Aretha—in her yellow gown—turned "green" with envy, and was getting "redder" with anger by the moment. Once the fireworks started, it became quite colorful indeed!

To throw some more fuel to the fire, Beyoncé was quoted by *Fox News* that evening as considering Tina Turner her "ultimate icon." (10)

Two days after *The Grammy Awards* telecast, Aretha issued a public statement. Fox News on-line headlined their story "Aretha Franklin Slams Beyoncé For Calling Tina Turner 'The Queen' at Grammys." The Queen of Soul proclaimed, "I am not sure of whose toes I may have stepped on or whose ego I may have bruised between the Grammy writers and Beyoncé. However, I dismissed it as a cheap shot for controversy." (10) She then half forgave the incident by stating, "love to Beyoncé anyway." (11)

When the Associated Press approached Beyoncé's camp for a statement, she declined an interview about the matter. So, Beyoncé's father / manager, Matthew Knowles, stated in an interview with CelebTV.com, "I am not taking something this ridiculous to Beyoncé. Beyoncé referred to Tina Turner as a 'queen.' Not Queen of Gospel, Queen of Soul, Queen of Blues, Queen of England. I consider my wife a queen and sometimes call her that. Does Aretha have a problem with that?" (11) When the item was picked up by *The New York Daily News*, the story spread all over the internet.

Gary Susman in *Entertainment Weekly* perfectly summed up the event by stating, "Hell hath no fury like an R&B diva scorned, especially at the Grammys. First there was Natalie Cole opening fire on Amy Winehouse. Now, in a statement released Tuesday, Aretha Franklin revealed that she, too, was incensed at a young upstart: she didn't appreciate that Beyoncé, in her introduction of Tina Turner at Sunday's awards show, referred to Turner as 'The Queen.' There's only one Queen of Soul, Franklin implied, and she was not amused." (12)

Matthew Knowles called Franklin's remarks "ridiculous . . . childish . . . [and] unprofessional." Ouch! (12)

Several months later, *The National Enquirer* headlined a story: "CLASH OF THE TITANS: Tina Turner vs. Aretha Franklin Feud Has Festered for Twenty-five Years." According to that article, "While Arista Records president Clive Davis was masterminding Aretha's career comeback in the early 1980s, Tina came along with her smash *Private Dancer* album. Tina instantly surpassed Aretha on the charts, and she was furious! Aretha felt that Tina stole her thunder and she's never forgiven her for it." (13)

For quite some time Tina Turner remained quiet about this whole matter. By autumn of 2008, the "Queen of Rock & Roll"—Tina Turner—finally got into the fray, and Aretha and Tina Turner were at it again.

At the time Tina was about to launch a high-profile comeback concert tour. She was looking hot, and she was selling out concerts right and left.

Not one to mince words, Tina announced in the press that Aretha had a huge ego. When *USA Today* interviewed her about her return to the concert road, they couldn't resist inquiring about her battle with Aretha. According to Tina: "Aretha has always been like that. We've always accepted that from her. She's the Queen of Soul, and I'm the Queen of Rock & Roll. There were so many kings and queens there that night. Her ego must be so big to think she was the only one. That's how queens are!" (14)

When Aretha read this in the September 30 issue of *USA Today*, she got in contact with the newspaper, and demanded that she get her say. They gave her the space to do so, and in their October 8, 2008 issue they headlined it, "ARETHA SPEAKS OUT: Aretha Franklin's Response to Tina Turner Statement in *USA TODAY*." According to Franklin, "I have always appreciated what Tina Turner has to offer and had quietly cheered her on after Ike and her subsequent success. However, with respect to her statement concerning my ego (in saying, 'Her ego must be so big to think she was the only one . . . that's how queens are') clearly she was talking about herself as she described herself as the 'Queen of Rock' and saying 'that's what Queens do'—particularly since she does not have a clue as to who I am in view of the fact that we have never met. I never figured her to resort to tacky press just to sell a few tickets. I understand and I know that the concert market is down where ticket sales are concerned. I really had put her in a different class—higher than that. Finally, no one has been more gracious or complimentary to their peers than I have and I am confident and secure enough to do so, unlike some others. I wish Ms. Turner all the best, as I always have. Perhaps one day we will meet." (15)

While all of this high profile headline-grabbing drama was transpiring, the year 2008 turned out to be one which brought further acclaim and honors to Aretha. On February 14, Franklin was given the Vanguard Award at the presentation of the NAACP Image Awards. On May 4, Franklin was given the Key to the City of Memphis at the 2008 "Memphis in May International Music Festival." It was presented by Mayor Dr. Willie Herenton amidst her on-stage performance that day. In their September 13 issue, *Billboard* magazine ranked Aretha at Number Nineteen on their "*Billboard* Hot 100 All-Time Top Artists." And, in November, Franklin was named by *Rolling Stone* magazine as the Number One "All-Time Best

Singer of the Rock Era." This honor was voted on by the publication's survey of 179 musicians, producers, *Rolling Stone* editors, and other music industry insiders.

With the exception of her two compilation albums in 2007 and her appearance on tribute albums, it had been five years since Aretha released a full album of new material. In late 2008, Aretha released her first official holiday album, *This Christmas, ARETHA*. It was originally released as a Borders Bookstore exclusive offering, however the following year it was released to wider distribution by the DMI / Rhino Records label. Several of the tracks are of the solemn and religious category, including "Ave Maria," "Silent Night," and "Angels We Have Heard on High." However the most truly successful song is the joyous "Christmas Isn't Christmas (Without the One You Love)" which was written by Kenneth Gamble and Leon Huff, and produced by Tena Clark.

Aretha being Aretha, she cannot help but include at least one snippet of impromptu dialogue on the album, and a hysterical one-sided telephone conversation—a la "Jump to It"—with her gossiping and talking about two of her favorite topics: her family and food. We hear Aretha laughing about how she was not going to make her soul food "chitlins" as part of her holiday meal at Christmas, since they nearly killed her "last year." Clearly, Aretha does have a fun sense of humor about herself when she lets herself go.

On the subject of food-related Aretha stories, one of the most amusing ones from this era came right after *The Grammy Awards* show. Celebrity photographer Charles Moniz was present at one of Aretha Franklin's concerts at the Nokia Theater in Los Angeles on February 16, 2008. He laughingly recalls, "For the opening of the second act of the show, Aretha returned to the stage, donning a Pink's Hot Dog stand baseball cap on top of her beehive hairdo. She then verbally carried on about one of the best things about being back in Los Angeles, was being able to go to Pink's for their famous hot dogs. She then proceeded to have several men come out on-stage, carrying cases of Pink's hot dogs, which they distributed to the audience. Not only did she share the hot dogs with the audience, but she herself ate one on-stage as part of her endorsement. She said that she had picked up nine Pink's hot dogs while she was there, but qualified it by explaining that she didn't eat them all at once!" (16)

On a completely sad note, in 2008 two of the most influential men in Aretha's musical career passed away: Clyde Otis and Jerry Wexler. Both these men considered their work with Aretha to be amongst their greatest achievements. Their talents will be missed, but the music they have created will always be fondly remembered.

Without a doubt, the decade's crowning achievement for Aretha Franklin was her performance on the steps of the Capitol Building in Washington, D.C., for President Barack Obama's inauguration on January 20, 2009. Aretha was personally invited to the historic event to sing her expressive version of the song "My Country 'Tis of Thee."

Since the event is held outdoors in the coldest month of the year, everyone attending had to be bundled up in very warm outfits. For this occasion Aretha commissioned a stylish grey wool overcoat and matching grey hat—which was decorated with a huge grey bow sitting atop it. The hat in question came from Mr. Song Millinery in Detroit, and was created by Luke Song, who has been designing ladies hats for twenty-five years. The bow was decorated with Swarovski crystals and cost Miss Franklin $179.

Aretha made such a huge sensation with that iconic hat, that it was one of the most memorable aspects of the entire event. People were standing around water coolers at work that week discussing "Did you see that hat Aretha Franklin wore at the inauguration?" It was such an attention-getter that Aretha sold it to the museum collection at the Smithsonian Institute, for an incredible—reported—$2 million. Not bad for a $179 investment. Again, the Queen of Soul had conquered, in a fashion sense, and financially as well!

Throughout 2009 Aretha kept busy making personal appearances and concert engagements. On May 2, she got the chance to wear another one of her hats, this time around at the Kentucky Derby in Louisville, Kentucky. Amongst her most notable concerts that year was a visit to the Hollywood Bowl on June 26. That night she not only performed several of her signature songs—from "Respect" to "Freeway of Love"—but she also tackled the perfect Hollywood-themed song—"As If We Never Said Goodbye" from the Andrew Lloyd Weber Broadway musical *Sunset Boulevard*. On October 30, 2009, Aretha was one of the performers to take part in the *25th Anniversary Concert for the Rock &*

Roll Hall of Fame, held at Manhattan's Madison Square Garden. Also on the bill during that two night all-star concert were Bruce Springsteen, Mick Jagger, Paul Simon & Art Garfunkel, Jerry Lee Lewis, Lou Reed, Annie Lennox, Sting, David Crosby, Graham Nash, Stephen Stills, John Fogerty, and Stevie Wonder. Amongst the highlights of the concerts and the resulting DVD was Aretha's duet with Annie Lennox on the song "Chain of Fools."

As the holiday season came along, on December 2 Aretha was in New York City to help officially light the Christmas tree in Rockefeller Center. For that occasion she wore a huge fur coat, complete with a strange-looking fur hood that seemed to bury her. It was so odd-looking that it was lampooned on *Saturday Night Live*, where comedian Seth Meyers commented that it looked like Aretha had been engulfed by the coat. While a photo of Aretha in the huge fur coat flashed on the screen, Meyers satirically explained, "This Wednesday the Rockefeller Christmas tree was illuminated. However the occasion was marred when Aretha Franklin was caught in a bear's mouth." (17)

One of the sad things that happened in 2009, was the death of Aretha's half-brother, Vaughn Franklin. Vaughn had been the son of Barbara Siggers, but he was adopted by Reverend C.L. Franklin shortly after he married Barbara. At this point, all of Aretha's siblings were deceased, and she was now the oldest member of her immediate family.

In February 2010, Aretha turned the tables on everyone and presented the most humorous performance of her entire career. Rarely does she so blatantly show the public her sense of humor. However, in a 30-second TV commercial for Snickers candy bars, Aretha and Liza Minnelli poke fun at themselves for being temperamental "divas." In the context of the commercial, four college-age men are amidst a "road trip" in a cramped car. In the backseat is Aretha in a yellow dress, complaining about the air conditioning. The young man next to him offers diva-like "Aretha" a Snicker's bar, and she takes a bite, then instantly turns back into the character of "Jeff" who is wearing a yellow tee-shirt, admitting that he feels himself again, thanks to the candy bar. Then the cranky person in front of him complains about knees poking him in the back of his seat, and it is another diva in need of a Snickers candy bar: Liza Minnelli.

Although the locale of the exterior shots make it look like the commercial was filmed in California, the interior shots of Aretha and Liza were shot in the Detroit area—in Farmington Hills, Michigan—at Grace & Wild Studios. The hysterically funny commercial proved to be so popular that it was actively shown on television over the next two years.

During this era Aretha continued to make personal appearances at hotels, concert venues, and casinos. On April 30, 2010, she was booked to perform at the annual New Orleans Jazz and Blues Festival. The day of her appearance, she canceled, giving the very unhappy promoters less than ten hours notice. The group Earth, Wind & Fire were quickly contacted to perform in her place. This was the second year in a row that Aretha had "stiffed" the "Jazz Fest," as she had also been booked for the same festival in 2009, and likewise she had canceled at the last minute.

On May 24, Aretha Franklin received another honorary music degree, this time from Yale University. Although everyone hoped that she would grace the commencement ceremonies with a song, she didn't sing that day. The closest the crowd came to a concert that day came when the band played a few bars of the song "Respect." However, on-stage Aretha Franklin was fittingly honored by Yale President Richard C. Levin, who conferred upon her the honorary "Doctor of Music" degree.

According to Levin that day at Yale, "We know royalty when we see it, and you are, without question, the 'Queen of Soul.' . . . From gospel to pop, from blues to hip-hop, your voice expresses our feelings." (18)

"Dr. Aretha" was on a roll! Aretha's most high-profile 2010 concert performance came in Philadelphia, on July 28, when she appeared in concert, on the bill with former Secretary of State, Condoleezza Rice, an accomplished classical piano player. For Miss Franklin and Miss Rice, the event was a special one-time-only concert, held to raise money for arts and for the Mann Center—the summer home of the Philadelphia Orchestra.

Ann Midgette of *The Washington Post* wrote of the evening, "Putting Aretha Franklin and Rice together on the stage had a kind of goofy brilliance. It was evidently Franklin who decided that the two should perform together; she may have sensed, with the same stage-animal instinct she demonstrated throughout the evening, that Rice would provide curiosity value to augment, or even showcase, Franklin's entertainment value." (19)

It was a chance for Rice to show off the fact that she was actually an accomplished piano player, and for Franklin it was a chance to show off the fact that she actually has ten operatic arias in her repertoire. Aretha had been studying with Mary Callaghan Lynch, a Detroit classical soprano. It was Lynch who first coached Franklin when Pavarotti enticed her to sing "Nessun Dorma" in 1998. Rice showed off her talents during the first act of the evening, tackling such classics as Mozart's "Piano Concerto in D Minor, K. 466."

After the intermission, Aretha presented a one-and-three-quarter-hour, sixteen-song set. Franklin had been working on classical arias for over twelve years. She had started with "Nussen Dorma" from Puccini's *Turandot*, the year that she ended up substituting for Pavarotti on *The Grammy Awards* telecast. Now she was ready to debut some new arias. So, for the first time in public, Aretha sang "Che faro" from Gluck's *Orfeo ed Euridice*.

Reported Midgette in her review of the evening, "In 'Che faro,' the result was a bit of a train wreck as Franklin struggled to free herself from the regular beat of the orchestra. But she produced a cover of 'Ombra mai fù' from Handel's *Xerxes*, to her own piano accompaniment, that came from the heart." (19)

For her classical portion of the show, Aretha wore opera-length gloves. As though she was doing a bit of a strip-tease, she removed them one finger at a time. Then she sat down to play and sing her own classic: "Dr. Feelgood." On the non-classical side of Aretha's show, she performed several of her own hits in her sixteen-song set, including "Respect" and "(You Make Me Feel Like) A Natural Woman," and a duet version of "The Way We Were" with Ronald Isley of The Isley Brothers.

Naturally, the show had to have at least one duet performance between Rice and Franklin. It came on the song "I Say a Little Prayer," with Condoleezza on piano, and Aretha handling her trademark vocals on the Burt Bacharach and Hal David composed song. Playing with the audience, Aretha laughingly joked, "You didn't think she could play it, right?" Reportedly, the crowd of approximately 8,000 concert-goers was thrilled by both the classical and the rocking proceedings that evening.

The second half of 2010 found Aretha Franklin all over the media, and the majority of the press coverage that she received was mainly about her various health issues. It started in August of 2010 when it was reported that Aretha fell in the shower and fractured three of her ribs. According to a statement by her publicist, "Due to fractured ribs and pain in the abdomen, it was necessary for Ms. Franklin to cancel and reschedule the two concerts." (20)

In the same press release Aretha claimed, "I was very much looking forward to being in Brooklyn and having a foot-long hot dog at Coney Island. Hopefully I will get it before the end of August." (20)

Since Aretha was scheduled to sing at politician Charlie Rangel's eightieth birthday party in New York City amidst that same trip, her statement also announced, "I will really miss that nice slice of cake from Congressman Charlie Rangel's birthday party and singing 'Happy Birthday' to him." (20)

In his witty gossip column in *The Village Voice*, Michael Musto cited the press release about the Coney Island hot dogs and the birthday cake comments from Franklin, and subsequently entitled his article about it, "Aretha Cancels Concerts, Will Miss the Food." Claimed Musto, "Our hearts are with her, but it's obvious that the woman hasn't become that unglued by this cancellation, seeing as she's still thinking about the food ops [opportunities] that are being lost as a result of it." (21)

In their September 20 issue, *The National Enquirer* put Aretha and other stars on its cover story entitled "Hollywood's Deadliest Diets." The magazine claimed that Franklin now tipped the scales at nearly three hundred pounds, although she only stands five-feet five-inches tall.

Also in September 2010, Aretha issued an elaborate press release proclaiming that the actress she would most like to portray her in a projected film about her life, would be Halle Berry—who is admittedly gorgeous, and weighs approximately 120 pounds. Franklin also stated that she would like Denzel Washington to portray her father in the film if it is to be done. The statement claimed that Denzel "was very interested in the role," and said that she "also had a very positive response from her in-person conversations" with other actors on her wish list. (22) She also claimed that she wanted Terrence Howard to play young Smokey

Robinson in the film. However, it was the crazy idea of Halle Berry playing Aretha, that caused the story to spread like wildfire on the internet.

While all of this was taking place, Aretha's son, Eddie, found his name splashed all over the newspapers, when it was disclosed that on September 21, 2010 he was "allegedly" attacked by three people, reportedly at a Detroit area gas station. According to the news coverage, Eddie was hospitalized for his injuries, and released. There is a lot of conjecture and confusion regarding the event, as there was no gas station at the exact location of the reported attack. Eddie mysteriously left the hospital abruptly, and very conspicuously avoided talking to the police.

Mike Helms in *The Detroit Free Press*, reported, "Gwendolyn Quinn, a spokeswoman for Motown legend Aretha Franklin, issued a news release Tuesday morning saying Eddie Franklin, 52, was attacked by two men and a woman late Monday and underwent emergency surgery. She said no other information about the attack was available. Police said they have been unable to confirm details of the attack or talk to Eddie Franklin. What's more, Franklin was said to have been attacked as he left a gas station in that area, but Sgt. Eren Stephens, a police department spokeswoman, said there is no gas station in the area where the attack took place. 'He has not yet made a report,' Stephens said. 'Right now, we're waiting on him to make a report so we can find out what happened. A spokeswoman for Sinai-Grace Hospital confirmed Eddie Franklin was treated and released from the hospital but said his treatment did not require surgery." (23)

Also, according to the article, "Eddie Franklin was a suspect in a fall 2002 fire at a $1.6 million Bloomfield Township mansion his mother used for storage, but an investigation by Michigan Attorney General Mike Cox's office later cleared him. Lost in the fire were Grammy Awards, dresses and other items Aretha Franklin had intended to donate to the Smithsonian Institution or similar groups." (23)

The whole story about the attack on Edward seemed very suspicious indeed. Edward claimed to be attacked at a gas station, where no gas station existed, and when the police wanted to question him, he avoided them. Then Aretha threw herself in the middle of the story. Karu F. Daniels in *BlackSpin News* reported, "Franklin claimed the cops 'gave the media the impression that [her] son was not being cooperative.' Police said they failed to take a statement from him in the hospital. 'After observing my son on Tuesday, it was clear that he was unable to communicate with anyone after such a traumatic attack and with his jaw wired,' Franklin told *The Detroit News* newspaper. 'The officer probably would not have been able to give a statement if he had been attacked by three men the very next day, either, and it was totally unreasonable to expect Eddie to do so as if he were not being cooperative.'" (24)

In November of 2010, Aretha was heard on the debut solo album by Ronald Isley of the Isley Brothers, entitled *Mr. I*. The duet that she sang on Ronald's album was the Carole King song, "You've Got a Friend." It was so well received that it was eventually nominated for a Grammy Award, although it did not win it.

On November 4, 2010, the ongoing Aretha Franklin story shifted gears and became one of deep concern for her health. It was publicly announced that Aretha was canceling all of her public appearances, due to strict orders from her doctor. This would mark the beginning of several months of alarming concerns and conflicting reports about the status of Franklin's health.

The Detroit Free Press reported that Aretha left Sinai-Grace Hospital in Detroit, on October 30. She had been hospitalized for several days and that she had an undisclosed medical condition.

With stories appearing around the globe, even Australia's *Herald Sun* proclaimed, "Legendary soul singer Aretha Franklin has been ordered by her physicians to cancel all concerts and appearances for six months following a recent hospitalization. Doctors' orders have required her to cancel all concert and personal appearances through May 2011." (25) Amongst the canceled concert appearances was a planned Christmas concert, and two shows in February at New York City's Radio City Music Hall.

Through her publicist, Tracy Jordan, the press received word that, "Franklin is resting comfortably at home, but is anxious to get back on the road to perform for her countless fans around the world." According to the same press release, Aretha appreciatively stated, "I would like to thank my friends, fans and supporters for all the beautiful flowers and their many well wishes." (24)

To give her side of the story, Aretha chose to grant a telephone interview with *Jet* magazine's Clarence Waldron. "I am doing OK," she said amidst the interview. "I am getting the best of care. I have a superb team of doctors. I also have a Greater Authority. He is the doctor of doctors and I am standing on His promises . . . I'm not feeling 100-percent, but I'm not feeble or senile. You can print that," she laughed. (26)

She averted all questions about her exact health condition, merely explaining that more tests needed to be done. According to Aretha, she had prayed along with her friends, gospel singer Karen Clark-Sheard, Reverend Donald Parsons, and Bishop Paul Morton. "I know they can pray; they can sure 'nuf go to the Lord in prayer," claimed the soul diva. She ended her interview with, "I feel pretty good. My doctors and I are on it. God is good." (26)

On December 1, in downtown Detroit, City Councilwoman JoAnn Watson and several other Aretha friends gathered to hold a "Prayer Vigil" for Aretha's mysterious medical procedure she was due to have the following day. *The National Enquirer* online stated on December 2, that "Rumors have swept the blogosphere that Franklin may be suffering from a form of throat cancer." (27)

On December 8, 2010, Rev. Jesse Jackson gave an interview with Associated Press, and reported that he had been to Aretha's house, and that she is "recovering very well . . . She's conscious, communicating and taking daily walks up and down the hall . . . She has amazing strength—body, religion and faith. It's what keeps her going." (27)

That very same day, *The National Enquirer* reported that Aretha's mystery illness is in fact incurable pancreatic cancer. Whatever Aretha's ailment was, she was keeping it a guarded secret for as long as she could. In a cover story headlined "ARETHA CANCER STORY" the article claimed, "The Queen of Soul has only six to eight months to live, according to experts . . . But the surgery was not for gastric bypass—it was specifically for the pancreatic cancer she's been battling . . . Surgeons had to remove over half of her stomach . . . Insiders say the Queen of Soul underwent the standard operation for pancreatic cancer—called the 'Whipple' procedure." (28)

Since it was also *The National Enquirer* who had so accurately predicted and covered the pancreatic cancer of Patrick Swayze, it was assumed that this prognosis is 100-percent accurate. To add to the air of mystery about what her health problem was, or was not, Aretha wasn't telling. Nor did anyone in her camp ever say that the *Enquirer* had the story wrong, so it was universally presumed to be true.

In a subsequent issue of *The National Enquirer*, it was reported that sixty-eight-year-old Aretha was rushed back to Sinai-Grace Hospital on December 21, after she collapsed in her home. The article claimed that she was in fact suffering from dehydration. After several days she left the hospital.

From the end of December and the beginning of January, Aretha decided to take up residence in the Grand Penthouse Suite of the MGM Grand Hotel in downtown Detroit. In an article about Aretha in the January 24 issue of *The National Enquirer*, the magazine showed the aftermath of the gala party that Aretha threw for herself in her luxury suite. Reportedly the bar was stocked with Veuve Clicquot, Cristal, and Dom Pérignon champagnes, Grey Goose and Stolichnaya vodkas, and there was a smorgasbord of everything from lobster and shrimp to filet mignon and prime rib. The party astonishingly cost a reported $180,000. Did this mean that Aretha was literally "partying like there is no tomorrow?" This all seemed most alarming.

Access Hollywood reporter Shaun Robinson was granted a telephone interview with Aretha on January 13, 2011. With regard to her health crisis, Aretha explained, "Well, there was just so many wild things out there and just so many things being said that weren't true. I just felt I needed to address it a little." (29) In the "so many things being said that weren't true" category, this likely refers to the original rumor that she had "throat cancer."

However, she still refused to admit what it was that she was suffering from. What she did say was, "I went through a number of procedures before I knew what was wrong." (29)

She admitted to Sean that she had felt a pain in her side. "Yeah, the pain was so hard it almost brought me to my knees," Aretha explained. "I was in Birmingham and then Boston and after that concert the same pain hit me again. I really just began to not feel good and I said, 'Oh, no this is it, I can't do any more concerts till I know what the problem is.'" (29)

And, what about the reports of pancreatic cancer? All Aretha would say was, "I don't know where 'pancreatic cancer' came from. I was sitting there reading the newspaper and it was saying someone in my family said that. No one in my family ever said that to anybody." (29)

She then explained that her doctor said to her, "The surgery that you just had is going to add fifteen to twenty more years to your life." That was about it for her frank disclosures. She had basically danced around the whole issue again. (29)

What she would talk about was that she had heard from President Barack Obama. "I got a wonderful and beautiful letter from the President," Aretha proudly admitted. "And nobody does it like him!" (29)

She also claimed that she had been losing weight. According to Aretha, "I'm down to a rockin' [size] sixteen–eighteen." (29)

On January 16, 2011, Halle Berry was one of the glittering stars to attend the annual *Golden Globe Awards* in Hollywood. On the red carpet, Berry was asked by a reporter from *E! News* about Aretha Franklin's September 2010 announcement that she would like to have petite Halle portray her on the big screen. Halle let the Queen of Soul know that she was not interested in portraying her, by graciously stating, "If I could carry a tune, I'd consider it. Someone should tell Aretha that I can't do her justice." (30)

Aretha was surprised that Halle turned her down on national television but explained, "She was my first, but not my only choice. Everything is subject to negotiation and she shouldn't underestimate her own talent. There are a number of other leading ladies out there that can definitely handle the role . . . I never expected Halle Berry to sing, she's an actress, not a singer. Many actors have portrayed vocalists by lip-syncing to the artist's original recordings." (30)

Following months of seclusion, on February 11, 2011 Aretha suddenly made a surprise public appearance. She attended a Detroit Pistons basketball game, held at the Palace of Auburn Hills in Michigan. For that particular game the local team was playing against the Miami Heat.

That evening, Aretha was dressed in a long-sleeve leopard-print top. She had obviously lost a lot of weight in just over two months. It was later reported that the amount of weight she had dropped since December was eighty-five pounds. That night at the basketball game, Aretha sat in the second row with her date of the evening, Rev. Jesse Jackson. During the first quarter there was a break in the game and the cameras hit Aretha and her face was projected on the big screen, and her music played over the speaker system. That evening Detroit was both happy and proud to have their Queen of Soul up and about again.

She spoke briefly to the press that evening. *The Detroit News* reported that she said, "I'm feeling really great. Loving the game, loving the game." According to her, this was, "My first night out. My downtime was over about three days ago." (31)

The biggest public outpouring of concern and tribute came on February 13, 2011, at the 53rd annual *Grammy Awards* telecast. With an audience of over twenty-six million television viewers, the spotlight was firmly placed upon Aretha Franklin and seven of her most classic songs, with an all-star soul / gospel / country / pop divas salute.

The segment that opened the show, featured singer / actor LL Cool J presiding over the segment. He reverently announced, "Aretha Franklin is, and always will be the Queen of Soul. Tonight she is the queen of our hearts too, and the Queen of the Grammys. We're talking about a legend who has received eighteen Grammys so far. Aretha is at home tonight in Detroit, getting better, so until our Queen comes back to us, some of our most talented musical princesses are coming together to show their R-E-S-P-E-C-T for Aretha and this Grammy house that she helped build." (32)

With that, he introduced Greg Phillinganes, conducting a full orchestra to accompany Christina Aguilera, Jennifer Hudson, gospel singer Yolanda Adams, country star Martina McBride, and Florence Welch of Florence & the Machine. Hudson opened the Aretha musical medley with the first lines of "(You Make Me Feel Like) A Natural Woman," upon which all of the ladies joined in, each taking a stanza of the lyrics. They proceeded to include in their tribute: Christina's over-the-top version of "Ain't No Way," Martina's rocking "Until You Come Back to Me," Florence's sassy "Think," Jennifer's impassioned "Respect," and Yolanda's gospel-flavored "Spirit in the Dark." The musical tribute concluded with all five musical divas rocking out on "Sisters Are Doin' It For Themselves."

After the segment of songs, Grammy viewers were treated to a pre-taped spot by Aretha Franklin herself. Looking thinner than she had been in years, Aretha was dressed in a flattering pale pink satin shoulderless gown, with perfectly coiffed hair, and a double string of pearls. She was taped in the living room of her Bloomfield Hills, Michigan, house. Behind her was dramatic fireplace, a black grand piano, and upon the classic instrument was a crystal vase filled with the soul queen's favorite flowers: red and pink, long-stemmed roses.

In her segment a heartfelt Aretha proclaimed, "Thank you ladies, I love you all. Good evening ladies and gentlemen, and members of the Grammy Academy. I cannot tell you how thrilled I am to be with you this evening. And to whom do I have to thank for this very special moment? The longtime producer and visionary of *The Grammy Awards*, Mr. Ken Ehrlich. Thank you so much Ken. And I especially want to thank all of you who took the time to send me Get Well cards and flowers—beautiful flowers; and, most importantly, your prayers during my time of hospitalization. I also want to especially thank Mr. Clive Davis for his concern and his wonderful letter to me. I wish that I could have been with you all tonight, but since I couldn't, mmmmmm, next year. OK? To all of the Grammy nominees tonight, 'Good luck to you all.' Thank you so much, I love you. Have a good evening." (32)

After watching the tribute to her, off camera Aretha told the press that she was highly flattered by the whole event. "I loved it!" she proclaimed. "The ladies all sounded so wonderful and they looked fabulous! All of them were dressed to the nines! I enjoyed each and every performance, especially Yolanda doing 'Spirit In the Dark' and Christina's rendition of 'Ain't No Way.' Loved them all! They all looked beautiful, I really liked Jennifer's outfit, those epaulettes on her shoulder pads were too sharp! Bravo ladies!!!" (33)

In a program which featured such name performers as Barbra Streisand, Bob Dylan, Mick Jagger, Usher, Justin Beiber, and Lady Gaga, the eleven-minute tribute to the Queen of Soul was truly the highlight of the entire show. It was classy, exciting, and absolutely electrifying to see and to hear. And, the public's curiosity to catch a glimpse at the—reportedly—"three dress sizes slimmer" Aretha, truly piqued everyone's interest.

The photos of the new slimmer 2011 version of Aretha that were released that week on the internet showed a radiant Franklin with toned skin. Although it was essentially the same Aretha that millions of television audiences saw on *The Grammy Awards* pre-taped segment, the later "still" photos were clearly heavily airbrushed. The new versions of Aretha had a redefined neck and jaw line to make her appear healthier than she clearly was. Since the public still knew nothing of what Miss Franklin's true health problems were, it made it all the more alarming.

It was quite fitting that *The Grammy Awards* telecast should happen on the 13th of February, the eve of Valentine's Day. It served as a sincere tribute to everyone's favorite soul-singing Valentine, Aretha. The spotlight it placed on her was a sincere one, but it was also one that made everyone wonder what was really going on with Aretha. Was she just in the hospital to have her stomach reduced or blocked to cause her dramatic weight loss? Or, was this new slimmer look merely the sign of a truly grave health crisis? Were people scrambling to show their "respect" to Aretha for fear that she might be nearing the end of her long and eventful reign as the "Queen of Soul?"

Someone who Aretha has previously performed with, Fantasia, went to the press to make a statement about how she felt snubbed by *The Grammy Awards* telecast. Although she was nominated, and won a Grammy for "Best R&B Vocal Performance, Female" for her song "Bittersweet" that evening, she boycotted the show and refused to attend. According to her, she was mad that she wasn't invited to be part of the Aretha Franklin tribute on the show, and to demonstrate her hurt feelings, she decided to skip *The Grammy Awards* altogether.

According to Fantasia, "They were honoring someone who is my idol, Aretha Franklin, and there is no way I could have sat there and not got the happy feet and wanting to jump on the mike because she is my favorite. So I felt like, you know, at the end of the day I should have been on that stage so, I kind of did my own little thing last night." (32) Speaking of huge diva egos, Fantasia obviously had one too!

Aretha was reportedly "unhappy" when she heard Fantasia's rant to the press. According to Franklin, "I was sorry to hear that Fantasia was upset because she did not get the opportunity to participate in my

Grammy Tribute this year. I recall that in the past, Fantasia participated in both my MusicCares Person of the Year tribute and my United Negro College Fund tribute. Fantasia is still young in the business and although we all love and appreciate her, she must understand that in this business of show business, she will not always get to participate in everything she would like participate in. I'm sure it was not an intentional omission. I will see Fantasia over the summer here in Detroit." (34)

TV talk show hostess Wendy Williams snagged a real coup when she got Aretha to grant an in-person interview with her. The diva had phoned Wendy Williams on the air in January to say "hello," so she felt very comfortable with the idea of appearing on the talk show. When Wendy reached out to book Franklin for a TV interview, Aretha agreed, and Wendy flew off to Detroit to have a formal tea with Aretha.

The interview aired on *The Wendy Williams Show*, March 2 and 3, 2011. While they sipped tea at the Townsend Hotel in Birmingham, Michigan, Aretha mainly talked about her weight loss, food, *Dancing with the Stars*, Whitney Houston's self-destructive drug problems, Halle Berry, her sister Carolyn, and several other non-medical topics.

At the top of the interview Franklin admitted to Wendy that she had lost an astonishing total of eighty-five pounds since December, she still claimed that it was all due to a healthier diet. According to her, "I was looking at a lot of pictures, and I was saying, 'You are entirely too fat for words!'"

When Wendy said to her, "We all found out that you were having abdominal surgery."

Aretha said, "Is that what you heard?"

"Well that's what was said," admitted Williams.

Then Aretha replied, "O.K. Well a lot of things were said. I've left that behind. I'm feeling wonderful. I'm feeling great. And, I couldn't be feeling any better than I'm feeling right now." (35)

Apparently, Williams was granted one—and only one—question about Aretha's health problems. She had gotten it in, Aretha answered it the way she wanted to, and then it was on to much lighter topics.

To match the progressively growing interest in the singer, Aretha's three main record companies quickly began to put together musical compilations of her music. The first one to fully jump on the bandwagon was Columbia Records, and their massive twelve disc boxed-set called *Take a Look: Aretha Complete on Columbia.* In addition to all of Aretha's original albums for Columbia, for the first time ever, the set included a planned but never released album called *A Bit of Soul*, a stripped down studio version of Franklin's jazzy LP *Yeah!!!*, a DVD of some of her early sixties television performances on *The Steve Allen Show*, and an historic and rare audio dialogue of teenage Aretha in the recording studio with John Hammond and Ray Bryant at the time she recorded her first non-gospel album, in 1960.

According to Marc Myers in *The Wall Street Journal*, the *Take a Look: Aretha Complete on Columbia* album was a total hit. "Before Aretha Franklin became the Queen of Soul, she was a budding Princess of Pop. Fresh from Detroit in 1960, the 18-year-old gospel singer signed with Columbia Records and went to work recording the American songbook—combining Ella Fitzgerald's lyricism with Mahalia Jackson's earth-moving passion . . . Clearly, the pre-'Respect' Franklin could ace anything the label put before her—from Hoagy Carmichael's 'Skylark' to Neal Hefti's 'How to Murder Your Wife.' But as the years passed, Columbia's outdated pop strategy for Franklin gained little traction with the exploding youth culture and civil-rights movement . . . Yet this set provides an illuminating look back at the superstar's awakening," he claimed. (36)

Susan Whitall of *The Detroit News* glowingly assessed the boxed-set by stating, "As the DVD of her appearances on *The Tonight Show* [a/k/a *The Steve Allen Show*] illustrate, Franklin was a poised, satin-clad chanteuse, at ease with singing any part of the classic American songbook. Her jazz training and musicianship have not always been acknowledged, but she has the respect of musicians because she is not 'just' a singer, but one of them, a gifted pianist and arranger . . . There are also times when she accompanies herself on piano on a song like Jimmy Reed's 'Trouble In Mind,' that you can hear the stirrings of a new sound, the soulful, gospel-infused music that would soon explode for her and the entire country." (37)

At the same time that the *Take a Look: Complete on Columbia* album was released, Columbia / Sony Records also released a new single CD collection of the soul diva's jazz era music, entitled *The Great American*

Songbook. It took eighteen of her tracks from her Columbia career, and gave them a new spin. Several of the tracks are different mixes, and alternate takes on her early sixties music.

When Clyde Otis was originally interviewed for this book, I asked him if he remembered, "What nightclub was Aretha's *Yeah!!!* album recorded in?" He replied that he couldn't recall. It was revealed in the *Take a Look: Aretha Complete on Columbia* album that *Yeah!!!* was in fact a "live" studio recording, and that the applause and audience sounds were actually added to make it sound like she was performing in a jazz club. The 2011 boxed set and *The Great American Songbook* album both feature songs from *Yeah!!!* with the "ambient sound" and applause removed.

On March 25, 2011, Aretha Franklin was feeling well enough to celebrate her sixty-ninth birthday at a star-studded gala at the Helmsley Park Lane Hotel in New York City. Dressed in a white, loose-fitting dress with gold-colored accents, she danced, sang, and greeted guests who included Bette Midler, Tony Bennett, Smokey Robinson, and TV personalities Gayle King and Wendy Williams. Also on hand were two of the loves of her life, Willie Wilkerson, and Dennis Edwards of the Temptations.

She not only felt well enough to blow out the candles on her two-tiered flower-lined birthday cake, when Dennis decided to serenade her with his version of the song "The Way We Were," she joined in on the singing. This marked her first publicly sung song since her dramatic health scare of the previous year.

Bette Midler, who once recorded the Aretha-associated song "Drinking Again," proclaimed of Aretha, "She was in fine form. It's wonderful to see that she had such a good time."

Gayle King commented with delight, "There was a lot of love directed her way, and she appeared very touched by it all."

The Queen of Soul herself reassuringly proclaimed to her guests, "I'm feeling fine and blessed to be here!" (38)

After all of the recent talk about her health, Aretha's guests were just relieved that she had made it to this point. Already the concerned speculation had begun, with the public wondering if she would indeed make it to her seventieth birthday. According to one of the party attendees that night, there wasn't a dry eye in the house that evening.

On May 3, 2011, Aretha's album *A Woman Falling Out of Love* was released on her custom label, Aretha's Records, initially for sale exclusively at Wal-mart stores. Obviously, she had taken the album's title from her favorite song on her last Arista album, Burt Bacharach's "Falling Out of Love." To publicize the album she went to New York City to appear on *The View* on April 28. On the show she sang two songs: one track from the new album—"How Long I've Been Waiting," and one classic Aretha hit—"Think." The following night, Aretha appeared on *Late Night with Jimmy Fallon*, where she chatted about and previewed the new album with "Sweet Sixteen," and closed the show with "Freeway of Love."

On *The View* Aretha looked especially comfortable chatting with Whoopi Goldberg, and the other hostesses, having "girl talk." The only mention of Aretha's health was Whoopi carefully stating, "We know you don't want to talk about what was wrong, but how you feeling?"

According to Aretha, "I'm feeling wonderful. Fabulous . . . The weight loss came from the surgery. It was not bariatric surgery . . . I feel wonderful. I've got more energy. I changed my diet; going to Whole Foods [grocery store] now; getting all the best stuff. I dropped the chitlins, dropped the ham hocks, dropped all that stuff and I get some—I won't say 'better' food—but 'other' food." (39)

When *A Woman Falling Out of Love* was released, for Aretha there had been an eight-year gap between non-holiday studio albums. She had been announcing both it, and her own record label—Aretha's Records—for the past five years, and nothing ever came of either of them. Finally, with all of the publicity that her health issues had stirred up, she was able to secure a distribution deal in America through Wal-mart stores, and on the Wal-mart website. The fact that she "executive produced" the album herself instantly spelled out the precautionary words "train wreck." Indeed, the album ends up with the train off-of-the-tracks most of the time amidst its twelve-song road. However, she still delivers a few solid performances here.

Two major mistakes really mar this album. The first one is giving one of her sons a solo in the middle of her album. Her fans don't want to buy this album to hear Eddie Franklin sing "His Eye is on the Sparrow," they want to hear Aretha sing it. The second major mistake, is ending the album with "My Country 'Tis of Thee." It is the 2008 studio recording she produced for President Barack Obama's inaugural. This song is lushly orchestrated, but it ends the album on a somber note.

As an album, *A Woman Falling Out of Love* is a patchwork quilt of divergent styles. It varies from heartfelt blues on B. B. King's "Sweet Sixteen," to invigorating pop on "New Day." Along the way she also delivers two over-produced but interesting new versions of pop classics: "Theme from *A Summer Place*" and "The Way We Were." Aretha enlisted actor Billie Dee Williams to do a surprising little spoken-word passage in the middle of "A Summer Place," and on "The Way We Were" she duets with Ronald Isley of the Isley Brothers. Unfortunately, neither of these men are credited or thanked on the album in any way. Omissions like this never happened at Arista! Or, was there some behind-the-scenes drama between Aretha, Williams, and Isley that made her purposely remove their names?

The big pre-release hype on the album was the promise that Aretha sings an incredible gospel song on it with Karen Clark-Sheard, called "Faithful." Aretha must have mixed the vocal tracks, because it is mostly Franklin warbling by herself while Karen barely gets in a line or two underneath her. For all the big "wall of sound" effects, the song is ultimately more overwrought than inspiring. Both voices are lost in what sounds like a gospel shouting match.

"New Day" is the album's strongest track by far. The song was written by Aretha's son, Kecalf Franklin Cunningham, along with Norman West. It has a more of a memorable "hook" to it than any of the other new songs on *A Woman Falling Out of Love*. With a strong chorus line, and catchy beat to it, it shows Aretha's voice off well, and is light and refreshing in sound.

While *A Woman Falling Out of Love* features some very strong songs, especially "New Day" and "Sweet Sixteen," it also hits several wrong notes along the way. It bounces too abruptly from blues, to pop, to eighties retro, to gospel, to romantic, to patriotic. There are way too many mood swings here. Listening to it makes one long to have Clive Davis take the reigns of her recording career again. He knows how to pick out a hit song, and he knows how to structure an Aretha album that has a strong beginning, middle, and ending.

The press reviews for *A Woman Falling Out of Love* were mixed. According to Thomas Conner in *The Chicago Sun-Times*, "On 2003's *So Damn Happy*, her last album with Arista, Franklin made a stab at updating her music to fit the times, and it mostly worked. For *A Woman Falling Out of Love*, however, she's in retreat. The songwriting is '70s, the production is '80s, the arrangements are pure '90s smooth jazz. Instead of a contemporary queen, we get an unsettling Eartha Kitt-enish cougar anthem ('How Long I've Waited,' one of two songs here Franklin wrote and produced), clumsy jazz-club scat singing ('U Can't See Me'), an icy reading of 'Theme from *A Summer Place*.'" (40)

In a review entitled, "For Aretha Franklin Fans, These Are Trying Times," Allison Stewart in *The Washington Post* claims of *A Woman Falling Out of Love*, "Executive-produced by Franklin, recorded for Franklin's own label and appears to indulge every wrong musical instinct Franklin has ever had. This is the sound of a legend doing exactly as she pleases, which in Franklin's case means plenty of lite R&B ballads and underdone covers of overdone standards, such as 'The Way We Were.' . . . a muddy-sounding *hot mess* of an album!" (41)

Likewise, *Rolling Stone* gave *A Woman Falling Out of Love* a low rating. Will Hermes in his review found it full of "unmemorable songs and overcooked arrangements." (42)

It was instantly acknowledged in the music business that Aretha had made a huge mistake with *A Woman Falling Out of Love*. One her biggest fans on the radio side of things is Tom Cuddy, who helped turn New York City's WPLJ into a hit-making force in broadcasting. According to Cuddy, "It's been eight years since we were treated to a new Aretha CD with all new material, and as gifted as she is, now that the album is out, I feel let down. I believe she needs to let down her guard and trust a gifted producer to find the right material for her and to make sure it's produced to 2011–2012 standards. She still has the voice, the attitude, and the aural charisma, but she needs to have faith in someone like David Foster, who's a specialist at working with strong-willed women singers (Whitney Houston, Barbra Streisand, Toni Braxton). Or I'd love to see and hear how Jimmy Iovine would produce her." (43)

A Woman Falling Out of Love sadly became an album which failed to find an audience. In *Billboard* magazine in the U.S., it debuted on the charts at its peak Number of Fifty-Four pop, and Number Fifteen R&B.

On May 17, 2011, Aretha was in Chicago at the United Centre in front of a crowd of 13,000, as part of a star-studded television taping for the final week of *The Oprah Winfrey Show*. For the past twenty-five years—since 1986—Winfrey was the hostess of a top-rated TV talk show. The five-episodes-a-week American-based show also aired in 148 other countries around the world, including Germany, France, China, and Japan. The pair of special "farewell" shows, which were billed as *Surprise Oprah! A Farewell Spectacular*, featured such special guests as Tom Cruise, Halle Berry, Will Smith, Jada Pinkett, Stevie Wonder, Usher, Patti LaBelle, and Madonna, and also included a touching musical tribute to Winfrey by the Queen of Soul.

Aretha was dressed in a flowing sleeveless white dress with a single strap, and her ensemble was accented with some very sophisticated jewelry. While an emotional and tearful Winfrey watched from the audience, the soul diva sang a heartfelt rendition of "Amazing Grace." The episode with Ms. Franklin aired to an audience of millions on May 24, 2011.

It had been only eight months since her huge health scare, and again Aretha encountered another physical dilemma. However, this time around her injury was self-inflicted. She had gone to Texas to perform at a non-public event when she fell down in her hotel room and injured her left foot.

As Aretha later explained, "I was in Dallas, Texas, doing a private party for a billionaire there. After the concert, I had a pile of shoes; Jimmy Choos [designer shoes] right in the middle of the floor. You have to picture this: The couch is 'here,'" she said while marking out imaginary spots in a hotel room with her hands. "The pile of shoes are 'there,' and the cocktail table that sits in front of the couch was 'here.' I went to step over the pile of shoes, and I don't know—today—how I came down on the shoes, but my foot was really killing me. And, I stepped like on one of the heels, I guess." (44)

The injury she sustained was to her left index toe, which she explained, "hurt like heck for a minute but seemed to subside." (45) She decided not to seek immediate medical attention, and chose to see if it would heal on its own. On her road trip north from Texas, she decided to get it X-rayed at Community North Hospital in Indianapolis, Indiana. The X-ray revealed that she had indeed fractured that particular toe, and she was fitted with a wood-soled and blue Velcro-strapped medical shoe to hold the injured toe and her foot safely in place until it could mend itself. Once a diva, always a diva: since it seemed that Aretha's main concern with this was vanity-based. She complained in the press: "How am I supposed to match my new Marc Jacobs gown with this wooden blue hospital shoe?" (46)

She then spoke on more of a practicality issue, stating: "I'm so grateful it wasn't my right piano pedal foot, I have a gig on July 27th at the Jones Beach Theatre in New York!"

In the July 8, 2011 edition of *The New York Times Sunday Magazine*, an entertaining article about the Queen of Soul appeared under the title of "A-R-E-T-H-A," which was written by entertainment reporter Rob Hoerburger. The actual interview segment of the article wasn't all that revealing in a personal nature, and Hoerburger claimed in print: "Sooner or later, almost everything we discussed came back to food, and it was clear that Franklin is as obsessed with it as she ever was." (47)

Indeed, amidst the article Aretha was more forthcoming about life's dining possibilities than about any other topic. "May I recommend something?" the diva asked the writer: "The shrimp-and-avocado salad. I've had it four times this week." Later in their conversation she reminisced about New York City and all of the cuisines that it contains: "You remember certain things about the city that aren't here anymore. There was a great little steak place next to the Apollo where I'd go between shows to have my lunch and dinner." Regarding her much publicized weight loss she revealed, "Falling out of love is like losing weight. It's a lot easier putting it on than taking it off . . . I learned that I wouldn't starve if I had one hot dog instead of two." (47)

With regard to shopping, Aretha proclaimed, "I love Wal-Mart, and not just because my record is there. You can get some things there that you cannot find at Saks or Bergdorf's or other upscale stores." (47)

Most amusingly, Hoerburger's meeting with the Aretha came with strict parameters about what topics were not to be asked, and that included her medical issues. He claimed, "she would throw up that filter of formality throughout our lunch if a question cut a little too close. I'd also been told beforehand that she would not discuss the nature of the medical procedure or anything reported in *The Queen of Soul*, an unauthorized biography by Mark Bego that, like most unauthorized biographies, sometimes presents its subject in less-than-flattering lights." (47) The "diva" had spoken!

While Aretha has an incredibly strong reputation for being a first class singer, her track record as a businesswoman is not so highly revered. Unfortunately, starting her own record label, Aretha's Records, has yielded a sea of new problems. Not only was her album, *A Woman Falling Out of Love* a sales and critical disappointment, in July of 2011 it also became a legal problem.

Music publishing rights are a complicated issue for veterans of record labels, let alone artists who self-release their own material. In July of 2011, Aretha's music publishing company, Springtime Publishing, was sued by the writer of the song "Put It Back Together Again" and co-writer of "New Day," Norman D. West. His legal suit claimed that Aretha had refused to sign a royalty agreement for the first song, yet she issued both songs on her *A Woman Falling Out of Love* album, without properly and legally agreeing to obtain the rights to one of them.

Furthermore, West was also the writer of the song "Watch My Back," which Aretha had recorded on her 1998 album *A Rose is Still a Rose*. In addition, his lawsuit included unresolved "copyright infringement" claims over that song as well. Although Franklin had not come to an agreement with West, he claimed that she continued to record his material without agreeing to proper arrangements to compensate him. The suit was filed on July 15, 2011 in Detroit Federal Court.

According to Norman D. White's lawyer, Jeffrey Thennisch, "These are two parties that have a long-standing working collaboration. Mr. West has the utmost respect for Springtime and everyone associated with it. Mr. West has told me that he owes much of his career to Aretha Franklin and that he views her as both a mentor and a guiding force in his career." (48) However, even the strongest friendship can be strained when money becomes involved.

The Queen of Soul was atypically un-amused. Speaking to the press Aretha claimed that she was "extremely disappointed" by West's actions, in his attempts to be paid by the diva. She proclaimed that he had displayed "unmitigated gall" by filing this lawsuit against her and her company. (49)

During the summer of 2011 Aretha continued to make television appearances to promote her *A Woman Falling Out of Love* album, and to show the public that she was in good health. Although she definitely weighed less than she had before her health scare of 2010, she was clearly packing on the pounds again.

When she arrived at ABC-TV studios in New York City to appear on the popular morning show, *Live with Regis and Kelly*, she and Willie Wilkerson pulled up in a chauffer-driven limousine. According to eye-witnesses, she sat inside the automobile snacking on potato chips prior to her appearance.

Press photographer Derek Storm was one of the people on the sidewalk waiting for her to come out of the car before she walked into the studio entrance. According to him, "Aretha spent about ten minutes in her town car, waiting for the segment to begin taping. She had a tube of Pringles potato chips in her purse that she kept munching on. When she got out of the car, she put on a pair of huge Jackie Onassis-style sunglasses. She was actually quite friendly with the crowd, as she signed autographs. However, she moved very carefully—most likely because of the broken toe—and she was very soft-spoken. She was not the energetic Aretha I am used to seeing." (50)

On the show she performed the song "How Long I've Been Waiting" from her new album. Dressed in a white pant suit, she wore a sandal on her right foot, but on her left foot she had on a medical shoe to protect her recently-broken toe.

Aretha also sat down to chat with the show's hosts, Regis Philbin, and Kelly Ripa. Although she was seen eating a can of Pringles potato chips in her limousine prior to the TV taping, she proceeded to go on camera during the interview segment of the television show, and to speak about how her startling weight loss was due to her new and more sensible diet.

When Regis said to her, "You look great. You lost a few pounds," Aretha admitted, "A few pounds. All together, yeah, about 85 pounds, all together. Not at one time, though. It wasn't all at one time. It was gradual." (44)

Kelly looked down at Aretha's odd-looking left shoe and asked her, "What happened to your foot?"

"I don't know how I did it," Aretha replied. She proceeded to tell the tale of tripping over her stack of designer shoes in Dallas, laughingly concluding with the amusing quip, "You would think that at [the age of] '46,' you wouldn't stumble on your shoes and things like that."

In a humorous dialogue with Franklin, Regis confessed, "I can't get into the computer, and the Twitter, and the texting, and all that, but I understand you have become a fan of that stuff."

Aretha explained, "I did graduate from the fax, I went to the laptop. I don't go on Facebook, I don't Twitter. I don't do any of that, I text. But, I forget to check my texts. I'm so used to faxing, I never go to the texts. And when I do, there's like 500 messages." (44)

The diva also revealed that she had just completed a duet with Tony Bennett for his forthcoming album, *Duets II*. She told Regis and Kelly, and their viewing audience, that they could look forward to hearing her with Bennett performing the song "How Do You Keep the Music Playing."

On July 25, 2011 Franklin continued to add to her high-profile list of television performances by appearing on *The Today Show* with Kathie Lee Gifford and Hoda Kotb. Although she was not interviewed in-depth, she chatted a bit, and again she sang the song that she was promoting from her latest album, "How Long I've Waited." It was one of the songs she was not being sued over.

The previous year, Aretha had cancelled two scheduled concerts in the Brooklyn / Long Island area of New York due to her failing health. When she had done so, she vowed that she would come back and make them up. In late July / early August of 2011, Lady Soul made good her promise. One of the dates was performing at the outdoor concert facility at Jones Beach, the other one was an open air "free admission" concert where 10,000 fans happily crowded into the Seaside Concert Arena at Coney Island.

Regarding her July 27 concert, Jon Parales wrote in *The New York Times*, "Aretha Franklin isn't letting medical problems sideline her anymore. At Jones Beach Theater on Wednesday night she let fly a voice with its power, range and improvisational spirit fully alive . . . She sang about earthly and divine ecstasy, and she sang simply to exult in her voice." (51)

On August 4, 2011, the Queen of Soul finally made it out to Coney Island. In his review of Aretha Franklin that night, in *The New York Post* Dan Aquilante claimed, "There couldn't have been a more perfect fit than the Queen of Soul in Kings County last night . . . The crowd was so large, it overflowed onto the adjoining boardwalk and beach . . . Whether the song was soul, gospel, rock or funk, Franklin was stunning." (52)

Since the beginning of 2011 Aretha had done all that she could to prove that she still had some more fire and sparkle in her soul, and that her singing career and her musical creativity were far from over. There were definitely some awkward and unsatisfying moments as witnessed by her *A Woman Falling Out of Love* album, its blasé sales and critical reception, the embarrassing lawsuit it brought, and her falling over in Dallas resulting in a fractured toe.

However, her dazzling performance on *The Oprah Winfrey Show*, playing sold-out dates that provided her with some of the strongest concert reviews she had seen in the past ten years, and the general outpouring of love that Aretha received from television show hosts, from concert goers, and from her fans, by far outweighed any of the temporary missteps.

Through her most recent 2011 concert and television performances, Aretha proved time and time again that although she was again gaining weight and having some physical problems, her voice was still amazingly strong, agile, and expressively dramatic. Her millions of fans were thankful and happy to see and hear that she was not only alive and well, but that the instrument that is her amazing voice was still as good and as strong as it ever was.

Now it was time for the living legend to go back to her home base and to show Detroit that the Motor City's reigning diva still had the magic, the talent, and the vocal power that had originally made her a star. And, that is exactly what she did.

CHAPTER TWELVE

HOW DOES ARETHA KEEP THE MUSIC PLAYING?

It is August 25, 2011, and it is a warm and somewhat overcast evening in the Detroit, Michigan area. I am seated on a picnic blanket on a hillside in the suburban town of Clarkston, at the outdoor amphitheater that is universally known as Pine Knob, although it now is officially entitled DTE Energy Music Theater. In spite of the venue's commercial new title, to many people—including Aretha—it will always be known as "Pine Knob," since that is the name of the winter ski resort where it is located. This has been an arena that has presented a glittering roster of musical stars since 1972 when it was originally built. It has played host to everyone in the music business from rock and soul stars like Joni Mitchell, War, Alice Cooper, The Four Tops, Bob Dylan, and Stevie Wonder; to jazz, folk and pop stars like The Carpenters, Andy Williams, and Ella Fitzgerald. Tonight however, the entire tree-lined venue belongs to the phenomenal and legendary Queen of Soul: Aretha Franklin.

Tonight's program isn't just a concert or a mere musical show, it is a triumphant "return," a revival, and a testimony to one woman's talent, and her perseverance. It seemed for many months that the reigning diva who calls herself "Lady Soul" was on death's doorstep. Her extreme weight problems, her mysterious health dilemmas, and the early deaths of all of her four siblings, made her fans fear that she might not make it to her 70th birthday. This evening, nearly 10,000 Detroit-area fans of soul music, gospel music, and rock & roll have gathered to see the often-controversial and universally-beloved singer. It was her first Detroit concert since 2009, and the anticipation was high. Some people came to see what her physical health was like, or to hear how she would sound, or simply to see what kind of show she would give. No one quite knew what to expect.

The crowd that gathered at DTE to see Aretha on this evening was as diverse as her music. An older crowd came to hear the classic songs of their youth. Middle-aged people came to hear her latter day hits like "Freeway of Love." Teenagers came to see the woman they knew from the Snickers candy bar commercials. And, members of her church-going audience came to hear some gospel. Everyone who was gathered here had expectations and hopes that they would hear the Queen of Soul sing their favorite tunes.

With the exception of a revue of six scantly clad Brazilian dancers in feathered Carnival costumes who danced and shimmied through the aisles prior to the show, there is no opening act this evening. Although it was entertaining in a fashion, this dance troupe had nothing to do with Aretha's music or legend. The crowd began to get restless for the main event, and began to wonder how late Aretha would be for her curtain, originally called for at 7:30 p.m. Finally, twenty minutes later, "The Aretha Franklin Orchestra" conducted by Fred Nelson III, took the stage. It was a twenty piece orchestra with five strong-voiced background singers. In an effort to redirect the atmosphere into a more "Aretha-centric" mode, they launched into an instrumental overture of the Franklin hits "Jump to It," "(You Make Me Feel Like a) Natural Woman," "Think," and "Respect."

Finally, a commanding voice came over the loudspeakers to announce: "The greatest voice of all times . . . Your queen, my queen, the queen of all time . . . ," and at a slow-but-steady pace there she was: Aretha was being carefully led out of the wings of "stage right" by a pair of handlers. As she arrived at center stage, she loudly and confidently announced to her adoring hometown crowd, "Hello Detroit, you're looking wonderful!"

She was dressed in a floor-length apple green gown, which was decorated with pink cloth carnations. Over the top of it she wore a short but voluminous pink jacket that covered her upper arms. The top of the dress featured her trademark low-cut front, and a sparkling double string of beads hung around her neck and fell onto her décolletage.

Launching into her lively version of Jackie Wilson's "(Your Love Keeps Lifting Me) Higher and Higher," Aretha sang with such enthusiasm and confidence that all fears that she no longer had her trademark vocal power melted away.

It was instantly evident that Aretha is not at all successful at keeping off the weight that she lost from December 2010 and February 2011. As she shimmied and sashayed at center stage, she made it clear that—regardless of what her weight was—she has all of her legendary singing strength.

As she launched into Curtis Mayfield's classic from the film *Sparkle*, "Something He Can Feel," she began to hit her stride. Bobbing her head to the music and showing off her a cute and sporty short haircut, she commandingly entreated the audience: "If you feel like partying, just get up in your seat!" Whether they were seated on the lawn, or in the assigned theater seats closer to the stage, the crowd began to do exactly that.

In the next hour and a half, Aretha was about to hit every phase of her incomparably long and exciting career. Turning to her Arista Records songbook she dedicated her third song to: "My friend Luther Vandross . . . let's get it right!" As she sang the energetic "Get It Right," she took the enthusiastic crowd back to 1983 when she and Luther rocked the charts as a dynamic producing and singing team. She then turned back the clock to sing the Stevie Wonder song that she had made famous in 1973, "Until You Come Back to Me."

As the sun continued to set in the Michigan sky, the evening's temperature began to cool, which is very much to Aretha disliking, causing her to insist on concert halls and television studios being kept warm for her. However, the warmth that she was creating on-stage was enough to keep her happy.

She also seemed to be in a good frame of mind, and she was obviously relieved to have her mysterious illness behind her. After she finished her sparkling rendition of the Stevie Wonder song, she turned her attention to another one of her favorite songwriters by stating, "We're gonna look back and remember my sister Carolyn." With that came the familiar sounds of the song "Angel," which drew an enthusiastic round of applause.

"This is Detroit's own, how do you like the band?" Franklin shouted out to the crowd, which again elicited an appreciative round of applause. It was clearly an all-Aretha / all-Detroit music fest this evening, and she confidently reconfirmed her claim to the title of being the queen of her Motor City realm.

While the diva sang, huge projection screens flashed illustrations of her glorious life, including photos of her with former Detroit Mayor Coleman Young and her late father: Reverend C. L. Franklin, as well as snapshots of her with Bette Midler, and with Tony Bennett from her highly-publicized sixty-ninth birthday party in New York City in March of 2011.

Since she was originally known as a teenage gospel singer growing up in downtown Detroit, it seemed fitting that for her sixth song of the evening, she should take the proceedings into a gospel vein with a lively rendition of the song "I Came to Lift Him Up." Singing the song with full-force gospel power, she had the first several rows of the audience standing up, dancing and figuratively "going to church."

Next, she began to delve deeper into her Atlantic Records classics to sing a beautiful version of her 1967 R&B classic "Ain't No Way." In the middle of the song Aretha proclaimed: "Cousin Brenda back there," referring to the hefty girl standing with the background singers hitting the distinctive high note that Cissy Houston performed on the original recording.

Aretha then moved forward to 1970 to present a rousing version of her Number One R&B hit "Don't Play That Song (For Me)." As she sang with incredible vocal power, three young female dancers in cheerleader outfits came out of the wings and began dancing while the commanding diva sang. While they performed, Aretha took off her short pink jacket, slung it over her shoulder, and placed it on the piano as she exclaimed, "Don't play it! I don't want to hear it!"

It was 8:35 p.m. and as she turned to leave the stage she announced, "I'm just going away for a moment to have a Snickers," amusingly referring to the wildly popular candy bar television commercial she made with Liza Minnelli. As she left the stage, she introduced a young man she announced was "my grandson, Jordan." The slim young man took the stage, and presented a couple of politely-received but forgettable rap songs. When he was finished, Aretha returned to the stage in a form-fitting sleeveless silver sequined floor-length gown and instantly regained the spotlight.

"Did someone say 'Grandma?'" she laughingly asked the audience. As she returned to her position at center stage, her background singers started crooning: "Woman, woman, strong woman." Franklin announced as a commercial plug for her most recent album: "My newest single . . . exclusively at Walmart.com." With that she sang the first cut from her newest album: "How Long I've Waited." Although she sounded in great voice on the tepid song, she demonstrated again how this song from *A Woman Falling Out of Love* dramatically paled in comparison to the dynamically appealing hits of her past. When she finished it, she only received a soft and polite round of applause. By now, the audience had heard enough gospel, her grandson's rap, and other filler, and we were clearly getting restless to hear the songs that made Aretha famous.

Fortunately, the Pine Knob audience was about to get exactly what they wanted. As the familiar intro the song "Chain of Fools" began, it caused an audible ripple of ecstatic anticipation. Now this is what we came for! As Aretha delivered a searing version of this dynamic Number One 1967 hit, she had her fans on their feet, singing and dancing along with her. This is what her hometown audience wanted, and Franklin presented it with all of the fire and excitement that she became world-renown for delivering.

For her eleventh song of the evening, Aretha sat down at the grand piano that was at "stage right" and she proceeded to play while she sang. "From the book of Simon & Garfunkel," the diva announced as she played the familiar long and slow introduction to the song that won her the sixth Grammy Award of her career, "Bridge over Troubled Water." The crowd roared with excited approval to hear this selection, which is one of the most beloved hits of her entire career.

As she played the song she asked the crowd, "Did you notice that ugly shoe is gone?" referring to the wooden protective medical shoe that she had worn since June of that year. "It took me ten weeks," she explained. "This is the first pair of heels I've had on in ten weeks!" According to her, "I said, 'I gotta put my heels on, I'm going to Pine Knob!'" The hometown crowd laughed along with Aretha who was so comfortable on stage, that her comments were delivered in a fashion that made her sound like we were all seated in her Bloomfield Hills living room.

While she was sitting at the grand piano and masterfully playing the keyboards, a close-up shot of her hands flashed on the projection screens. At first glance, the close-up mainly showed off a large square ring on her right middle finger, with a blue stone on it. However, as she played to accompany her singing, what we were witnessing was her incredibly creative talent as a musician. "Sing it 'Ree!" someone enthusiastically shouted to Franklin from the audience.

As she showed off the keyboard work that she had been displaying since she was a young preacher's daughter in downtown Detroit, she provided the most moving, exciting, and satisfying segment of the show. It was her emotional and soulful version of "Bridge over Troubled Water," that truly demonstrated the sheer musical genius that is Aretha Franklin.

Like Jerry Wexler once said, the key to unleashing the power of Aretha's voice was to sit her down at the piano and have her play while she sang. As I sat there on the lawn of Pine Knob, I could hear Jerry Wexler's words echoing in my ears, "I took her to church, sat her down, and let her be herself."

This extended version of "Bridge over Troubled Water" really took the crowd back to a time in the 1970s when every song that Aretha chose to sing was instantly a smash. Tonight she really jammed on the keyboards, and drew the song out. Finally, she stood up from the piano bench, and danced in her high heeled shoes as the orchestra continued to vamp on this emotion-filled performance of "Bridge over Troubled Water."

When the song came to a conclusion, she received a heartfelt and joyfully cheering standing ovation that had the flavor of a church "revival meeting." While she had the audience in a church-going mood, Aretha presented her twelfth song, "One Night with the King," the gospel ballad she recorded on her 2009 Christmas album. According to the song, "One night with the king" certainly "changes everything." However that night in suburban Detroit, it was the "Queen" who changed everything. After she finished the song, she announced, "Ladies and gentlemen, I've had a wonderful, wonderful evening tonight." Then she turned to leave the stage.

As she moved towards the wings of the huge outdoor amphitheater, she announced, "My son Eddie got on the freeway and is here tonight." She also pointed to one her guitar players, who was another of her sons: "Teddy is up here on the stage, he is a graduate of Michigan State [University]," she proudly proclaimed. Tonight, surrounded by her hometown crowd of family and friends, Aretha wasn't just the star of the show, she was also the local suburban mom and grandmother.

As she was led off-stage, the appreciative Detroit crowd was on its feet, cheering with enthusiasm for their one and only Queen of Soul. Fortunately for them, she returned to the stage and said, "Let's get on the freeway!" With that, there was a huge anticipatory roar of enthusiasm from the audience. "Did you come up I-75?" Aretha asked, referring to Detroit's main freeway.

Unquestionably, Ms. Franklin was about to musically take her throng of Motor City fans down the fabled "Freeway of Love." As she sashayed on center stage, she announced that she was about to deliver "A major throwdown!" while she boogied all of us to the entrance ramp to the freeway. She proceeded to sing a rousing version of her gigantic award-winning song from 1985, which was all about big pink Cadillacs and several other fun Detroit-oriented images.

After an extended and exciting version of "Freeway of Love," she waved to the crowd and said "Good night!" It was 9:30 p.m. at this point, and the audience made it clear they were not ready to get on I-75 and leave the Pine Knob area yet. This crowd of thousands of her local hometown fans were on their feet cheering and applauding wildly for more.

As Aretha disappeared from the stage again, the cover of her latest album flashed on the huge projection screens as the orchestra vamped. "The Queen!" proclaimed the announcer over the loudspeakers. And again, Franklin came back to the stage. As she returned, she again moved to center stage, this time wearing a full-length satin jacket over her silver sequined dress, to do an encore chorus of "Freeway of Love."

"She has to do 'Respect' doesn't she?" I heard someone in the audience inquire of the person next to them. Just as the question was asked, the music for Aretha's signature hit began to play. It was her fourteenth song of the evening, and she fittingly used "Respect" as her encore number. It was delivered with all of the fire that she had put into the original version of the song that topped the charts in 1967, and welded her into rock & roll and soul history. As the song came to an end, Aretha proclaimed, "I want to thank you," which drew a huge round of applause. She continued, "I've been to London, been to Paris, to Germany. But there is no place like Detroit, Michigan!" Franklin then blew a kiss to the cheering crowd as she exited stage right. However, the applause and cheering continued so wildly that she came back for another bow before exiting the stage one last time. (1)

Aretha had come home, and all of the Motor City was glad to have her back. Her show only lasted an hour and a half, and only encompassed fourteen songs, yet it proved beyond a doubt that she was in incredibly strong voice. Those fourteen songs were all that it took to let all of us Detroit fans know who our hometown queen is, and that she was far from finished with her soulful reign.

She had overcome her physical illness of the previous year. Her broken toe had healed enough to allow her to wear her beloved high heeled shoes again. She had proven to audiences in various parts of the country that she had her voice and her strength back together again. Now it was time to show the world that her recording career could be somehow "jump started" again. In September of 2011 she was about to prove that in a most interesting way. And it took the classiness of Tony Bennett and the production mastery of Phil Ramone to do it.

Tony Bennett had recorded and released an album in 2006 called *Duets: An American Classic*. It became a hugely successful album, and featured Bennett singing songs with such luminaries as Barbra Streisand, James Taylor, Elton John, Billy Joel, and Paul McCartney. The original album was produced by well-respected music man Phil Ramone. When it won a Grammy Award and was certified Platinum, it seemed to be a winning musical formula worth repeating.

It was decided that it would be released to commemorate Tony Bennett's recent 85th birthday (August 3), and that it would contain a various group of fresh new voices, and some classic recording artists as well. For Tony's duet partners on his 2011 *Duets II* album, the list of singers he chose really ran the gamut—from newcomers like Lady Gaga,

John Mayer, and Amy Winehouse—to more established acts like Willie Nelson, Natalie Cole, and Aretha Franklin. Again it was the wonderfully talented Phil Ramone who produced this album's classy and snappy music.

For the Aretha Franklin and Tony Bennett duet, the beautiful Michel Legrand / Alan Bergman / Marilyn Bergman song "How Do You Keep the Music Playing" was chosen. It proved to be the perfect selection for the pair.

Unlike the famed *Duets* and *Duets II* albums that Phil Ramone produced for Frank Sinatra in the 1990s, this time around all of the vocalists were actually in the recording studio with Tony Bennett. To accomplish this, Bennett and Ramone literally flew around the world to record many of these songs.

The brilliance of this strategy is especially evidenced in the Lady Gaga, Amy Winehouse, and Aretha Franklin tracks. On each of these songs, you can tell that Tony is having a lot of fun in the recording studio adlibbing with his singing partners.

Released on September 20, 2011, Tony Bennett's *Duets II* received a huge sales push on television, and it really knocked the project "through the goal post" in terms of sales. Listening to the beautiful and excitingly orchestrated and lushly produced duet between Aretha and Tony, it is immediately evident that it is vastly better than any track on her Wal-Mart album. It so clearly benefits from being overseen by a producer like Phil Ramone who knows what to do with two such classic—yet very different— voices as Tony's and Aretha's.

The press reviews were instantly glowing. *Rolling Stone* magazine proclaimed, "Aretha Franklin and Bennett blow the roof off 'How Do You Keep the Music Playing.'" (2) In *The Los Angeles Times* Mikael Wood wrote, "It's a beautiful bummer to hear Winehouse do her best Billie Holiday in 'Body and Soul.' A clunky, chemistry-free collaboration with John Mayer . . . Bennett fares better in gorgeous duets with k.d. lang and Aretha Franklin." (3) And, *CBS News* beamed about, "Norah Jones gorgeously singing in just above a whisper on 'Speak Low'; Mariah Carey showing unusual restraint on 'When Do the Bells Ring For Me,' and Aretha Franklin pushing Bennett to a rousing climax on 'How Do You Keep the Music Playing.'" (4)

The week of October 1, 2011, the Tony Bennett *Duets II* album debuted on the *Billboard* magazine Hot 200 album chart at Number One! Surprisingly, *Duets II*, is the first and only Number One non-soundtrack pop album that Aretha Franklin has ever recorded or appeared on in her entire career. She has had ten Number One R&B albums in the past, and *Waiting to Exhale* hit Number One in the nineties, but she had never appeared on a Number One pop album on the *Billboard* charts in America that wasn't tied to a film. This became a dazzlingly brilliant new high point in her career, and it was a class act like Tony Bennett who gave her this wonderful distinction. In a year of many missteps, this album set a creative new Twenty-First Century high-water mark for Aretha. The Queen of Soul was officially back on top of the charts where she belonged!

What is it that makes Aretha Franklin great? Is it the individual songs? Is it the individual albums? Is it the inspiring sound of her voice? Is it the inspiring concerts she has delivered? Is it her diva attitude? Or is it because she is a colorful and a bigger-than-life pop music icon? In a way, it is "all of the above."

Aretha has had five major phases to her career. First there was the gospel prodigy phase she lived from the age of fourteen to the time she was eighteen. Then came her jazz / pop diva era at Columbia Records. Next came her reign as the Queen of Soul at Atlantic Records from the late sixties—starting with song "Respect." Her fourth era was her twenty-three year run as a huge hit-maker at Arista Records. And ever since 2003 when she left Arista Records, Aretha has been in her "legend" phase. It is an era where she only occasionally makes record-breaking music, yet she dabbles in new music from time-to-time, and happily shows up to receive awards, or to be saluted by her peers, or she hangs out in Detroit and has record producers or TV crews come to her.

It seemed that when her major health crisis began in 2010, it put the spotlight squarely on Aretha again, after seven years of resting on her laurels. With a hit-filled, and dramatic life lived for over fifty years in the spotlight, Aretha Franklin is a true legend, and an incredible survivor.

It is not easy being the Queen of Soul. It is acknowledged that for many years Aretha has been the victim of many of the men in her life. Her father dominating her as a child, the two children she had by the time she was sixteen years old, her reportedly abusive first marriage, her many emotional struggles, and her sons' legal battles, somehow have only made her stronger.

Not everyone was sure that she could survive all of the challenges that were put upon her. When Clyde Otis was interviewed for this book in 1988, he explained, "I did hear many a wild tale . . . I'm surprised that she is still alive today, and didn't just jump off a roof somewhere." (5) However, whatever the challenges were, Aretha stood tall and faced them.

Not only did Aretha survive the traumas and dramas of her early life, she managed to turn her life experiences into some of the most dramatic and memorable songs of the Twentieth Century. She has made a mark on the world of popular culture and soul music that will never be forgotten.

After her initial reign of hit records and ten Grammy Awards while at Atlantic Records in 1960s and 1970s, when disco music ruled the airwaves, she could have easily faded away as a nostalgia act. Instead, in 1980 she moved to Arista Records to score the biggest selling records of her career, and to be presented with another ten Grammy Awards.

When the word "diva" started to become associated with female performers outside the world of the opera—in the 1980s—Aretha was instantly classified as a "diva" supreme. According to definition, a "diva" is a talented and expressive singer who is also a "prima donna." In all fairness, Aretha has worked overtime to become a "diva" in every sense of the word. She has staunchly defended her crown as the Queen of Soul, as witnessed by her many competitive battles with other divas, including: Patti LaBelle, Martha Reeves, Diana Ross, Natalie Cole, Mavis Staples, Whitney Houston, Beyoncé, and most recently—Tina Turner.

Many of her diva peers in the music business have been following Aretha's career since the very beginning, especially the singers and musicians who also lived in the Motor City. Freda Payne started out singing and recording jazz albums in the sixties, and then became a pop and rock star in the seventies with a string of hits including "Band of Gold." Freda fondly recalls, "When I grew up in Detroit, I knew who Aretha was because we had a mutual friend whose name was Donald Meadows. He always told me what Aretha was up to, and he told her what I was up to as well. It was the 1950s, and we were both around twelve years old at the time. Detroit was 'in its heyday' back then. I remember the first time I heard Aretha sing. It was in the early sixties, and the song was 'Today I Sing the Blues.' I was instantly impressed with her musicianship, her voice, and the extreme soulfulness of her singing style. I always knew that she had 'it.' Aretha sang standards, jazz, and blues, but it wasn't until she signed with Atlantic Records in the sixties her legendary rise to fame began. Before that it was Diana Washington who was known as the Queen of the Blues, until her death. Aretha's music was so moving and wonderful. And, from the beginning, it has always been very well produced. Then, her big break finally came with the release of 'Respect.'" (6)

With regard to Aretha's personality, Freda explains, "When I first met her, I found her to be a very private person and not very friendly. It was almost as if there were a wall up. Since that time she has been more friendly with me. In fact, I felt we could be girlfriends being as we're in the same age group and we have experienced so much in our careers. I was highly flattered when she hired me to perform at her birthday party back in the nineties, and I got to know her a little better." (6)

According to Payne, "Aretha will always be special in my mind because her recordings are flawless and for years to come, they will leave an unforgettable historical impression for America." (6)

Sarah Dash, whose big post-LaBelle disco hit was "Sinner Man," has known Aretha since the sixties. Sarah recalls, "The first time I saw Aretha was on television, and then live at Madison Square Garden. I was greatly impressed with her voice and her ability to slam those gorgeous chords on the piano. Her music was very uplifting, especially the song 'Ain't No Way.' When I first met her she was very gracious and soft spoken. Her father was with her. She has surpassed all in the industry. She has become 'The Queen' over all singers. Aretha will always be special to me because, like her, I started singing in the church. Both being P.K.'s (Preacher's Kids), we've still managed to keep our faith in God. We both came from a strong church upbringing, and then went into show business. I also admire her for having the ability to cross over into opera as well. I got to see her perform with Condoleezza Rice, and Aretha was nothing short of awesome. She *is* the best." (7)

According to Mary Wilson of The Supremes, "Whenever she opens her mouth to sing, there is no question that Aretha is, and always will be, 'The Queen.'" (8)

Aretha Franklin has taken her claim to the title as Queen of Soul very seriously. She has defended her territory staunchly, and she wears her crown very proudly. She also remains something of an enigma and a mystery. While she reveals her emotions freely in her songs, she is not so generous with her deepest, darkest secrets. When Jerry Wexler described Aretha as "the mysterious lady of sorrow," he truly struck a chord of clarity and honesty. (9)

In 2010 and 2011 Aretha had a new set of problems to address. However, they were not career problems or relationship problems. They were far more serious concerns, since they were about her own health. When the subject of cancer was brought up, it was a major concern, especially since her sisters—Carolyn and Erma—both died of cancer.

Still, Aretha refused to talk about the reason she was in the hospital. She went so far as to tell *People* magazine in April 2011, "I read the rumors, and they were just ridiculous. I feel fabulous." (10) She might have found the rumors to be "ridiculous," but she never once used the words "cancer" or "untrue." The Aretha health mystery continued.

A well-known doctor at Cedars Sinai Hospital in Los Angeles, who treated Patrick Swayze in his losing battle with pancreatic cancer, spoke about Aretha's health condition. According to him, "She has all the classic signs of pancreatic cancer: dramatic weight loss, followed by some swelling." He also said that Aretha's weight loss—85 pounds from a 300 pound woman in less than three months—"would not happen in this period of time simply by suddenly eating salads." With regard to Aretha being a thirty- to forty-year tobacco chain smoker, he said, "That can increase her risk of having pancreatic cancer by 75-percent." (11)

When the world first found out that it she was having health problems, TV producers, record companies, and publications started scrambling to put together tributes to Aretha. It suddenly became a time to show Franklin just how much her talent and her vocal artistry is appreciated.

Throughout 2011, Aretha Franklin continued to proclaim that she is now healthy and fit, and feeling well. As she maintained her silence about what kind of operation she did or did not have, her fans around the world hoped and prayed for her recovery and her health. To demonstrate how healthy she felt, she even went so far as to begin to set up her first concert dates since her health issues arose.

As a further affirmation of her good health, Aretha began 2012 with a dramatic announcement: that she intended to marry her longtime boyfriend Willie Wilkerson. According to Franklin, they became engaged over the 2011 holidays. She claimed that the wedding was to take place in the summer of 2012 in Miami, Florida. Unfortunately, it was not to be. According to a statement that Franklin sent to the press, "Regretfully, to Our Friends and Supporters: Will and I have decided we were moving a little too fast, and there were a number of things that had not been thought through thoroughly. There will be no wedding at this time."

In 2014 RCA Records released Aretha's final studio album "Aretha Franklin Sings the Great Diva Classics." It was to be the last musical high point for the living legend. Although she announced in 2017 she was due to retire from concerts, and was going to release one last album during her lifetime, that did not happen.

On August 12, 2018 it was announced that Aretha was gravely ill, and that it was only a matter of time before the end. Finally, on the morning of August 16, at the age of seventy-six, Aretha Franklin passed away, and the mourning began.

Although Aretha is no longer with us, some things are definite and will remain unchanged. One of those things is the incredible legacy that Franklin built in her many years as a recording artist. She was a pop singing diva. She was a rock and roll legend. She was the peerless singing star of gospel music, soul music, jazz, and even arias. There is no diva quite like her. Aretha Franklin was and always will be known as "The Queen of Soul."

QUOTE SOURCES

Quote Sources for the 1989 Chapters of *Aretha Franklin:*
The Queen of Soul:

At the time that this book was originally done, the original publisher was not interested in publishing a list of the sources for the quotes so no master list was made. Several sources were used, including magazines, newspapers, television telecasts, press releases, and my own interviews.

The largest single source of the quotes from Aretha Franklin, came from my in-depth in-person interview with her, at her home in Bloomfield Hills, Michigan, on July 24, 1985.

With the exception of three instances, all of the quotes from Jerry Wexler came from my interview with him on May 2, 1988.

Unless otherwise noted, all quotes in the 1989 version of this book from the following people, are from my personal interviews with them in 1988 and 1989: Clyde Otis, Clive Davis, Ray Bryant, Ted White, Billy Davis, Barbara Shelley, Ken Reynolds, Dennis Fine, Tisha Fein, Dan Hartman, Greg Porto, Bob Altshuler, Rita Griffin, Bob Margouleff, Cathy Mahoney, Gary Graff, Peter Max, and Mary Wilson.

The Martha Reeves episode was told to me in 1993 for the book Martha and I wrote together called *Dancing In the Street: Confessions of a Motown Diva*. The story from Randy Jones of the Village People was told to me in 2011.

QUOTE SOURCES for Chapter Ten: A Rose is Still a Rose—
The 1990's and Beyond

(1)   *Rolling Stone, What You See Is What You Sweat* album review by Stephen Holden, 1992

(2) *Entertainment Weekly, What You See Is What You Sweat* album review by Amy Linden, 1992

(3) *Dayna* television show, Detroit, Michigan, July 10, 1991

(4) *Duets* television special, Fox Television, taped on April 27, 1993, first broadcast on May 9, 1993

(5) *The Tucson Daily Star*, "People" column, item from the Knight-Rider newswire, December 28, 1991

(6) *Time*, "Soul Sister 2000: Aretha On Her Past, Her Future, And Her Fabulous New Album" by Christopher John Farley, March 2, 1998

(7) *Ebony*, "Aretha Talks About Men, Marriage, Music and Motherhood," April 1995, by Laura B. Randolph

(8) *USA Today*, "Fur Out In Full Force For Inauguration," "Letters [to the editor]" column, January 22, 1993

(9) *USA Today*, "Respect 'Fur' Franklin," "Letters [to the editor]" column, February 4, 1993

(10) *Vanity Fair*, "Soul Of The Queen," by James T. Jones IV, March 1994

(11) *Entertainment Weekly*, "100 Best CD's," DB, Ty Burr, Bob Cannon, David Hajdu, Michelle Romero, and Greg Sandow, November 5, 1993

(12) *Interview*, "Aretha Gets Respect From Babyface," March 1994

(13) *USA Today*, "Aretha's Aria: A Time Of Triumph For Queen Of Soul," March 10, 1998

(14) *USA Today*, "Franklin's Encore For The Clintons" by James T. Jones IV, June 21, 1994

(15) *USA Today*, "A Silent Reign For Queen Of Soul," by Toriano Boynton, June 22, 1994

(16) *USA Today*, "Pete Seeger Still Swinging The Hammer Of Justice," by Jeannie Williams, December 5, 1994

(17) *Jet*, "Kennedy Center Honors Go To Queen Of Soul," December 19, 1994

(18) *USA Today*, "Kennedy Honors Full Of Love And R-E-S-P-E-C-T," by Jeannie Williams, December 5, 1994

(19) Author's interview with Detroit health worker, November 22, 1998, Tucson, Arizona

(20) *Christmas Here With You* record album by the Four Tops, liner notes, Motown Records 1995

(21) *USA Today*, "*'Exhale'*: Voices Let Loose," by James T. Jones IV, October 17, 1996

(22) *USA Today*, "Torch Continues Trek Through Great Lakes," August 9, 1996

(23) *The Detroit News*, "Detroit's Queen Of Soul Aretha Franklin Has No Plans To Give Up Crown" by Kevin Ransom, August 30, 1997

(24) *Detroit Free Press*, "Aretha Franklin And The Detroit Symphony Orchestra Prepare To Rock The House" by Brian McCollum, November 25, 1998

(25) *USA Today*, "40th Annual Grammy Awards: Music, Majesty And A Little Mayhem," February 26, 1998

(26) *Ebony*, "Aretha Roars Back And Gets R-E-S-P-E-C-T," by Lynn Norment, August 1998

(27) *Rolling Stone*, "Aretha Franklin Stakes Claim To The Nineties," album review by James Hunter, March 19, 1998

(28) *People*, album reviews, by Steve Dougherty, March 16, 1998

(29) *Blues Brothers 2000* feature film, 1998

(30) *VH1 Divas Live*, TV special 1998

(31) *The New York Times*, "As The Categories Blur, One Diva Clearly Rules" by Albert Innuarato, May 24, 1998

(32) *People*, "Rock On: The Sons And Daughters Of Rock's First Families Find A Rhythm Of Their Own As They Break Into The Music Biz," July 24, 1997

(33) *The Detroit Free Press*, "Singer's Son Gets Probation For Drugs: His Clean Record Keeps Him Out Of Jail," by L. L. Brasier, June 12, 1998

(34) *The Detroit Free Press*, "Limo Company Files Suit Against Queen Of Soul," by Erin Lee Martin, December 5, 1998

(35) *Star* magazine, "When Queen Of Soul Wants Take Out, She Pays Big Time," December 22, 1998

(36) *The Detroit Free Press*, "Aretha Franklin Gives Classical Debut," by Gary Graff, November 30, 1998

(37) *The Detroit Free Press*, "Queen Of Soul, DSO Make A Blend Of Sass And Class" by Brian McCollum, November 28, 1998

(38) *The Wall Street Journal*, "Queen Of Soul's Symphony Of Sound" by Greg Sandow, December 9, 1998

(39) *The Chicago Tribune*, "R-E-S-P-E-C-TED Singer Takes Firm For A Ride," December 31, 1998

(40) *The Chicago Tribune*, "Aretha Franklin Sings At Hospital," January 1, 1999

(41) *Time*, "The Best & Worst Of The Year," December 21, 1998

(42) *The Detroit Free Press*, "Aretha Franklin: Income Comes From Many Sources," February 15, 1999

(43) *Aretha: From These Roots*, Villard Books, New York City, Aretha Franklin with David Ritz, 1999

(44) *Detroit Free Press*, "Aretha Hums and Haws, But Readers Want Details," a book review by Lisa R. Manns, October 1, 1999

(45) *Entertainment Weekly*, "Do Right Woman," a book review by Tom Sinclair, October 1, 1999

(46) *Vanity Fair*, "The Music Portfolio," November 2000

QUOTE SOURCES for Chapter Eleven: So Damn Happy

(1) *Entertainment Weekly*, "Do Right Woman," by Gary Susan January 31, 2003

(2) *www.ClickonDetroit.com*, "Defenders: Aretha Franklin's House Fire Remains Unsolved," July 11, 2003

(3) *The New York Times*, "Aretha, So Damn Happy About Her New Album," by Bernard Weinraub, September 28, 2003

(4) *Rolling Stone*, "Aretha Franklin So Damn Happy," by Andrew Dansby, September 9, 2003

(5) *Rolling Stone*, review of *So Damn Happy*, by Barry Walters, September 9, 2002

(6) *The Guardian*, review of *So Damn Happy*, by Betty Clarke, October 3, 2003

(7) *All Music Guide*, review of *So Damn Happy*, by John Bush, 2003

(8) *BBC*, review of *So Damn Happy*, by Jack Smith, November 7, 2003

(9) *The Washington Post*, "Aretha Franklin: The Queen of Soul Still Rules," by J. Freedom du Lac, July 7, 2007

(10) *Fox News / Associated Press*, "Aretha Franklin Slams Beyoncé For Calling Tina Turner 'The Queen' at Grammys," February 13, 2008

(11) *The New York Daily News / Associated Press,* "Beyoncé's Dad Chimes in on Feud with Aretha Franklin," February 14, 2008

(12) *Entertainment Weekly,* "Another Stupid Grammy Feud: Aretha vs. Beyoncé," by Gary Susman, February 13, 2008

(13) *The National Enquirer,* "Clash of the Titans: Tina Turner vs. Aretha Franklin Feud Has Festered for 25 Years," by Michael Glynn, October 27, 2008

(14) *USA Today,* "The Lights Go Back Up for Turner's Encore," by Edna Gundersen, September 30, 2008

(15) *USA Today,* "Aretha Speaks Out: Aretha Franklin's response to Tina Turner statement in *USA Today,*" October 8, 2008

(16) Author's interview with Charles Moniz, Palm Springs, California, April 30, 2011

(17) *Saturday Night Live,* "Weekend News," by Seth Meyers, December 7, 2009

(18) *The Hartford Courant,* "Aretha Franklin Gets Honorary Degree," by Kathleen Megan, May 24, 2010

(19) *The Washington Post,* "Condoleezza Rice, Aretha Franklin: A Philadelphia show of a little R-E-S-P-E-C-T," by Anne Midgette, July 29, 2010

(20) *www.CNN.com,* "Aretha Franklin Cancels Concerts Because of Fractured Ribs, Pain," by the CNN Wire Staff, August 4, 2010|

(21) *The Village Voice,* "Aretha Cancels Concerts, Will Miss the Food," by Michael Musto, August 4, 2010

(22) *The Huffington Post,* "Aretha Franklin: Halle Berry Should Portray Me in Film," by Mike Householder, September 10, 2010

(23) *The Detroit Free Press,* "Aretha Franklin's Son Severely Beaten in Detroit," by Mike Helms, September 21, 2010

(24) *BlackSpin News / Black Voices Entertainment Newswire,* "Aretha Franklin Release From Hospital Under Cloud of Mystery," by Karu F. Daniels, November 3, 2010

(25) *Herald Sun* [Australia], November 5, 2010, "Fears for Aretha Franklin's Health"

(26) *Jet,* "Aretha Franklin On Her Health," by Clarence Waldron, November 4, 2010

(27) *The Oakland Press* [via Associated Press], "Jesse Jackson: Aretha Franklin 'Recovering Well;' Reports Indicate She Has Cancer," by Mike Householder, December 8, 2010

(28) *The National Enquirer* "Aretha Cancer Story," by Patricia Shipp, and Lynn Allison, December 20, 2011

(29) *Access Hollywood*, "Aretha Franklin Sets The Record Straight On Her Health," interview by Shaun Robinson, January 13, 2011

(30) *USA Today*, "Aretha Franklin: Halle Berry Was 'Not My Only Choice," by Ann Oldenburg, January 25, 2011

(31) *The Detroit News*, "Aretha Franklin Attends Pistons Game," February 11. 2011

(32) *The Grammy Awards*, CBS-TV, February 13, 2011

(33) *BlackSpin News / Black Voices Entertainment Newswire*, "Aretha Franklin Reveals New Look, Shares Her Thoughts On Star-Studded Grammy Tribute," by Karu F. Daniels, February 13, 2011

(34) *The Hollywood Reporter*, "Aretha Franklin 'Sorry' Fantasia Was Upset By Grammy Tribute," by Lindsay Powers, February 23, 2011

(35) *The Wendy Williams Show*, "Interview with Aretha Franklin, March 3, 2011

(36) *The Wall Street Journal*, "The Search for Aretha's Sound," a review of *Take a Look: Aretha Franklin Complete on Columbia*, by Marc Myers, March 11, 2011

(37) *The Detroit News*, "Aretha Franklin's Columbia Recordings Reveal a Young Singer Finding Her Voice," by Susan Whitall, March 16, 2011

(38) *The National Enquirer*, "Happy 69th Birthday, Aretha!," by Bob Hartlein, April 11, 2011

(39) *The View*, ABC-TV, April 28, 2011

(40) *The Chicago Sun-Times*, review of *A Woman Falling Out of Love*, by Thomas Conner, May 3, 2011

(41) *The Washington Post*, review of *A Woman Falling Out of Love*, by Allison Stewart, May 2, 2011

(42) *Rolling Stone*, review of *A Woman Falling Out of Love*, by Will Hermes, May 26, 2011

(43) Author's e-mail dialogue with Tom Cuddy, May 10, 2011

(44) Aretha Franklin on the TV show *Live with Regis and Kelly*, July 21, 2011

(45) *US* magazine, "Talk About a Fashion Emergency," June 21, 2011

(46) *CNN Style News*, "Aretha Franklin Breaks Toe After Tripping Over a Shoe," June 24, 2011

(47) *The New York Times Sunday Magazine*, "A-R-E-T-H-A," by Rob Hoerburger, July 8, 2011

(48) *The Toledo Blade*, "Aretha Franklin's Company Sued," July 17, 2011

(49) *Billboard*, as reported via the Associated Press, "Aretha Franklin Criticizes Songwriter Over Rights Lawsuit," August 2, 2011

(50) Author's conversation with Derek Storm, July 21, 2011

(51) *The New York Times*, "A Fount of Soul, Full Throttle," by Jon Pareles, July 28, 2011

(52) *The New York Post*, "The Queen of Kings," by Dan Aquilante, August 5, 2011

QUOTE SOURCES for Chapter Twelve: How Does Aretha Keep the Music Playing?

(1) Author's eyewitness report of Aretha Franklin at DTE Music Center, Clarkston, Michigan, August 25, 2011

(2) *Rolling Stone*, review of *Tony Bennett Duets II*, by Jody Rosen, September 29, 2011

(3) The *Los Angeles Times*, album review of Tony Bennett's *Duets II*, by Mikael Wood, September 19, 2011

(4) *CBS News Celebrity Circuit*, "Tony Bennett Reaches Out To a New Generation," September 20, 2011

(5) The author's interview with Clyde Otis, March 3, 1988

(6) Author's e-mail dialogue with Freda Payne, May 8 and 9, 2011

(7) Author's e-mail dialogue with Sarah Dash, May 16, 2011

(8) Author's conversation with Mary Wilson, Los Angeles, September 27, 2011

(9) The author's interview with Jerry Wexler, May 2, 1988

(10) *People*, "Aretha Franklin: I Feel Fabulous," by Rennie Dyball, May 2, 2011

(11) The author's interview with an anonymous doctor from Cedar's Sinai Hospital, Los Angeles, April 21, 2011

ARETHA FRANKLIN DISCOGRAPHY

Albums
On Chess Records

Songs of Faith (Chess Records / 1956)
(also released as *Aretha Gospel* on Checker Records, 1982; and as a shortened
   CD version called *Precious Lord* on Laserlight Digital, 2001)
Produced by Joe Von Battles
"There is a Fountain Filled with Blood"
"Precious Lord (Part One)"
"Precious Lord (Part Two)"
"You Grow Closer"
"Never Grow Old"
"The Day Is Past and Gone"
"He Will Wash You White as Snow"
"While the Blood Runs Warm"
"Yield Not to Temptation"

On Columbia Records

Aretha (Columbia Records / 1961)
[Also released as *The Great Aretha Franklin—The First 12 Sides* on
   Columbia Records, 1972]
Produced by John Hammond
"Won't Be Long"

"Over the Rainbow"
"Love Is the Only Thing"
"Sweet Lover"
"All Night Long"
"Who Needs You?"
"Right Now"
"Are You Sure"
"Maybe I'm a Fool"
"It Ain't Necessarily So"
"By Myself"
"Today I Sing the Blues"

The Electrifying Aretha Franklin (Columbia Records / 1962)
Produced by John Hammond
"You Made Me Love You"
"I Told You So"
"Rock-A-Bye Your Baby with a Dixie Melody"
"Nobody Like You"
"Exactly Like You"
"It's So Heartbreakin'"
"Rough Lover"
"Blue Holiday"
"Just For You"
"That Lucky Old Sun"
"I Surrender Dear"
"Ac-cent-tchu-ate the Positive"

The Tender, The Moving, The Swinging Aretha Franklin
    (Columbia Records / 1962)
Produced by Robert Mersey
"Don't Cry, Baby"
"Try a Little Tenderness"
"I Apologize"
"Without the One You Love"
"Look for the Silver Lining"

"I'm Sitting on Top of the World"
"Just For a Thrill"
"God Bless the Child"
"I'm Wandering"
"How Deep Is the Ocean"
"I Don't Know Anymore"
"Lover Come Back To Me"

Laughing on the Outside (Columbia Records / 1963)
Produced by Robert Mersey
"Skylark"
"For All We Know"
"Make Someone Happy"
"I Wonder (Where You Are Tonight)"
"Solitude"
"Laughing on the Outside"
"Say It Isn't So"
"Until the Real Thing Comes Along"
"If Ever I Would Leave You"
"Where Are You"
"Mr. Ugly"
"I Wanna Be Around"

Unforgettable—A Tribute to Dinah Washington (Columbia Records /
    1964)
Produced by Robert Mersey
"Unforgettable"
"Cold, Cold Heart"
"What a Diff'rence a Day Makes"
"Drinking Again"
"Nobody Knows the Way I Feel This Morning"
"Evil Gal Blues"
"Don't Say You're Sorry Again"
"This Bitter Earth"
"If I Should Lose You"

"Soulville"
["Lee Cross" was later added to the 1995 CD version of this album, because it came from one of the studio sessions that produced this album]

Runnin' Out of Fools (Columbia Records / 1964)
Produced by Clyde Otis
"Mockingbird"
"How Glad I Am"
"Walk On By"
"Every Little Bit Hurts"
"The Shoop Shoop Song (It's in His Kiss)"
"You'll Lose a Good Thing"
"I Can't Wait Until I See My Baby's Face"
"It's Just a Matter of Time"
"Runnin' Out of Fools"
"My Guy"
"Two Sides of Love"
"One Room Paradise"

Yeah!!! (Columbia Records / 1965)
Produced by Clyde Otis
"This Could Be the Start of Something"
"Once in a Lifetime"
"Misty"
"More"
"There Is No Greater Love"
"Muddy Water"
"If I Had a Hammer"
"Impossible"
"Today I Love Ev'rybody"
"Without the One You Love"
"Trouble in Mind"
"Love for Sale"

ARETHA FRANKLIN DISCOGRAPHY **361**

Soul Sister (Columbia Records / 1965)
Produced by Clyde Otis, Robert Mersey, and Bob Johnston
"Until You Were Gone"
"You Made Me Love You"
"Follow Your Heart"
"Ol' Man River"
"Sweet Bitter Love"
"A Mother's Love"
"Swanee"
"(No, No) I'm Losing You"
"Take a Look"
"Can't You Just See Me"
"Cry Like a Baby"

Take It Like You Give It (Columbia Records / 1967)
Produced by Clyde Otis, Bob Johnston, Robert Mersey, and Bobby Scott
"Why Was I Born?"
"I May Never Get to Heaven"
"Tighten Up Your Tie, Button Up Your Jacket (Make It for the Door)"
"Her Little Heart Went to Loveland"
"Lee Cross"
"Take It Like You Give It"
"Only the One You Love"
"Deeper"
"Remember Me"
"Land of Dreams"
"A Little Bit of Soul"

Take a Look (Columbia Records / 1967)
Produced by Clyde Otis, John Hammond, Al Kasha, and Robert Mersey
"Lee Cross"
"Operation Heartbreak"
"Bill Bailey, Won't You Please Come Home"
"I'll Keep On Smiling"
"I Won't Cry Anymore"

"Take a Look"
"Won't Be Long"
"Until You Were Gone"
"Blue Holiday"
"Follow Your Heart"

Aretha Franklin's Greatest Hits (Columbia Records / 1967)
Produced by Clyde Otis, John Hammond, and Robert Mersey
"Rock-A-Bye Your Baby with a Dixie Melody"
"Today I Sing the Blues"
"Cry Like a Baby"
"Without the One You Love"
"One Step Ahead"
"Evil Gal Blues"
"Runnin' Out of Fools"
"Try a Little Tenderness"
"Sweet Bitter Love"
"God Bless the Child"
"If Ever I Would Leave You"

Aretha Franklin's Greatest Hits Volume II (Columbia Records / 1967)
Produced by Clyde Otis, and Robert Mersey
"Lee Cross"
"Say It Isn't So"
"Skylark"
"Take It Like You Give It"
"Take a Look"
"Soulville"
"Every Little Bit Hurts"
"Don't Cry, Baby"
"All Night Long"
"Just for a Thrill"

Queen of Soul (Columbia/Harmony Records / 1968)
Produced by Robert Mersey, Clyde Otis, Bobby Scott, and John Hammond

"You Made Me Love You"
"Follow Your Heart"
"Love for Sale"
"I Surrender, Dear"
"Bill Bailey, Won't You Please Come Home?"
"What a Diff'rence a Day Makes"
"I May Never Get to Heaven"
"I Apologize"
"It's Just a Matter of Time"

Once in a Lifetime (Columbia/Harmony Records / 1969)
Produced by Robert Mersey, Clyde Otis, Bobby Scott, and John
    Hammond
"(Blue) By Myself"
"Look for the Silver Lining"
"I May Never Get to Heaven"
"My Guy"
"Once in a Lifetime"
"Moon River"
"Exactly Like You"
"If I Had a Hammer"
"Unforgettable"

Soft and Beautiful (Columbia Records / 1969)
Produced by Clyde Otis
"Only the Lonely"
"I Wish I Didn't Love You So"
"(Ah, the Apple Trees) When the World Was Young"
"Shangri-la"
"A Mother's Love"
"My Coloring Book"
"Jim"
"Friend Persuasion (Thee I Love)"
"But Beautiful"
"People"

Two Sides of Love (Columbia/Harmony Records / 1970)
Produced by Clyde Otis, Bobby Scott, Robert Mersey, and
    John Hammond
"Two Sides of Love"
"Friendly Persuasion"
"Hands Off"
"Johnny"
"Drinking Again"
"Lover Come Back to Me"
"Where Are You?"
"Won't Be Long"
"Here's Where I Came In (Here's Where I Walk Out)"

In the Beginning—The World of Aretha Franklin, 1960–1967
    (Columbia Records / 2-Record Set / 1972)
Produced by John Hammond, Clyde Otis, and Robert Mersey
"Today I Sing the Blues"
"Cry Like a Baby"
"Without the One You Love"
"One Step Ahead"
"Evil Gal Blues"
"Lee Cross"
"Skylark"
"Take It Like You Give It"
"Take a Look"
"Every Little Bit Hurts"
"Don't Cry, Baby"
"Just for a Thrill"
"Soulville"
"Mockingbird"
"People"
"Runnin' Out of Fools"
"Try a Little Tenderness"
"Sweet Bitter Love"
"God Bless the Child"
"If Ever I Would Leave You"

Today I Sing the Blues (Columbia Records Limited Edition / 1975)
Produced by Clyde Otis, Robert Mersey, and John Hammond
"Walk On By"
"One Room Paradise"
"Take a Look"
"Evil Gal Blues"
"Every Little Bit Hurts"
"Won't Be Long"
"Without the One You Love"
"Trouble in Mind"
"Rough Lover"
"Today I Sing the Blues"

Aretha Franklin—The Legendary Queen of Soul (Columbia Records /
    2-Record Set / 1981)
Produced by Clyde Otis, Robert Mersey, and John Hammond
"Mockingbird"
"How Glad I Am"
"Walk On By"
"You'll Lose a Good thing"
"Every Little Bit Hurts"
"I Can't Wait Until I See My Baby's Face"
"You Made Me Love You"
"Nobody Like You"
"Rough Lover"
"Lee Cross"
"Runnin' Out of Fools"
"Won't Be Long"
"Until You Were Gone"
"Blue Holiday"
"One Room Paradise"
"Cry Like a Baby"
"Can't You Just See Me"
"Two Sides of Love"
"I Won't Cry Anymore"
"I Keep Smiling"

Sweet Bitter Love (Columbia Records / 1982)
Produced by Robert Mersey, Clyde Otis, John Hammond,
    and Bobby Scott
"All Night Long"
"Ac-cent-tchu-ate the Positive"
"Nobody Like You"
"Today I Sing the Blues"
"Sweet Bitter Love"
"Try a Little Tenderness"
"Skylark"
"Johnny"
"God Bless the Child"
"If Ever I Should Leave You"

Aretha Sings the Blues (Columbia Records / 1985)
Produced by Clyde Otis, Robert Mersey, and John Hammond
"Drinking Again"
"Today I Sing the Blues"
"What a Diff'rence a Day Makes" (on CD only)
"Without the One You Love"
"Trouble in Mind"
"Muddy Water"
"Only the Lonely"
"I Wonder (Where You Are Tonight)"
"Laughing On the Outside (Crying On the Inside)"
"Take a Look"
"Nobody Knows the Way I Feel This Morning"
"Evil Gal Blues" (on CD only)
"This Bitter Earth" (on CD only)
"Maybe I'm a Fool"

After Hours (Columbia Records / 1987)
Produced by Robert Mersey, and Clyde Otis
"This Bitter Earth"
"Once in a Lifetime"
"Misty"

"There Is No Greater Love"
"Unforgettable"
"If I Should Lose You"
"Don't Cry, Baby"
"Just For a Thrill"
"I'm Wandering"
"Don't Say You're Sorry Again"
"Look for the Silver Lining"

Aretha Franklin: Jazz to Soul (Columbia Legacy Records / 2-Disc Set / 1992)
Produced by John Hammond, Bob Johnston, Robert Mersey, Clyde Otis, and Bobby Scott

DISC ONE
"Today I Sing the Blues"
"(Blue) To Myself"
"Maybe I'm a Fool"
"All Night Long"
"Blue Holiday"
"Nobody Like You"
"Sweet Lover"
"Just For a Thrill"
"If Ever I Would Leave You"
"Once in a While" [Previously Unreleased]
"This Bitter Earth""
"God Bless the Child"
"Skylark" [Previously Unreleased Alternate Version]
"Muddy Water"
"Drinking Again"
"What a Diff'rence a Day Makes"
"Unforgettable"
"Love For Sale"
"Misty"
"Impossible" [Previously Unreleased Alternate Take]
"This Could Be the Start of Something"

DISC TWO
"Won't Be Long"
"Operation Heartbreak"
"Soulville"
"Runnin' Out of Fools"
"Trouble in Mind"
"Walk On By"
"Every Little Bit Hurts"
"Mockingbird"
"You'll Lose a Good Thing"
"Cry Like a Baby"
"Take It Like You Give It"
"Land of Dreams"
"Can't You Just See Me"
"(No, No) I'm Losing You"
"Bit of Soul"
"Why Was I Born"
"Until You Were Gone"
"Lee Cross"

Aretha Franklin: The Early Years (Columbia Records / 1997)
Produced by John Hammond, Robert Mersey, Clyde Otis,
      and Bobby Scott
"This Bitter Earth"
"Without The One You Love"
"Cry Like a Baby"
"Trouble in Mind"
"Muddy Water"
"Walk On By"
"Skylark"
"Drinking Again"
"Evil Gal Blues"
"Laughing On the Outside"
"God Bless the Child"
"Take a Look"

"Nobody Knows the Way I Feel This Morning"
"I Wonder (Where You Are Tonight)"

Aretha Franklin Sings Standards (Sony Records / 1997)
Produced by John Hammond, Robert Mersey, Clyde Otis,
    and Bobby Scott
"How Deep Is the Ocean"
"Until the Real Thing Comes Along"
"Look For the Silver Lining"
"Exactly Like You"
"Where Are You?"
"Say It Isn't So"
"That Lucky Old Sun"
"I Apologize"
"For All We Know"
"Moon River"

Aretha Franklin: This Is Jazz #34 (Columbia / Legacy Records /
    1998)
Produced by Robert Mersey, Clyde Otis, and John Hammond
"Evil Gal Blues"
"Today I Sing the Blues"
"Skylark"
"Nobody Knows the Way I Feel This Morning"
"Unforgettable"
"Love For Sale"
"Only the Lonely"
"Muddy Water"
"God Bless the Child"
"All Night Long"
"It Ain't Necessarily So"
"What a Diff'rence a Day Makes"
"Over the Rainbow"
"Maybe I'm a Fool"
"Drinking Again"

"Trouble in Mind"
"This Bitter Earth"

Aretha Franklin: The Queen in Waiting (Columbia / Legacy / Sony
    Records / 2-Disc Set / 2002)
Produced by John Hammond, Robert Mersey, Clyde Otis, Bobby Scott,
    and Bob Johnston

DISC ONE
"Nobody Like You"
"Once in a While"
"Maybe I'm a Fool"
"Muddy Water"
"Bill Bailey, Won't You Please Come Home?" [Alternate Version /
    Previously Unreleased]
"Hard Times (No One Knows Better Than I)" [Previously Unreleased]
"Today I Sing the Blues"
"Won't Be Long"
"Nobody Knows the Way I Feel This Morning"
"Evil Gal Blues"
"Lee Cross"
"Walk On By"
"I Wonder (Where Are You Tonight)"
"God Bless the Child"
"Blue Holiday"
"Looking Through a Tear" [Previously Unreleased]
"Tiny Sparrow" [Previously Unreleased]
"Here Today and Gone Tomorrow" [Previously Unreleased]
"Little Brown Book" [Previously Unreleased]
"Without the One You Love"

DISC TWO
"This Bitter Earth"
"Just for a Thrill"
"Skylark"

"Skylark" [Alternate Version]
"Trouble in Mind"
"Runnin' Out of Fools"
"Drinking Again"
"Laughing On the Outside"
"What a Diff'rence a Day Makes"
"Soulville"
"You'll Lose a Good Thing"
"Take a Look"
"Cry Like a Baby"
"I Wish I Didn't Love You So"
"Only the Lonely"
"People"
"Mockingbird"
"Until You Were Gone"
"My Coloring Book"
"Try a Little Tenderness"

Joy to the World (Sony / BMG Records / 2003)

[NOTE: Comprised of several tracks from the Columbia catalog and tracks from the Arista gospel album *One Lord, One Faith, One Baptism*]

Produced by Aretha Franklin, Robert Mersey, John Hammond,
        Bobby Scott, and Belford C. Hendricks
"Joy to the World"
"Oh Happy Day"
"Over the Rainbow"
"Winter Wonderland"
"The Christmas Song (Chestnuts Roasting On an Open Fire)"
"Kissin' By the Mistletoe"
"Ac-cent-tchu-ate the Positive"
"God Bless the Child"
"The Lord's Prayer"
"Ave Maria"

The Essential Aretha Franklin: The Columbia Years (Columbia /
    Legacy / Sony Records / 2-Disc Set / 2010)
Produced by John Hammond, Robert Mersey, Clyde Otis, Bobby Scott,
    and Bob Johnston

DISC ONE
[Identical to DISC ONE of *The Queen in Waiting* above]

DISC TWO
[Identical to DISC TWO of *The Queen in Waiting* above]

*The Essential Aretha Franklin: The Columbia Years / Special Edition
    3.0* (Columbia / Legacy / Sony Records / 3-Disc Set / 2010)
Produced by John Hammond, Robert Mersey, Clyde Otis, Bobby Scott,
    and Bob Johnston

DISC ONE
[Identical to DISC ONE of *The Queen in Waiting* above]

DISC TWO
[Identical to DISC TWO of *The Queen in Waiting* above]

DISC THREE
"In My Solitude"
"Love for Sale"
"Ac-cent-tchu-ate the Positive"
"Unforgettable"
"All Night Long"
"Every Little Bit Hurts"
"Sweet Bitter Love"
"If Ever I Would Leave You"

Aretha Franklin: The Great American Songbook (Columbia / Legacy /
    Sony Records / 2011)
Produced by John Hammond, Robert Mersey, Clyde Otis, Bobby Scott,
    and Al Kasha
"Little Brown Book"
"Trouble in Mind" [Mono Mix]

"Try a Little Tenderness"
"It Ain't Necessarily So"
"How Deep Is the Ocean"
"Cold, Cold Heart"
"Love for Sale"
"How Glad I Am"
"Skylark"
"This Bitter Earth"
"Ac-cent-tchu-ate the Positive"
"What a Diff'rence a Day Made"
"Only the Lonely"
"Rock-A-Bye Your Baby with a Dixie Melody"
"God Bless the Child"
"Say It Isn't So"
"Are You Sure"
"That Lucky Old Sun (Just Rolls Around Heaven All Day)"

Take a Look: Aretha Franklin: Complete On Columbia (Columbia /
    Legacy / Sony Records / 11-Disc + 1 DVD Boxed Set / 2011)
Produced by John Hammond, Robert Mersey, Clyde Otis, Bobby Scott,
    Bob Johnston, Terry Melcher, Al Kasha, Billy Jackson, and Belford
    C. Hendricks

DISC ONE
"Won't Be Long"
"Over the Rainbow"
"Love Is the Only Thing"
"Sweet Lover"
"All Night Long"
"Who Needs You?"
"Right Now"
"Are You Sure"
"Maybe I'm A Fool"
"It Ain't Necessarily So"
"By Myself"
"Today I Sing the Blues"

"Are You Sure" [Bonus Track / Rehearsal Version]
"Who Needs You?" [Previously Unreleased / Bonus Track / Take 9]
"Right Now" [Previously Unreleased / Bonus Track / Take 1]
"Maybe I'm A Fool" [Previously Unreleased / Bonus Track / Take 4]
"By Myself" [Bonus Track]
"Won't Be Long" [Bonus Track]
"All Night Long" [Bonus Track]
"Love Is the Only Thing" [Bonus Track]
"Right Now" [Bonus Track]
"Today I Sing the Blues" [Bonus Track]

DISC TWO
"You Made Me Love You"
"I Told You So"
"Rock-A-Bye Your Baby with a Dixie Melody"
"Nobody Like You"
"Exactly Like You"
"It's So Heartbreakin'"
"Rough Lover"
"Blue Holiday"
"Just for You"
"That Lucky Old Sun"
"I Surrender, Dear"
"Ac-cent-tchu-ate The Positive"
Introduction to "Hard Times" [Bonus Track]
"Hard Times (No One Knows Better Than I)" [Bonus Track]
"When They Ask About You" [Bonus Track]
"Operation Heartbreak" [Bonus Track]
"I Surrender, Dear" [Bonus Track]
"Rough Lover" [Bonus Track]
"Kissin' By the Mistletoe" [Bonus Track]

DISC THREE
"Don't Cry, Baby"
"Try a Little Tenderness"
"I Apologize"

"Without the One You Love"
"Look For the Silver Lining"
"I'm Sitting on Top of the World"
"Just For a Thrill"
"God Bless the Child"
"I'm Wandering"
"How Deep Is the Ocean"
"I Don't Know You Anymore"
"Lover Come Back to Me"
"Trouble in Mind" [Mono Mix]
"Without the One You Love" [Mono Mix]
"Don't Cry, Baby" [Mono Mix]
"I'm Wandering" [Mono Mix]
"Try a Little Tenderness" [Mono Mix]
"I Apologize" [Mono Mix]
"Lover Come Back To Me" [Mono Mix]
"I Don't Know You Anymore" [Mono Mix]

DISC FOUR
"Skylark"
"For All We Know"
"Make Someone Happy"
"I Wonder (Where Are You Tonight)"
"Solitude"
"Laughing On the Outside"
"Say It Isn't So"
"Until The Real Thing Comes Along"
"If Ever I Would Leave You"
"Where Are You?"
"Mr. Ugly"
"I Wanna Be Around"
"Ol' Man River" [Bonus Track]
"You've Got Her" [Bonus Track]
"Here's Where I Came In (Here's Where I Walk Out)" [Bonus Track]
"Say It Isn't So" [Bonus Track]

DISC FIVE
"Here Today and Gone Tomorrow"
"Please Answer Me"
"Harbor Lights"
"I May Never Get To Heaven"
"Moon River"
"I Won't Cry Anymore"
"Bill Bailey, Won't You Please Come Home"
"My Little Brown Book"
"Tiny Sparrow"
"Johnny"
"Looking Through a Tear"
"Bill Bailey, Won't You Please Come Home"
"Johnny"

DISC SIX
"Unforgettable"
"Cold, Cold Heart"
"What a Diff'rence a Day Made"
"Drinking Again"
"Nobody Knows the Way I Feel This Morning"
"Evil Gal Blues"
"Don't Say You're Sorry Again"
"This Bitter Earth"
"If I Should Lose You"
"Soulville"
"Lee Cross" [Mono Mix]

DISC SEVEN
"I'll Keep on Smiling"
"Shangri-la"
"Zing! Went the Strings of My Heart"
"People"
"A Mother's Love"
"Friendly Persuasion (Thee I Love)"

"But Beautiful"
"That's Entertainment"
"Take a Look"
"(Ah, The Apple Trees) When the World Was Young"
"Jim"
"Sweet Bitter Love"
"Only the Lonely"
"My Coloring Book"
"I Wish I Didn't Love You So"
"People" [Mono Mix]
"A Mother's Love" [Mono Mix]

DISC EIGHT
"Mockingbird"
"How Glad I Am"
"Walk on By"
"Every Little Bit Hurts"
"The Shoop Shoop Song (It's in His Kiss)"
"You'll Lose a Good Thing"
"I Can't Wait Until I See My Baby's Face"
"It's Just a Matter of Time"
"Runnin' Out of Fools"
"My Guy"
"Two Sides of Love"
"One Room Paradise"
A General Market Advertisement from Columbia Records [Bonus Track]
A Special Ad for Christmas [Bonus Track]
"The Christmas Song (Chestnuts Roasting On an Open Fire)"
    [Mono Mix]
"Winter Wonderland" [Mono Mix]

DISC NINE
"Follow Your Heart"
"Only the One You Love"
"One Step Ahead"

"Can't You Just See Me"
"How to Murder Your Wife"
"A Little Bit of Soul"
"Cry Like a Baby"
"Her Little Heart Went to Loveland"
"Remember Me"
"Land of Dreams"
"Little Miss Raggedy Ann"
"Deeper" [Bonus Track]
"I Still Can't Forget" [Bonus Track]
"Rose of Washington Square" [Bonus Track]
"Take It Like You Give It" [Bonus Track]
"Follow Your Heart" [Bonus Track]
"Only the One You Love" [Bonus Track]
"One Step Ahead" [Bonus Track]
"How to Murder Your Wife" [Bonus Track]
"A Little Bit of Soul" [Bonus Track]
"Cry Like a Baby" [Bonus Track]
"Her Little Heart Went To Loveland" [Bonus Track]

DISC TEN
"This Could Be the Start of Something"
"Once in a Lifetime"
"Misty"
"More"
"There Is No Greater Love"
"Muddy Water"
"If I Had a Hammer"
"Impossible"
"Today I Love Ev'rybody"
"Without the One You Love"
"Trouble in Mind"
"Love For Sale"
"Bill Bailey, Won't You Please Come Home"
    [Previously Unreleased Version]

"Misty" [Previously Unreleased Version]
"Love For Sale" [Previously Unreleased Version]
"Once in a Lifetime" [Previously Unreleased Version]
"Today I Love Ev'rybody" [Previously Unreleased Version]
"Impossible" [Previously Unreleased Version]
"This Could Be the Start of Something" [Previously Unreleased Version]
"More" [Previously Unreleased Version]
"There Is No Greater Love" [Previously Unreleased Version]
"If I Had a Hammer" [Previously Unreleased Version]
"Muddy Water" [Previously Unreleased Version]
"Without the One You Love" [Previously Unreleased Version]
"Trouble in Mind" [Previously Unreleased Version]

DISC ELEVEN
"Tighten Up Your Tie, Button Up Your Jacket (Make for the Door)"
"(No, No) I'm Losing You"
"Why Was I Born?"
"Hands Off"
"Swanee"
"You Made Me Love You"
"Until You Were Gone"
"Mockingbird"
"Can't You Just See Me"
"Today I Sing The Blues"
"Walk On By"
"One Room Paradise"
"Every Little Bit Hurts"
"Evil Gal Blues"
"Rough Lover"
"Trouble in Mind"
"Without the One You Love"
"Won't Be Long"
"Take a Look"
"Runnin' Out of Fools" [Previously Unreleased]
"Skylark" [Previously Unreleased]

DISC TWELVE
(DVD of Aretha on TV's *The Steve Allen Show*)
"Lover Come Back to Me" [Live]
"Rock-A-Bye Your Baby with a Dixie Melody" [Live]
"Won't Be Long" [Live]
"Skylark" [Live]
"Evil Gal Blues" [Live]

[NOTE: By the 1990's and into the 2000's, Sony Records began ownership of both Columbia Records and Arista Records, so some of the compilations—especially the Columbia releases—have appeared on Sony Records]

On Atlantic Records

I Never Loved a Man the Way I Love You (Atlantic Records / 1967)
    [Platinum]
Produced by Jerry Wexler
"Respect"
"Drown in My Own Tears"
"I Never Loved a Man (The Way I Love You)"
"Soul Serenade"
"Don't Let Me Lose This Dream"
"Baby, Baby, Baby"
"Dr. Feelgood (Love Is a Serious Business)"
"Good Times"
"Do Right Woman—Do Right Man"
"Save Me"
"A Change is Gonna Come"

Aretha Arrives (Atlantic Records / 1967)
Produced by Jerry Wexler
"Satisfaction"
"You Are My Sunshine"

"Never Let Me Go"
"96 Tears"
"Prove It"
"Night Life"
"That's Life"
"I Wonder"
"Ain't Nobody (Gonna Turn Me Around)"
"Going Down Slow"
"Baby, I Love You"

Lady Soul (Atlantic Records / 1968) [Platinum]
Produced by Jerry Wexler
"Chain of Fools"
"Money Won't Change You"
"People Get Ready"
"Niki Hoeky"
"(You Make Me Feel Like) A Natural Woman"
"Since You've Been Gone"
"Good to Me As I Am to You"
"Come Back Baby"
"Groovin'"
"Ain't No Way"

Aretha Now (Atlantic Records / 1968) [Platinum]
Produced by Jerry Wexler
"Think"
"I Say a Little Prayer"
"See Saw"
"Night Time Is the Right Time"
"You Send Me"
"You're a Sweet Sweet Man"
"I Take What I Want"
"Hello Sunshine"
"A Change"
"I Can't See Myself Leaving You"

Aretha in Paris (Atlantic Records / 1968)
Produced by Jerry Wexler
"(I Can't Get No) Satisfaction"
"Don't Let Me Lose This Dream"
"Soul Serenade"
"Night Life"
"Baby, I Love You"
"Groovin'"
"(You Make Me Feel Like) A Natural Woman"
"Come Back Baby"
"Dr. Feelgood (Love Is a Serious Business)"
"(Sweet Sweet Baby) Since You're Been Gone"
"I Never Loved a Man (The Way I Love You)"
"Chain of Fools"
"Respect"

Soul '69 (Atlantic Records / 1969)
Produced by Jerry Wexler and Tom Dowd
"Ramblin'"
"Today I Sing the Blues"
"River's Invitation"
"Pitiful"
"Crazy He Calls Me"
"Bring It on Home to Me"
"Tracks of My Tears"
"If You Gotta Make a Fool Out of Somebody"
"Gentle on My Mind"
"So Long"
"I'll Never Be Free"
"Elusive Butterfly"

Aretha's Gold (Atlantic Records / 1969)
Produced by Jerry Wexler
"I Never Loved a Man (The Way I Love You)"
"Do Right Woman—Do Right Man"

"Respect"
"Dr. Feelgood (Love Is a Serious Business)"
"Baby, I Love You"
"Chain of Fools"
"Since You're Been Gone (Sweet Sweet Baby)"
"Ain't No Way"
"Think"
"You Send Me"
"The House that Jack Built"
"I Say a Little Prayer"
"See Saw"

This Girl's in Love with You (Atlantic Records / 1970)
Produced by Jerry Wexler, Tom Dowd, and Arif Mardin
"Son of a Preacher Man"
"Share Your Love with Me"
"Dark End of the Street"
"Let It Be"
"Eleanor Rigby"
"This Girl's in Love with You"
"It Ain't Fair"
"The Weight"
"Call Me"
"Sit Down and Cry"

Spirit in the Dark (Atlantic Records / 1970)
Produced by Jerry Wexler, Tom Dowd, and Arif Mardin
"Don't Play That Song (For Me)"
"The Thrill Is Gone (From Yesterday's Kiss)"
"Pullin'"
"You and Me"
"Honest I Do"
"Spirit in the Dark"
"When the Battle Is Over"
"One Way Ticket"

"Try Matty's"
"That's All I Want from You"
"Oh No Not My Baby"
"Why I Sing the Blues"

Aretha Live at Fillmore West (Atlantic Records / 1971) [Gold]
Produced by Jerry Wexler and Arif Mardin
"Respect"
"Love the One You're With"
"Bridge over Troubled Water"
"Eleanor Rigby"
"Make It with You"
"Don't Play That Song (For Me)"
"Dr. Feelgood (Love Is a Serious Business)"
"Spirit in the Dark" [Solo]
"Spirit in the Dark" [Duet with Ray Charles]
"Reach Out and Touch (Somebody's Hand)"

Aretha's Greatest Hits (Atlantic Records / 1971)
Produced by Jerry Wexler, Tom Dowd, and Arif Mardin
"Spanish Harlem"
"Baby, I Love You"
"(You Make Me Feel Like) A Natural Woman"
"Don't Play That Song (For Me)"
"Dr. Feelgood (Love Is a Serious Business)"
"Let It Be"
"Do Right Woman—Do Right Man"
"Respect"
"Chain of Fools"
"I Say a Little Prayer"
"Bridge over Troubled Water"
"I Never Loved a Man (The Way I Love You)"
"You're All I Need to Get By"
"Call Me"

Young, Gifted and Black (Atlantic Records / 1972) [Platinum]
Produced by Jerry Wexler, Tom Dowd, and Arif Mardin
"Oh Me Oh My (I'm a Fool for You Baby)"
"Day Dreaming"
"Rock Steady"
"Young, Gifted and Black"
"All the King's Horses"
"A Brand New Me"
"April Fools"
"I've Been Loving You Too Long"
"First Snow in Kokomo"
"The Long and Winding Road"
"Didn't I (Blow Your Mind This Time)"
"Border Song (Holy Moses)"

Amazing Grace (Atlantic Records / 2-Record and 2-Disc Set / 1972)
    [Double Platinum]
Produced by Jerry Wexler, Arif Mardin, and Aretha Franklin
"Mary, Don't You Weep"
"Precious Lord, Take My Hand"
"You've Got a Friend"
"Old Landmark"
"Give Yourself to Jesus"
"How I Got Over"
"What a Friend We Have in Jesus"
"Amazing Grace"
"Precious Memories"
"Climbing Higher Mountains"
"Remarks by Reverend C. L. Franklin"
"God Will Take Care of You"
"Wholly Holy"
"You'll Never Walk Alone"
"Never Grow Old"

Hey Now Hey (The Other Side of the Sky) (Atlantic Records / 1973)
Produced by Quincy Jones and Aretha Franklin
"Hey Now Hey (The Other Side of the Sky)"
"Somewhere"
"So Swell When You're Well"
"Angel"
"Sister from Texas"
"Mister Spain"
"That's the Way I Feel About Cha"
"Moody's Mood"
"Just Right Tonight"
["Master of Eyes (The Deepness of Your Eyes)" added to the 1994 CD
issue of this album, as it came from the same Quincy Jones sessions, and
the song won a Grammy Award]

Let Me in Your Life (Atlantic Records / 1974)
Produced by Jerry Wexler, Tom Dowd, Arif Mardin, and Aretha Franklin
"Let Me in Your Life"
"Every Natural Thing"
"Ain't Nothing Like the Real Thing"
"I'm in Love"
"Until You Come Back to Me (That's What I'm Gonna Do)"
"The Masquerade Is Over"
"With Pen in Hand"
"Oh Baby"
"Eight Days On the Road"
"If You Don't Think"
"A Song for You"

With Everything I Feel in Me (Atlantic Records / 1974)
Produced by Jerry Wexler, Tom Dowd, Arif Mardin, and Aretha Franklin
"Without Love"
"Don't Go Breaking My Heart"
"When You Get Right Down to It"
"You'll Never Get to Heaven"

"With Everything I Feel in Me"
"I Love Every Little Thing About You"
"Sing It Again—Say It Again"
"All of These Things"
"You Move Me"

You (Atlantic Records / 1975)
Produced by Jerry Wexler and Aretha Franklin
"Mr. D.J. (5 for the D.J.)"
"It Only Happens (When I Look at You)"
"I'm Not Strong Enough to Love You Again"
"Walk Softly"
"You Make My Life"
"Without You"
"The Sha-La Bandit"
"You"
"You Got All the Aces"
"As Long as You Are There"

Sparkle (Atlantic Records / 1976) [Gold]
Produced by Curtis Mayfield
"Sparkle"
"(Giving Him) Something He Can Feel"
"Hooked on Your Love"
"Look into Your Heart"
"I Get High"
"Jump"
"Loving You Baby"
"Rock with Me"

Ten Years of Gold (Atlantic Records / 1976)
Produced by Jerry Wexler, Tom Dowd, Arif Mardin, Quincy Jones,
    Curtis Mayfield, and Aretha Franklin
"I Never Loved a Man (The Way I Love You)"
"Respect"

"Baby, I Love You"
"(You Make Me Feel Like) A Natural Woman"
"Think"
"See Saw"
"Spanish Harlem"
"Rock Steady"
"Day Dreaming"
"Angel"
"Until You Come Back to Me (That's What I'm Gonna Do)"
"(Giving Him) Something He Can Feel"

Sweet Passion (Atlantic Records / 1977)
Produced by Lamont Dozier, Marvin Hamlisch, Carole Bayer Sager,
    Marty Paich, and David Paich
"Break It to Me Gently"
"When I Think About You"
"What I Did for Love"
"No One Could Ever Love You More"
"A Tender Touch"
"Touch Me Up"
"Sunshine Will Never Be the Same"
"Meadows of Springtime"
"Mumbles"
"I've Got the Music in Me"
"Sweet Passion"

Almighty Fire (Atlantic Records / 1978)
Produced by Curtis Mayfield
"Almighty Fire (Woman of the Future)"
"Lady, Lady"
"More Than Just a Joy"
"Keep on Loving You"
"I Need You Baby"
"Close to You"
"No Matter Who You Love"

"This You Can Believe"
"I'm Your Speed"

La Diva (Atlantic Records / 1979)
Produced by Van McCoy, Charles Kipps, Skip Scarborough,
    and Aretha Franklin
"Ladies Only"
"It's Gonna Get a Bit Better"
"What If I Should Ever Need You"
"Honey I Need Your Love"
"I Was Made for You"
"Only Star"
"Reasons Why"
"You Brought Me Back to Life"
"Half a Love"
"The Feeling"

Aretha's Jazz (Atlantic Records / 1984)
Produced by Jerry Wexler, Tom Dowd, Quincy Jones,
    and Aretha Franklin
"Ramblin'"
"Today I Sing the Blues"
"Pitiful"
"Crazy He Calls Me"
"Bring It on Home to Me"
"Somewhere"
"Moody's Mood"
"Just Right Tonight"

The Best of Aretha Franklin (Atlantic Records / 1984)
Produced by Jerry Wexler, Tom Dowd, Arif Mardin, and Aretha Franklin
"Chain of Fools"
"I Say a Little Prayer for You"
"(You Make Me Feel Like) A Natural Woman"
"Think"

"Rock Steady"
"Until You Come Back to Me (That's What I'm Gonna Do)"
"Respect"
"Spanish Harlem"
"Dr. Feelgood (Love Is a Serious Business)"
"Do Right Woman—Do Right Man"
"I Never Loved a Man (The Way I Love You)"
"Save Me"

Aretha Franklin—30 Greatest Hits (Atlantic Records / 2-Disc Set / 1986)
Produced by Jerry Wexler, Tom Dowd, Arif Mardin, and Aretha Franklin

DISC ONE
"I Never Loved a Man (The Way I Love You)"
"Respect"
"Dr. Feelgood (Love Is a Serious Business)"
"Do Right Woman—Do Right Man"
"Save Me"
"Baby, I Love You"
"(You Make Me Feel Like) A Natural Woman"
"Chain of Fools"
"(Sweet Sweet Baby) Since You've Been Gone"
"Ain't No Way"
"Think"
"I Say a Little Prayer"
"The House That Jack Built"
"See Saw"
"The Weight"
"Share Your Love with Me"
"Eleanor Rigby"

DISC TWO
"Call Me"
"Spirit in the Dark"
"Don't Play That Song (For Me)"

"You're All I Need to Get By"
"Bridge over Troubled Water"
"Spanish Harlem"
"Rock Steady"
"Oh Me Oh My (I'm a Fool for You Baby)"
"Day Dreaming"
"Wholly Holy"
"Angel"
"Until You Come Back to Me (That's What I'm Gonna Do)"
"I'm in Love"

Aretha Franklin: Queen of Soul—The Atlantic Recordings
(Rhino Atlantic Records / 1992) [Four CD Boxed Set]

DISC ONE
"I Never Loved a Man (The Way I Love You)"
"Do Right Woman, Do Right Man"
"Save Me"
"Respect"
"Baby, Baby, Baby"
"Dr. Feelgood (Love Is a Serious Business)"
"(You Make Me Feel Like) A Natural Woman"
"Soul Serenade"
"Drown in My Own Tears"
"Chain of Fools"
"Baby, I Love You"
"Ain't Nobody (Gonna Turn Me Around)"
"Since You've Been Gone (Sweet Sweet Baby)"
"You Are My Sunshine"
"Going Down Slow"
"Never Let Me Go"
"I Wonder"
"Prove It"
"Good Times"
"Come Back Baby"
"A Change"

"You're a Sweet Sweet Man"
"Good As I Am to You"
"People Get Ready"
"Ain't No Way"

DISC TWO
"Think"
"See Saw"
"The House That Jack Built"
"Night Time Is the Right Time"
"I Say A Little Prayer"
"You Send Me"
"My Song"
"I Take What I Want"
"I Can't See Myself Leaving You"
"Night Life" [Live Version]
"Today I Sing The Blues"
"Pitiful"
"Tracks of My Tears"
"River's Invitation"
"Share Your Love with Me"
"It Ain't Fair"
"Sit Down and Cry"
"Honest I Do"
"The Weight"
"When the Battle Is Over"
"Eleanor Rigby"
"One Way Ticket"
"Call Me"
"Pullin'"

DISC THREE
"Son of a Preacher Man"
"Try Matty's"
"The Thrill is Gone (From Yesterday's Kiss)"
"Dark End of the Street"

"You and Me"
"Let It Be"
"Spirit in the Dark"
"Why I Sing the Blues"
"Don't Play That Song (For Me)"
"Young, Gifted and Black"
"Border Song (Holy Moses)"
"A Brand New Me"
"You're All I Need to Get By"
"Spanish Harlem"
"Rock Steady"
"Oh Me Oh My (I'm A Fool for You Baby)"
"Day Dreaming"
"All the King's Men"
"Bridge over Troubled Water"
"Angel"

DISC FOUR
"Spirit in the Dark" [Aretha Franklin Live, Reprise with Ray Charles]
"How I Got Over"
"So Swell When You're Well"
"Master of Eyes (The Deepness of Your Eyes)"
"Somewhere"
"I'm in Love"
"Ain't Nothing Like the Real Thing"
"Until You Come Back to Me (That's What I'm Gonna Do)"
"Every Natural Thing"
"Without Love"
"With Everything I Feel In Me"
"Mr. D.J. (5 for the D.J.)"
"Look into Your Heart"
"Sparkle"
"Rock with Me"
"Break It to Me Gently"
"Something He Can Feel"

The Definitive Soul Collection
(Rhino / Atlantic Records / 1993)
Identical track listing as *30 Greatest Hits*

The Very Best of Aretha Franklin, Volume One, The '60's
(Rhino / Atlantic Records / 1994) [Platinum]
"Respect"
"Baby, I Love You"
"Never Loved a Man (The Way I Love You)"
"Chain of Fools"
"Do Right Woman, Do Right Man"
"(You Make Me Feel Like) A Natural Woman"
"Since You've Been Gone (Sweet, Sweet Baby)"
"Ain't No Way"
"Think"
"See Saw"
"The House That Jack Built"
"I Say a Little Prayer"
"The Weight"
"Eleanor Rigby"
"Share Your Love with Me"
"Call Me"

The Very Best Of Aretha Franklin, Volume Two
(Rhino / Atlantic Records, 1994)
"Rock Steady"
"Spanish Harlem"
"Don't Play That Song (For Me)"
"Spirit in the Dark"
"The Border Song (Holy Moses)"
"You're All I Need (To Get By)"
"Bridge over Troubled Water"
"Brand New Me"
"Day Dreaming"
"All the King's Horses"

"Angel"
"Master of Eyes (The Deepness of Your Eyes)"
"Oh Me Oh My (I'm A Fool for You Baby)"
"Until You Come Back to Me (That's All I'm Gonna Do)"
"I'm in Love"
"Something He Can Feel"

Aretha Franklin Love Songs
(Rhino / Atlantic Records / 1997)
"Baby I Love You"
"Say A Little Prayer"
"You and Me"
"(You Make Me Feel Like) A Natural Woman"
"Day Dreaming"
"This Girl's in Love"
"You and Me"
"Call Me"
"A Brand New Me"
"Oh Me, Oh My"
"I'm in Love"
"Look into Your Heart"
"If You Don't Think"
"Ain't Nothing Like the Real Thing"
"Something He Can Feel"

The Delta Meets Detroit: Aretha's Blues
(Rhino / Atlantic Records / 1998)
"Today I Sing the Blues"
"Ramblin'"
"Pitiful"
"I Never Loved a Man (The Way I Love You)"
"Nightlife"
"I Wonder"
"Takin' Another Man's Place"
"Night Time is the Right Time"

"River's Invitation"
"Good to Me As I Am to You"
"It Ain't Fair"
"Going Down Slow"
"Drown in My Own Tears"
"You Are My Sunshine"
"Dr. Feelgood (Love is a Serious Business)"
"The Thrill is Gone (From Yesterday's Kiss)"

Aretha Franklin Live at Fillmore West [Full Length] (Atlantic / Rhino
    Records / 2-Disc Set / 2006)
Produced by Jerry Wexler, and Arif Mardin

DISC ONE
"Respect"
"Love the One You're With"
"Bridge over Troubled Water"
"Eleanor Rigby"
"Make It with You"
"Don't Play That Song (For Me)"
"Dr. Feelgood (Love Is a Serious Business)"
"Spirit in the Dark" [Solo / Unedited Version]
"Spirit in the Dark" [Duet with Ray Charles / Unedited Version]
"Reach Out and Touch (Somebody's Hand)"

DISC TWO
"Respect"
"Call Me"
"Mixed-Up Girl"
"Love the One You're With"
"Bridge over Troubled Water"
"Share Your Love with Me"
"Eleanor Rigby"
"Make It with You"
"You're All I Need to Get By"
"Don't Play That Song (For Me)"
"Dr. Feelgood (Love Is a Serious Business)"

"Spirit in the Dark"
"Spirit in the Dark" [Reprise]

***Rare & Unreleased Recordings from the Golden Reign of The Queen
    of Soul*** (Atlantic / Rhino Records / 2-Disc Set / 2007)
Produced by Jerry Wexler, Tom Dowd, Arif Mardin, Quincy Jones, and
    Aretha Franklin

DISC ONE
"I Never Loved a Man (The Way I Love You)" [Demo Version]
"Dr. Feelgood (Love Is a Serious Business)" [Demo Version]
"Sweet Bitter Love" [Demo Version]
"It Was You" [Outtake]
"The Letter" [Outtake]
"So Soon" [Outtake]
"Mr. Big" [Outtake]
"Talk to Me, Talk to Me" [Outtake]
"The Fool on the Hill" [Outtake]
"Pledging My Love / The Clock" [Single B-Side]
"You're Talking Up Another Man's Place" [Outtake]
"You Keep Me Hangin' On" [Outtake]
"I'm Trying to Overcome" [Outtake]
"My Way" [Outtake]
"My Cup Runneth Over" [Outtake]
"You're All I Need to Get By" [Take 1]
"You're All I Need to Get By" [Take 2]
"Lean on Me" [Single B-Side]

DISC TWO
"Rock Steady" [Alternate Mix - Outtake]
"I Need a Strong Man (The To-To Song)" [Outtake]
"Heavenly Father" [Outtake]
"Sweetest Smile and the Funkiest Style" [Outtake]
"This Is" [Outtake]
"Tree of Life" [Outtake]
"Do You Know" [Outtake]
"Can You Love Again" [Outtake]

"I Want to Be with You" [Outtake]
"Suzanne" [Outtake]
"That's the Way I Feel About Cha" [Alternate Version—Outtake]
"Ain't But the One" [Duet with Ray Charles]
"The Happy Blues" [Outtake]
"At Last" [Outtake]
"Love Letters" [Outtake]
"I'm in Love" [Alternate Vocal / Outtake]
"Are You Leaving Me" [Demo Version]

Oh Me Oh My: Aretha Live in Philly 1972 (Atlantic / Rhino Records / 2008)
Produced by Jerry Wexler
"Introduction: 'Also Sprach Zarathustra' / 'Rock Steady'"
"This Girl's in Love with You"
"Medley: 'I Never Loved a Man (The Way I Love You)' / 'I Say a Little Prayer'"
"Medley: 'Day Dreaming' / 'Think'"
"Spanish Harlem"
"Medley: 'Chain of Fools' / 'See Saw'"
"Don't Play That Song (For Me)"
"Respect"
"Medley: 'Bridge over Troubled Water' / 'We've Only Just Begun'"
"Young, Gifted and Black"
"Oh Me Oh My (I'm A Fool for You Baby)"
"That's the Way I Feel About Cha"
"April Fools"
"Spirit in the Dark"

On Arista Records

Aretha (Arista Records / 1980)
Produced by Chuck Jackson, Arif Mardin, and Aretha Franklin
"Come to Me"
"Can't Turn You Loose"

"United Together"
"Take Me with You"
"Whatever It Is"
"What a Fool Believes"
"Together Again"
"Love Me Forever"
"School Days"

Love All the Hurt Away (Arista Records / 1981)
Produced by Arif Mardin, and Aretha Franklin
"Love All the Hurt Away" [Duet with George Benson]
"Hold On I'm Comin'"
"Living in the Streets"
"There's a Star for Everyone"
"You Can't Always Get What You Want"
"It's My Turn"
"Truth and Honesty"
"Search On"
"Whole Lot of Me"
"Kind of Man"

Jump to It (Arista Records / 1982) [Gold]
Produced by Luther Vandross, and Aretha Franklin
"Jump to It"
"Love Me Right"
"If She Don't Want Your Lovin'"
"This Is for Real"
"(It's Just) Your Love"
"I Wanna Make It Up to You" [with the Four Tops]
"It's Your Thing"
"Just My Daydream"

Get It Right (Arista Records / 1983)
Produced by Luther Vandross
"Get It Right"
"Pretender"

"Every Girl (Wants My Guy)"
"When You Love Me Like That"
"I Wish It Would Rain"
"Better Friends than Lovers"
"I Got Your Love"
"Giving In"

Who's Zoomin' Who? (Arista Records / 1985) [Platinum]
Produced by Narada Michael Walden, Aretha Franklin, and
    Dave Stewart (of Eurythmics)
"Freeway of Love
"Another Night"
"Sweet Bitter Love"
"Who's Zoomin' Who"
"Sisters Are Doin' It for Themselves" [with Eurythymics]
"Until You Say You Love Me"
"Push" [Duet with Peter Wolf of J. Giles Band]
"Ain't Nobody Ever Loved You"
"Integrity"

Aretha (Arista Records / 1986) [Gold]
Produced by Narada Michael Walden, Aretha Franklin, and Keith Richards
"Jimmy Lee"
"I Knew You Were Waiting (For Me)" [Duet with George Michael]
"Do You Still Remember"
"Jumpin' Jack Flash"
"Rock-A-Lott"
"An Angel Cries"
"He'll Come Along"
"If You Need My Love Tonight" [Duet with Larry Graham]
"Look to the Rainbow"

One Lord, One Faith, One Baptism (Arista Records / 2-Album 2-Disc
    Set / 1987)
Produced by Aretha Franklin

"Walk in the Light"

"Prayer Invocation by Rev. Cecil Franklin (July 27)"

"Introduction of Aretha and the Franklin Sisters by Rev. Jesse Jackson"

"Jesus Hears Every Prayer" [with the Franklin Sisters]

"Surely as God Is Able" [with the Franklin Sisters]

"The Lord's Prayer"

"Introduction of Aretha and Mavis Staples by Rev. Jesse Jackson"

"Oh Happy Day" [Duet with Mavis Staples]

"We Need Power" [Duet with Mavis Staples]

"Speech by Rev. Jesse Jackson (July 27)"

"Ave Maria"

"Introduction to 'Higher Ground' by Rev. Jaspar Williams"

"Higher Ground" [Duet with Rev. Jaspar Williams]

"Prayer Invocation by Rev. Donald Parsons"

"I've Been in the Storm Too Long" [Duet with Joe Ligon of the Mighty
    Clouds of Joy]

"Packing Up, Getting Ready to Go" [with Mavis Staples, Joe Ligon of
    the Mighty Clouds of Joy, and the Franklin Sisters]

[NOTE: The 2003 reissue of this album adds three new tracks: "Beams
of Heaven (Someday)," "Father I Stretch My Hands to Thee," and
"Packing Up, Getting Ready to Go" (Alternate Version).]

Through the Storm (Arista Records / 1989)

Produced by Narada Michael Walden, Aretha Franklin, Arif Mardin,
    Joe Mardin, Jerry King, and Aaron Zigman

"Gimme Your Love" [Duet with James Brown]

"Mercy"

"He's the Boy"

"It Isn't, It Wasn't, It Ain't Never Gonna Be" [Duet with
    Whitney Houston]

"Through the Storm" [Duet with Elton John]

"Think (1989)"

"Come to Me"

"If Ever a Love There Was" [with the Four Tops]

What You See Is What You Sweat (Arista Records / 1991)
Produced by Luther Vandross, Narada Michael Walden, Burt Bacharach,
    Carole Bayer Sager, Bruce Roberts, David "Pic" Conley, Elliot
    Wolff, Oliver Leiber, Aretha Franklin, Michel Legrand
"Everyday People"
"Ever Changing Times" [Duet with Michael McDonald]
"What You See Is What You Sweat"
"Mary Goes Round"
"I Dreamed a Dream"
"Some Else's Eyes"
"Doctor's Orders" [Duet with Luther Vandross]
"You Can't Take Me For Granted"
"What Did You Give"
"Everyday People (Remix)"

Aretha Franklin Greatest Hits 1980–1994 (Arista Records / 1994)
    [Platinum]
Produced by Luther Vandross, Narada Michael Walden, Kenny
    "Babyface" Edmonds & Daryl Simmons, Chuck Jackson, Robert
    Clivillés & David Cole, Burt Bacharach & Carole Bayer Sager,
    Ken Ehrlich, David "Pic" Conley
"Freeway of Love"
"I Knew You Were Waiting (For Me)" [Duet with George Michael]
"Jump To It"
"Willing To Forgive"
"Doctors Orders" [Duet with Luther Vandross]
"United Together"
"Who's Zoomin' Who"
"A Deeper Love"
"Honey"
"Get It Right"
"Another Night"
"Ever Changing Times" [Duet with Michael McDonald]
"Jimmy Lee"
"You Make Me Feel (Like a Natural Woman)" [Trio with Bonnie Raitt
    and Gloria Estefan]
"I Dreamed a Dream"

A Rose Is Still a Rose (Arista Records / 1998) [Gold]
Produced by Lauryn Hill, Sean "Puffy" Combs, Daryl Simmons,
    Jermaine Dupri, Dallas Austin, Michael J. Powell, Narada Michael
    Walden, Aretha Franklin
"A Rose Is Still a Rose"
"Never Leave You Again"
"In Case You Forgot"
"Here We Go Again"
"Every Lil' Bit Hurts"
"In the Morning"
"I'll Dip"
"How Many Times"
"Watch My Back"
"Love Pang"
"The Woman"

Aretha Franklin: Platinum and Gold Collection (Arista Records / 2003)
Various Producers from Atlantic and Arista Records
"Respect"
"Think"
"I Knew You Were Waiting (For Me)" [Duet with George Michael]
"Who's Zoomin' Who"
"It Isn't, It Wasn't, It Ain't Never Gonna Be" [Duet with
    Whitney Houston]
"Freeway of Love"
"Jump to It"
"Jimmy Lee"
"A Rose is Still a Rose"
"Sisters Are Doin' It for Themselves' [with Eurythmics]
"Get It Right"
"Jumpin' Jack Flash"

So Damn Happy (Arista Records / 2003)
Produced by Troy Taylor, Ron Lawrence, Jimmy Jam, Terry Lewis, James
    Wright, Aretha Franklin, Burt Bacharach, Gordon Chambers, Barry
    J. Eastmond, and Norman West
"The Only One Missin'"

"Wonderful"
"Holdin' On"
"No Matter What"
"Everybody's Somebody's Fool"
"So Damn Happy"
"You Are My Joy"
"Falling Out of Love"
"Ain't No Way"
"Good News"
"You Are My Joy (Reprise)"

Jewels in the Crown: All-Star Duets with The Queen (Arista Records / 2007)
Produced by Keith Richards, Dave Stewart, Narada Michael Walden, Phil Ramone, the Underdogs, Devo Springsteen, Ken Erlich, Luther Vandross, Burt Bacharach, Carole Bayer Sager, Sean Murphy, Babyface, and Arif Mardin
"Jumpin' Jack Flash" [with Keith Richards on lead guitar]
"Sisters Are Doin' It For Themselves" [with Eurythmics]
"I Knew You Were Waiting (For Me)" [Duet with George Michael]
"What Now My Love" [Duet with Frank Sinatra]
"Put You Up on Game" [Duet with Fantasia]
"What Y'All Came to Do" [Duet with John Legend]
"Never Gonna Break My Faith" [Duet with Mary J. Blige]
"Through the Storm" [Duet with Elton John]
"It Isn't, It Wasn't, It Ain't Never Gonna Be" [Duet with Whitney Houston]
"(You Make Me Feel Like) A Natural Woman" [Trio with Bonnie Raitt and Gloria Estefan]
"Doctor's Orders" [Duet with Luther Vandross]
"Ever Changing Times" [Duet with Michael McDonald]
"Chain of Fools" [Duet with Mariah Carey]
"Don't Waste Your Time" [Duet with Mary J. Blige]
"Love All the Hurt Away" [Duet with George Benson]
"Nessun Dorma" [with the New York Recording Orchestra]
"If Ever a Love There Was" [with the Four Tops and Kenny G]

Aretha Albums on Other Record Labels

This Christmas ARETHA (DMI / Rhino Records / 2009)
Produced by Tena Clark, and Aretha Franklin
"Angels We Have Heard On High"
"This Christmas"
"My Grown-Up Christmas List"
"The Lord Will Make a Way"
"Silent Night"
"Ave Maria"
"Christmas Ain't Christmas (Without the One You Love)"
"Angels"
"One Night with the King"
"Hark! The Herald Angels Sing"
"'Twas the Night Before Christmas"

A Woman Falling Out of Love (Aretha's Records / Wal-mart / 2011)
Executive Produced by Aretha Franklin. Produced by Aretha Franklin,
       Curtis Boone, Marty Paich, Brian Garrett, Joseph Hall,
       Jacqui Whittman
"How Long I've Waited"
"Sweet Sixteen"
"This You Should Know"
"U Can't See Me"
"Theme from *A Summer Place*" [with spoken word Billy Dee Williams]
"The Way We Were" [Duet with Ron Isley]
"New Day"
"Put It Back Together Again"
"Faithful" [featuring Karen Clark-Sheard]
"His Eye Is on the Sparrow" [piano by Aretha, sung by Eddie Franklin]
"When Two Become One"
"My Country 'Tis of Thee"

Aretha Franklin Sings the Great Diva Classics (**RCA Records / 2014**)
Co-Produced by Clive Davis and Aretha Franklin, Tracks produced by

Kenny "Babyface" Edmonds, Terry Hunter, Harvey Mason Jr., Eric
Kupper, and André 3000 Benjamin
"At Last"
"Rolling in the Deep (The Aretha Version)"
"Midnight Train to Georgia"
"I Will Survive (The Aretha Version)"
"People"
"No One"
"I'm Every Woman / Respect"
"Teach Me Tonight"
"You Keep Me Hangin' On"
"Nothing Compares 2U"

***A Brand New Me: Aretha Franklin with The Royal Philharmonic
Orchestra*** (Atlantic Records / 2017)
Producer: Nick Patrick
"Think"
"Don't Play That Song (You Lied)"
"I Say a Little Prayer"
"Until You Come Back to Me (That's What I'm Gonna Do)"
"A Brand New Me"
"(You Make Me Feel Like) A Natural Woman"
"Angel"
"Border Song (Holy Moses)"
"Let It Be"
"People Get Ready"
"Oh Me Oh My (I'm a Fool For You Baby)"
"You're All I Need to Get By"
"Son of a Preacher Man"
"Respect"

Aretha Franklin Appearances on Other Albums:

Here's Johnny—Magic Moments from "The Tonight Show"
    by Johnny Carson
(Casablanca Records / 1974)
"Until You Come Back to Me (That's What I'm Gonna Do)" by Aretha
    Franklin [live version]

The Blues Brothers [Soundtrack] by Various Artists
(Atlantic Records / 1980)
Produced by Bob Tischler
"Think" [New Version] by Aretha Franklin

Back Where I Belong by the Four Tops
(Motown Records / 1983)
Produced by Willie Hutch
"What Have We Got to Lose" by the Four Tops and Aretha Franklin

Indestructible by the Four Tops
(Arista Records / 1988)
Produced by Jerry Knight and Aaron Zigman
"If Ever a Love There Was" by the Four Tops and Aretha Franklin

I'm Gonna Git You Sucka! [Soundtrack]
(Arista Records / 1988)
Produced by Jerry Knight and Aaron Zigman
"If Ever a Love There Was" by the Four Tops and Aretha Franklin

A Very Special Christmas 2 by Various Artists
(A&M Records / 1992)
Produced by Marty & David Paich
"O Christmas Tree" by Aretha Franklin

White Men Can't Jump [Soundtrack] by Various Artists
(EMI Records / 1992)
Produced by Bennie Wallace
"If I Lose You" by Aretha Franklin

Duets by Frank Sinatra & Friends
(Capital Records / 1993)
Produced by Phil Ramone
"What Now My Love" by Aretha Franklin with Frank Sinatra

Sister Act 2: Back in the Habit [film soundtrack] by Various Artists
(Hollywood Records / 1993)
Produced by Robert Clivillés & David Cole
"Deeper Love" by Aretha Franklin

A Tribute to Curtis Mayfield by Various Artists
(Warner Brothers Records / 1994)
Produced by Arif Mardin
"The Makings of You" by Aretha Franklin

Tapestry Revisited / A Tribute to Carole King by Various Artists
(Lava / Atlantic Records / 1995)
Produced by Arif Mardin
"You've Got a Friend" by BeBe & CeCe Winans, featuring
     Aretha Franklin

Waiting to Exhale [film soundtrack] by Various Artists
(Arista Records / 1995)
Produced by Kenny "Babyface" Edmonds
"It Hurts Like Hell" by Aretha Franklin

Christmas Here with You by the Four Tops
(Motown Records / 1995)
Produced by Lawrence Payton, Levi Payton, Abdul Fakir, Obie Benson,
     and Ronnie McNeir
"Christmas Here with You"
The Four Tops featuring Aretha Franklin
"White Christmas"
The Four Tops featuring Aretha Franklin
"Silent Night"
The Four Tops featuring Aretha Franklin

Songs of West Side Story by Various Artists
(BMG/RCA Records / 1996)
Produced by David Pack
"Somewhere" by Aretha Franklin

Diana: Princess of Wales / Tribute by Various Artists
(Sony Records / 1997)
Produced by Aretha Franklin
"I'll Fly Away" by Aretha Franklin

Blues Brothers 2000 [Soundtrack] by Various Artists
(Universal Records / 1998)
Produced by Paul Shaffer
"R-E-S-P-E-C-T" (1998 version) by Aretha Franklin
"New Orleans" by Aretha Franklin

VH1 Divas Live by Mariah Carey, Gloria Estefan, Shania Twain, Aretha
      Franklin, and Celine Dion [special guest star: Carole King]
(Epic Records / 1998)
Produced by Wayne Isaak
"Chain of Fools" by Aretha Franklin and Mariah Carey
"A Natural Woman" by Aretha Franklin, Mariah Carey, Gloria Estefan,
      Shania Twain, Celine Dion, and Carole King
"Testimony" by Aretha Franklin, featuring Mariah Carey, Gloria Estefan,
      Shania Twain, Celine Dion, and Carole King

Ultimate Christmas by Various Artists
(Arista Records / 1998)
Produced by Belford C. Hendricks
"Winter Wonderland" by Aretha Franklin (1964 studio recording)

Ultimate Broadway by Various Artists
(Arista Records / 1998)
Produced by David "Pic" Conley
"I Dreamed a Dream" by Aretha Franklin

[NOTE: Although this is listed as being from "President Clinton's Inaugural Gala, 1993," it is still the studio recording that appears on both albums *What You See Is What You Sweat* and *Greatest Hits 1980–1994*. For the *Hits* album, the actual Inaugural intro was tacked onto the start of the 1991 studio recording. What is heard here is the end of the applause from the Inaugural, and then the same studio recording with a bit of echo added to it.]

So Amazing: An All-Star Tribute to Luther Vandross by Various Artists
(J Records / 2005)
Produced by Arif Mardin
"A House is Not a Home" by Aretha Franklin

Mr. I by Ronald Isley
(Def Jam Records / 2010)
Produced by Jerry "Wonda" Duplessis
"You've Got a Friend" [Duet by Ronald Isley and Aretha Franklin]

Duets II by Tony Bennett
(Columbia Records / 2011)
Produced by Phil Ramone and Dae Bennett
"How Do You Keep the Music Playing" [Duet by Tony Bennett and
     Aretha Franklin]

Anthologies and Repackaged Hits Albums
[NOTE: There are several compilations on the market that utilize Aretha recordings from her three major record labels. These are a few of the most significant ones.]

"Respect" and Other Hits (Rhino Records / 1997) [Gold]
"Respect"
"You Send Me"
"The Weight"
"Baby, I Love You"
"Do Right Woman—Do Right Man"
"Chain of Fools"

"Ain't No Way"
"My Song"
"Tracks of My Tears"
"I Never Loved a Man (The Way I Love You)"

"Natural Woman" and Other Hits (Rhino Flashback Records / 1997)
"(You Make Me Feel Like) A Natural Woman"
"The House That Jack Built"
"Son of a Preacher Man"
"Spirit in the Dark"
"I Say a Little Prayer"
"Bridge over Troubled Water"
"Ain't Nothing Like the Real Thing"
"Without Love"
"Eleanor Rigby"
"Rock Steady"

"Think" and Other Hits (Rhino Flashback Records / 1998)
"Think"
"Call Me"
"I Can't See Myself Leaving You"
"You're All I Need to Get By"
"(Sweet Sweet Baby) Since You've Been Gone"
"Don't Play That Song (For Me)"
"All the King's Horses"
"Master of Eyes (The Deepness of Your Eyes)"
"Look into Your Heart"
"I'm in Love"

Aretha Franklin: Greatest Hits
(Global Television/Warners / 1998) [England Only]

DISC ONE
"I Knew You Were Waiting (For Me)" [Duet with George Michael]
"Respect"
"I Say a Little Prayer"
"Think"

"(You Make Me Feel Like) A Natural Woman"
"I Never Loved a Man (The Way I Love You)"
"You're All I Need (To Get By)"
"Chain of Fools"
"Spanish Harlem"
"Angel"
"Let It Be"
"Until You Come Back to Me (That's What I'm Gonna Do)"
"Son of a Preacher Man"
"Don't Play That Song (For Me)"
"Rock Steady"
"See Saw"
"Ain't Nothing Like the Real Thing"
"Do Right Woman, Do Right Man"
"Save Me"
"The House That Jack Built"
"People Get Ready"
"Day Dreaming"

DISC TWO
"Sisters Are Doing It For Themselves" [with Eurythmics]
"A Deeper Love"
"What a Fool Believes"
"Who's Zoomin' Who?"
"Willing to Forgive"
"Jumpin' Jack Flash"
"Freeway of Love"
"Border Song (Holy Moses)"
"Oh No Not My Baby"
"Call Me"
"Ain't No Way"
"Since You've Been Gone (Sweet Sweet Baby)"
"Baby I Love You"
"The Long and Winding Road"
"Today I Sing the Blues"
"Love All the Hurt Away" [Duet with George Benson]

"It Isn't, It Wasn't, It Ain't Never Gonna Be" [Duet with
    Whitney Houston]
"Through the Storm" [Duet with Elton John]
"A Rose Is Still a Rose"

Aretha's Best
(Atlantic Records / 2001)
"Respect"
"Think"
"Freeway of Love"
"Baby, I Love You"
"(You Make Me Fell Like) A Natural Woman"
"Day Dreaming"
"I Say a Little Prayer"
"The House That Jack Built"
"(Sweet Sweet Baby) Since You've Been Gone"
"Spanish Harlem"
"Jump to It"
"I Knew You Were Waiting (For Me)" [Duet with George Michael]
"Chain of Fools"
"Rock Steady"
"Who's Zoomin' Who"
"Until You Come Back to Me (That's What I'm Gonna Do)"
"I Never Loved a Man (The Way I Love You)"
"Call Me"
"Do Right Woman, Do Right Man"
"Bridge over Troubled Water"

A Deeper Love: The Best of Aretha Franklin
(Sony Records / 2009) [Europe Only]

DISC ONE
"Freeway of Love"
"Who's Zoomin' Who"
"Willing to Forgive"
"Love All the Hurt Away" [Duet with George Benson]

"Another Night"
"Here We Go Again"
"Everyday People"
"Get It Right"
"Gimme Your Love" [Duet with James Brown]
"Rock-A-Lott"
"Sweet Bitter Love"
"If She Don't Want Your Lovin'"
"Jimmy Lee"
"It's Your Thing"
"It's My Turn"
"Love Me Right"

DISC TWO
"A Deeper Love"
"A Rose Is Still a Rose"
"Jump to It"
"Through the Storm" [Duet with Elton John]
"What a Fool Believes"
"Come to Me"
"United Together"
"If Ever a Love There Was" [with the Four Tops]
"Honey"
"Jumpin' Jack Flash"
"Never Leave You Again"
"This Is for Real"
"Ever Changing Times" [Duet with Michael McDonald]
"Every Girl Wants My Guy"
"Doctor's Orders"
"I Dreamed a Dream"

Since 2009 several more Aretha compilations and or boxed sets have been released including:

Sunday Morning Classics [Vinyl Only] (Columbia Records / 2009)

Great American Songbook: Aretha Franklin (Columbia Legacy
    Records / 2011)
More Gospel Greats (Rhino Records / 2011)
Take a Look: Aretha Franklin Complete on Columbia (Columbia
    Legacy Records / 2011)
Knew You Were Waiting: The Best of Aretha Franklin 1980–1998
    (Columbia Legacy Records / 2012)
Original Album Series Vol. 2 (Columbia Legacy Records / 2013)
The Queen's Greatest Hits (Sony Music / 2013)
The Queen of Soul (Atlantic / 2014)
The Real . . . Aretha Franklin—The Ultimate Collection (RCA
    Records / 2014)
The Atlantic Albums Collection (Atlantic Records / 2014)
The Atlantic Singles Collection (Atlantic Records / 2018)

SINGLE RELEASES:
"Today I Sing the Blues" (Columbia / 1960)
"Won't Be Long" (Columbia / 1961)
"Are You Sure" (Columbia / 1961)
"Operation Heartbreak" / "Rock-A-Bye Your Baby with a Dixie Melody"
    (Columbia / 1961)
"I Surrender, Dear" / "Rough Lover" (Columbia / 1962)
"Don't Cry, Baby" (Columbia / 1962)
"Just for a Thrill" / "Try a Little Tenderness" (Columbia / 1962)
"Trouble in Mind" (Columbia / 1962)
"Here's Where I Came In (Here's Where I Walk Out)" / "Say It Isn't So"
    (Columbia / 1963)
"Skylark" (Columbia / 1963)
"Kissin' by the Mistletoe" (Columbia / 1963)
"Soulville" (Columbia / 1964)
"Runnin' Out of Fools" (Columbia / 1964)
"The Christmas Song (Chestnuts Roasting on an Open Fire)"
    (Columbia / 1964)
"Precious Lord (Part One)" / "Precious Lord" (Part Two)"
    (Chess / 1964)

"Can't You Just See Me" (Columbia / 1965)

"One Step Ahead" (Columbia / 1965)

"(No, No) I'm Losing You" (Columbia / 1965)

"You Made Me Love You" (Columbia / 1965)

"Runnin' Out of Fools" / "Cry Like a Baby" (Columbia / 1965)

"A Mother's Love" / "Mockingbird" (Columbia / 1965)

"Tighten Up Your Tie, Button Up Your Jacket" (Columbia / 1966)

"Until You Were Gone" (Columbia / 1966)

"Follow Your Heart" / "Take a Look" (Columbia / 1966)

"I Never Loved a Man (The Way I Love You)" / "Do Right Woman-Do Right Man" (Atlantic / 1967) [Gold]

"Respect" (Atlantic / 1967) [Gold]

"Lee Cross" / "Until You Were Gone" (Columbia / 1967)

"Baby I Love You" (Atlantic / 1967) [Gold]

"Soulville" / "If Ever I Would Leave You" (Columbia / 1967)

"Take a Look" [Reissue] (Columbia / 1967)

"(You Make Me Feel Like) A Natural Woman" (Atlantic / 1967)

"Chain of Fools" (Atlantic / 1967) [Gold]

"Mockingbird" (Columbia / 1967)

"Soulville" [Reissue] (Columbia / 1967)

"Satisfaction" (Atlantic / 1968)

"(Sweet Sweet Baby) Since You've Been Gone" / "Ain't No Way" (Atlantic / 1968) [Gold]

"Think" / "You Send Me" (Atlantic / 1968) [Gold]

"The House That Jack Built" / "I Say a Little Prayer" (Atlantic / 1968) [Gold]

"See Saw" / "My Song" (Atlantic / 1968) [Gold]

"Jim" (Columbia / 1969)

"The Weight" / "Tracks of My Tears" (Atlantic / 1969)

"I Can't See Myself Leaving You" / "Gentle on My Mind" (Atlantic / 1969)

"Today I Sing the Blues" [Re-release] (Columbia / 1969)

"Share Your Love with Me" (Atlantic / 1969)

"Eleanor Rigby" (Atlantic / 1969)

"Call Me" / "Son of a Preacher Man" (Atlantic / 1970)

"Spirit in the Dark" / "The Thrill Is Gone (From Yesterday's Kiss)"
    (Atlantic / 1970)
"Don't Play That Song (For Me)" (Atlantic / 1970) [Gold]
"Border Song (Holy Moses)" / "You and Me" (Atlantic / 1970)
"You're All I Need to Get By" (Atlantic / 1971)
"Bridge over Troubled Water" / "A Brand New Me" (Atlantic / 1971)
    [Gold]
"Spanish Harlem" (Atlantic / 1971) [Gold]
"Rock Steady" / "Oh Me Oh My (I'm a Fool for You Baby)" (Atlantic /
    1971) [Gold]
"Day Dreaming" (Atlantic / 1972) [Gold]
"All the King's Horses" / "April Fools" (Atlantic / 1972)
"Wholy Holy" (Atlantic / 1972)
"Master of Eyes (The Deepness of Your Eyes)" (Atlantic / 1973)
"Angel" (Atlantic / 1973) [Gold]
"Until You Come Back to Me (That's What I'm Gonna Do)" (Atlantic /
    1973) [Gold]
"I'm in Love" (Atlantic / 1974)
"Ain't Nothing Like the Real Thing" (Atlantic / 1974)
"Without Love" (Atlantic / 1974)
"With Everything I Feel in Me" (Atlantic / 1975)
"Mr. D.J. (5 for the D.J.)" (Atlantic / 1975)
"You" (Atlantic / 1976)
"Something He Can Feel" (Atlantic / 1976)
"Jump" / "Hooked on Your Love" (Atlantic / 1976)
"Look into Your Heart" (Atlantic / 1977)
"Break It to Me Gently" (Atlantic / 1977)
"When I Think About You" (Atlantic / 1977)
"Almighty Fire (Woman of the Future)" (Atlantic / 1978)
"More Than Just a Joy" (Atlantic / 1978)
"Ladies Only" (Atlantic / 1979)
"Half a Love" (Atlantic / 1979)
"United Together" (Arista / 1980)
"What a Fool Believes" (Arista / 1980)
"Come to Me" (Arista / 1980)

"Love All the Hurt Away" [Duet with George Benson] (Arista / 1981)

"It's My Turn" (Arista / 1981)

"Livin' in the Streets" (Arista / 1982)

"Jump to It" (Arista / 1982)

"Love Me Right" (Arista / 1982)

"This Is for Real" (Arista / 1983)

"Get It Right" (Arista / 1983)

"Every Girl (Wants My Guy)" (Arista / 1983)

"Freeway of Love" (Arista / 1985)

"Who's Zoomin' Who" (Arista / 1985)

"Sisters Are Doin' It for Themselves" [with Eurythmics] (RCA / 1985)

"Another Night" (Arista / 1986)

"Freeway of Love" [Rerelease] (Arista / 1986)

"Ain't Nobody Ever Loved You" (Arista / 1986)

"Jumpin' Jack Flash" (Arista / 1986)

"Jimmy Lee" (Arista / 1986)

"I Knew You Were Waiting (For Me)" [Duet with George Michael] (Arista / 1987)

"Rock-A-Lott" (Arista / 1987)

"If You Need My Love Tonight" [Duet with Larry Graham] (Arista / 1987)

"Oh Happy Day" (Arista / 1988)

"If Ever a Love There Was" [with the Four Tops] (Arista / 1988)

"Through the Storm" [with Elton John] (Arista / 1989)

"It Isn't, It Wasn't, It Ain't Never Gonna Be" [Duet with Whitney Houston] (Arista / 1989)

"Gimme Your Love" [Duet with James Brown] (Arista / 1989)

"Everyday People" (Arista / 1991)

"Someone Else's Eyes" (Arista / 1991)

"What You See Is What You Sweat" (Arista / 1991)

"Ever Changing Times" [Duet with Michael McDonald] (Arista / 1992)

"Someday We'll All Be Free" (Arista / 1992)

"A Deeper Love" (Arista / 1994)

"Willing to Forgive" (Arista / 1994)

"Jump to It" [Re-release: CJ's Master Mix] (Arista / 1994)

"Honey" (Arista / 1994)
"It Hurts Like Hell" (Arista / 1996)
"A Rose Is Still a Rose" (Arista / 1998) [Gold]
"Here We Go Again" / "Nessun Dorma" (Arista / 1998)
"In Case You Forgot" (Arista / 1998)
"The Only Thing Missin'" (Arista / 2003)
"Wonderful" (Arista / 2003)
"Put You Up on Game" [Duet with Fantasia] (Arista / 2007)
"Angels We Have Heard on High" (DMI Records / 2009)
"How Long I've Been Waiting" (Aretha's Records / 2011)
"Rolling in the Deep (The Aretha Version)" (RCA Records / 2014)

[NOTE: The use of the terms "Gold" and "Platinum" in this book refer to record sales figures in the United States, as calculated by the Record Industry Association of America (RIAA). For singles, "Gold" refers to sales in excess of one million copies, and "Platinum" refers to sales in excess of two million copies. For albums, "Gold" refers to sales in excess of 500,000 copies, and "Platinum" refers to sales in excess of one million copies.]

ARETHA FRANKLIN ON DVD:
(Date refers to release of original material)

The Blues Brothers (1980)
Aretha Franklin: Live at Park West (1985)
VH1 Diva's Live (1998)
The Blues Brothers 2000 (1998)
Ladies & Gentlemen: The Best of George Michael (1999)
    Contains video of "I Knew You Were Waiting (For Me)"
Aretha Franklin: Live at Park West (1999)
25 Years of Hits: Arista Records 25th Anniversary (2000)
Rhythm, Love and Soul (2003)
Saturday Night Live: 25 Years of Music, Volume 4 (2003)
From the Heart: The Four Tops 50th Anniversary Concert (2006)
The Inauguration of Barack Obama: A Moment in History (2009)
Aretha Franklin: Live from Chicago (2009)
The Best of "Soul Train" (2010)
The 25th Anniversary Rock & Roll Hall of Fame Concert (2010)

ARETHA FRANKLIN'S GRAMMY AWARDS

1. "Respect" ("Best R&B Recording" / 1967)
2. "Respect" ("Best Female R&B Vocal Performance" / 1967)
3. "Chain of Fools" ("Best Female R&B Vocal Performance" / 1968)
4. "Share Your Love with Me" ("Best Female R&B Vocal Performance" / 1969)
5. "Don't Play That Song (For Me)" ("Best Female R&B Vocal Performance" / 1970)
6. "Bridge over Troubled Water" ("Best Female R&B Vocal Performance" / 1971)
7. *Young, Gifted and Black* [album] ("Best Female R&B Vocal Performance" / 1972)
8. *Amazing Grace* [album] ("Best Soul Gospel Performance" / 1972)
9. "Master of Eyes (The Deepness of Your Eyes)" ("Best Female R&B Vocal Performance" / 1973)
10. "Ain't Nothing Like the Real Thing" ("Best Female R&B Vocal Performance" / 1974)
11. "Hold On . . . I'm Comin'" [album track] ("Best Female R&B Vocal Performance" / 1981)
12. "Freeway of Love" ("Best Female R&B Vocal Performance" / 1985)
13. *Aretha* [album] ("Best Female R&B Vocal Performance" / 1987)
14. "I Knew You Were Waiting (For Me)" [with George Michael] ("Best R&B Performance—Duo or Group with Vocals" / 1987)
15. *One Lord, One Faith, One Baptism* [album] ("Best Soul Gospel Performance—Female" / 1988)
16. "Living Legend Award" [Special] / 1991

17. "Lifetime Achievement Award" [Special] / 1994
18. "Wonderful" ("Best Traditional R&B Vocal Performance" / 2003)
19. "A House Is Not a Home" ("Best Traditional R&B Vocal Performance" / 2005)
20. "Never Gonna Break My Faith" [with Mary J. Blige] ("Best Gospel / Soul Vocal Performance by a Duo or Group" / 2007)

[NOTE: Grammy Awards 16 and 17 above are "honorary" awards, so some tallies of Aretha's Grammys don't count these, since they are not attached to individual songs.]

INDEX

ABOUT THE AUTHOR

MARK BEGO is a professional writer who is called "The Number One Best-Selling Pop Biographer" in *Publishers Weekly* and has been referred to in the press as "The Prince of Pop Music Bios." He has authored over sixty-five published books involving rock & roll and show business. He has penned two *New York Times* bestsellers, a *Los Angeles Times* bestseller, and the *Chicago Tribune* bestseller *Dancing in the Street: Confessions of a Motown Diva* written with its subject, Martha Reeves of the beloved recording group: Martha & the Vandellas.

In 1984 Bego released his biography of Michael Jackson entitled: *Michael!* It hit the stores the week that Jackson's hair caught on fire filming a Pepsi-Cola commercial and Bego ended up selling three million copies of his book in the United States alone. It spent six weeks on *The New York Times* best-seller list, and was published in six foreign language editions.

In 1985, Bego wrote the million-selling *Madonna!* about the pop icon from his hometown of Pontiac, Michigan. It was so popular that he has twice expanded the book as *Madonna: Blonde Ambition* (1992 and 2001).

From 1978 to 1980, he was the Nightlife Editor for Manhattan's *Cue* magazine covering everything from the opening of Studio 54 to all of the jazz and cabaret clubs in the city. From 1983 to 1985 he was Editor-In-Chief of *Modern Screen* magazine. His writing has also appeared in *People, Us, Billboard, Record World, Cosmopolitan, The Star,* and *The National Enquirer*.

He has also written books with Micky Dolenz of the Monkees (*I'm a Believer*), Debbie Gibson (*Between the Lines*), and Jimmy Greenspoon of Three Dog Night (*One is the Loneliest Number*). Bego's book subjects have ranged from Elvis Presley, Bonnie Raitt, Julia Roberts, Whitney Houston, Joni Mitchell, Jackson Browne, Cher, and Bette Midler. Bego also authored the reference books *TV Rock* [The History of Rock & Roll on Television] and *The Rock & Roll Almanac*.

At the height of the box-office success of the film *Titanic*, Bego wrote the biography of the movie's star: *Leonardo DiCaprio: Romantic Hero*. It spent six weeks on *The New York Times'* best-seller list in 1998. He is frequently seen on television, speaking about show business on such shows as *Entertainment Tonight*, *Biography*, and *True Hollywood Story*.

In 2007 he published the book *Billy Joel: The Biography* and the following year he wrote *Macho Man* with Randy Jones of the Village People. His 2009 book *Elton John: The Bitch is Back* is Mark's most widely-read international book since the 1980s. Mark Bego published his own show business memoir in 2010 entitled *Paperback Writer*.

In 2012, Skyhorse Publishing released *Whitney Houston! The Spectacular Rise and Tragic Fall of the Woman Whose Voice Inspired a Generation*. Bego also released his first novel in 2012: *Murder at Motor City Records*. In 2014 he published his collaboration with Debby Campbell, entitled, *Life with My Father Glen Campbell*. It hit the best-seller list in Nashville's newspaper *The Tennessean*.

Mark made a big leap into a new arena with his 2017 celebrity cookbook: *Eat Like a Rock Star*, from Skyhorse Publishing. Bego gathered recipes from forty-six rock luminaries including Mary Wilson of The Supremes, Bill Wyman of The Rolling Stones, Boz Scaggs, Tanya Tucker, Joey Fatone, Richie Sambora, Micky Dolenz, Martha Reeves and dozens more.

In 2018 Mark has two new books: *Supreme Glamour!!!* with Mary Wilson, and *Living the Luxe Life* with millionaire Beverly Hills hotelier Efrem Harkham.

His official website is: *www.MarkBego.com*. You can write to him at: *MarkBego@aol.com*.

ABOUT "ARETHA FRANKLIN: THE QUEEN OF SOUL"

The 2018 version of *Aretha Franklin: The Queen of Soul*, features new photos, new never-before published material, and an updated discography. Long considered to be the ultimate biographical portrait of Aretha Franklin, the new edition takes the story even further than previous editions. It includes new material from the author's in-depth interviews with Jerry Wexler, Clyde Otis, Ted White, Clive Davis, Martha Reeves, and Aretha Franklin—the Queen of Soul herself.

Press reviews for *Aretha Franklin: The Queen of Soul* by Mark Bego:

The Library Journal
"Bego's detail-laden effort could well stand as the definitive reading of the Queen of Soul's life and career."

The Rock & Roll Reader's Guide by Gary Krebs
"Mark Bego does a magnificent job exploring the pieces of Franklin's life and Grammy-filled career . . . excellent photos contribute to this '. . . well rounded portrait.'"

Inside Books by Anne Raso
"Author Mark Bego—a former *Modern Screen* editor and author of a dozen celeb bios—does a nice and tidy job of telling Aretha's tale of many personal challenges. It's hard to hold back the tears through stories about Aretha's desertion by her mother at age six, her strict Baptist upbringing,

a teenage pregnancy, three unhappy marriages and the shooting death of her father who was a renown gospel preacher. Fortunately, there are plenty of humorous anecdotes to balance the negative in the R&B star's life . . . this is a colorful book—as colorful as the eccentric Queen of Soul herself."